The WEST GUIDE to WRITING:

Success through the Sequence from Community College to University

Katherine Boutry • Clare Norris-Bell • Holly Bailey-Hofmann

Kendall Hunt
publishing company

Unless otherwise noted, all interior images © Shutterstock, Inc. Used under license.

Cover image © Shutterstock, Inc. Used under license.

Kendall Hunt
publishing company

www.kendallhunt.com
Send all inquiries to:
4050 Westmark Drive
Dubuque, IA 52004-1840

DEDICATION

DEDICATION
DEDICATION

We dedicate this book with much love to all of our students at West
Los Angeles College who teach us so much more than we teach them.

ACKNOWLEDGMENTS

ACKNOWLEDGMENTS

ACKNOWLEDGMENTS

The authors thank

Katherine Boutry: I wish to extend heartfelt gratitude to my wonderful colleagues in the English Department and to my co-authors for trusting me enough to take this leap with me. Thanks to our former chair, Betty Jacobs, for encouraging us always. The rock stars at the West library, Judy Chow, Ken Lee, and Ken Lin, have my undying gratitude for their incredibly generous help with this project (and anything) no matter when I ask, and for their friendship. Finally, to my husband Vianney and my best creations to date: Max, Penelope, and Lily, no woman has ever been luckier than I, or felt more surrounded by love. Even our lab Violette kept me company on so many long nights when the rest of the house was in bed. I don't deserve you all, and I know it.

Clare Norris-Bell: Infinite appreciation and love to my parents, Mary and Trusse Norris for fostering and supporting within me a love of language and literature. Thanks to my husband, Marcus Bell, for his unfaltering support and confidence in me. Thanks to Marianne Steverson for exposing me to new literacy concepts and offering her expertise to our book. I also acknowledge the following colleagues, friends, and family members for generously accepting my request for feedback: Sarah Beams, Mary-Jo Apigo, Sharon Brooks, Joanne Griffith Poplar, and Holly Norris. Thanks, finally, to Betty Jacobs for recognizing my potential.

Holly Bailey-Hofmann: Loving gratitude to my parents, David and Rosemary Bailey, for purposefully raising me to appreciate books, learning, and for encouraging my writing; heartfelt thanks to my brother Nathan Bailey and to Christa Leight, Rosalynde Vas Dias, Jerry Flores, and Richard Grenville Clark for years of uninterrupted, relentless encouragement; and much appreciation to the following colleagues: Celena Alcala for her angelic support, and Richard Bilsker, Rick Mayock, Marianne Steverson, and Katherine Tyszkiewicz for reviewing various sections of this book.

The authors thank Carol Alexander, Luis Cordova, Judy Chow, Kathryn Hansen, Betty Jacobs, Ken Lee, Ken Lin, Fran Leonard, David Spielman, Sylvia Spielman-Vaught, Kimberly Manner, Courtney Cottom, Tori Dunlap, and Rebekah Brandes..

AUTHOR BIOS

AUTHOR BIOS
AUTHOR BIOS

 Dr. Katherine Boutry got her PhD in English at Harvard University where she taught for ten years, first as a graduate teaching fellow and then as a lecturer after earning her degree. While at Harvard, she served as Assistant Director of Undergraduate Studies, advising English Majors and seeing firsthand what made for successful students. She won numerous teaching awards at Harvard and was a Derek Bok Writing Fellow. She first taught writing as a tutor in the Writing Lab at MIT. She got her BA and MA in English at Georgetown University and spent a post-graduate semester at the Sorbonne in Paris. As a graduate student, she had a Fulbright Scholarship to the Czech Republic. Dr. Boutry is also a produced television writer. She has loved teaching the students at West Los Angeles College since 2006 and preparing them for transfer.

 Clare Norris-Bell is a fourth generation educator. She earned her BA in Social Relations with an English minor from the University of California, Riverside, her MA in English from the University of Texas, San Antonio, and her certificate in Postsecondary Reading and Learning from California State University, Fullerton. She taught elementary school before earning her MA and has been tutoring and teaching community college students since 2002. She was selected as the faculty chair for West's student success efforts and has traveled around the country networking and participating in professional development opportunities connected to student success. She has taught virtually all levels of English at West, and she especially loves supporting students as they blossom into college-level writers.

 Holly Bailey-Hofmann has a BA in English from St. Mary's College of Maryland, where she studied poetry with Lucille Clifton. She earned her MA in English from the University of Cincinnati and specializes in language, linguistics, and learning strategies. Once her high school's graduating Latin scholar, she enjoys teaching students effective techniques for memorization, learning, and test-taking. Holly teaches the range of classes in the English sequence, from grammar and composition to literature and creative writing. In 2010 she founded the college's annual research poster fair, which she directed for many years. She has served as both vice president and president of the Academic Senate, and in 2016 began pursuing her doctorate in Educational Leadership at UCLA.

TABLE OF CONTENTS

TABLE OF CONTENTS
TABLE OF CONTENTS

APPENDIX

INTRODUCTION FOR INSTRUCTORS
INTRODUCTION FOR INSTRUCTORS
INTRODUCTION FOR INSTRUCTORS

Dear Instructor,

As fulltime English professors with a combined thirty years of teaching at both the community college and university levels, we wanted to create the kind of textbook we have always been looking for: affordable, compact, comprehensive, timely, and accurate. *Voila*!
We proudly present to you ***The West Guide to Writing: Success through the Sequence from Community College to University***.

Having ourselves skipped many a textbook introduction, we've boiled down the essential differences between *The West Guide* and all the other composition textbooks on your shelves.

THE ONLY COMPOSITION TEXTBOOK STUDENTS WILL EVER NEED

The most unique feature of *The West Guide* is that it can be used at any level in the composition sequence, from the foundational classes to advanced classes such as "Critical Thinking and Composition" and "Introduction to Literature." While there is more material than any one instructor should need, it's meant to be used in portions as needed.

NOT TOO MANY READINGS

We have our own favorite books and articles to teach, and we know you have yours. Thus, we've kept this edition light on readings, including only some favorite standards to illustrate concepts.

UNIQUE STUDENT SUCCESS AND LEARNING TOOLS

We are very proud of the learning and student success tools we've created. You will find sections on Time Management, Learning Styles, Active Reading, Student and Class Success Strategies, as well as some one-of-a-kind Memorization Techniques, and some other surprises that will supplement composition content to enhance students' entire educational experience.

NOT TOO MUCH, NOT TOO LITTLE GRAMMAR

In our experience, most adult learners work continuously to master grammatical concepts and rules. We've noticed that many students come to college with some gaps, even if they place into higher level classes; and in higher level classes, instructors can't always make time to address every issue that arises for every student. For this reason we wanted a guide that is at once a composition textbook and an

MLA/APA/Chicago Style guidebook, with basic grammatical concepts, to help students improve their skills. While our grammatical section is not comprehensive, it covers the basics that come up for our own students again and again. With certain grammatical concepts around which there has emerged debate—can a sentence start with a coordinating conjunction? Is that serial comma necessary?—we have tried to indicate the various approaches without straying from the most common, traditionally taught rules of usage which will make students competitive.

NOT TOO MUCH, NOT TOO LITTLE MLA/APA/CHICAGO STYLE GUIDANCE

With so much formatting and documentation information now available free on the web, we don't want students to pay for an additional, expensive guide that includes every possible citation situation. Thus, we've included the essentials that we find ourselves teaching over and over, and have pointed students to online resources for the rest.

AUTHOR EXPERTISE

With over thirty combined years of college classroom and online teaching in both private and public colleges, we've written this book as a collaborative effort to share the student learning and success tools we've developed for students at every level of the college experience. Katherine Boutry served for five years as the Assistant Director of Undergraduate Studies in the English Department at Harvard University, where she saw firsthand what skills are most fundamental to successful students. As co-chair of West Los Angeles College's Student Success Committee at West, Clare Norris-Bell leads a team of faculty in devising effective strategies to help all students attain their educational goals. Holly Bailey-Hofmann's "Seven Rules of College-Level Writing," Chapter 15 in the *West Guide* first edition, has been used online for over ten years by instructors of varied disciplines across the country.

WRITING ACROSS THE CURRICULUM

As our forebears in the English discipline first realized, writing is a strength—or weakness—for students in all their classes, so becoming a successful writer gives students an advantage in all their classes. This is not just an English textbook. We believe all the components of *The West Guide* are helpful with most classes, and we welcome your feedback about how you use it with your students.

Yours in student success,

Katherine Boutry, Clare Norris-Bell, and Holly Bailey-Hofmann

INTRODUCTION FOR STUDENTS
INTRODUCTION FOR STUDENTS
INTRODUCTION FOR STUDENTS

Greetings, Scholar!

We are excited that our book has landed in your lap, and we are equally excited that you're reading our introduction! We are committed that our book, *The West Guide to Writing: Success through the Sequence from Community College to University*, will make a difference in your education.

THE ONLY COMPOSITION TEXTBOOK YOU WILL EVER NEED

The most unique feature of *The West Guide* is that it can be used at any level in your college's composition sequence. We designed the book to cover all the skills you'll need in your college composition classes. That means that no matter which English class you start with, this book is meant to carry you through to graduation or transfer. We plan to use *The West Guide* with our students in various levels of English classes from the foundational class at our college to the advanced Critical Thinking and Composition class along with literature and creative writing classes. Our intent is to save you money and provide a text that you use from your first semester in college until you fulfill your educational goals. We want you to get familiar with *The West Guide* in your first college English course and then to return to it for each subsequent course so that you know exactly where to look to review the skills you need again and again.

UNIQUE STUDENT SUCCESS AND LEARNING TOOLS

We are proud of the learning and student success tools we've built in to guide you through elements of your classes and college writing that other books don't cover. You will find sections on time management, learning styles, active reading, and note taking, student and class success strategies, as well as ways to take advantage of your college community.

NOT TOO MUCH, NOT TOO LITTLE GRAMMAR

You may be aware that many students come to college with some gaps in their knowledge and reading and writing skills. Your instructors can't always make time to address every individual student's needs. As a result, we created a guide that is a composition textbook and an MLA/APA/Chicago guidebook, with basic grammatical concepts, designed to give you access to all the information you need to work to build your skills in all of those areas.

NOT TOO MUCH, NOT TOO LITTLE, MLA/APA/CHICAGO

With so much formatting and documentation information now available free online, we don't want you to have to pay for an additional, expensive guide that includes every possible citation situation. Thus, we've included the essentials that we teach over and over and offer you directions to online resources for the rest.

We know that becoming an effective writer gives you an advantage in all of your classes. We intend the components of *The West Guide* to offer material that can direct you through writing assignments for most classes. Again, we are committed to the idea that this text will make a difference in your education, and we welcome your feedback about when, where, and how you use it.

Yours in student success,

Katherine Boutry, Clare Norris-Bell, and Holly Bailey-Hofmann
boutryk@wlac.edu; norrisc@wlac.edu, baileyHH@wlac.edu

I

BE A SUCCESS IN CLASS

CHAPTERS

CHAPTER 1

Making Time for College: Scheduling Yourself for Success

CREATE A SCHEDULE THAT WORKS

You are a smart and capable human being. Like you, the vast majority of college students we have taught have had the necessary abilities to pass and often to ace their classes. However, some of them still did not pass. Why is that? One word: TIME! Thriving in college takes time. An academic environment is rigorous and requires students to dedicate adequate time to gain the skills and knowledge necessary to move on to the next level. Too many students miss this important basic fact about being a successful student, so let us repeat it. THRIVING IN COLLEGE TAKES TIME, probably more time than you expect, so in this section, we are going to help you get a handle on exactly how much time you need to dedicate to your studies to come out on top.

Fun Fact: Did you know that two to three hours of study/homework time for every one hour you spend in class is a standard expectation across colleges and universities? That means that each of your instructors expects you to spend that amount of time studying. And that means that in order for you to gain the skills and knowledge you need, you should spend that amount of time outside of class reading, writing, preparing, practicing, discussing, studying, etc. Your instructor designs the class around that expectation, so if you do not spend adequate time, you are much less likely to gain the skills and knowledge you need to pass the class.

So, let's think about this.

1 hour in class per week (1 unit) = 2–3 study hours out of class per week

A standard 3-unit class meets for 3 hours per week. For that class, you would need to spend 6–9 hours studying.

Let's consider an example. Autumn is taking four college classes this semester: English 101 (3 units), College Algebra (3 units), Health 11 (3 units), and Astronomy 1 (3 units). She is enrolled in twelve units, which means she is in class twelve hours per week. She filled in the formula this way:

AUTUMN

How many hours do you spend in class each week (units)? __12__ × __2__ = 24

That means that 24 is the *minimum* number of hours Autumn should spend studying per week. She may need to spend as many as (12 x 3=) 36 hours per week studying and preparing for her classes. If she does not do that, Autumn risks not gaining the skills and knowledge she needs to pass her classes and having to retake them.

Next, Autumn will complete a Time Management Table to ensure that she has enough time in her schedule to pass all four of her classes. Examine Autumn's Time Management Table. Has she dedicated enough study time to develop her knowledge and skills and pass her classes?

Time Management Table   Name *Autumn*

	Monday	Tuesday	Wednesday	Thursday	Friday	Saturday	Sunday
6-7am	Get up	Sleep	Get up	Sleep	Sleep	Sleep	Sleep
7-8	Bus	Sleep	Bus to school	Sleep	Get up	Get up	Sleep
8-9	Math	Get up	Math	Get up	Bus to Work	Bus to Work	Get Up
9-10	Math	Bus	Math	Bus	Work	Work	Church
	Bus to work	Health	Bus Home	Health			
10-11	Work	Health	Babysit	Health	Work	Work	Church
11-12pm	Work	English	Babysit	English	Work	Work	Church
12-1	Work	English	Babysit/ Lunch	English	Work	Work	Church
		Bus to Work		Lunch			
1-2	Work	Work	Babysit	Study	Work	Work	Cook
2-3	Work	Work	Bus to Work	Study	Work	Work	Sunday Dinner
3-4	Work	Work	Work	Study	Work	Work	Sunday Dinner
4-5	Work	Work	Work	Study	Work	Work	Free Time
5-6	Work	Work	Work	Astronomy	Bus home	Bus home	Free Time
6-7	Bus Home	Work	Work	Astronomy	Eat	Eat	Free Time
7-8	Dinner/TV	Work	Work	Astronomy	TV	Babysit	Free Time
8-9	Study	Bus Home	Work	Astronomy	TV	Babysit	Study
				Bus Home			
9-10	Study	TV	Work	TV	Out	Babysit	Study
10-11	Study	Study	Bus home	Study	Out	Babysit	Study
11-12am	Study	Study	TV	Study	Out	Sleep	Study
12-1	Sleep	Sleep	Study	Study	Out	Sleep	Sleep
1-2	Sleep	Sleep	Sleep	Sleep	Sleep	Sleep	Sleep
2-3	Sleep	Sleep	Sleep	Sleep	Sleep	Sleep	Sleep
3-4	Sleep	Sleep	Sleep	Sleep	Sleep	Sleep	Sleep
4-5	Sleep	Sleep	Sleep	Sleep	Sleep	Sleep	Sleep
5-6	Sleep	Sleep	Sleep	Sleep	Sleep	Sleep	Sleep

____12____ hours in class   ☐ study/homework hours

Now, what feedback would you give Autumn on her schedule? Does she have enough time to study? Write her a note on the sticky note below advising her about her study time for the semester.

Next, you will complete your own Time Management Table. Remember your goal of 2–3 hours of study time for each hour you are in class per week. Start with the formula:

1 hour in class per week (1 unit) = 2–3 study hours out of class per week

How many classes are you taking this semester? _____

How many hours do you spend in class each week (units)? _____ × 2 = [   ]

In the blue box is the **minimum** number of hours you should spend studying per week.

Now, fill in the entire time management table with a realistic weekly schedule for yourself. Be sure to add up your hours in class and study hours and write them at the bottom of the page. Keep in mind all of your commitments including work and family obligations. Then, revisit this table every few weeks of the semester to see if you are maintaining your study schedule and monitor changes in your schedule.

Time Management Table

Name _____   Class _____

	Monday	Tuesday	Wednesday	Thursday	Friday	Saturday	Sunday
6-7am							
7-8							
8-9							
9-10							
10-11							
11-12pm							
12-1							
1-2							
2-3							
3-4							
4-5							
5-6							
6-7							
7-8							
8-9							
9-10							
10-11							
11-12am							
12-1							
1-2							
2-3							
3-4							
4-5							
5-6							

[   ] hours in class   [   ] study/homework hours

Did you reserve for homework/studying at least the number of hours you wrote in your blue box? If not, revise the table until you have allotted adequate study hours. If your schedule outside of school does not allow you to dedicate an adequate number of hours per week to studying, this is a great time to reevaluate your class schedule. Are you taking too many classes for your lifestyle? Consider discussing this matter with a counselor at your college. It may be worth it to take *fewer* classes in which you can gain the required knowledge and skills instead of trying to do too much and ultimately having to retake classes.

Remember, THRIVING IN COLLEGE TAKES TIME. Don't cheat yourself. You are a smart and capable human being. Just carve out the time to show it!

Bedrin/Shutterstock.com

MAKE TIME FOR ASSIGNMENTS

Now that you have established that you have two to three hours per week to study and prepare outside of class for every hour you are in class, let's get down to specifics for your English class.

Most likely your English class is a three-unit class. That means you meet three hours a week if it is an on-campus class or you have three hours' worth of online activities to complete per week if it is an online class. That also means that your instructor expects you to spend six to nine hours per week outside of class working on assignments. You may have this gut reaction: WHAT?!? SIX TO NINE HOURS PER WEEK ON ENGLISH ASSIGNMENTS?!?! THAT'S CRAZY!!!

Well, hear us out. Think about your English class. In a class titled "College Reading and Composition" or "Composition and Critical Thinking" what types of assignments are you likely to get? List three examples below:

1)

2)

3)

You probably listed assignments like these: writing essays; reading books, articles, or sections from your textbook; defining vocabulary words; or completing grammar practice exercises. Now, before we start talking about how much time you should spend on those types of assignments, let's think about learning **outcomes**. What are the learning outcomes you should attain as a result of successfully completing an English class at your college? Try listing five here, even if you're not sure:

1)

2)

3)

4)

5)

Now compare your list to these sample lists of English class outcomes from a few different colleges:

1) At the end of the course, a successful student will be able to argue a point (thesis) and support it in writing using extensive evidence from outside sources.

2) At the end of the course, a successful student will be able to cite sources both in-text and on a works cited page following MLA guidelines.

1) Students will be able to read critically for literal and implied meaning, identify main ideas, organizational strategies, and authors' writing strategies as well as summarize, paraphrase, and analyze written works.

2) Students will use the writing process to write, in proper MLA format, academic essays, including a documented research paper, using appropriately chosen details, organizational strategies, more complex sentence variety, and sufficiently correct grammar, punctuation, effective word choice, and style.

3) Students will evaluate and ethically use primary and secondary academic sources to avoid plagiarism and will use the library's resources, including online databases, to locate appropriate academic source material.

1) Students will employ the writing process in order to understand and complete the writing task.

2) Students will employ critical thinking concepts to evaluate arguments.

3) Students will employ critical thinking concepts to write coherent, logical arguments.

4) Students will demonstrate critical engagement with outside sources.

5) Students will write in prose style characterized by clarity, complexity, and variety.

6) Students will adhere to the conventions of standard written English, including MLA format.

Those are just a few examples of skills your instructor will expect you to be able to demonstrate at the end of your semester in an English class at your college. Those lists probably look similar to the list of outcomes you made. You probably wrote something about improving your reading skills, writing better essays, maybe improving your vocabulary, spelling, and grammatical skills. If you did, you were right on.

So, what will you need to do in order to acquire those skills? How much time will it take?

Of course, that will depend on you. It will depend on your current skill level and exactly which class you're taking. But we can give you some basic tips and guidelines here. Keep reading!

ENGLISH CLASS TIME MANAGEMENT TIPS

1) The more time you spend, the better results you will get.

   The more you rush through your assignments, the less likely you are to gain the skills your class is designed to teach you.

2) The more undivided attention you give your assignments, the less time they will take. Multitasking will slow your learning!

   If you want to spend your time wisely and efficiently, turn off the TV, stay away from Facebook and Twitter, and put your phone down while you read and write for your English class. If you want to have to spend MORE time studying and doing homework, then multitask away.

3) Time yourself to gauge how much time you will need.

   Try this. Look at the clock. Make a note of the time. Then, read the first three to five pages of your reading assignment. Read it closely and take notes. Review your notes. Now look at the clock again. How long did that take you? Fifteen minutes? Thirty minutes? An hour? Now, how long is your full reading assignment? Calculate how long your entire reading assignment should take. Then, be sure to allow that amount of time for you to complete your assignment.

▌READING

Below is an example reading assignment from Jason's English class. When he reads the assignment, he assumes it will take him about two hours to complete.

1) Read *Between the World and Me* pp. 5–39.

2) While reading, highlight at least three important ideas in the text.

3) While reading, briefly summarize each important idea or main point in the margin and then also in the margin, make a note of a connection to something you already know, a prediction about what will come next, or a question you have about the idea or point.

4) While reading, highlight at least three challenging passages that you find difficult to understand from different parts of the text, and in the margin, make a note of what makes each passage difficult to understand. (You might note if the author refers to something you're not familiar with or uses a word or words you don't know.)

5) Highlight one golden line (One or two sentences that you think are important to the text and stand out to you.) in the text and make a note of why you selected it as your golden line.

6) Highlight at least five unfamiliar words in the text, and write the dictionary definition of each word in the margin.

This assignment requires Jason to read 34 pages from the book *Between the World and Me* by Ta-Nehisi Coates, so Jason will time himself to figure out approximately how long this assignment will take him. He looks at the clock, and it is 3:30pm. Then, he reads pp. 5–12 in *Between the World and Me*. As he is reading, he highlights three new words. Then, he highlights Coates's most important ideas in those pages, and summarizes one in the margin. Then, he writes a question about that idea. He checks the clock again when he's done. It is 4:15. It has taken him about 45 minutes to complete this task for 7 pages of text. If he has 35 pages to read, how long will it take him to complete the entire reading portion of this assignment? If you said 225 minutes, you were correct! How many hours is that? That is almost four hours, which is less than half of Jason's allotted study time for the week. He should have plenty of time to read and annotate the text as well as complete any further homework assignments for his English class.

Now, think about Jason's process, and answer the questions in Exercise 1.

Exercise 1:

1. How long did Jason learn his assignment was likely to take once he timed himself reading?

2. As you can see, Jason's guess of two hours was not accurate. How far off was he?

3. Why do you think he guessed incorrectly?

4. Have you ever underestimated the time you thought an assignment would take?

5. If so, what was the impact of your incorrect guess?

6. What would have been the impact on Jason if he had only spent two hours on this assignment?

7. What would have been the impact on Jason if he had been multitasking (watching videos, texting, scrolling through Instagram) as he worked on this assignment?

Time management is the key to completing college classes and attaining the knowledge and skills necessary to move on to the next level. The likelihood is great that by spending an adequate amount of time on homework and studying, you will pass your classes and move on to the next level. Just remember not to overdo it, and plan ahead. Everyone at your college is rooting for you!

FINAL RECOMMENDATIONS FOR COLLEGE TIME MANAGEMENT

1) Use a calendar.

   You may have a calendar on your phone, or try using a Google or Yahoo calendar. Open a Gmail or Yahoo account, and you immediately have access to a calendar. You can sync it to your phone and set it to alert you when an event or task is approaching.

   You can also use a paper calendar especially if you don't have a smart phone and don't spend a lot of time on a computer. Student planners or calendars are likely sold at your college bookstore.

2) Use your syllabus to plan ahead.

   Write assignment due dates in your calendar. Schedule necessary homework and study time into your calendar too, so you won't be able to use the "I forgot" excuse.

3) Make lists.

   A lot of people find making "to do" lists useful. They feel a sense of accomplishment when they can cross off items on their lists. Some people make daily or weekly lists. You might make lists in your planner or you may have a notepad application on your phone you can use.

   Remember that as the title of this chapter suggests, you CAN schedule yourself for success in college. Make the time, and you will thrive!

CHAPTER CHAPTER CHAPTER

2

CLASS SUCCESS STRATEGIES:
USE YOUR COLLEGE COMMUNITY

Sometimes a student will try to deal with all of life's challenges by herself as though she is alone in the world. Fortunately, in your English class, and in the rest of college, you are not alone. You have an entire community of people available to support your success.

Academic counselors on your campus offer a wealth of knowledge to guide you in succeeding in college. They are the experts in your college community who will support you in overcoming obstacles and in taking the best classes to accomplish your goals.

In your individual classes, each professor is an expert resource to support your success. Your classmates can also support you in achieving your goals. In addition, most

colleges have libraries and learning centers or labs where you can find librarians and tutors whose purpose is to support students academically.

PROFESSORS:
EXPERTS IN YOUR COMMUNITY

Building relationships with your college professors will certainly aid in your completing your classes successfully. Your professors' office hours are the weekly hours they have committed to be available for their students. These hours are included in your professors' salaries and are generally held during a reasonable time when students are likely to be on campus.

SEVEN REASONS TO VISIT YOUR PROFESSOR'S OFFICE HOURS:

1) Introduce yourself.

2) Get to know your professor.

3) Give your professor a chance to get to know you.

4) Ensure clarity on assignment directions and due dates.

5) Ask for feedback on a draft of an assignment.

6) Ask for an explanation of a grade on a returned assignment.

7) Check on your progress in the class.

While we recommend visiting all of your professors in their office hours, visiting your English professors can make an immense difference in your attaining the knowledge and skills you need to move successfully to the next level.

WHY VISIT YOUR ENGLISH PROFESSOR?

Get feedback on drafts of your papers before you submit them for grades.

> Your English professor knows how you can improve your writing. He writes comments on your essays *after* you've turned them in. Why not get those comments *before* the essays are due so you can demonstrate all the skills you need to in order to earn the best grade possible?

Ask for an explanation of a grade on a returned assignment.

> Sometimes you may earn a grade on an assignment but not understand why you earned that grade. Office hours provide the perfect opportunity for your professor to explain the rationale for the grade you earned on a writing assignment and for you to find out what to do on future writing assignments to demonstrate your skills and earn the best possible grade.

Ask for an explanation of professors' comments on returned assignments.

> Your professors' comments can be an invaluable tool for improving your writing. Many students do not know the best ways to use those comments. When you read a professor's comments, you may not understand something, and office hours are a great time to get clarification.

One interesting thing about college composition (writing) classes is that they are different from many other college courses. In a composition class, you are learning and practicing a skill just like you would if you were taking a dance class. In a dance class, the instructor shows you some steps, and then you practice them until you get better at them. Your dance instructor is available to give you tips and pointers along the way to ensure your dancing is as good as it can be. Like dance lessons, the vast majority of composition class content is skill-based. As a result, visiting your composition professor's office hours is critical as you develop and practice this skill of college level academic writing. Just like you would with a dance instructor, you want to give yourself an opportunity to ask questions and get directions from the expert, your professor, one-on-one, especially since getting that crucial individual attention is often difficult in a classroom setting.

WHAT YOU GAIN: BENEFITS OF VISITING A PROFESSOR IN OFFICE HOURS

Practice interacting in an academic or professional setting.

> Sometimes students are intimidated by the idea of visiting a professor during his office hours. However, these visits provide great practice for future job inquiries or interviews in which you might also feel intimidated but need to take action and interact with someone new in order to accomplish your goals.

Nuggets of information that your professor may not reveal during class time.

> Some professors share information with students in their office hours that they have not shared or will not share in a classroom setting. This may be information about upcoming assignments or their expectations or their styles of grading. This information can be invaluable for your success in the class.

An opportunity to show your professor your commitment to your education.

> Professors may not glean a student's level of commitment from their interaction in class. Take advantage of office hours to communicate this commitment to your professor. Show him what you've been doing toward his class. Ask questions that show you've been thinking about the course content.

UNIQUE CIRCUMSTANCES

If you're not available during your professor's office hours, don't despair. Ask her about making an appointment. You might ask before or after class or send an e-mail. Don't let your busy schedule cause you to miss out on the opportunity to get one-on-one time with your professor.

Some online professors hold online office hours. Those may be hours when you can chat online with the professor in real time, or you may have the opportunity to video chat with your professor. That one-on-one real time interaction can be as valuable as office hours in person. On the other hand, some online professors are only available via e-mail or phone. If this is the case, do everything you can to speak to the professor on the phone at least once during the semester. If you have a specific question, e-mail the professor first with the question, and then follow up with a call so the two of you can discuss your question in real time.

If e-mail is your only option, make it work for you. Asking your professor questions via e-mail can work as well as asking them face-to-face and sometimes even better because you will have the answers in writing and you can refer back to them at a later date. See "E-mail Correspondence" for details on professional e-mail etiquette.

The bottom line is that you will reap the benefits of meeting with your professors one-on-one. Use the table below to record your professors' office hours. Then, schedule in your calendar time to visit each of them at least once this semester.

Professor's Name	Phone Number/E-mail	Class	Office Hours Day and Time	Date I'll Visit
1)		English		
2)				
3)				
4)				
5)				

Now, add your professors' phone numbers and e-mail addresses to your phone so you will always have them with you. That way, if you encounter an emergency and need to contact a professor to notify her of anything, you will be able to do so.

One more benefit of getting to know your professors during their office hours is that when you need a recommendation letter for your transfer application or a scholarship, you will have a number of professors to ask. If you contact a former professor a few semesters later, he will likely want to see previous essays or other assignments to remind him of the quality of your work, so be sure to keep those materials accessible to make writing that recommendation as easy as possible.

CLASSMATES:

GET PEER SUPPORT IN YOUR COMMUNITY

Your classmates provide a valuable resource in class and outside of class. At the beginning of the semester, identify some students with whom you will study and engage with them right away. "Study" time for an English or composition (writing) class is not usually spent doing traditional studying for exams. For your English classes, that study time is often spent doing one or more of the following:

- reading from textbooks like this one, articles, essays, or other books to be discussed in class or written about for class assignments
- writing compositions, essays, or research papers
- completing other types of assignments like grammar practice or exercises

As a result, students often think that there is no point in forming "study groups" or finding "study partners" for English classes. However, study groups or study partners can be vital for your success in English classes.

FIVE THINGS TO DO WITH YOUR ENGLISH CLASS STUDY GROUPS OR STUDY PARTNERS:

1) Discuss and identify main points in reading assignments.
2) Prepare for quizzes.
3) Help each other with research.
4) Review each other's writing.
5) Support each other in completing assignments.

Don't underestimate your classmates as a resource. They may not be professionals at composition or writing, but they will see your writing from an objective point of view. Also, since they are in the class with you, they have exposure to the assignments and incentive to complete them with you. When you build a community in your class, you are more likely to attend, and you have support if you have to miss. Plus, creating a community of classmates will make going to class more fun! (We have even seen students meet their boyfriends/girlfriends in our classes through this process.)

TUTORS:

ANOTHER RESOURCE IN YOUR COMMUNITY

Some people are not comfortable asking for help. They may see asking for help as a sign of weakness or an admission that they can't do something alone. However, one valuable lesson available to you in college is that asking for help is an opportunity for empowerment. Some members of your community available to empower you to ask for help are the faculty and staff members of your college's Center for Learning Support or Student Success Center or Learning Center or Writing Lab. Those members of your community are available to provide you with academic support for your English classes (and usually others as well). Most academic support centers offer English or writing tutoring. Sometimes you will encounter one-on-one tutoring and sometimes small-group tutoring, and either way, seeing a tutor has value because of the individualized attention you get from someone more versed in the subject than you. Here are some things to remember when you see an English or writing tutor:

1) If your college's learning support center takes appointments, call ahead for an appointment. Go and look up your college's center and find the hours and the phone number. Write them in the table below.

Name of Center:		
Location on Campus:	Phone Number:	Hours:

Now add the center's phone number to the contacts in your phone so you'll always have it with you.

2) If you have an appointment, be on time. Avoid the risk of losing your spot in line.

3) Come to the tutoring session prepared: Bring the assignment sheet or book or syllabus that explains the assignment. If the assignment is based on a reading, bring the reading (book, article, essay, etc.) Bring pen and paper unless you will be using a computer. Bring any relevant notes from class or on your reading. Bring previous graded writing assignments.

4) If you bring the tutor a draft of your work, come to the session far enough in advance of the due date for you to take full advantage of the feedback you get from the tutor.

5) Bring questions to ask the tutor. Since the session's purpose is to benefit your learning and help you accomplish the outcomes of your class, you can lead the session. Talk to the tutor about your concerns and areas that have given you trouble in the past.

6) Take full responsibility for your assignment. Know that when it comes down to it, the essay is yours, not the tutor's, so make sure you understand all suggestions before you implement them. The tutor will not do the assignment for you, nor will he edit it for you. Remember that the tutor provides learning support, so he will support you in demonstrating that *you* have attained the outcomes for your course.

LIBRARIANS:

ONE MORE GREAT RESOURCE TO FOSTER YOUR SUCCESS

In a college level English class you will have to write one or more essays with research components. Your English professors are getting you ready to apply research strategies in your other classes as you advance in your college career. You may think that your English professor is an expert in research, and she is. However, who is the real research expert on campus? The librarian is, of course. Your college library invariably has at least one reference librarian whose job it is to help students conduct research. Take advantage of this librarian's expertise. As soon as you get a research assignment, go to the librarian for tips on where to find the best sources for your topic and how to use those sources once you've found them.

We cannot reiterate it enough. Take advantage of your college community to foster your success in English classes and beyond. Remember that you are a smart and capable human being. Seeking help from others in your college community will underscore your abilities and give you the opportunity to take them to the next level.

FIND YOUR VOICE AND MAKE IT COUNT: THE IMPORTANCE OF CLASS PARTICIPATION

Critical thinking and effective communication are likely learning outcomes at your college and in the English class for which you are using this textbook. Many of the skills you develop in a college composition class are tied to critical thinking and effective communication:

- using strategies to present a persuasive argument
- using evidence to support your point
- acknowledging your opponents' views

Both writing essays and participating in class give you the opportunity to sharpen and practice these skills. Class discussions build your critical thinking and effective communication skills as you practice articulating your ideas. The ability to speak persuasively is a very useful skill. Even if you never write another essay after this semester, you will have to convince someone verbally in the future: whether it is negotiating your pay for a new job, getting visitation rights with your children, or selecting a movie with a friend. Participating in class discussions will prepare you for all of these scenarios. We also recommend taking a Communication Studies or Speech class to build those same skills.

Class discussions also provide opportunities to show your instructor your commitment to your education, and for you to practice your leadership skills. Students often have questions, but are afraid to ask them. The student who participates in the discussion by asking questions provides a service for his or her more timid classmates.

Be bold. Participate actively in your classes. That participation will serve you well in the long-term.

LEARN HOW YOU LEARN

LEARNING AND TEACHING MODES

The traditional mode of pedagogy (teaching) in college has always been lecture; professors deliver a stream of information while students listen and take notes, although professors are increasingly moving away from this model. It's vital, therefore, that you not only learn how to learn from this teaching style, but learn how to compensate for what may be the differences in your own learning style.

Not every teaching style works for every learner. Many researchers have distinguished several distinct modes of learning such as learning by seeing, learning by hearing, and learning by doing. Some students learn best from seeing content visually, while some learn best by hearing. Others learn best by doing: either reading and/or writing about the information, or through direct experience, like role play.

In our experience, all of these modes, when used together to reinforce one another, can enhance everyone's learning experience. It is important to determine what your learning style is, and identify the gap, if applicable, between the system that works best for you, and the system each of your professors is using. While you can't expect professors to change their styles, by understanding what you need best to learn, you can learn to provide it for yourself.

For example, if your professor uses lecture, and your dominant learning modes are hearing (aural) and seeing (visual), you will easily benefit from your professor's teaching style. However, as a visual learner, you could enhance your experience even more by drawing while the professor is speaking—drawing the concepts being described. Or, if it is more important to get the information down in notation form, you could draw the concepts as a study tool. As a visual learner, you would also benefit from paying close attention to images, graphs, and charts in your textbooks as learning tools. In addition, if you obtain the professor's consent to record the class, you can listen to the material again and again at your convenience. If the professor will not allow sound recording—some will, and some won't—you can make your own recording by reading yourself the content out of the textbook or out of your notes. Both the process of recording it, and of listening to it, will be beneficial to you.

However, if you don't learn particularly well by hearing, nor by reading or writing, the traditional mode of lecture and reading/writing homework may be quite a challenge for you. Once you've identified what mode(s) work best for you, you can think about how you can enhance the learning experience for yourself. If you learn by doing, you might be able to create some experiments during your study time that will help you conceptualize the material. Perhaps you and a study partner could act out a skit between characters—perhaps a proton and a neutron—in which they talk to each other and argue about their "jobs" inside the nucleus. Many instructors offer a number of supplemental materials (study guides, Power-Points, videos, interactive software, etc.) that can also reinforce the material.

Below are some specific tools that can supplement the classroom lecture experience.

MEMORIZATION TOOLS

There are many mnemonic (memory) devices that can be used to aid learning and memorization. **One useful technique is to store information in a picture.** This could be a picture you hold in your mind, like the mental image of Grandma's kitchen, or it could be a picture that you find and use for this purpose. Terms, equations, definitions, and so forth can be stored at different places in the drawing. For example, I might store helping verbs in Grandma's kitchen. I'll put "am," "is," "are," "was," and "were" in the oven. I'll put "be," being," and "been" in the cookie jar. I'll put "could," "should," "shall," and "will" in the sink, and "do,"

Four Most Common Comma Usages

Before a FANBOYS

After intro material

Items in a series

Around interrupters

Nathan Bailey

You can store information in a picture to aid memorization.

© Canoneer/Shutterstock.com

12 11 1
to at during
10 of on 2
9 behind until 3
8 with in 4
onto after into
7 6 5

I'm a simple sentence!

I'm a complex sentence!

"does," and "did" in the potato bin. Now when I am taking my test, and stressed out, the chances are greater than I can remember this data even under stressful conditions—because who can forget Grandma's kitchen?

In the image, a student has stored the four most common uses of a comma on a picture of chairs he had handy on his laptop or phone. Now he can quickly recall the information by recalling the picture and which "use" was stored on each chair.

Likewise, we can store information on the face of a clock. Take a look at this preposition clock image at left. Although the clock face isn't big enough to store all the common prepositions, it can certainly store twelve of the most common ones, which is twelve more than I might be able to remember otherwise!

This popsicle image (left) was created to remember the difference between types of verbs. It is at once a drawing and at once a skit. The double content layer, together with the very act of creating it, inscribes the information in the brain.

STUDY PARTNERS

Study partners are an indispensable tool in succeeding in any class. Because we all learn differently, study groups are a chance to re-experience the material from our classmates' perspectives. This creates another layer of learning on top of the initial lecture/textbook experience. You might benefit from their note-taking skills, while they might benefit from your accurate aural (hearing) memory or whatever your particular skills are.

LEARNING DIFFERENCES

Students with learning differences (often called disabilities) sometimes have an even greater challenge in benefitting from the traditional mode of classroom delivery. Most colleges have an office to accommodate for specific physical or learning needs, once you test into the program. Benefits can include, but are not limited to, free note-takers, extra time on tests, test taking in a distraction-free environment, American Sign Language interpreters, hearing devices, visual magnification tools, or even just a seat up front to hear the professors' words more clearly. Accommodations vary by school, and by the degree of difference or disability you demonstrate. If you already have an IEP from high school, request a copy sent to your college to speed the process.

TAKE YOUR LEARNING INVENTORY

In conclusion, whether or not you have a learning difference that qualifies you for special accommodations, you can become an expert about your learning process and take the experience of each classroom to a whole new level. You can also teach others what you've learned. First, you must determine the learning modes that are most useful to you. There are many diagnostic resources online, but you can start by taking an informal "inventory."

How do you best retain information? How useful are written words to you in recalling information? How useful are pictures or sound? Are one of these three more useful than the others? Would direct experience—a field trip, as applicable, or role play—be even more useful than the other three? You can take your own learning inventory just by paying attention to the modes that work best for you.

ACE IN-CLASS PRESENTATIONS

Students are often asked to make in-class presentations as a part of their responsibilities in English class. The reasons for this are many. More and more, the ability to speak publically and clearly about a project is a necessary and useful job skill recognized by many employers. If you get the opportunity to speak at a student conference, having confidence in your speaking abilities will ensure that it is a rewarding experience. Practicing in class is a great way to start. Often we professors find that some students show quite a flare for presenting and blossom when asked to do so. Let us help you make the most of the experience.

Here are a few pointers to help you through what doesn't have to be a nerve-wracking process:

© Matej Kastelic/Shutterstock.com

1) Familiarize yourself with the assignment. Know what is expected.

2) Allow enough time to fully understand and **research your topic sufficiently**. There is nothing worse than not feeling prepared. Know your topic so that you can field any questions your professor or classmates might throw your way.

3) **When narrowing your topic, be sure to consider the length of time you will be speaking**. The difference between a five- and a twenty-minute presentation is significant. **Time yourself at home in front of the mirror. Speak slowly and carefully**. Don't try to cram too much information into a short time span by speaking a mile a minute. Your points will be lost and you will get out of breath. In presentations, sometimes less is more. This is especially true if you will be submitting a written component of the assignment. If that is the case, you can focus on the key points in the presentation and leave the nuances and exceptions for the written version. Listeners may have difficulty taking in too much information, and reducing to the key points will ensure that your message gets across.

4) **Know your surroundings**. If you can, practice in the room you will be speaking in when it is empty. Students always say that the classroom looks very different from the front than the back! Practice using the podium and decide if you like it or not. If you are in an unknown place, for example at a student conference, try to find out where you will be speaking and sneak a peek at the room. Having an accurate mental picture of the space can help relax you. If permitted, bring a bottle of water with you to combat nervous dry mouth during longer presentations.

5) If it gives you confidence to do so, write out your presentation and memorize it. **Practice enough that you can deliver your speech in a conversational way that doesn't feel too artificial**. Ironically, the more you rehearse, the more "natural" you will sound because you will be comfortable. Also, memorizing at least the introduction will help you get through the first minutes of your talk (which is the part that most presenters find the most difficult). Once you get going, you will gain confidence.

6) **Stay professional and retain an appropriately formal tone**. A little humor is great. Slang and vulgar words are not.

7) **Ask your professor if you are permitted to read or bring notes**. Having the notes in front of you will help if you temporarily lose your train of thought. Generally, it is preferable not to read your presentation. However, if your paper is complicated or long, reading may be the best option. If you do read, look up often and make eye contact with your audience so that it feels almost like a conversation. You might even write in when to look up and when to take a sip of water for longer presentations to keep yourself on track.

8) As you go through your presentation, just as you would do in a written essay, be sure to **state your thesis explicitly. Make transitions** between different points and remind your audience of how each point fits into your thesis.

9) Do not neglect your introduction or your conclusion. As in writing, a strong introduction will capture your audience's attention. Likewise, a snappy conclusion will leave them feeling they have heard a good presentation.

10) **Use a PowerPoint presentation or visual aids if your professor allows them**. Having visuals can help make a point to an audience member who processes information visually. Moreover, having a PowerPoint can help deflect some of the audience's attention from you and might help you focus on your talk rather than on your nerves. **Remember to keep slides simple and visual. Don't have too much text on a slide**. Viewers will get lost trying to read small print. Ideally, make your point verbally with a compelling argument or statistic and illustrate it with a picture. You might isolate and enlarge the strongest or most shocking statistic or quote on one slide for maximum impact. **Be sure to proofread your slides for spelling and grammatical errors before presenting.** Practice your presentation with the slides to get the flow of information coordinated ahead of time.

11) **Group Presentations**: If you are presenting with a group, practice together to be sure each member knows what he or she should be saying and in what order. Arguing about whose turn it is will be distracting for the audience. Delegate jobs so that everyone plays a part. Assign one person to advance the slides, another to distribute hand-outs, another to ask questions, etc. You can also delegate research to different group members, but be sure each person knows the subject well and can field questions from the professor or students no matter when they come.

12) **Pause periodically to ask a question of the audience if appropriate**. This can keep listeners engaged and participating in your talk. Give the audience time to respond. Wait a moment for answers, but if none are forthcoming, don't let that throw you. Be prepared to forge ahead gracefully.

13) **If the professor interrupts your presentation**, he or she is likely trying to help you make a point to the class or clarify a mistake you may have made. Don't be surprised. Appreciate the interruption to gather your thoughts and be prepared to continue on with the presentation.

14) **Dress in appropriate clothing that fits and is comfortable**. You might feel foolish putting on a tie and a jacket for a ten-minute presentation, and that probably isn't necessary. However, class presentation day is not the time to try out a risky fashion statement or low-cut blouses or low-riding pants. They will be distracting to you and to your audience. You don't want to be fidgeting or uncomfortable. You want the focus on your words!

15) **Breathe and have fun!** Everyone wants you to do well, especially your professor.

MAKE THE MOST OF YOUR ONLINE CLASSES

Distance learning has revolutionized education. Online classes have provided many students who work or who could not commute to a campus access to an education, and more students than ever before are being educated thanks to technology. Being in a virtual classroom is different from a "face-to-face" class, however. We want to share a few tips to help you make the most of your online experience.

© Elnur/Shutterstock.com

1) First, know what you're getting into. Online classes work best for students who will have the discipline and the commitment to keep to the schedule of assignments. Not having set times to do your work is both a blessing and a curse. If you have a complicated work or life schedule, online classes can open up a whole new world of learning opportunities to you. Keep a schedule to avoid forgetting about assignments or responsibilities.

> "The advice I would give is to not take online classes if you don't have enough free time. I learned this the hard way because I was a full time student and full time worker."
>
> English 101 Student

2) Get your technical difficulties taken care of **before** the semester starts. Don't buy a new laptop the day the semester opens. Your instructor expects you to be familiar with the computer skills and computer you will need to succeed in the course. Do not send fifty e-mails to your instructor in a panic before you have tried to solve the technical issue yourself. The campus Distance Learning office is always another source of help.

3) The very first week, take the time to complete the tutorial available for your college's courseware. Get versed in all the ins and outs **before** a deadline is looming. Have fun looking around the site and getting to know its features. Find out how to post assignments and comments on the discussion board as well as retrieve comments and grades. Know how to contact your professor in both private and public messages. Test the features out in advance.

4) Once the class has started, check in daily. Being away from the class for more than a day can spell trouble in an online class. New assignments, posts, and announcements accumulate and can quickly become unmanageable if left even for a couple of days. Stay on top of it!

5) Awaken your inner blogger. Participate in online discussions and generate enthusiasm for the course material. Most courses have a requirement that you participate in discussions. Read the assignment before you contribute. This is not the place to expound upon your personal philosophies if they are not relevant to the discussion.

6) Practice good netiquette. Be polite and respectful of your classmates. Never use vulgar language or insult another student's views, and do not respond in anger if someone else doesn't follow the same practice. Remember, your professor will be reading the posts. Keep it professional. If you get upset at something a classmate has said, log off for awhile and cool down rather than reacting immediately. It may be appropriate to message the instructor.

7) This should go without saying, but never try to sell anything to your classmates or use their e-mail addresses to circulate any information unrelated to the course content.

8) The great advantage to online courses is that you can carefully compose your arguments before you post. In a classroom, you might be put on the spot. Online you have time to think. Use this opportunity to be eloquent and persuasive.

9) Proofread your posts before they go out. Spelling and grammar mistakes are embarrassing and will take away from the excellent points you want to make.

10) Always save a copy of your work on your computer first and submit it online from there. Don't work directly inside the submission box in case it times out.

11) Keep your folders and drafts organized. This will make your life much easier. Label drafts correctly and don't assume you'll remember which is the correct version.

Have fun and enjoy coming to class in your pajamas!

TAKE STUDENT ADVICE

Don't just take it from us. Here's what our best students are saying...

We asked students the following question on a survey: "What advice would you give to a nervous new student who was starting her first day of college? What do you wish someone had told you on your first day?" Many students voiced the same concerns and shared some great advice.

Here are some of their responses:

Time Management

> "Pace yourself. Never wait till the last minute for anything. In high school, teachers are on top of the student. But in college, it's up to you to do your work and do it well."

- "Read a little of the books assigned every day. There have been studies that show that cramming does not work as well as twenty minutes every day."
- "Don't wait till the last minute to get readings or papers done. Make sure you actually read the book that is given to you in class."
- "If you have a full time job, don't try to take a lot on. I wish I had known how to use my time better."
- "Arrive on time to class...you'll gain the respect of your teachers."

Using Your Community

> "Visit a counselor every semester to keep you on track for where you want to go."

- "See a counselor and make an SEP (Student Educational Plan). Have an idea of what four-year university you would like to attend. Some universities require different classes depending on your major."
- "Approach every course as if it were your major. Don't be afraid to seek out help, whether it be from tutors, teachers, or fellow classmates."

- "If you're having problems in a class, go to office hours! The instructor won't come after you."
- "Don't be afraid to ask questions!! Especially when in the middle of tests, teachers can clarify confusing questions."

Knowing What to Study

- "Start early and finish! Take summer and winter courses also because it will help you to be done faster and to get the GE requirements done."
- "Get to know the college and different services that are available for you in college; basically get comfortable in college before you start taking more classes and harder classes."
- "Register for core classes ASAP! Math and English are two subjects that are hard for some students and getting them out of the way is one of the best things you can do."

Attitude

"Breathe. Even pacing and a deliberate approach may serve you better than six 5-hour energy drinks. Too often we see the next step in our lives as something to be overcome as quickly as possible. The true knowledge comes not in the end result, but in the journey." –Erin Paul

- "Don't be afraid of other students. Be humble, kind, and understanding.
- "No matter what happens throughout one's educational journey, remain strong-willed and never give up or give in! Think 'mind over matter' because success is a lifelong journey."

"Don't doubt yourself or feel you aren't as smart as everyone else. Remember, we are all here for the same reason, to learn."

Workload/Hard Work

- "You really need to study! If you don't, you won't pass your class. My test scores improved a lot when I studied for days before my exams."

"Set goals. When you don't, it's easy to get distracted."

- "It'd be helpful to do a little research on the book and author that you're reading. This background would help to understand the reading better."
- "Attend class."
- "I wish I had set out a timeline and realistic goals. Fifteen and eighteen units are too much if you're going to work and school and expect to do well."

"If you're not excited about college, don't sign up. Wait a semester or more until you personally are ready for it. You'll be more motivated to be here and you'll do better over all."

- "Add all your classes on time and be well prepared for the first day of school. Check e-mail regularly for classroom changes and updates."

Getting Involved in College Activities

- "Clubs and special interest groups are a great way to make friends with people who share your interests, and can help you develop a support system."
- "Join the honor societies!"

"I wish I had realized that going to school, having had kids, is not an impossible goal. A friend introduced me to all the resources the school has to offer to assist me in accomplishing my goals."

Financial Assistance

- "Don't be ashamed to get financial aid. College is really expensive and every little bit of free money helps."
- "Financial aid should be your very best friend. Apply for it early!"
- "I wish I had known all the locations and opportunities for work and financial assistance and the internships."

Additional Advice

- "Don't wait till the last minute to buy your books!"
- "Also, surround yourself with focused people because it's motivating being around that energy."

II

START WITH A GOOD FOUNDATION

CHAPTERS

CHAPTER 3

READING

This chapter was written in collaboration with Marianne Steverson, literacy expert and Senior Director, Smar^{2}tel Foundations.

▌READING FUNDAMENTALS

In her book, *Beginning to Read: Thinking and Learning About Print*, Marilyn Jager Adams famously said, "most of our formal education is acquired through language." Think about it. Most of what you learn in school does not come from your looking at pictures or listening to music. Instead, it comes from your listening to someone talk, your talking, or most often—from your reading texts (books, articles, essays, stories, poems, etc.). This underscores the need for successful col-

lege students to have mastery over reading, writing, and talking about texts. If you have trouble reading college level texts, this chapter will give you some tools to improve your vocabulary, reading fluency, and comprehension and to remove any barriers that exist between your current level of skills and your overall education.

In 2009, the Council of Chief State School Officers and the National Governors Association for Best Practices spearheaded an effort to develop a commonly-shared set of standards that would ensure that all students across the nation have access to the knowledge and skills necessary to succeed in their chosen careers.

The following table outlines the anchor **reading standards** in which a student should be proficient by the end of Grade 12. As you read through these standards, look for any thing on the list that is challenging for you, and as you continue through this chapter, choose ways to build those skills.

COLLEGE AND CAREER READINESS ANCHOR STANDARDS FOR GRADES 6 – 12 IN READING

Key Ideas and Details

1) Read closely to determine what the text says explicitly and to make logical inferences from it; cite specific textual evidence when writing or speaking to support conclusions drawn from the text.

2) Determine central ideas or themes of a text and analyze their development; summarize the key supporting details and ideas.

3) Analyze how and why individuals, events, and ideas develop and interact over the course of a text.

Craft and Structure

4) Interpret words and phrases as they are used in a text, including determining technical, connotative, and figurative meanings, and analyze how specific word choices shape meaning or tone.

5) Analyze the structure of texts, including how specific sentences, paragraphs, and larger portions of the text (e.g., a section, chapter, scene, or stanza) relate to each other and the whole.

6) Assess how point of view or purpose shapes the content and style of a text.

Integration of Knowledge and Ideas

7) Integrate and evaluate content presented in diverse formats and media, including visually and quantitatively, as well as in words.

8) Delineate and evaluate the argument and specific claims in a text, including the validity of the reasoning as well as the relevance and sufficiency of the evidence.

9) Analyze how two or more texts address similar themes or topics in order to build knowledge or to compare the approaches the authors take.

Range of Reading and Level of Text Complexity

10) Read and comprehend complex literary and informational texts independently and proficiently.

Reading and Spelling Multi-syllabic Words

As you read in college, you will have to know the words' sounds (phonemes), but with more advanced words, you may need to break them into parts (syllabication) in order to read and spell them. Try this word "**antidisestablishmentarianism**." It looks difficult, but there are some strategies we can apply to words like this. We break them into syllables also known as sound (phonological) parts—

> an / ti / dis / es / tab / lish / men / tar / i / an / ism—

> Now it is not so difficult.

> But let us start with some easier words and ideas.

Syllabication

A phonological or sound syllable is a word part that contains only one sounded vowel. The word "slapped" has only one sounded vowel /ă/ (the letter "e" is not sounded as a vowel), so it is made up of one syllable. The word "abrupt" has two sounded vowels —/ə/ and /ŭ/, so it has two syllables (a/brupt).

We syllabicate, or break words into syllables, for two reasons, 1) **to read and spell them or** 2) **to understand their meanings**. First we are going to learn a strategy for breaking words into syllables in order to read and spell them. It is important that you understand this concept because you will see words divided into syllables in different ways. You may see words broken up into sound bytes (fas-ter) or meaning bytes (fast-er). We will begin with sound bytes.

Dividing Words into Syllables to Read and Spell (Sound Bytes)

1) Separate any prefixes or suffixes (You will read more about these later):

   a. In "introduction," "in" and "tro" are prefixes; "tion" is a suffix, and many times the word will be easily broken up: **in** / **tro** / duc / **tion**.

2) Identify your vowels and break between the vowel and the consonant: **o/p**en; if that doesn't work, break between the consonant and the vowel: ca**b/i**n.

3) Break between double letters: co**m/m**em/or/ate.

4) Keep vowel teams and consonant teams together: in/**str**uc/**tio**n/al.

Exercise 1:

Choose five words from the list below and divide them into syllables in the boxes. See the sample done for you.

inextricably	pseudoscientific	infallible	proliferating
utilitarian	ruminate	boycotted	farcical
altruistic	staunchest	peripheries	ambiguous
respite	lament	rectify	disenfranchisement

dis	en	fran	chise	ment

Once you have broken the words into syllables, you can examine the vowels because the vowels give you important information on how to pronounce the syllables. Use the Syllable Type chart below to identify the characteristics of each syllable type for pronunciation. Try saying the word, and if it doesn't sound like a word you know, consult *Dictionary.com* and listen to the audio pronunciation of the word for help with the correct accent (syllable emphasis) and to confirm your pronunciation.

More on Syllables

In order for a word to be a word, it must have at least one vowel sound. When a word has more than one vowel sound, it is a multisyllabic word. The pronunciation for each syllable is guided by the vowel sound in that syllable.

Vocabulary Acquisition: Understanding Word Parts

According to Richard Anderson et al., a high school graduate should know at least 60,000 words. Most students enter first grade knowing about 5,000 words; thus, in order to reach 60,000 by Grade 12, a student must learn approximately 4,000 new words per year to reach that goal.

Instead of learning all of those words one word at a time, students often learn about different types of word parts to help them know many more words than they could simply memorize.

Words are made up of meaning parts called **morphemes**. A morpheme is the smallest unit of meaning in a word. We break words into morphemes to assist us in understanding the function and meaning of a word. The following word may look difficult, but we can apply a number of strategies to help us understand it. Hint: Try looking for meaning parts in this word.

pneumonoultramicroscopicsilicovolcanoconiosis

If we break the word into meaning (morphological) parts—

pneumono (having to do with the lungs)

ultra-micro-scopic (too small to be seen with the eye)

silico (silica or quartz particles)

volcano (from a volcano)

coniosis (a disease)

— it is not so difficult to figure out the meaning (*a disease of the lungs caused by inhalation of microscopic silica particles found in volcanos*).

Now try breaking the word into syllables (phonemes) to help you pronounce it.

Let's get a common understanding of some specific word parts or morphemes. Structure and meaning of the whole word helps you to know whether a word part is a morpheme. The chart below also gives you the characteristics of three basic word parts, prefixes, roots, and suffixes, and examples of each.

Word Part Characteristics		
Morpheme (Meaning Part)	**Function**	**Example**
Prefix	Syllable at the beginning of a multisyllabic word that adds or changes the meaning of root words; bound prefixes must be attached to another word part.	Un-, re-, dis-, in-
	*Spelling may change to match first letter of root or assist in pronunciation (Ad can be spelled *ac, af, al, an, ap, ar, as, at,* but they all have the same meaning).	**Ad** is the prefix but spelling changes in words like: accept, affair, allow, annex, appear, arrive, assign, attend
Root	Syllable in a multisyllabic word that carries the primary meaning of the word; bound roots must be attached to another word part.	
	• Latin (used in literature)	port, scribe, dic, form
	• Greek (math, science, literature)	tele, micro, phobia, scope, drama
	• Anglo Saxon (common everyday words)	ground, build, clean, friend
Suffix	Syllable at end of multisyllabic word; indicates part of speech; adds meaning; cannot stand alone.	Introduc*tion (noun)*
	• Noun	-ation, -ism, -ment, -ence
	• Verb	-ate, -fy, -ize
	• Adjective	-al, -ful, -ious, -ative
	• Adverbial	-ly, -ways
	• Inflectional (changes tense, number, person, etc.)	-ed, -s, -es, -ing, -er, -est
	• Derivational (changes function or part of speech or makes new words)	-fy, -ist, -able

Exercise 3:

Practice identifying morphemes. Choose five words from the list below and identify each morpheme in each word. Then, write the word's definition. You may use your dictionary and what you know about prefixes, roots, and suffixes. If you have access to the Internet, you may also use *TheCognātarium.com*. See the sample done for you.

IN SUMMARY: TACKLING UNFAMILIAR WORDS

altruistic	ambiguous	boycotted	disenfranchisement
farcical	inextricably	infallible	lament
peripheries	proliferating	pseudoscientific	rectify
respite	ruminate	staunchest	utilitarian

in	fall	i	ble
in (not)	fall (failing, false)	ible (able)	
Infallible—not able to fail, not able to be false			

Prior to reading text that contains unfamiliar multisyllabic words, scan the pages and pull those words out so that when you begin to read, you don't have to stop and interrupt your thoughts. Utilizing these steps will also help you become a more fluent reader. Follow these steps to help you pronounce unfamiliar words:

Pronouncing Unfamiliar Words

1) Divide the word into syllables.

2) Identify the vowel pattern (see syllable type chart).

3) Say each syllable and then combine them all into a word.

4) Look up the pronunciation of the word in a dictionary.

5) If you are still not sure, go to *Dictionary.com* and listen to the pronunciation.

6) Practice pronouncing the word alone and as it appears in the text.

Part of our goal in this section is to help you read **fluently**. According to the National Reading Panel (NRP), fluent reading is the ability to read text quickly, accurately, and with proper expression (prosody).

Read the characteristics of fluent reading below and determine how fluent a reader you are:

1) automatic recognition of words (no thought given to decoding words)

2) reading at a rate similar to talking

3) reading with appropriate pitch, stress, pauses, and phrasing (Phrasing is a key element in grasping meaning)

4) reading with 98-100% accuracy

5) engaging with text to promote comprehension

If you have determined that you are not a fluent reader, don't despair. Keep reading to find a number of tips to help you build your reading fluency. As you become a more fluent reader, your reading comprehension will improve as well.

You may have noticed that the language in books, especially your college textbooks, is different from conversational language. The language in academic books and articles tends to be denser than conversational language, containing more prepositions and unfamiliar words. Authors of academic texts use more formal grammar and rarely repeat themselves. As a result, students, especially students new to college or returning after years out of school, often have difficulty reading fluently and comprehending their academic textbooks.

Linnea Ehri found in 1998 that students who had heard words spoken were more likely to read those words fluently even the first time they saw the words in print. Thus, one way to improve your reading fluency is by simply hearing on a regular basis more advanced, college-level words. Try some of these strategies:

Build Reading Fluency

- Listen to audiobooks.
- Listen to public radio.
- Watch public television.
- Find an audio version of a book you're reading, and listen along as you read.

- Check out DVDs and written versions of books and plays from the library and read along with the actors. Here are some great options:

Fences (Wilson)	*A Raisin in the Sun* (Hansberry)
Death of a Salesman (Miller)	*Glengarry Glen Ross* (Mamet)
Angels in America (Tony Kushner)	*Wit* (Edson)
Sense and Sensibility (Austen)	*Six Degrees of Separation* (Guare)

- See plays at your local theater. Theaters often have last-minute student rush tickets at affordable prices.
- Watch lectures on your areas of interest on Youtube.
- Watch and listen to TED Talks online at www.ted.com/talks.
- Practice reading aloud. (Use *Dictionary.com*'s audio pronunciation feature to hear the pronunciations of unfamiliar words.)

Understanding Word Meaning

In order to be a fluent reader, you not only have to pronounce words correctly, you also must know what the words mean as you are reading. So, before you begin reading, scan the text for words whose meaning and/or context you do not understand.

1) Check for word parts (prefixes, roots, suffixes) with meanings you know.
2) Look up the word's meaning in a dictionary.
3) Check the word's part of speech.
4) Identify a synonym and antonym of the word.
5) Read the sentence that contains that word and substitute a synonym for it.
6) Practice using the word.

COMPREHENSION

Many students have trouble comprehending what they read. We have heard countless students report that they read several pages from an assignment and have no idea what they just read, so they have to go back and start over. To fully comprehend any text that you read, you must complete a two-stage process:

- Identify each word and meaning in context (automatically).
- Interpret and consider relationships between terms and concepts as you use your own background knowledge.

To fully comprehend as you read, you must be *fully engaged* and *actively relate* what is written in the text to your own ideas, knowledge, and experiences. So, after gaining some proficiency with identifying words and their meanings, you must now gain an understanding of how those words fit together.

Five Elements That Affect Readers' Comprehension

In-Text Elements	Environmental Elements
1. Parts of Speech	4. Behavior
2. Syntax	5. Purpose
3. Punctuation	

1. Parts of Speech

In English class, you study parts of speech not just because you need to identify nouns and verbs but to help you understand that each word in a sentence has a "job" to perform. The label helps you know a word's job. (See Chapter 3, "Parts of Speech.") The words in the sentence tell us "who or what" (noun/subject); "did what" (verb); and may elaborate a little more by telling us "what it looks like" (adjective); "when they did it;" "where" (preposition); "how" (adverb); and "why." Knowing the function of each word gives you information that will help you comprehend and actively relate to what you read as you read it—who, did what, when, where, why, and how.

2. Syntax

In your English classes, you also may study sentence construction. Why? **Syntax,** or the rules for the arrangement and order of words in a sentence, provides us with those guidelines and helps us build our mental pictures in memory. Understanding this ordering also gives us clues regarding each word's job and helps us to understand what we are reading.

In this sentence the word "bats" is the verb:

"Jose bats flies."

In this sentence the word "flies" is the verb:

"Jose flies bats."

Notice the difference word order makes in the meaning of the sentence.

3. Punctuation

Understanding punctuation and its effects on reading comprehension is critical. Read the following sentences and explain how the lack of commas influences your ability to interpret them:

- In the field below the brook gurgled merrily.
- Instead of two five teachers made the trip.

Punctuation marks tell you how to read. Those marks create meaning. Notice the difference in meaning just based on punctuation: Marcus is a musician. Marcus is a musician! Marcus is a musician?

See Chapter 4, "Punctuation" for more on how punctuation can affect meaning.

4. and 5. Behavior and Purpose

Finally, you can improve your reading comprehension by being aware of your behavior and intentions. Research shows that the environment in which you read, along with your awareness of your purpose for reading, heavily impact your ability to comprehend. Earlier we mentioned that you must be *fully engaged* in order to comprehend challenging texts. Think of what being "fully engaged" means to you. Visualize yourself fully engaged with a text. Where are you? What does your environment look like? What behaviors are you engaged in to foster engagement? Consider how you will realize that visualization the next time you tackle a reading assignment.

Exercise 4:

Think about all the reading assignments you must complete over the next two weeks in your classes. Now think about the purpose of each assignment. Is it to do well on a test or quiz? Is it to write in response to what you've read? Is it simply to learn the material to be able to recall it at a later date? List four of those assignments and their purposes below:

Reading Assignment 1	
Purpose	
Reading Assignment 2	
Purpose	
Reading Assignment 3	
Purpose	
Reading Assignment 4	
Purpose	

Next, consider the purposes you wrote above. What is the ideal reading environment to accomplish those purposes? What does it look like? What does it sound like? What does it feel like? Describe it in detail below:

What is your actual reading environment like? What does it look like? What does it sound like? What does it feel like? Describe it in detail below:

Notice the differences between your ideal reading environment and your actual reading environment. What actions can you take to eliminate some of those differences so that your actual reading environment is more like your ideal reading environment? Write at least three actions below.

1)

2)

3)

Once you take those actions, you will be on your way to more effective reading comprehension!

THE READING PROCESS

1) Select or create an environment conducive to full engagement with the text.

2) Identify your purpose for reading.

3) Preview the text.

4) Read the text.

5) Review the text.

THE READING PROCESS

1) **Select or create an environment conducive to full engagement with the text.**

   a. Be sure your reading environment will support your comprehension.

   b. Eliminate distractions that might hinder your reading comprehension like the television, social media, your cell phone, etc.

   c. Gather tools that will assist you in your reading task like pens and pencils, highlighters, colored sticky tabs, etc. Anything that you don't have right at hand is an excuse to interrupt your reading later.

2) **Identify your purpose for reading.**

   a. Consider what you want to learn from the text.

   • Are you reading to earn a certain grade on a quiz, test, writing assignment, or course?

   • Are you reading to prepare yourself for a task, job, or meeting?

   • Will you share what you got from the text with a friend, classmate, or colleague?

   b. Review the assignment in your syllabus and your lecture notes, as well as any review material, like a study guide or PowerPoint lecture, distributed in class or online by the professor. This will signal to you the topics and terms that are emphasized by the professor and thus are likely to appear on a test. This step will also ensure that you are following your professor's directions and will help you hone in on the purpose of the assignment.

3) **Preview the text.**

   a. Look at the author's name, title, and subtitles. Are you familiar with the author? If so, think about what you know about him/her. If not, consider what his/her profession tells you about him/her. Is the author a professor, a politician, a private citizen, etc., and what context can that offer? Based on the title, consider what the text might be about.

   b. Look at any graphics, images, or charts on the cover or within the text. What is signaled by these images? Textbooks are enhanced with a number of features which facilitate efficient navigation. Subject headings throughout each chapter signal a change in topic. Important terms and sometimes their definitions are in bold font, making them stand out. Often there is a chart which summarizes the important terms in one place, while the discussion may be spread out over several pages. Locating and using these features can accelerate and invigorate your reading process.

c. Skim the subject headings in the chapter. Do any of these match the terms or topics from the class material? Highlight definitions and memorable sentences, but do not highlight so much that the important concepts no longer stand out. Rather, make note in your notebook or laptop the same definitions you highlight in that section.

d. Skim the first and last paragraphs of the text to get a better sense of the content.

e. Skim through the first sentences of a few paragraphs in the text. Also, look for any lists or headings, and read those as well.

f. Keep an eye out for unfamiliar and key words in the texts. Look them up and take down their definitions, so you can refer back to them when you read the full text.

g. Read review or exercise questions associated with the text. What clues do they provide about the content of the text?

h. Make notes of your overall first impressions of the text.

4) **Read the text.**

a. Break the text into sections before or as you read. Notice how the author has segmented the text into chapters or smaller segments, and focus on one section at a time. Before you read each section, though, skim through and note the bold-face words. Then come back to the beginning and read the entire section word for word. Repeat the process of writing down what you've highlighted. Then, come back to any difficult section you already read once, and read it again. When you read the section for the second time, you are likely to notice things you missed the first time. Each of these steps helps enforce the concepts. Should you be interrupted at any point in this process, your learning will be less disrupted because you already read several of the sections in the preview stage and because you are reading (and thus learning and processing the material) in *chunks*.

b. Another helpful technique, especially in a book, is to jot down a phrase or sentence at the top of each page which summarizes its content. This forces you to stop at the end of every page and mentally distill the information into a chunk—a phrase or sentence. (For example, at the top of page 10 you might scribble: "Author claims that erosion occurs at twice the anticipated rate.")

c. Another useful reading technique is to complete the following chart, often called a memory matrix, while you read. It accomplishes the same function as noting down highlighted terms in a notebook, but organizes key concepts more holistically, so you can see the whole (chapter or book) at a glance. The great part about this tool is that you can make it as large as necessary by copying it on different sizes of paper at a copying store, or by customizing it yourself in Microsoft Word or Excel. Likewise, it can expand and contract as necessary, for an entire book, or simply one chapter.

Memory Matrix

Fences Ch. 1	Pages 1–5	Pages 6–10	Pages 11–15
Key Terms			
Main Claims			
Unfamiliar Terms			
Memorable Quotes			
Characters/People			
Questions			

d. Use what you already know about reading, and apply it to your reading of the text. You are likely already an expert at reading and comprehending some type of text: Facebook posts, emails, Tweets, menus, magazine articles, song lyrics, user manuals, online news sources, or something else. Think about how you approach those familiar texts, and see how you can apply those strategies as you read for your classes.

e. Use your prior knowledge of the topic, and apply it to your reading of the text. This relevant prior knowledge is called **schema**. Effective readers apply and build on their schema each time they read something new about a topic.

f. Look for context clues and signal words that clue you in about a writer's intention in phrases, sentences, and paragraphs. **Contrast words** like "however", "conversely" and the phrase "on the other hand" suggest the writer is creating a contrast between two or more things—it's your job to figure out what. Likewise, **cause and effect** words and phrases like "therefore" or "as a result" signal that one thing was caused by something else. See the chart below for a full list of these helpful textual clues!

g. Be patient with yourself and persist even if the text confuses or bores you. Just like any skill, reading takes practice, and the more you do it, you will develop endurance for reading longer and more complex texts.

5) **Review the Text**

    a. Reread the text's headings and unfamilar terms. Review the graphics, and read your notes.

    b. Discuss the text with your classmate, your roommate, your boyfriend, your mom, or all of the above. Ask them questions about the topic. Encourage them to ask you questions. Share with them what you learned from the text. Talk to them about what confused you and what was most interesting and applicable to your experiences. This process of engaging in conversation about your text will be invaluable for your comprehension and recall.

You may not realize it, but you've now come full circle from feeling like a passenger in an unending line of words to a front seat driver! Once these reading strategies become automatic for you, your reading and comprehension process will accelerate, and you'll have a powerful skill to teach to others.

Signal Words and Phrases for Finding Context and Meaning

Contrast	Comparison	Cause& Effect
but	both	after
conversely	comparatively	as a result
despite	in the same way	because
however	just as	consequently
in contrast	like, likewise	if…then
instead	similarly	when, whenever
even though		since
nevertheless		thus
on the contrary		therefore
on the other hand		
other than		
though		
unlike		
yet		
whereas		
while		

Additional Detail	Explanation	Sequential
additionally also another furthermore moreover	e.g. (Latin for "for example") for example for instance i.e. (Latin for "that is") specifically such as that is	first second, secondly third, thirdly next then finally ultimately

Exercise 5:

In the following sentences, underline the signal words and phrases you see and identify the category of meaning they signify (addition, cause and effect, explanation, etc.). Use the chart to help you.

1) Tamir intended to meet the deadline; however, he misunderstood the directions and submitted his letter to the wrong recipient.

2) Like online magazines and newspapers, e-books are easy and quick to access.

3) Whereas Kindle readers and iPads need to be charged and require power cords, print books are cordless and don't run out of power.

4) Because I had not backed up my data before my computer crashed, I had to pay a lot of money to have it retrieved from the hard drive.

5) Write your own sentence using sequential signal words/phrases to describe the things you did over the weekend.

_____

_____

6) Write your own sentence using contrast signal words/phrases to contrast two classes you have taken.

_____

_____

Writing a summary of something you've read like an article, essay, or book provides a great opportunity to practice and demonstrate your comprehension of a text. A summary is simply a *condensed version* of a piece of writing. Summarizing is an invaluable strategy to use when reviewing materials for an exam or writing a research assignment. Ultimately, for your English classes, a summary is a necessary tool when you write in response to a text. It is useful to recap what the writer of that text has said for your reader before you respond to his/her points.

Teachers in college often assign summaries, but students are rarely taught explicitly how to write them. We intend to provide that guidance here so you can use it for the rest of your college career.

Start by Being a Committed and Serious Reader

Your ability to summarize what someone else has written is dependent on your reading and comprehending what that person has said first. Use the guidance we provided earlier in this chapter to strengthen your reading skills. Use other tools and knowledge you have about reading to help you comprehend what you read. Finally, take adequate time to read your text before you summarize.

Why Write a Summary?

Now that you've gotten some reading fundamentals and know how to be a critical reader, you can take those skills a step further. You can recreate your understanding of what you read into a summary. Usually students do this to position themselves into a conversation with the writer. They summarize what the writer has said in order to later respond to the writer by agreeing, disagreeing, analyzing, or comparing what the writer has said to something else.

Writing a summary is also a standard way to introduce a traditional five-paragraph persuasive essay in response to a text.

Basic Guidelines

1) Start your summary with the title, author's full name (spelled correctly), and date of the text. You should include the source title as well. Remember if you are summarizing an article, place the title in quotation marks, and italicize the source (newspaper, journal, book, magazine, etc.) title.

2) After you have introduced the basic information about your text, the content of your summary should begin by providing the reader with the main idea or overall purpose of the text. Here are two examples of opening sentences:

a. **Article with named author:**

In his 1999 *New York Times* article, "The Singer Solution to World Poverty," Peter Singer argues that middle class people have the moral obligation to donate any money they do not spend on necessities to save the lives of poor people around the world.

b. **Article with no named author:**

The 2006 *Facts on File* article "Black History Month," provides some history of the annual commemoration of African-American History in Febuary and describes the controversy over Americans continuing to obsesrve that cultural heritage month.

3) Use your own words throughout most of your summary. Be sure to place any exact words or phrases from your text in quotation marks. Limit your use of quotations in the summary to the author's words or expressions that cannot be condensed or stated in your own way.

4) Your summary should contain *only* the main points of the text and avoid mentioning minor details. For example, if you are summarizing an article that describes the history and controversy around African-American History Month, *specific statistics* outlining percentages of students who assert the value or lack of value in celebrating Black History Month are **too** *specific* for a short summary.

5) Your summary must, however, include *all* of the main points in the text. Don't leave out anything important. One way to make sure of this is to divide the text that you are summarizing into sections. For a very short article, you might just divide into paragraphs while for a longer article, you would group the paragraphs into sections, and when summarizing an entire book, you might look at each chapter. Read the text one section at a time, and sum up the author's major point from each section in one or two sentences.

6) Remember that a summary has no room for your own opinion of the text or the issue. Save your opinion for essay writing, persuasive speeches, or arguments with your friends. In a summary you are just summing up what someone else has written, not writing your own opinion.

7) Leave out any information that is not directly from the text.

8) After naming the author in the opening sentence of your summary, intersperse the author's last name along with the words "the author" throughout the summary to remind the reader that the ideas belong to the author. Use signal phrases like these throughout the summary:

a. According to _____,

b. _____ also states,

c. _____ adds,

d. _____ points out that

e. _____ asserts

(Notice the comma used after some of the above phrases. Be sure to include those commas in your summary when appropriate.)

9) Be sure to preserve the balance of the article in your summary. Emphasize certain issues and examples in proportion to the author's emphasis. For example, Peter Singer's article, "The Singer Solution to World Poverty," starts with a description of a movie, *Central Station*. The article contains twenty-seven paragraphs including a three-paragraph introduction. He spends about five paragraphs talking about that film. So, if you are summarizing that article, how much of your summary should be spent on the film? Half of the summary? A quarter of the summary? Probably not even that much. You could even calculate it mathematically. The proportions of five paragraphs out of an approximately twenty-five-paragraph article are these: 5/25=1/5. That means that only one fifth of your summary should talk about the film *Central Station*. Thus, if your summary is ten sentences long, two sentences should be about the film. The rest of your summary should cover Singer's other points.

10) If the text (article, chapter, essay, book) you are summarizing presents two sides to an issue, your summary should also clearly present both sides. You might say something like this: According to _____, opponents of _____ argue _____ while supporters of _____ argue _____.

Now you are prepared to write your own summary. When your instructor asks you to summarize a text (for any class), use these guidelines! Keep this book nearby and open to this section as you type so you can refer to it. You will be reading texts at least until you graduate from college, and the ability to effectively summarize those texts will benefit you all along the way.

Read the sample summary below. (See the entire Sascha de Gersdorff article in the Appendix.)

Sample Summary

Sacha de Gersdorff's 2005 article "Fresh Faces" is about the growing prevalence and acceptance of elective cosmetic surgical procedures among American teens. De Gersdorff names transformation-centered reality television shows like *Extreme Makeover* and *The Swan* as contributing to the trend. In recent years, plastic surgery has become especially attractive to young people ages 18-24, 34% of whom say "they would definitely consider surgery for themselves." Some healthcare professionals blame the bombardment of idealized media images of "supposedly ideal-looking Americans" for driving so many young people to cosmetic procedures. De Gersdorff lists risks like preoccupation with instant gratification and addiction to surgery that concern parents and some doctors. One example, Kristen, who had rhinoplasty at fifteen, says that she would be open to future cosmetic procedures that could make her feel better about herself if there was something she wanted to change. Without hesitation, she says, "I would do it."

Note: After any quotation in a summary, be sure to cite the page number(s) if you use a print source. The article summarized here was accessed from the Internet. Therefore, the author did not include page numbers.

Exercise 6:

Test your newfound skills! Read the article, "The Singer Solution to World Poverty," found in the Appendix of this book. Identify ten unfamiliar words, and break them into syllables. Look them up in the dictionary and if necessary, use *Dictionary.com* for help with pronunciation. Then, summarize the article.

CHAPTER 4

PARTS OF SPEECH

Knowing a word's job in a sentence helps readers comprehend. If you understand the functions of each word, you'll know who did what, when, where, why, and how. However, just as people take on different identities in different situations, words often do double duty, performing additional functions. Once you learn the primary uses of these parts of speech, you'll be ready to detect them in all contexts. When in doubt, look up a word in the dictionary to see all its possible roles.

NOUNS / SUBJECTS / OBJECTS

A **noun** is a person, place, or thing. Since persons, places, and things can consist of varying amounts, (e.g., one "dog" or two "dogs") nouns can be either **singular** or **plural** ("dog" is singular, "dogs" is plural). Nouns serve sentences primarily as **subjects** that "do" or "act" the verb and **objects** that "receive" the action of the verb but can also double as adjectives if they are used to describe other nouns (e.g., a "hair cut," in which the noun "hair" is used to describe the noun "cut.") Sometimes a subject comprises more than one person place or thing, and we call that a **compound subject**. Sometimes the subject can be a gerund, which is a verb acting as a noun (by using an "–ing" ending, like in the sentence, "Studying is the key to academic success.")

SOME COMMON ENGLISH NOUN ENDINGS					
-ade	-age	-ance	-ant	-ard	-arian
-ary	-ation	-cle	-cy	-dom	-ee
-ence	-ency	-ent	-er	-ery	-hood
-ics	-ine	-ion	-ism	-ity	-ment
-mony	-ness	-ology	-ty		

There are many types of nouns, in the same way that ice cream has many flavors. Proper nouns, collective nouns, abstract nouns, and so on are like extra flavors of the same essential thing: a person, place, or thing. When the person, place, or thing is/has a name, it is a **proper noun** (for example, Los Angeles, Zimbabwe, Aunt Ruth, Pop-Tart). We make this distinction to remember to capitalize proper nouns. **Collective nouns** are nouns which are singular but imply a plural group (class, family, bank, band, army). **Abstract nouns** are intangible things (again, a noun is person, place, or thing) like concepts and qualities which are harder to identify as nouns because we can't see them or touch them (for example, truth, wisdom, integrity, doubt, beauty, love).

PRONOUNS

In simplest terms, a **pronoun** is a smaller word that "stands in" to represent a noun (so that noun need not be repeated multiple times.) It can even allow us to refer to a noun that isn't physically present in the sentence. Like nouns, pronouns themselves come in many distinct flavors: subject pronouns, object pronouns, relative pronouns, demonstrative pronouns, etc. They can be singular or plural, definite or indefinite. Take a look.

Subject Pronouns		Object Pronouns		Possessive Pronouns	
Singular	**Plural**	**Singular**	**Plural**	**Singular**	**Plural**
I	we	me	us	my	our
you	you	you	you	your	your
he/she	they	him/her	them	his/her	their

Demonstrative Pronouns		Indefinite Pronouns	Reflexive Pronouns	
Singular	**Plural**	(all singular)	**Singular**	**Plural**
this	these	all, any, anyone, anybody, both, everyone, everybody, each, either, few, nobody, none, no one, one, some, several	myself	ourselves
that	those		yourself	yourselves
			himself	themselves
			herself	

Relative Pronouns		Interrogative Pronouns	Absolute Possessive Pronouns	
Subject	**Object**	who, which, what, where, how	**Singular**	**Plural**
who	whom		mine	ours
which	that		yours	yours
			his/hers	theirs

For tips on using pronouns correctly in essays by maintaining pronoun agreement and consistent pronoun/ subject reference, see Chapter 5.

▌VERBS

A verb serves an important job in the sentence: it is the "action" that the subject "does." We've said that a subject is usually a noun (unless it is a gerund); what is the subject *doing*? That is our verb. Let's look at an example.

The dog devours his juicy bone.

In this example, "dog" is the subject of the sentence; the sentence is about him. What is he doing? What action does the dog perform? The dog "devours" (verb) his bone (object.) Therefore "devours" is the verb.

The	dog	**devours**	his	juicy	bone.
	Sub.	**Verb**			**Obj.**

In sentences in which the subject "does" more than one thing (for example, the dog first "buries" and later "devours" his bone) we have what we call a **compound verb**.

COMMON VERB ENDINGS IN ENGLISH

-ate	-er	-fy	-ificate	-ise	-ize

▎HELPING (AUXILIARY) VERBS

The sentence "The dog devours his juicy bone" is very straightforward. However, we don't always write or talk in such simple sentences. Sometimes, the verb can consist of more than one word—in other words, it may take several words to express one verb. The main verb might enlist the aid of one or more **helping verbs** such as "am," "is," "are," "was," "were," or "be," "being," "been."

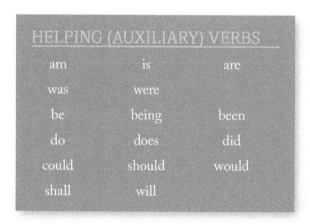

HELPING (AUXILIARY) VERBS		
am	is	are
was	were	
be	being	been
do	does	did
could	should	would
shall	will	

Helping verbs (officially called auxiliary verbs) have their name because their job is to help express the main verb. Let's refer back to our dog and his bone.

The   dog   **<u>is</u>**   **<u>devouring</u>**   his   juicy   bone.

Sub. HV Main Verb

In the above example, the same idea is being expressed as in the first example, but in this case the helping verb "is" assists the word "devour" (in a slightly different form, what we call the present participle) to express the verb completely. Together the helping verb and the main verb, in its participle form, become what we call the **verb phrase**.

Helping verbs can even help change the verb's tense in order to express the action in a different time (the past, the present, or the future.) Look at the next example.

The   dog   **_was_**   **<u>devouring</u>**   his   juicy   bone.

Sub. HV   Verb

By exchanging the helping verb "is" for "was," we have expressed the past tense (actually past continuous) rather than the present (continuous) tense. For a fuller discussion of verb tenses, visit Chapter 7.

LINKING VERBS

Sometimes helping verbs can help out by standing in for the main verb completely and doing the job all by themselves! In this case, they are often called **linking verbs** since they link the subject of the sentence to the information about what the subject is doing. In this example, "is" links the subject, Snoopy, to the information about the subject that he's "a loyal dog."

Snoopy <u>**is**</u> a loyal dog.

Sub.   Verb

In this case, we recognize that the helping/linking verb "is" is the only verb present in the sentence, and therefore it is the sentence's main verb in this sentence.

Note: When sentences become compound and complex—that is, they consist of more than one phrase or clause (a phrase is a group of words, a clause is a phrase with a subject and a verb)—they may have several verbs, in one or both clause(s). So when you are trying to identify all the verbs and verb phrases, don't forget to read to the end of a sentence to find them all!

Simple sentence (one subject/verb combination):

<u>Snoopy</u>   <u>barked</u>   at   the   door.

Sub.   Verb

Compound Sentence (double subject/verb combination):

<u>Snoopy</u>   <u>barked</u>   at   the   door,   but   the   <u>door</u>   <u>stayed</u>   silent.

Sub.   Verb   Sub.   Verb

Complex Sentence (double subject/verb combination with a subordinating conjunction):

<u>Although</u>   <u>Snoopy</u>   <u>barked</u>   at   the   door,   the   <u>door</u>   <u>stayed</u>   silent.

Sub.Conj.   Sub.   Verb   Sub.   Verb

(A subordinating conjunction is also called a dependent word because it makes the clause it precedes dependent (on the attached clause) for meaning. For more on the ways to combine sentences phrases and clauses, and how to punctuate them, see Chapter 6.)

INFINITIVE VERBS

A verb in its most basic form is an infinitive verb. In English, the infinitive verb is simply the verb preceded by the word "to," like "to write" or "to read." Many students learning verbs in a second language encounter verbs first in the infinitive form. In many languages, like Spanish and French, for example, the infinitive form of a verb is simply one word (e.g., *hablar*, *parler*.) In English, it is two words (e.g., "to speak," "to eat.")

Note: Be careful not to confuse an infinitive verb with a prepositional phrase. When the word "to" is followed by a verb, it is an infinitive verb ("to walk," "to stand," "to run") but when the word "to" is followed by a noun, it is a prepositional phrase ("to the store," "for the present," "on her birthday.")

ADJECTIVES

An adjective's job is to describe a noun. Adjectives are the words that color our imaginations. Did you just catch sight of a *hot* guy or a *sexy* girl? Do you have a *mean* landlord, or a *kind* one? Adjectives are what we use to describe people and places. Any word you can use to describe a person, place, or thing is an adjective. Adjectives answer the questions, "Which one?", "What kind?" and "How many?"

When we use two adjectives at once to describe a noun, like "one-eyed" man or "two-legged" creature, we hyphenate the two adjectives. However, if they can be used interchangeably, we use commas: "little, brown monkey" could also be stated as "brown, little monkey" with no change in meaning, whereas "eyed-one" man makes no sense.

Note: Sometimes a noun can also work as an adjective. For example, we said earlier that words can do "double duty." If "duty" is a noun, then any word used to describe it is going to be an adjective. "Double" can be a noun or a verb. An identical twin has a double (noun), or I can double (verb) my money in the stock market. When we use "double" to describe what kind of duty (noun) a word can do, it is serving as an adjective. So the word "double" can actually do triple duty!

Exercise:

With a partner, or on your own, list as many adjectives as you can to describe what you see in the photo.

ADVERBS

The main job of adverbs is to describe how verbs are performed. How does the robot walk (verb)? Methodically? Awkwardly? Or capably? Adverbs can describe not only verbs, but also "How?", "When?", "Where?" adjectives, ("very hot") and even other adverbs ("too quickly"). In this sense, adverbs have more "weight" or power than adjectives do, since adjectives typically describe only a noun. Adverbs also answer the questions "How?" "When?" "Where?" and "How much?"

You may have noticed that adverbs often end in the letters "-ly." However, not all adverbs do; this is only a general guideline. Because English takes words from other languages, we have many words that are exceptions. For example, "lovely" looks like an adverb, but is actually an adjective because it can only describe a noun, not a verb. Likewise, the word "very" doesn't look like an adverb but it is, because it describes verbs and other adjectives and adverbs.

SOME ADJECTIVES THAT LOOK LIKE ADVERBS					
friendly	godly	likely	lonely	manly	lovely
costly	silly	timely	worldly		
SOME ADVERBS THAT DON'T END IN –LY					
almost	aloud	alright	also	always	far
less	more	often	never	not	quite
too	very	well			

Some other non-typical adverbs are conjunctive adverbs, which are used between phrases and sentences, often as what we call "transitional words." Details on conjunctive adverbs follow in our section on "Conjunctions."

PREPOSITIONS

Prepositions are words that add extra details to our sentences by anchoring phrases that give additional information. Prepositional phrases answer the questions, "Which one?" "What kind?" "How?" "Where?" "When?" Prepositions themselves usually imply a question that gets answered by the "object" of the prepositional phrase, the noun. For example, consider the common prepositions "with," "for," and "to." Confronted with these words, we wonder, "To *what*? With *what*? For *what*?" A prepositional phrase contains the question and the answer: "To the store. With the list. For the party."

SOME COMMON PREPOSITIONS

above	across	after	against	among	around
at	before	behind	below	beneath	beside(s)
between	by	down	except	for	from
in	into	like	near	of	off
on	onto	over	past	than	through
to	toward	with	without	under	underneath
until	up				

Although prepositional phrases don't get the same publicity as nouns and verbs, and aren't as flashy as adjectives and adverbs, they give sentences a lot of important information. Prepositions are the quiet, hardworking, unrecognized heroes of sentences! Let's say your boss cut you a check, and you need it now. It's therefore critical to know where he put it! Is it *in* the mail? *On* your shelf? *With* the manager? *Beneath* the time clock? All these prepositional phrases convey important information that is just as important to us as the nouns and verbs!

Another great thing about prepositions and prepositional phrases is that they can be very helpful to you in identifying sentence parts. Let's say you are trying to identify the parts of speech in the following sentence.

He told me to walk to the car.

Right away you notice that "car" is a noun: that's easy! A car is a thing, so you are thinking maybe it's the subject, since subjects are usually nouns, right? While that's true, not all nouns are subjects. You are about to walk into a trap!

Of course, at this point you might also begin to ask yourself what the verb is, and who is doing it, which would take you back to the true subject ("He") and verb ("told") of the sentence. But had you recognized that "to" was a preposition, and that "to the car" was a prepositional phrase, you would have known you would never find your main subject and verb of the sentence there, and left the prepositional phrase alone to do its job. Many instructors teach students to simply cross out prepositional phrases, either on the page, or in your mind, in order to avoid mistaking them for other parts of speech.

Likewise, in our example, your knowledge of prepositions and prepositional phrases would remind you that "to walk" must be an infinitive verb, the kind of verb that often seems to look like a prepositional phrase, but which is not, since "to" followed by a verb is always an infinitive verb.

<u>He</u>   <u>told</u>   <u>me</u>   ~~to walk~~   ~~to the car.~~

subj.   verb pronoun   infinitive verb   prepositional phrase

Once I've crossed out the infinitive verb and the prepositional phrase, I can easily find the subject and verb!

Finally, many grammar books and instructors teach student not to end a sentence in a preposition. By this rule, "We couldn't tell what he threw the rock <u>at</u>" would be better rephrased as "<u>at what</u> he threw the rock," embedding the preposition inside the sentence.

Exercise:

Nathan Bailey

With a partner, or on your own, list as many prepositional phrases as you can to describe what you see in the photo.

ARTICLES

There are only three articles in English: "a," "an," and "the." "A" and "an" are called indefinite articles and "the" is a definite article. You will encounter more variations on articles in other languages. In English, we do not need to make articles agree with nouns—one small compensation for all the other exceptions we have to remember in our language! The only thing to remember with articles is to use "an" before a noun beginning with a vowel. This makes the vowel sound easier to pronounce, and is something most native English speakers do intuitively. For example, we say, "*an* apple," not "*a* apple." See Chapter 7 for more on the use of articles.

INTERJECTIONS

Often speakers "interject" words that aren't any other part of speech; they are exclamations to show emotion, such as "Wow!" or "Oops!" Some words used as interjections do have day jobs as another part of speech, such as "Well," or "Really," (which are both adverbs) but many of them don't. (Some are **onomatopoeia**, or sounds we use as words, such as "Oops!") Often an interjection is attached to the beginning of a sentence with a comma. Sometimes it's in the middle. Here are some examples.

"<u>Wow</u>, that's a beautiful puppy!"

"<u>Well</u>, I'm not sure yet."

"I'd like to, but <u>oh</u>—I don't know."

Note: We encourage you not to use interjections in essays. Interjections usually only appear in informal speech, in short stories or screenplays, or in interview transcripts.

CONJUNCTIONS

Conjunctions have the admirable job of connecting sentence parts. They are assisted in this task by punctuation marks, which are described at length in our Punctuation section. There are two kinds of conjunctions: subordinating and coordinating conjunctions. **Subordinating conjunctions** are often referred to as "dependent words," and include words like "after," "since," "until," and "whenever." Subordinating conjunctions, or dependent words, often subordinate one clause to another, meaning that they create a dependent relationship between a dependent clause, often explanatory in nature, and an independent clause, which could function on its own as a complete sentence without the dependent clause. Take a look at the following examples.

<u>Whenever</u> I am late for work, I have to miss lunch.

I have to miss lunch <u>whenever</u> I am late to work.

In the first example, the subordinating conjunction "whenever" makes the entire clause subordinate to the second clause which follows after the comma; in fact, it makes the first phrase what we call a dependent clause. This dependent clause could not be a complete sentence on its own. It wouldn't make sense if you tapped someone on the shoulder and said, "Whenever I am late for work!" The person would naturally be confused, and unsure what you were trying to communicate.

In the second example, the subordinating conjunction is used in the middle of the two clauses, functioning as a hinge to hold both clauses together. When a subordinating conjunction is used in this way no punctuation is needed.

DEPENDENT WORDS/SUBORDINATING CONJUNCTIONS			
after	although	as	as if
because	before	even if	even though
if	in order to	once	since
that	though	unless	until
whatever	when	whenever	where
wherever	whether	which	while

Coordinating conjunctions are often referred to by the acronym FANBOYS (which spells them out, "for / and / nor / but / or / yet / so." Coordinating conjunctions connect two independent clauses, usually with the aid of a comma. When a woman tries to match her shoes to her shirt or pants, we say that the pieces "coordinate" or that she looks very "coordinated." This might be a good way for you to remember the job of coordinating conjunctions; coordinating conjunctions help coordinate or match one clause to another so that they work together to form a complete package: in this case, a complete sentence.

for, and, nor, but, or, yet, so

We can also connect two clauses with a **conjunctive adverb**. Like adverbs, conjunctive adverbs answer the questions "how," "when," and "to what degree." To punctuate them properly, see Chapter 4.

COMMON CONJUNCTIVE ADVERBS					
accordingly	also	anyway	although	besides	certainly
consequently	finally	furthermore	hence	however	incidentally
indeed	instead	likewise	meanwhile	moreover	namely
nevertheless	next	nonetheless	now	otherwise	still
then	similarly	thereafter	therefore	thus	undoubtedly

CONNECTIONS AMONG LANGUAGES

As we have said, parts of speech exist in every language. They are a constant in every grammatical system. Although not every language has every part of speech another language does (one language, for example, may not have a way of expressing cardinal numbers like "first" or "second,") when a part of speech is the same, it has the same job in each language. This can be very handy for language learners.

Since the mind learns effectively with the use of schemas, we can build a schema around the parts of speech and use it to align vocabulary words in a new language alongside the words in the languages we already know. Some languages have standard endings for parts of speech where English does not. Here is a chart which illustrates this.

Common Adverb Endings		
English	**Spanish**	**French**
quick<u>ly</u>	rapida<u>mente</u>	rapide<u>ment</u>
tru<u>ly</u>	verdadera<u>mente</u>, real<u>mente</u>	vrai<u>ment</u>
faithful<u>ly</u>	fiel<u>mente</u>	fidèle<u>ment</u>

Common Adjective Endings		
English (no rule)	**Spanish (masc., fem.)**	**French (masc., fem.)**
discreet	discret<u>o</u>, discret<u>a</u>	discret, discrèt<u>e</u>
fat	gord<u>o</u>, gord<u>a</u>	gros, gross<u>e</u>
beautiful	bonit<u>o</u>, bonit<u>a</u>	beau, bell<u>e</u>

While this chart simplifies matters considerably, it is meant to illustrate how students can use commonalities to align patterns across languages. We can observe here that Spanish adjective endings are fairly standard, with an "o" ending for the masculine and the "a" ending for female, although there are of course exceptions and irregulars. Likewise, the most obvious pattern in French adjective endings is in the female ending, which typically adds an "e," whether or not it doubles the ending consonant.

Inasmuch as English has any regular adjective endings, they are "-able/-ible," "-al," "-ful," "-ic" and "-ive" (for example: capable, illegible, functional, youthful, terrific, rustic, creative, inventive.) But for as many adjectives in English that follow this pattern, there are just as many that do not.

Many English words can be identified by the language they came from. For example, nouns from French often end in "-age", "ence" or "tion," while nouns from Greek might end in "-(ph)obia." Nouns from Latin often in "-ium" and thus change to "a" or "ae" in the plural. Knowing which suffixes are associated with which language allows us to understand how to form their plurals.

Parent Language	Noun, Singular Form	Noun, Plural Form
Latin	datum, curriculum, medium	data, curricula, media
Greek	criterion, thesis, crisis, parenthesis	criteria, theses, crises, parentheses

Parts Of Speech Exercises

1) Underline the nouns in the following sentences.

   The little grey mouse rode a pink bicycle to the library.

   During the weekend, the local playground is filled with screaming children.

2) Underline the pronouns in the following sentences.

   Rudi said the nametag was hers, but I told him that it was mine.

   He gave it to me, but I think it belongs to you.

3) Underline the verbs in the following sentence.

   My dog chewed my flip flops and shredded a box of tissues before he fell asleep.

4) Underline the verbs in the following sentence, and circle any infinitive verbs.

   I like to visit Ocean City, swim in the Atlantic Ocean, and eat saltwater taffy.

5) Underline the adjectives in the following sentence.

   In summer, Pennsylvania is hot and humid, but the trees are lush and green.

6) Underline the adjectives in the following sentence.

   In a popular children's book, a man in a yellow hat owns a little brown monkey.

7) Underline the adverbs in the following sentence.

   Often the monkey behaves mischievously, but his owner is very understanding.

8) Underline the adverbs in the following sentence.

   The graduates cheered excitedly, cheered wildly, and joyfully accepted applause.

9) Underline the articles in the following sentence.

I don't want the sandwich; can I have an apple?

10) Underline the articles in the following sentence.

The school's new sports mascot needs a name.

11) Circle the prepositions, and underline the prepositional phrases, in the following sentence.

In San Francisco, I saw a Chinese dragon, a man carrying a heavy bag of golf clubs up a steep hill, and a car with two people in it drive into the bay.

12) Circle the prepositions, and underline the prepositional phrases, in the following sentence.

Howard put the briefcase with documents in it under the bed and placed the suitcase with his clothes in the bathroom.

13) Underline any interjections in the following sentence.

Hey, are you going to pick that stuff up?

14) Underline any interjections in the following sentence.

The sunset is breathtaking tonight; wow, it's just beautiful.

15) Underline any coordinating conjunctions in the following sentence.

James is the big brother, and Charlotte is the little sister.

16) Underline any coordinating conjunctions in the following sentence.

We heard Mom say we could have a candy bar, but she denies saying it.

17) Underline any subordinating conjunctions in the following sentence.

Whenever Mia visits Los Angeles, she has Tito's Tacos for lunch.

18) Underline any subordinating conjunctions in the following sentence.

> I didn't get to eat breakfast since I was running late to work.

19) Identify and label each of the words in the following sentences according to its part of speech.

> Brandy is very excited; she got a full scholarship to UC Berkeley.

> Many people do not realize it, but the law requires drivers to use turn signals.

20) Review the "Common Noun Endings" chart in Noun section of Chapter 3 and list the first ten nouns you can think of that have any of these endings.

21) Review the "Common Verb Endings" chart in Verb section of Chapter 3 and list the first ten verbs you can think of that have any of these endings.

For Speakers of Romance Languages

22) Take sentences no. 4 and no. 5 above and translate them into Spanish, French, or Italian. What happens to the infinitive verb? What happens to the prepositional phrase? (Trick question.) How can you use this difference to remember how to form these in English?

23) Review the "Common Adjective Endings" and "Common Adverb Endings" charts on pages 47 and 48. If you speak Spanish or French, list five other adjectives and five other adverbs in one of those languages that have the same endings as those listed here. If you speak a language other than Spanish or French, expand the chart to list some common adjective and adverb endings in your own language, if applicable (some languages may have common endings for certain parts of speech but not others. (You may find a language dictionary helpful for this. Look up a word in your language you think is an adjective or adverb and confirm its part of speech. Then brainstorm any other adjectives or adverbs with similar endings. In fact, this can be done for any/all parts of speech.)

CHAPTER 5

PUNCTUATION

In her fun book on punctuation *Eats Shoots and Leaves: A Zero Tolerance Approach to Punctuation*, British writer Lynn Truss says about punctuation that "without it there is no reliable way of communicating meaning" (20). That may be difficult for you to believe, but she offers a number of cases in which punctuation can affect meaning. Here is one of our favorites:

A woman, without her man, is nothing.

A woman: without her, man is nothing.

(Truss 9)

Notice the impact of the punctuation on these two sentences. The words are exactly the same, but the meanings are opposite.

While the use of punctuation may affect the writer's meaning, the correct use is sometimes ambiguous. This is likely why so many students have such trouble using punctuation marks effectively. As a result, we want to start this chapter on punctuation with a warning: punctuation is not math. While some rules are well established and definite, punctuation can sometimes be seen as an art which you apply using your good judgment.

Your job in college is to master the basic, most concrete, comprehensible punctuation rules. That way, in graduate school or in your career, you will have these basics mastered and be able to use your good judgment and common sense to punctuate effectively when there is not an absolute rule. You will also ensure that poor punctuation never obscures your meaning. Remember that in writing, your first priority is communicating clearly. Keep in mind that your ignorance of the most effective uses of punctuation will stand out to potential employers in your application or cover letter, to professors in your psychology or biology research papers, and even to your friends on *Facebook* or *Twitter*, especially if the rule-breaking is chronic. This chapter is your opportunity to brush up on these most effective uses of punctuation and ultimately master them.

© advent/Shutterstock.com

COMMAS ,

You will find many rules or uses for the comma in grammar and English textbooks. However, four uses are most beneficial for students to grasp fully in order to write effectively:

1) Use commas to separate items in a list or series.

2) Use a comma to separate two complete thoughts (independent clauses) joined by a coordinating conjunction.

3) Use a comma to separate introductory information from the main part of a sentence.

4) Use a comma to separate interruptors from the main part of the sentence.

You will notice that commas are generally used to separate parts of sentences from each other. That may be why many students are taught to place a comma at a point in a sentence where the reader would naturally pause. This use of the comma in the English language goes back over 400 years. Here is how Richard Mulcaster described the comma in 1582: "a small, crooked point, which in writing followeth some small branch of the sentence, & in reading warneth [u]s to rest there, & to help our bre[a]th a little" (Truss 71). While it might still be useful to think of a comma as following "some small branch of the sentence," this "rule" about placing commas at any pause in a sentence is not adequate since people speak differently and pause at different places. Thus, we need a concrete understanding of the ways to use the comma effectively.

1) **Use a comma to separate items in a list or series.**

This use of the comma is generally easiest for students to understand and to apply. We rarely see errors of this kind in student writing. You are probably familiar with the idea that when you are listing items in a sentence, you must place a comma between each item.

Example:

> The article "Black History Month" describes the origins of the month, the criticisms of the month-long celebration, and the justifications for its existence.

Each item in the list is underlined.

> Many Americans spend their money on luxury items like video games, vacations, name-brand shoes, and lattes.

Now, write your own sentence in which you place commas between items in a list. (Consider using a sentence from your most recent writing assignment.)

Students often ask about that last comma that comes before the word "and" in a series. Technically, that comma is optional. However, we encourage students to use it because it cannot hurt, and sometimes it is useful in making your sentence clearer. Here is an example.

Unclear:

My favorite sandwiches are turkey, salami, peanut butter and jelly and tuna.

Notice the difference in this version with the additional comma:

Clear:

My favorite sandwiches are turkey, salami, peanut butter and jelly, and tuna.

This comma, sometimes called the "Oxford comma" or "serial comma," can ensure clarity in the items you are listing.

2) **Use a comma to separate two complete thoughts (independent clauses) joined by a coordinating conjunction (FANBOYS).**

Coordinating conjunctions: FANBOYS

for, and, nor, but, or, yet, so

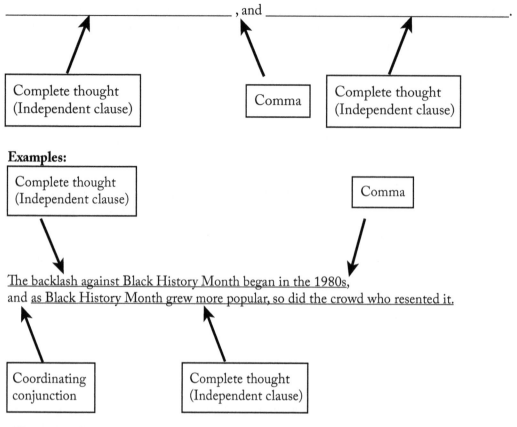

Examples:

The backlash against Black History Month began in the 1980s, and as Black History Month grew more popular, so did the crowd who resented it.

Exercise 1:

Now, practice on the sentence below.

1) Add the comma before the coordinating conjunction that joins the two complete thoughts:

> In 1926 Carter Woodson created "Negro History Week" and on its 50th anniversary, the weeklong celebration was expanded to a whole month.

2) Write your own sentence that contains **two complete thoughts** joined by the coordinating conjunction "so:"

3) Write your own sentence that contains **two complete thoughts** joined by the coordinating conjunction "but:"

4) Write your own sentence that contains **two complete thoughts** joined by the coordinating conjunction "or:"

Sometimes students think that they must always place a comma before the word "and." This is a misconception. In fact, there are many circumstances that do not require a comma before the coordinating conjunction "and."

Example:

> Peter Singer argues that middle class people should stop buying luxuries and start donating to charities that save lives.

Why doesn't this sentence call for a comma before the word "and"?

If you said that the word "and" does not come between two complete thoughts, you're right. Good work.

A sentence calls for a comma before the word "and" when it **joins two complete thoughts** (independent clauses).

Note: Be sure to avoid a very common mistake, and never place just a comma between two complete thoughts, a comma splice. You need to use a coordinating conjunction (FANBOYS) for the sentence to be correct. A comma will not work between two complete thoughts all by itself. See Chapter 5 for more on comma splices.

Incorrect:

> As Michael Pollan recommends, I always shop along the outer edges of the supermarket, I find fresh bread, meat, produce, and dairy products there.

Correct:

> As Michael Pollan recommends, I always shop along the outer edges of the supermarket, **for** I find fresh bread, meat, produce, and dairy products there.

3) **Use a comma to separate introductory information from the main part of the sentence. Introductory information includes an introductory word, phrase, or clause.**

a. Introductory Word

A comma goes after an introductory word like "also" because it introduces the main part of the sentence.

Example:

Also, one reason for some scholars' criticism of Black History Month is that they think it is too short.

    i. **Main part of the sentence:** one reason for some scholars' criticism of Black History Month is that they think it is too short.

    ii. **Introductory word:** Also,

Exercise 2:

Write a sentence using each of the following introductory words:

1) Lastly,

2) Unfortunately,

3) However,

b. Introductory Phrase

A comma goes after an introductory phrase like "According to the article" because it introduces the main part of the sentence.

Example:

According to the article, President Gerald Ford officially designated February as Black History Month in 1976.

    i. **Main part of the sentence:** President Gerald Ford officially designated February as Black History Month in 1976.

    ii. **Introductory phrase:** According to the article,

Exercise 3:

Write a sentence using each of the following introductory phrases:

1) After a while,

2) In conclusion,

3) For example,

Note: A comma also goes after a phrase that introduces a quotation.

Example:

| comma after introductory phrase |

The author says, "Many opponents of Black History Month allege that the story of African Americans' past is far too detailed and complex to present to audiences in a few weeks' time" ("Black History Month").

Hint: This does not apply if the phrase includes the word "that."

Example:

| no comma |

The author says that "[m]any opponents of Black History Month allege that the story of African Americans' past is far too detailed and complex to present to audiences in a few weeks' time ("Black History Month").

c. Introductory Clause

A comma goes after an introductory (dependent) clause like "Although supporters and opponents disagree about the month-long celebration" because it comes before the main part of the sentence.

Example:

Although supporters and opponents disagree about the month-long celebration, they agree that African-American history should be taught and integrated into American history throughout the year.

    i. **Main part of the sentence:** they agree that African-American history should be taught and integrated into American history throughout the year.

    ii. **Introductory clause:** Although supporters and opponents disagree about the month-long celebration,

An introductory clause will start with a subordinating conjunction, also known as a dependent word. The following words are examples of subordinating conjunctions (dependent words):

DEPENDENT WORDS/SUBORDINATING CONJUNCTIONS			
after	although	as	as if
because	before	even if	even though
if	in order to	once	since
that	though	unless	until
whatever	when	whenever	where
wherever	whether	which	while

Exercise 4:

Now, write a sentence that begins with an introductory clause starting with the subordinating conjunction *when*.

Hint: Remember that the comma does **not** belong immediately after the subordinating conjunction "when." **The comma belongs after the entire introductory clause**. Then, the sentence should be completed with an independent clause, the main part of the sentence.

1) When _____, _____.

Now, choose four more subordinating conjunctions from the list above, and write four more sentences that start with introductory clauses.

2)

3)

4)

5)

4) **Use a comma to separate interrupters from the main part of the sentence.**

As you just learned, use the comma sets off a word group that comes **before** the main part of the sentence. In the same way, the comma sets off an interrupting word group that comes **in the middle** of the main part of the sentence. This example should look familiar as an example with an introductory phrase:

> According to the article, President Gerald Ford officially appointed February as Black History Month in 1976.

We can rearrange this sentence to see the fourth use of the comma: separating the interrupter from the main part of the sentence:

> President Gerald Ford, according to the article, officially appointed February as Black History Month in 1976.

i) **Main part of the sentence:** President Gerald Ford officially appointed February as Black History Month in 1976.

ii) **Interrupter:** according to the article

Here is another example. In this case we have an introductory word separated from the main sentence with a comma:

> Unfortunately, African-American history still does not garner the attention it should in mainstream US history curricula.

Again, we can rearrange the sentence to turn the introductory information into an interrupter using commas to separate the interrupter from the main part of the sentence.

> African-American history, unfortunately, still does not garner the attention it should in mainstream US history curricula.

i. **Main part of sentence:** African-American history still does not garner the attention it should in mainstream US history curricula.

ii. **Interrupter:** unfortunately

Exercise 5:

Now you try. Here is a sentence that starts with a phrase that introduces the main sentence:

> For instance, David Walker and his *Appeal to the Colored Citizens of the World* were excluded from my education on American history.

Rewrite the sentence so that the introductory phrase "for instance" becomes an interrupter in the middle of the main part of the sentence.

Some interrupters are called appositives. An **appositive** explains who or what a noun is in the sentence. Here is an example:

> Carter Woodson, the originator of Negro History Week, wanted the special February observance of African-American history to end once Black history became a fixture in mainstream history curricula.

Notice that we could reverse the order of the appositive and noun and we would still need the commas:

> The originator of Negro History Week, Carter Woodson, wanted the special February observance of African-American history to end once Black history became a fixture in mainstream history curricula.

OTHER COMMA USES

Obviously, commas are used in ways other than just the four we covered here. You probably know to **use a comma to separate the day from the year in a date:**

Negro History Week was first observed February 12, 1926.

You also probably know to **use commas in an address to separate the street address from the city and the city from the state:**

9000 Overland Avenue, Culver City, CA 90230

Also, don't forget to **use a comma to separate a city name from its state or country name in a sentence:**

Carter Woodson was born in New Canton, Virginia.

AVOIDING COMMA PITFALLS

- There is no need to place a comma before a subordinating conjunction (dependent word) when the dependent clause occurs in the second half of the sentence. Here is an example:

    Michael Pollan recommends that people avoid foods that contain high fructose corn syrup because those foods tend to be processed foods.

    ↑ no comma

    Because is not a coordinating conjunction (FANBOYS). It is a subordinating conjunction.

- Avoid placing a comma before a coordinating conjunction (FANBOYS) that does not join two complete thoughts:

    Michael Pollan suggests that we avoid cereals that change the color of our milk and that we "shop on the peripheries of the supermarket" (27).   no comma ↑

    Notice that the second part of that sentence that comes after the conjunction "and" is NOT a complete thought (independent clause), so there is no need for a comma.

Exercise 6:

Add or remove commas in the following sentences. (One sentence is correct.)

1) Although some people think Black History Month is not necessary it actually helps to educate people on African-American culture.

2) Black History Month activities can teach people about little-known events from the Civil Rights Movement about unrecognized African-American inventors about Black artists and about the history of education in the African-American community.

3) According to the article "Black History Month" some supporters of Black History Month argue that it "can teach children valuable lessons about adversity" but opponents argue that the month "represents an opportunity for groups to express token appreciation for the legacy of African-Americans."

4) Carter Woodson wanted to end the February observance of African-American history after Black history became adequately recognized by mainstream American society.

5) First of all the heritage of African-Americans is too vast to cover in just one month.

6) Also many African-Americans object to the celebration of Black History Month.

7) Some argue that Black History Month should be observed, because it draws the nation's attention to uncomfortable elements of its history.

THE APOSTROPHE ,

The apostrophe is a mark of punctuation that stumps many students. We have encountered countless talented, brilliant writers who flub using the apostrophe. Students often do not include necessary apostrophes:

Incorrect:

> The full understanding of African Americans detailed past will lead to a multicultural country which appreciates all races.

Do you see where the apostrophe is missing?

Correct:

> The full understanding of African Americans' detailed past will lead to a multicultural country which appreciates all races.

Students also include unnecessary apostrophes:

Incorrect:

> Some African-American's are offended by the observance of Black History Month.

Incorrect:

> Some African-Americans' are offended by the observance of Black History Month.

Do you see why these apostrophes are not necessary?

The word "African-Americans" in this sentence is plural. The writer is just referring to more than one African-American.

Once you master the correct uses of the apostrophe, you will observe its misuse everywhere. In England, an Apostrophe Protection Society even exists to protect the correct use of the apostrophe. On the Society's website, people post pictures of signs wielding messages containing apostrophe errors like these:

Saint Pauls Square   **No Swimming. Jet Ski's Only**   **Gift's Direct**

This section of Chapter 4 will provide you with the tools to help you avoid getting a picture of your sign or document posted on the Society's website. You can learn to use the apostrophe flawlessly!

COMMON USES FOR THE APOSTROPHE

The apostrophe has two common uses that will probably sound at least a little familiar to you.

1) Use an apostrophe in contractions in place of omitted letters.

2) Use an apostrophe to show possession (ownership).

These two uses sound straightforward, but many students encounter difficulty using this little mark correctly.

1) **Use an apostrophe in contractions in place of omitted letters.**

Most students do pretty well using apostrophes in contractions.

Exercise 1:

List the common contractions below for the sets of words they replace. The first one is done for you.

do not = **don't**	I am =	would have =
cannot =	have not =	it is =

| she is = | they are = | let us = |
| I will = | we have = | will not = |

Notice that in almost every case, the apostrophe goes where the letters have been removed from the words. The thing to remember about contractions is that they connote an *informal* tone. You will learn more about the best tones to use in college writing in Chapter 6, but as a rule, college essays use a formal tone, so you want to avoid using contractions in your college writing. While some instructors forbid the use of contractions, others do not. Just keep in mind that contractions are best reserved for informal speaking and writing.

2) **Use an apostrophe to show possession (ownership).**

Add an apostrophe and an "s" to singular nouns, and just an apostrophe to plural nouns that end in "s" to indicate possession or ownership.

This second use of the apostrophe tends to be more challenging. Some students mistakenly use an apostrophe when it's not necessary:

Incorrect	**Correct**
The boy's have great mothers.	The boys have great mothers.
The boys' have great mothers.	
The boys have great mother's.	
The boys have great mothers'.	

The mothers do belong to the boys in these sentence, so you might think one of the above apostrophes is appropriate.

In fact, **none of those apostrophes is necessary**. To show possession or ownership, use an apostrophe to show that one noun owns the noun immediately following:

Correct

The boy's <u>mother</u> is great.	The mother belongs to the one boy, so we add an apostrophe and an "s" to communicate that ownership.
The boys' <u>mothers</u> are great.	In this case, the mothers belong to the two or more boys, so we add an apostrophe to the word boys (which already ends in "s") to communicate the ownership.
The boys' <u>mother</u> is great.	In this case the boys share the same great mother. (Hence, they must be brothers.)

Exercise 2:

Where necessary add an apostrophe and "s" in the sentences below to show possession:

1) Shawn burns were not as severe as Alvaro.
2) The university reputation for safety was impacted by the fire.
3) Angie grades were excellent even through Alvaro hospital stay.
4) Saint Barnabas Hospital burn unit was known throughout the world.
5) Hani Mansour first experience with a burn victim had a profound impact on him.

Now that you've practiced the basic apostrophe used to show possession before the "s," let's move on to something a little trickier.

WHEN DO YOU PUT THE APOSTROPHE *AFTER* THE S?

The apostrophe belongs after the "s" when you still want to indicate possession but the possessor is a plural noun that ends with "s." Basically, you just add the apostrophe to the plural word that already ends with an "s." For example, the sentences earlier describing the mothers of the boys as great:

The boys' mothers are great.   The boys' mother is great.

(Remember these boys share the same mother)

There is more than one boy, so the word "boys" already ends with an "s." Then, you add the apostrophe to show that two boys *own* or *possess* the mothers or mother. The mothers *belong* to the boys.

Here's another example:

The nurses' favorite television star is Lucille Ball.

In the book *After the Fire*, many nurses love Lucille Ball. Thus, the word "nurses" already ends with an "s" because it is plural. Also, the word "nurses'" needs the apostrophe because the favorite television star *belongs* to the nurses.

Exercise 3:

Now, where necessary in the sentences below about Ishmael Beah's book *A Long Way Gone*, add apostrophes to the **plural** nouns:

1) In the forest, the pigs loud snorts startled Ishmael.
2) When the chief saw Ishmael and his friends rap tapes, he let the boys live.

3) The fisherman helped nurse the boys wounds.

4) The soldiers drug use helped to numb their pain.

5) In the rehab center, all of the residents withdrawal symptoms were severe.

HOW DO YOU SHOW POSSESSION WITH PLURAL NOUNS THAT DO NOT END IN "S"?

Students also ask about using the apostrophe to show possession with words that are plural but do not end in "s" like "women" and "children." To make those types of words possessive, add the apostrophe, then "s" just like in singular nouns.

Examples:

> Parents should pay close attention to their children's eating habits to help them follow Michael Pollan's food rules.
>
> Many life-saving charities help increase impoverished women's ability to feed their families by providing loans so those women can start their own businesses.

HOW DO YOU USE THE POSSESSIVE APOSTROPHE WITH SINGULAR NOUNS ENDING IN "S"?

In this case you have options!

Correct

Frances' friends	Frances's friends
Mr. Jones' lawyer	Mr. Jones's lawyer
Curtis' touchdown	Curtis's touchdown
the toss' angle	the toss's angle
his kiss' meaning	his kiss's meaning

You may use your judgment about whether to add the "s" after the apostrophe in singular nouns that end in "s." Just be sure to be consistent throughout your document.

ADDITIONAL USES FOR THE APOSTROPHE

While contractions and possession are the most common uses for the apostrophe, a few others do exist, and since questions do come up regarding those other uses, we have included some of them briefly below. Bear in mind, however, that some of those uses are only appropriate in an informal setting.

1) **Use an apostrophe when you omit numbers from a date.**

Example:

> I graduated from high school in '04 and worked for many years before enrolling in college.

This sentence is fine in an informal context like an e-mail to a friend or a verbal conversation with a classmate, but in a college essay, you would just write "2004," so there would be no need for the apostrophe.

2) **Use an apostrophe to make numbers, letters, abbreviations, and words plural.**
(This apostrophe use is often optional and calls for good judgment.)

Examples:

- Black History Month gained prominence in the 1980's and 1990's.

  Or

- Black History Month gained prominence in the 1980s and 1990s.
- Shawn was proud of himself for earning A's and B's when he returned to school after the fire.

We have included a number of apostrophe exercises to give you adequate practice to master the use of the apostrophe.

Exercise 4:

Add the necessary apostrophes to the following sentences. One sentence is correct.

1) In *A Long Way Gone*, Ishmaels home country is Sierra Leone.
2) The womans baby was shot dead while strapped to her back.
3) When the rebels attacked the village, the boys were separated.
4) The villages imam was killed by the rebels.
5) Ishmael and his friends were awed by Freetowns cars and big buildings.

Exercise 5:

Correct the apostrophe errors in the sentences below taken directly from student essays. One sentence is correct.

1) Another reason Black History Month should continue is because Black history doesnt get adequate attention in standard history curricula.

2) Woodsons goal was for African-American history to be integrated into mainstream history.

3) Nothing will take the place of the American observances of African-American History Month in schools and businesses around the nation.

4) Opponents objections to Black History Month vary from wanting Black history to be studied throughout the year to thinking Black history gets too much attention.

5) Some critics in the nations academic community assert that the integrity of Black history is compromised by attempts to educate people on such a broad topic in a month.

Exercise 6:

Add and remove apostrophes when necessary. Some sentences may be correct.

1) Peter Singer argues that American's and people in other wealthy nations should donate more money instead of buying things we don't need.

2) His article made me think about the things I buy that are luxurie's that I don't really need.

3) For example, last week I bought three pairs of shoes for my kid's.

4) I also bought a sweater for my daughters dog.

5) A dogs sweater is certainly not more important than a childs life.

Exercise 7:

Correct each apostrophe error. One sentence is correct.

1) In Toni Morrisons *The Bluest Eye*, the Breedlove familys constant bickering and poverty pressure Pecola into a constant depression and defeat.

2) Pecola is a young girl who moves in with nine-year-old Claudia and ten-year-old Frieda because Pecola's father tries to burn his families' house down.

3) She goes to the whore's house and asks them about their love lives.

4) Claudia is the MacTeer's youngest daughter.

5) Maureen is nosy when it comes to her peer's personal lives.

6) Maureens knee socks never fall down.

7) Claudia and Frieda call Maureen names because the girls are jealous of her.

8) Geraldines cats blue eyes fascinate Pecola.

9) Mr. Henrys behavior enrages Friedas parents.

10) Pecola knocks over her mothers cobbler.

11) When Pauline Breedlove is young, she doesnt have many friends.

12) Pauline and Chollys marriage starts out happily.

13) Paulines pregnancy pleases Cholly.

14) After learning White Americas standards of beauty, Pauline determines that shes ugly.

15) Paulines job at the Fishers home gives her a sense of pride.

Exercise 8:

Add the necessary apostrophes to or remove the unnecessary apostrophes from the following paragraph. (There are four errors).

> First of all, one of Michael Pollans food rules says that people should "eat only foods that have been cooked by humans;" however, a lot of my favorite snack's were made in factories (37). Pollan argues that food corporations products are not healthy. He says, "In general, corporations cook with too much salt, fat, and sugar, as well as with preservatives, colorings, and other biological novelties" (37). Even though I know that each company's goal is just to make money, most of my favorite foods are made by corporations. At least once a week I eat a big pack of Oreo's made by the Nabisco Corporation. I also eat Cheetos and Doritos from the Frito Lay Corporation all the time.

END PUNCTUATION

PERIOD •

Use a period to indicate the closure of a complete sentence (independent clause).

Example:

Eat food.

–Rule #1 in Michael Pollan's *Food Rules*

EXCLAMATION POINT !

> Use an exclamation point in place of a period to indicate strong emotion or loud volume.

Example:

> Angie yelled "Al!" as she was searching for Alvaro in the chaos of the fire (Fisher 10).

Note: You are more likely to use exclamation points in writing dialogue or in informal writing than in academic writing for your college classes.

QUESTION MARK ?

> Use a question mark to indicate the closure of a direct question.

Example:

> Should people resent Black History Month?

Question marks can sometimes be misused when a question is embedded in the sentence.

Example:

> Some people ask why Black History Month exists.

There is no question mark here because the entire sentence is a statement, not a question. This is often referred to as an indirect question.

QUOTATION MARKS

> 1. Use quotation marks to indicate a writer or speaker's exact words.
> 2. Use quotation marks to indicate a title of a short text like a short story, song, poem, chapter title, article, or essay.
> 3. Use quotation marks to indicate that a word or phrase is being used with a definition that may not be universally accepted.

1) **Use quotation marks to indicate a writer or speaker's *exact* words.**

> In her book *Eats, Shoots, and Leaves*, Lynn Truss says, "There is a huge amount of ignorance concerning the use of quotation marks" (149).

Students often ask how to indicate a direct quotation from a text that contains its own quotation. In those cases, place single quotation marks around the quotation within the quotation.

> In her book *After the Fire*, Robin Gaby Fisher writes, "Shawn had other ideas. 'Give me two weeks and a couple of days, and I'll be out of here,' he promised Andy Horvath" (86).

2) **Use quotation marks to indicate a title of a short text like a short story, song, poem, article, or essay.**

"The Singer Solution to World Poverty"   "Letter from a Birmingham Jail"

"The Gilded Six Bits"   "Oh Captain! My Captain!"

3) **Use quotation marks to indicate that a word or phrase is being used with a definition that may not be universally accepted.** (A rule of thumb: if you can place "so-called" in front of the word or phrase, you might put it in quotation marks.)

Peter Singer applies this use of quotation marks in his article "The Singer Solution to Poverty." His point is that the notion of "fair share" that people use as an excuse not to donate to save the lives of others is not universally accepted.

> Thus, we know that the money we can give beyond that theoretical "fair share" is still going to save lives that would otherwise be lost.
>
> -Peter Singer "The Singer Solution to World Poverty"

Exercise 1:

Add the necessary quotation marks to these examples from student work:

1) In the article The Singer Solution to World Poverty from *The New York Times Magazine,* the author, Peter Singer, describes how wealthy and middle class people should donate all of their extra money to save lives instead of spending it on luxuries.

2) In the article Singer says, Since there are a lot of desperately needy children in the world, there will always be another child whose life you could save for 200 dollars.

3) The moral obligation that Singer claims people have to donate money, does not really exist.

▌SEMICOLON ;

Remember that, for the most part, semicolons are not technically necessary. You could write an entire 1000-page book without using one, and it could be grammatically correct. However, semicolons give you some dexterity in your writing once you have mastered their nuances, so read on to find out exactly how to use them correctly.

> 1. Use a semicolon between two related complete thoughts (independent clauses).
>
> 2. Use a semicolon to separate items in a list that contains other punctuation marks.

The first use is pretty straightforward:

1) **Use a semicolon like a period between two related sentences (independent clauses).**

Here is a student example:

> Special February events like television shows and performances about African-American culture have educated people. For example, I went to a Cultural Arts Extravaganza at my college that was educational for me; the performances I saw were beautiful; there was also a sculpture that represented the struggles that African-Americans have experienced.

Notice how this student used semicolons *between related complete sentences* in this excerpt of her essay.

Exercise 1:

Now you try. Insert semicolons between the sets of sentences below:

(1) My college hosted several Black History Month events this year I attended the talk on Malcom X.

(2) I also went to see the screening of the film, *Glory* I learned about African-American soldiers who fought in the American Civil War.

(3) Before I saw this film, I did not even know Black soldiers fought in the Civil War observing Black History Month clearly has value since my college's Black History Month observance gave me the opportunity to learn about this important element of American History.

A semicolon is often presented as an option for correcting run-on sentences and comma splices because sometimes students place just a comma or nothing at all between two related sentences (independent clauses).

The second use of the semicolon is a little more complex and unusual:

2) **Use a semicolon to separate items in a list that contains other punctuation marks (usually commas).**

Here is a student example of a list of items containing other punctuation marks separated with just commas.

Unclear:

> This year during Black History Month, I saw three exhibits at the African-American museum: Places of Validation, Art & Progression, Women: Game Changers, Less Known, Here Celebrated, and Justice, Balance and Achievement: African Americans and the California Courts.

Separated by just commas, the items in that list of exhibits is indecipherable. You can't even tell how many exhibits the writer saw. Here is the correct version with semicolons.

Clear:

> This year during Black History Month, I saw three exhibits at the African-American museum: Places of Validation, Art & Progression; Women: Game Changers, Less Known, Here Celebrated; and Justice, Balance and Achievement: African Americans and the California Courts.

Much better!

Now, before we move on to the colon, here is some practice for you.

Exercise 2:

Below are some sentences from real student compositions. All but one contain two related complete thoughts/independent clauses/sentences. One sentence includes a list of items that contains other punctuation marks. Add semicolons to make them correct.

1) In *After the Fire*, Shawn's mom, Christine, encourages Shawn even when he is discouraged she supports him through his worst days.

2) I also experienced a near-death experience I was hit by a car, and I went into a coma.

3) My auntie exposes my cousin to new things when she reads books to her like *Goodnight, Goodnight, Construction Site It's a Big World, Little Pig Isabella: Girl on the Go* and *Me . . . Jane.*

4) Christine is also compassionate she is so patient with Shawn when he thinks he smells smoke.

5) In the end, all mothers have different qualities, but being caring is one of the best nothing makes someone more of a mother than being caring.

Before we finish with the semicolon, one of the most beautiful and famous examples of an artistic use of semicolon that contributes to meaning is by Martin Luther King Jr. in "Letter from a Birmingham Jail." Scholars suggest that Dr. King's use of semicolons replicates the feeling of waiting for segregation to end. In response to the suggestion that Civil Rights leaders should just patiently bide their time, Dr. King here makes the audience wait for the end of his sentence just as African-Americans had to wait for the end of segregation.

"But when you have seen vicious mobs lynch your mothers and fathers at will and drown your sisters and brothers at whim; when you have seen hate filled policemen curse, kick and even kill your black brothers and sisters; when you see the vast majority of your twenty million Negro brothers smothering in an airtight cage of poverty in the midst of an affluent society; when you suddenly find your tongue twisted and your speech stammering as you seek to explain to your six year old daughter why she can't go to the public amusement park that has just been advertised on television, and see tears welling up in her eyes when she is told that Funtown is closed to colored children, and see ominous clouds of inferiority beginning to form in her little mental sky, and see her beginning to distort her personality by developing an unconscious bitterness toward white people; when you have to concoct an answer for a five year old son who is asking: "Daddy, why do white people treat colored people so mean?"; when you take a cross county drive and find it necessary to sleep night after night in the uncomfortable corners of your automobile because no motel will accept you; when you are humiliated day in and day out by nagging signs reading "white" and "colored"; when your first name becomes "nigger," your middle name becomes "boy" (however old you are) and your last name becomes "John," and your wife and mother are never given the respected title "Mrs."; when you are harried by day and haunted by night by the fact that you are a Negro, living constantly at tiptoe stance, never quite knowing what to expect next, and are plagued with inner fears and outer resentments; when you are forever fighting a degenerating sense of "nobodiness"--then you will understand why we find it difficult to wait."

"Letter from a Birmingham Jail"

COLON :

The first thing to remember about the colon is that it almost always **follows a complete thought (independent clause)**. Because they have learned that a colon often precedes a list, many students misuse the colon in this way.

Incorrect:

Shawn and I share qualities such as: bravery, thoughtfulness, and strength.

Read the word group that comes before the colon. That is certainly not a complete sentence. See this revised version where the colon follows a complete thought and is used correctly.

Correct:

Shawn and I share several characteristics: bravery, thoughtfulness, and strength.

A colon at the end of a complete thought sets the reader up for what is coming. It leaves the reader with a sense of anticipation. Here is another example of student work in which the student uses the colon before a quotation that has been set up in the preceding complete sentence (independent clause).

> There are many ways that freedom of religion is defined. President Barack Obama in his book *The Audacity of Hope—Thoughts on Reclaiming the American Dream,* defines it this way: "We value a faith in something bigger than ourselves, whether that something expresses itself in formal religion or ethical precepts...These values are rooted in a basic optimism about life and a faith in free will" (Obama 54-5).

Exercise 1:

Insert colons into the following sentences:

1) I share several characteristics with Shawn Simmons we are both caring, brave, and we know how to be good friends.

2) Americans should continue to observe African-American history month for several reasons February is a time for educational enlightenment, people participate in African-American cultural events, and great people involved with African-American history are emphasized.

3) A good mother must have a number of characteristics, but these three are the most important she must be attentive, dependable, and compassionate.

4) I eat a number of foods regularly that do not follow Michael Pollan's food rules Twinkies, Chicken Mcnuggets, Taco Bell tacos, Skittles, Fritos, Pop Tarts, Fruit Loops, and Lunchables.

THE HYPHEN -

1. Use a hyphen to join two or more words to aid in understanding.
2. Use a hyphen to connect two or more words joined into an adjective before a noun.
3. Use a hyphen with certain prefixes and suffixes.
4. Use a hyphen to separate certain compound words that would be unreadable without the hyphen.

1) **Use a hyphen to join two or more words to aid in understanding.**

Hyphens can affect meaning in certain words like cross-reference and re-mark. The hyphenated versions may have different meanings than the compound versions. Note the example below:

> The instructor **remarked** that she would need to **re-mark** the essays she graded after drinking several glasses of wine the previous night.

> After the temperamental employee **resigned** from his job, he was hired back and **re-signed** his contract.

The same applies to numbers.

Seventy-three = 73   Seventy three = 70, 3

One-third = 1/3   one third = 1, 3rd

2) **Use a hyphen to connect two or more words joined into an adjective before a noun.**

| slow-moving train | high-fat diet | one-eyed monster |
| low-income family | half-cooked noodles | spikey-haired rocker |

3) **Use a hyphen with certain prefixes and suffixes.**

self-conscious	all-inclusive	ex-girlfriend
resident-elect	mid-July	post-Vietnam

4) **Use a hyphen to separate certain compound words that would be unreadable without the hyphen.**

Crossstitch	➔	Cross-stitch	deice	➔	de-ice
deemphasize	➔	de-emphasize		

Remember to consult the dictionary if you're not sure whether a compound word calls for a hyphen.

DASH —

1. Use a pair of dashes to set aside and emphasize additional information in a sentence.
2. Use one dash to indicate a sudden interruption in the writer's thought or a dramatic separation between one part of a sentence and another.

The hyphen and the dash are often mistaken for each other. Remember that the hyphen is short and goes directly between two words while the dash is longer and may have a space before and after it.

1) **Use a pair of dashes to set aside and emphasize additional information in a sentence.**

Two dashes can serve a similar purpose as parentheses or a pair of commas. The difference is that information between parentheses is de-emphasized as you will see below while information between two dashes is accentuated.

Notice the difference between this sentence and the examples in the next section on parenthesis:

> Carter Woodson—an African-American educator—started Negro History Week in 1926.

2) **Use one dash to indicate a sudden interruption in the writer's thought or a dramatic separation between one part of a sentence and another.**

Michael Pollan uses a dash in Rule #40 in his book, *Food Rules*:

"Be the kind of person who takes supplements—then skip the supplements" (87).

PARENTHESES ( )

Use parentheses to set aside additional information in a sentence.

Here is an example from Michael Pollan's *Food Rules*:

Most of these rules I wrote, but many of them have no single author. They are pieces of food culture, sometimes ancient, that deserve our attention, because they can help us. I've collected these adages about eating from a wide variety of sources. (The older sayings appear in quotes.) I consulted folklorists and anthropologists, doctors, nurses, nutritionists, and dietitians, as well as a large number of mothers, grandmothers, and great-grandmothers.

(Introduction xviii)

Parentheses sometimes act like commas to enclose interrupters or appositives:

Carter Woodson, an African-American educator, started Negro History Week in 1926.

Carter Woodson (an African-American educator) started Negro History Week in 1926.

Notice though how the parentheses set the information apart from the sentence and suggest it is less essential to the meaning of the sentence than when the information is set between two commas (or dashes). It is up to the writer to determine the best punctuation marks to use based on his/her meaning. The sentence must function on its own without the information in parentheses.

CHAPTER CHAPTER CHAPTER 6

GRAMMAR AND USAGE

| CAPITALIZATION

We have noticed an increase in capitalization errors as texting has increased in popularity. As a result, students today need to spend more time editing their writing for capitalization errors than previous generations of students. While there are many rules for capitalization, some of them are debated. In simplest terms, specific nouns—nouns with titles or names, called proper nouns—get capitalized while general (unspecific) nouns do not. For example, Grandma Lou is a specific person: the name that I call her is "Grandma Lou." When referring to her in general terms as "my grandmother" I am not being specific, so no capitalization is needed. Likewise "Disneyland" gets capitalized while "amusement park" does not. Referring to a large period of the calendar like the "summer" is unspecific, while month and day titles are specific: "the first Monday in July." Refer to the following chart for specific usages.

	Specific Nouns *Capitalize nouns when they have specific names.*	**Unspecific Nouns** *Don't capitalize nouns used in a general sense.*
1	**People's Names:** Mom, Uncle Max, Raul, Keisha, Professor Sander, Dr. Oz, Toni Morrison	**Types of People:** my mom, my uncle, my boyfriend, the professor, the doctor, an author
2	**Place Names:** Kenya, Brazil, Utah, Tito's Tacos, Main Street, Harlem, Stanford University, Disneyland	**Types of Places:** a city, a country, a state, a store, a college, a street, a neighborhood, a university, an amusement park
3	**Month, Day, Holiday Names:** Monday, June, Valentine's Day, Halloween, Easter	**Seasons:** winter, spring, summer, fall
4	**Product Names:** Black and Decker drill, Apple computer, Pop-Tarts, Hot Pockets	**Types of Products:** a drill, a computer, chocolate, candy, tax software
5	**Publication and Entertainment Names:** *New York Times Magazine*, *Love and Basketball*, *The Simpsons*, *The Color Purple*, "Still I Rise" (Titles of long works get italicized, short works get quote marks)	**Types of Publications and Entertainment:** a book, a movie, a television series, a newspaper, an article, a poem
6	**Company, Organization, and Religion Names:** Wells Fargo Bank, National Organization of Women, House of Representatives, Democratic Party, Rotary Club, American Federation of Teachers, Church of Latter-Day Saints, Jews, Monsanto, Oxfam	**Types of Companies, Organizations:** a club, a small business, a temple, a union, an association
7	**Names of Races, Nationalities, and Languages:** Asians, Native Americans, Italians, African Americans, Brazilian, Portuguese, Korean, Cantonese	**Colors Used To Describe People:** white, black. [*This usage is debated. Some books capitalize these, others don't. We suggest you pick one format and use it consistently.]
8	**Historical and Geographical Names:** Vietnam Way, World War II, the East Coast, the South, Reconstruction Era	**Geographic Directions:** Go west three miles; then proceed north.

Finally, there are two additional uses.

> **In opening and closing a letter:** "Dear Sir" and "Sincerely, Jose"
>
> **Specific School Courses:** Psychology 101, Environmental Science 74

Exercise 1:

Correct the errors in capitalization in the sentences below.

1) Ishmael Beah wrote a book called *A long way gone*, which was published in 2007 by sarah crichton books.

2) The book is about his experience during the civil war in sierra leone, Africa.

3) Beah's book starts with his first experience with war when he was Twelve years old.

4) On their way to a talent contest, Ishmael goes with his Brother and his friends through his Grandmother's village, kabati.

5) Ishmael likes to hear from his Father about sierra leone when it was a British colony. his father would often criticize Politics in Sierra Leone even after independence from the British.

Exercise 2:

1) I read the *facts on file* article "Black History Month" for my english class.

2) The article describes how certain People support the celebration of African-american History Month and others oppose it.

3) Morgan freeman is one famous African-American who opposes the existence of the month, calling it "ridiculous."

4) others argue that celebrating Black History Month gives students a chance to learn about historical figures like Charles drew, Mary McCleod Bethune, and Sojurner truth.

PRONOUN CHALLENGES

WHAT'S A PRONOUN?

We touched on pronouns in Chapter 3, but we decided to dedicate another section to pronouns because many students have difficulty using them correctly. English speakers use pronouns all day every day. It would probably be difficult for you to write or say three sentences in a row without using a pronoun. However, several aspects of correct pronoun use are especially tricky. Let's first make sure you are clear on what a pronoun is. A pronoun is a word we use to avoid naming a noun over and over again. For example, this sounds weird:

> Although wealthy and middle class people should not donate all of people's extra money to organizations that help solve world poverty, people should donate an amount that people feel people can afford to help end world poverty.

Notice how odd that paragraph sounds without the word "their" and "they." This is just one example of how much we depend on pronouns.

Here is our example again with the pronouns.

> Although wealthy and middle class people should not donate all of **their** extra money to organizations that help solve world poverty, people should donate an amount that **they** feel **they** can afford to help end world poverty.

Notice how much clearer it sounds with the pronouns "their" and "they" in place of the noun "people."

Here are some examples of other pronouns:

Subject Pronouns		Object Pronouns		Possessive Pronouns	
Singular	**Plural**	**Singular**	**Plural**	**Singular**	**Plural**
I	we	me	us	my	our
you	you	you	you	your	your
he/she	they	him/her	them	his/her	their

Demonstrative Pronouns		Indefinite Pronouns	Reflexive Pronouns	
Singular	**Plural**	(all singular)	**Singular**	**Plural**
this	these	all, any, anyone, anybody, both, everyone, everybody, each, either, few, nobody, none, no one, one, some, several	myself	ourselves
that	those		yourself	yourselves
			himself	themselves
			herself	

Relative Pronouns		Interrogative Pronouns	Absolute Possessive Pronouns	
Subject	**Object**	who, which, what, where, how	**Singular**	**Plural**
who	whom		mine	ours
which	that		yours	yours
			his/hers	theirs
			whose	

ANTECEDENTS

An **antecedent** is the noun to which the pronoun refers.

Here is an example of two sentences from a student essay in which the writer *does* use pronouns:

> Woodson was the creator of Negro History Week, which later became Black History Month. Overall, this creation was made to honor **African Americans'** accomplishments and **their** past struggles.

The pronoun is "their" and its antecedent is "African Americans'." When the writer says "**their** past struggles," you know she is referring back to **African Americans'** struggles.

Exercise 1:

Here is another example. Using the pronoun list above for help, circle the pronouns and their antecedents in this sentence. (Hint: One pronoun does not have a named antecedent.)

> Whether you support the continuation of Black History Month or oppose it, Black History Month should continue to be observed, and people should be proud that they have accomplished a month-long celebration after many years of persecution of African-Americans.

The pronouns in this sentence are "you," "it," and "they." The antecedent for "they" is "people." The antecedent for "it" is "the continuation of Black History Month." "You" is a special pronoun. It does not have an antecedent because it is understood that the pronoun "you" refers to the person reading or listening to what is being said, so there is no need for an antecedent.

THE SECOND PERSON PRONOUN "YOU"

As we mentioned earlier, the second person pronoun "you" refers to the person being directly addressed. However, in speaking, American speakers commonly use the second person pronoun "you" to refer to any person in general terms. Technically, we know that that second person pronoun "you" refers to the person being directly addressed, but sometimes students forget this and lapse into using the pronoun "you" when they mean someone other than the person being directly addressed. For example, a student might write something like this:

> **You** should not donate all of **your** extra money to charity because **you** might need that money for an emergency.

Now, if that student was talking to someone, that person might know that the student was not referring to him or her, and if that person was not sure, that person could ask the student to whom that pronoun "you" was referring. However, in writing, readers do not usually have the opportunity to ask the writer for clarification, so you (the writer) must be completely clear the first time. Let's consider whom the writer might mean by "you" in the above sentence. There are several possibilities:

Americans should not donate all of **their** extra money to charity because **they** might need that money for an emergency.

People in industrialized nations should not donate all of **their** extra money to charity because **they** might need that money for an emergency.

Wealthy and middle class people should not donate all of **their** extra money to charity because **they** might need that money for an emergency.

Notice how these examples give more useful information and are clearer than the original version that contained the second person pronoun "you." Generally, you (writers) should avoid using the second person pronoun "you" in your academic writing unless you are writing a process analysis paper which teaches the reader to do something (as we are in this book) or unless you are addressing your reader directly, like in an introduction or conclusion where you ask the reader a thought-provoking question.

Exercise 2:

Underline the second person pronouns in each sentence. Then replace those pronouns with clearer nouns.

1) Considering today's economic crisis, giving your family financial security makes more sense than giving all your extra money away.

2) Donating money to organizations can be very helpful in the fight against world poverty, but giving money is not the only way you can help.

3) You can never know how much your donation means to an extremely poor person overseas who may have been able to access clean, healthy drinking water because of your generosity.

Find *YOU*!

Follow these steps to identify any accidental cases of the second person pronoun "you" in your papers:

- Use the "Find" feature in your word processing program. (It's usually in the top right corner of your Home screen or in the Edit drop down menu in Microsoft Word.)
- Click "Find," and you can type the word "you" in the dialog box.
- Microsoft word will highlight the word "you" any time it occurs in your essay.
- Go through and decide whether to keep each "you" or change it to a clearer noun.

One common challenge that students encounter when using pronouns is being clear to whom or what their pronouns are referring. Here is a sample student sentence:

> Black History Month helps **us** understand and honor African-American culture.

The pronoun, "us," is bolded because whom the writer means when he says "us" is not clear. Does the writer mean Americans? People who observe Black history month? African-Americans? Students? Women? Men? The student could be referring to any group to which he belongs. That makes this sentence unclear. Remember that in writing, one of your highest priorities is to communicate meaning clearly and effectively. In this case, your reader cannot be sure exactly whom you mean, so you must revise this sentence. Replace the pronoun "us" with something more clear. Here are some options:

> Black History Month helps **Americans** understand and honor African-American culture.

> Black History Month helps **students** understand and honor African-American culture.

> Black History Month helps **everyone who observes it** understand and honor African-American culture.

> Black History Month helps **people in the United States** understand and honor African-American culture.

Notice how much clearer the writer's meaning is in the sentences above.

Exercise 3:

Underline each pronoun in the sentences from student essays below. Then, correct any unclear pronoun reference.

1) Even today, when we finally have a few new heritage months, Black History Month still gets the most attention.

2) With a year of teaching instead of a month, the full understanding of their detailed past will lead to a multicultural country which appreciates all races.

3) In recent years, prominent African-Americans have raised objections to celebrating Black History Month. Some supporters feel that it should be introduced throughout the year instead.

4) Another reason Black History Month should continue to be observed is because it is a time to honor their culture.

Pronouns must agree with their antecedents in case, gender, and number. (For definition of antecedent, see "Antecedents" section.)

You may wonder what it means that pronouns and antecedents must agree. By "agree," we do not mean that the pronoun and antecedent must never get into arguments. Instead, we mean that when the antecedent is masculine, the pronoun that refers to it must be masculine (and feminine for feminine). Likewise, when the <u>antecedent</u> is a <u>singular</u> noun, the <u>pronoun</u> that refers to it must be <u>singular</u>. Also, when the <u>antecedent</u> is a <u>plural</u> noun, the <u>pronoun</u> must be <u>plural</u>. Below are some examples of singular and plural antecedents; draw lines between the antecedents and the pronouns that would agree with them. Some of the antecedents can be matched correctly with two different pronouns.

Exercise 4:

Draw lines between the antecedents and the pronouns that would agree with them.

Antecedents	**Pronouns**
children	he/she
people's	its
student	they
money	his/her
someone's	their
school's	it

Now, read the sentence below. The pronoun and its antecedent are underlined.

Incorrect:

Morgan Freeman seems to think that any **person** who celebrates Black History Month is out of **their** mind.

In this sentence the word "person" is the antecedent for the pronoun "their." The pronoun and antecedent in this sentence <u>do not agree</u>. The antecedent "person" is singular. The pronoun "their" is plural and can only refer to a plural antecedent. When we speak, we often refer to singular antecedents using the pronouns "they," "them," and "their." However, even though this is common in spoken English, it is not correct. To make that sentence correct, we have several options. We might change the pronoun to make it singular so it agrees with the singular antecedent "person."

Correct:

Morgan Freeman seems to think that any **person** who celebrates Black History Month is out of **his or her** mind.

You might think this sentence sounds awkward and that you would never say it verbally this way, but it is correct. The pronouns "his" and "her" are both singular.

Here is the old fashioned way to say this same sentence:

Correct (but no longer commonly accepted):

Morgan Freeman seems to think that any **person** who celebrates Black History Month is out of **his** mind.

In this case, the pronoun and antecedent agree because they are both singular. However, this default to the male pronoun (he, him, his) is no longer common practice because it excludes girls and women. This is often referred to as sexist language or gender-bias, which you want to avoid. As a result, we resort to the awkward construction "his or her." Fortunately, you have another option:

Correct:

Morgan Freeman seems to think that **people** who celebrate Black History Month are out of **their** minds.

This option is to change the antecedent "person" and make it plural "people." Then, the plural pronoun "their" is correct.

Exercise 5:

Write one or two sentences using each of the following singular pronouns and antecedents:

1) a student   his/her

_____

2) a child   he/she

_____

3) a soldier   him/her

_____

4) a good friend   his/her

_____

5) a consumer   he/she

_____

The indefinite pronouns below are always singular and must be matched with singular pronouns.

SINGULAR INDEFINITE PRONOUNS				
another	anybody	anyone	anything	each
either	everybody	everyone	everything	neither
nobody	no one	nothing	one	somebody
something	someone			

Even though some of these words may seem like they should be plural (everyone, everything), all of the words above are **always** singular. These words are singular because they are referring to each body or thing **one at a time**. That means the only type of pronoun that will agree with them is a singular pronoun. Here is an example.

> **Incorrect:**
>
> **Each** of the opponents in the article presented **their** opinions about celebrating Black History Month.

In the sentence the word "each" is the antecedent for the pronoun "their." The pronoun and antecedent in this sentence <u>do not agree</u>. The antecedent "each" is singular. The pronoun "their" is plural and can only refer to a plural antecedent.

Note: To easily match your antecedent and pronoun in sentences like this one, cross out prepositional phrases like "of the opponents" and "in the article." See "Prepositions" in Chapter 3 for more information.

We might change the pronoun so that it agrees with the antecedent "each."

> **Correct:**
>
> **Each** opponent in the article presented **his or her** opinion about celebrating Black History Month.

This option is awkward for some students because many people would not say this if they were speaking the sentence aloud even though it is correct. The pronoun "his" is singular and the pronoun "her" is also singular.

Here is the old fashioned way to correct the error:

> **Correct (but not widely accepted):**
>
> **Each** opponent in the article presented **his** opinion about celebrating Black History Month.

This default to the male pronoun (he, him, his) is no longer common practice because it excludes girls and women. As a result, we resort to the awkward construction "his or her." A related emerging solution is to simply alternate between the masculine singular pronoun (he, him, his) and the feminine singular pronoun (she, her, hers) throughout a text. If you would like to try this option, check with your instructor first. Fortunately, you have another option:

> The **opponents** in the article presented **their** opinions about celebrating Black History Month.

This option of changing the antecedent and making it plural is often the preferable choice because it eliminates any sexist language and avoids awkward wording.

Exercise 6:

Below are a few sentences that came from real student essays. Underline the pronouns and their antecedents in each sentence. Then write "S" above any pronouns or antecedents that are singular and "P" above those that are plural. Finally, correct any pronoun agreement errors.

1) Peter Singer gives many reasons why each wealthy and middle class person should give all the extra money we have to help people suffering from poverty.

2) A person's responsibility is to their family before anything else.

3) For example, if someone had children, they should put extra money aside for their children or for when they have children later in life.

4) Everyone, whether wealthy or middle class, should donate all their extra money because the contributions go towards the children in need.

5) Singer stresses the fact that only $200 can save a child's life and get them from sick to healthy in about four years.

WHO, WHOM, WHICH, THAT: SUBJECT VERSUS OBJECT PRONOUNS

The form a pronoun takes depends upon how it is used in the sentence. For example, we don't say "Him called I," because these are the wrong usages of the subject and object pronoun forms. "He called me," is the only choice that sounds correct. We respect the subject and object forms because we need to indicate who is doing the action (the subject, "he") and who is receiving that action (the object, "me"). Otherwise, we might misunderstand the sentence as "I called him," which would mean the opposite of what we intended. In the same way, "who" and "whom" change depending on how they are used in a sentence (as subjects or objects).

Who, whom, which, and that are called "relative pronouns" because they give us more information that is "relative" or related to another noun in the sentence.

First, we must determine how the word "who" or "whom" is used in its own relative clause. These clauses are treated separately from the independent clause, but sometimes they are right in the middle of the sentence, which can make separating them difficult at first.

The relative clause of the sentence is in bold:

Example:

Students **who do their homework** are more likely to pass the class.

"Who" here refers to students and the dependent, relative clause, "who do their homework," tells us which students are more likely to pass the class. In this clause, "who" acts as the subject of the relative clause (the verb is "do"). The independent clause is "Students . . .are more likely to pass the class." Which students? The relative clause tells us.

If "who" were the object case in the sentence, it would have to change, just like "he" changes to "him" or "they" changes to "them."

Change "who" to "whom" when it is the object of a verb or a prepositional phrase.

Example:

The students **whom I appreciate the most** (direct object) are the ones who do their homework.

To whom do I owe the pleasure? (object of a preposition)

In this example, the bold relative clause is "whom I appreciate the most." Here, the subject of the relative clause is "I" (the verb is "appreciate"). Therefore, we use "whom" because it is the direct object of the relative clause.

Whom did she kiss? (direct object of the verb kiss)

To whom did you speak? (indirect object of the verb speak)

"Do not ask **for whom** the bell tolls." (object of a preposition for)

This plate of spaghetti was made **for whom**? (object of a preposition for)

The best test is to substitute "him" or "them" into the sentence to test whether "who" or "whom" would be appropriate. Try that in the above examples.

She kissed him. The bell tolls for him. The plate of spaghetti was made for him/them. That works; therefore we know we have the right form.

> Notice that in the object case, "him" and "them" end in "m." This can help us remember that we need to use "whom" in the same cases.

> Use "who" as a subject pronoun to refer to people.
>
> Use "that" as a subject or object pronoun to refer to things or animals.

Example:

The money **that was donated** went to digging wells. (Use "which" for nonessential clauses).

Which or That?

> Use "that" with essential clauses that are necessary for meaning.

Example:

I was studying plants **that lose their leaves.**

It is essential information to know which plants I was studying. Essential clauses are also known as "restrictive clauses."

> Use "which" as the pronoun in nonessential clauses.

Example:

I was studying plants, **which my mother could never understand.**

Exercise 1:

In the following exercise, fill in the blank with the appropriate word: whom, whom, which, or that.

1) _____ does he think he is? (Hint: Linking verbs are never used with direct or indirect objects.)

2) "To _____ it may concern, Rachelle is a wonderful student."

3) Adoption agencies love parents _____ embrace the challenges and joys of parenthood.

4) That man _____ hit my car ended up being very kind.

5) The museum to _____ I always take my kids is very educational.

6) The road _____ I always take is under construction.

7) To _____ does this umbrella belong?

8) All the kids _____ I have mentored through the program have gone on to prestigious universities.

9) He's been taking his studies seriously, _____ is a good thing.

10) Without a compass _____ can give us our direction, we will be lost.

11) Cows _____ chew their cuds digest grass faster than chickens _____ don't.

SUBJECT/VERB AGREEMENT

Just as pronouns and their antecedents must agree, subjects and verbs must agree. Students have the most difficulty with the third person singular subjects, so we will focus on those. A third person subject is anyone or anything other than the person speaking (I) or the person being spoken to (you). So *he, she, it, the student, Oprah Winfrey, my school, Los Angeles, the earth, my dog, Peter Singer,* and *high fructose corn syrup* are all third person singular subjects.

© PhuShutter/Shutterstock.com

	Subject
First Person Singular	*I*
Second Person Singular	*You*
Third Person Singular	*he* *she* *it*

→

the student
Oprah Winfrey
my school
Los Angeles
the earth
my dog
Peter Singer
high fructose corn syrup
etc.

Now, when we talk about any of those types of subjects in the present tense, we must use the correct form of the verb.

To agree with a third person singular subject, the verb always ends in "s."

Here is an example of a sentence from a student essay:

Incorrect

Morgan Freeman don't support celebrating Black History Month.

The subject in the sentence is Morgan Freeman. That subject is neither the person speaking (I) nor the person being spoken to (you), so you know that subject is in the third person.

Now, what is the verb? We often identify the verb in a sentence as the action that the subject is performing, and in this case the action is "support," but Freeman opposes Black History Month, so the sentence contains a helping verb to communicate his opposition. That helping verb is "do." Let's look at the sentence again and eliminate the contraction "don't." We will write it out as the full two words:

Incorrect

Morgan Freeman do not support celebrating Black History Month.

That may sound a little more odd to you because the subject, "Morgan Freeman" and the verb "do" do not agree. Notice that the verb "do" does not end in "s." Because "Morgan Freeman" is a third person singular subject, it requires a present tense verb that ends in "s." In this case, the verb should be "does."

Correct

Morgan Freeman does not support celebrating Black History Month.

Let's try another example. Let's examine what present tense verbs could follow the third person singular noun, high fructose corn syrup.

> **High fructose corn syrup is** found in many foods today.

> **High fructose corn syrup has** developed a bad reputation.

> Some people argue that **high fructose corn syrup gets** blamed for Americans' poor choices.

> Some researchers say that **high fructose corn syrup causes** our bodies to absorb more sugar.

> **High fructose corn syrup allows** Americans to enjoy many sweet snacks cheaply because of the cheap price of corn in this country.

Notice that the verb in each of those sentences ends in an "s" because any present tense verb that agrees with a third person singular subject always ends in "s." Try to prove us wrong.

Exercise 1:

Complete the charts below. The first one has been done for you.

	Subject	Present Tense Verb: HAVE
First Person Singular	I	*have class in an hour.*
Second Person Singular	You	*have beautiful hair.*
Third Person Singular	He	*has the same phone as I do.*
	She	*has two sons.*
	It	*has a great reputation.*
	Angie	*has a dilemma.*
	Singer	*has a controversial point of view.*
	Pollan	*has strong opinions about food.*

	Subject	Present Tense Verb: DO
First Person Singular	*I*	
Second Person Singular	*You*	
Third Person Singular		

	Subject	Present Tense Verb: GO
First Person Singular		
Second Person Singular		
Third Person Singular		

	Subject	Present Tense Verb: TO BE
First Person Singular		
Second Person Singular		
Third Person Singular		

	Subject	Present Tense Verb: THINK
First Person Singular		
Second Person Singular		
Third Person Singular		

Exercise 2:

Complete the tables below using your own verbs.

	Subject	Present Tense Verb:
First Person Singular	I	
Second Person Singular	You	
Third Person Singular		

	Subject	Present Tense Verb:
First Person Singular	I	
Second Person Singular	You	
Third Person Singular		

	Subject	Present Tense Verb:
First Person Singular	I	
Second Person Singular	You	
Third Person Singular		

	Subject	Present Tense Verb:
First Person Singular	I	
Second Person Singular	You	
Third Person Singular		

	Subject	Present Tense Verb:
First Person Singular	I	
Second Person Singular	You	
Third Person Singular		

CORRECTING RUN-ON SENTENCES, COMMA SPLICES, AND SENTENCE FRAGMENTS

Two different types of word groups make up all sentences in the English language: clauses and phrases.

CLAUSES

A clause is a group of words that contains a subject and a verb.

There are two types of clauses: independent clauses and dependent clauses.

An independent clause can stand alone as its own sentence. It is also known as a complete sentence, complete idea, or complete thought. Here are some examples of independent clauses:

> Shawn and Alvaro are roommates.
>
> They both escape the burning building.
>
> Alvaro's girlfriend, Angie, stands by him for many months.

Dependent clauses cannot stand alone. A dependent clause must attach to an independent clause in order to work. A dependent clause always begins with a subordinating conjunction (dependent word). Here are some examples:

DEPENDENT WORDS/SUBORDINATING CONJUNCTIONS			
after	although	as	as if
because	before	even if	even though
if	in order to	once	since
that	though	unless	until
whatever	when	whenever	where
wherever	whether	which	while

Here are some examples of dependent clauses:

> because Shawn and Alvaro are roommates
>
> when they both escape the burning building
>
> although Alvaro's girlfriend, Angie, stands by him for many months

Here is an example of a sentence that contains an independent clause and a dependent clause:

Shawn and Alvaro are roommates when they both escape the burning building.

PHRASES

Phrases are groups of words that do not contain a subject and a main verb. **A phrase cannot stand alone as its own sentence.** Some different types of phrases are gerund (-ing) phrases, infinitive phrases, and prepositional phrases. See the examples below.

Gerund Phrases (-ing Phrases)

eating so much processed food every day

going to the grocery store and shopping in the peripheral sections

Infinitive Phrases

to eat so much processed food every day

to go to the grocery store and shop in the peripheral sections

Prepositional Phrases

after eating so much processed food every day

in the peripheral sections of the grocery store

> The misuse of phrases and clauses can lead to two major pitfalls common in writing: sentence fragments and run-on sentences (including comma splices).

RUN-ONS

Students often think that a run-on sentence is a sentence that just goes on and on and on. However, a run-on sentence has a more technical definition. Below is a list of three run-on sentences from student essays. What error does each sentence have in common?

© Bokica/Shutterstock.com

1) George was an honest employee he never stole anything from the dry storage room.

2) Americans love nice things they enjoy eating the finest food and driving the fastest cars.

3) The problem is that her mood would change all the time sometimes she could be happy then she would be mad a few minutes later.

Do you see the common error in the sentences? If you said that each sentence contains more than one sentence joined together without anything separating them, you were right!

> A run-on sentence is a sentence that contains two or more independent clauses (complete thoughts) run together with no punctuation in between.

Let's look at the first example:

> George was an honest employee he never stole anything from the dry storage room.

Here is the first independent clause or complete thought in this run-on:

> George was an honest employee

Here is the second independent clause:

> he never stole anything from the dry storage room.

Each of these independent clauses can stand on its own and be its own sentence. It's also perfectly acceptable to combine the two clauses in one sentence, but you must do it correctly with a correct joining word or punctuation.

Correct a run-on sentence by inserting an appropriate punctuation mark and/or word between two independent clauses.

Between two independent clauses you may put any of the following:

1) A period.

> George was an honest employee. **He** never stole anything from the dry storage room.

2) A semicolon.

> George was an honest employee; he never stole anything from the dry storage room.

3) A comma + a coordinating conjunction (FANBOYS). **for, and, nor, but, or, yet, so**

> George was an honest employee**, so** he never stole anything from the dry storage room.

4) A subordinating conjunction (dependent word).

DEPENDENT WORDS/SUBORDINATING CONJUNCTIONS

after	although	as	as if
because	before	even if	even though
if	in order to	once	since
that	though	unless	until
whatever	when	whenever	where
wherever	whether	which	while

> George was an honest employee **if** he never stole anything from the dry storage room.

> **Because** George was an honest employee**,** he never stole anything from the dry storage room.

5) A colon (This is less common and only works to set up for an explanation, illustration, affirmation, or elaboration that comes in the second clause.)

> George was an honest employee**:** he never stole anything from the dry storage room.

Exercise 1:

Now, you try! Use those same strategies to correct this run-on sentence:

> Americans love nice things they enjoy eating the finest food and driving the fastest cars.

1) A period.

> Americans love nice things they enjoy eating the finest food and driving the fastest cars.

2) A semicolon.

> Americans love nice things they enjoy eating the finest food and driving the fastest cars.

3) A comma + a coordinating conjunction (FANBOYS). | for, and, nor, but, or, yet, so |

> Americans love nice things they enjoy eating the finest food and driving the fastest cars.

4) A subordinating conjunction (dependent word).

DEPENDENT WORDS/SUBORDINATING CONJUNCTIONS			
after	although	as	as if
because	before	even if	even though
if	in order to	once	since
that	though	unless	until
whatever	when	whenever	where
wherever	whether	which	while

> Americans love nice things they enjoy eating the finest food and driving the fastest cars.

5) A colon (This is less common and only works with certain types of clauses.)

> Americans love nice things they enjoy eating the finest food and driving the fastest cars.

To review, **a run-on sentence is a sentence that contains two or more independent clauses (complete thoughts) run together with no punctuation in between.** We just demonstrated five ways to correct a run-on sentence. Practice them in the exercises below.

Exercise 2:

Correct these run-on sentences using **a period and a capital letter** between the two independent clauses.

1) In *After the Fire*, Shawn's mom is caring she sits by his bedside for fourteen days and nights.

2) My mom supported me when I wanted to play the guitar, take cooking lessons, and act she is the most supportive mom ever.

3) I was also injured my mom showed her love by coming to the hospital and bringing me cards and kissing me on the forehead.

Exercise 3:

Correct these run-on sentences by inserting **a semicolon** between the two independent clauses.

1) My grandma showed her support when I was in high school she used to go to every game, not because she liked football, but to take care of me and make sure I didn't get hurt.

2) She is always there supporting me that is what makes a good mother.

3) My mom is always checking in on me I can count on her to call me at least once a week.

Exercise 4:

Correct these run-on **sentences by inserting a comma + a coordinating conjunction (FANBOYS)** between the two independent clauses.

for, and, nor, but, or, yet, so

1) My mom works two jobs she still makes time to play video games with me every Saturday.

2) My mother was always there when I needed her now I am available when she needs me.

3) All mothers have different qualities being caring is one of the best.

Exercise 5:

Correct these run-on sentences by inserting **a subordinating conjunction** (dependent word) between the two clauses **or** at the very beginning of the sentence and a comma between the two clauses.

DEPENDENT WORDS/SUBORDINATING CONJUNCTIONS			
after	although	as	as if
because	before	even if	even though
if	in order to	once	since
that	though	unless	until
whatever	when	whenever	where
wherever	whether	which	while

1) Daisy shows her dedication to Alvaro she comes to see him every day even though he does not know she is there.

2) My aunt might encounter a lot of <u>precarious</u> situations in her life she is still a generous mom.

3) She is devoted to me I am her only daughter.

Exercise 6:

Correct these run-on sentences by inserting a colon between the two independent clauses.

1) My grandma has been more than a grandma to me she is my mom.

2) Any good mother must have these three characteristics she must be sensitive, resourceful, and reliable.

3) My friend Jamal's mom sacrificed so much for him she worked long hours at a job she hated so he could go to college.

COMMA SPLICES

What does it mean to splice two things together? Think of electrical wires or 8mm film. If you don't know, look up the word "splice" in a dictionary.

Now, based on that definition, what do you think a comma splice is?

The sentences below are comma splices from student essays. What error do these sentences have in common?

1) I started working for Pizza Hut, the management only tested me for drugs once.

2) One of the restaurants where Ehrenreich works is Jerry's, she describes Jerry's as smoke-filled, very dirty, and generally a bad place to work.

3) I can work the hours I want to work, the time or day does not matter.

> Do you see the common error in the sentences? If you said that each sentence contains more than one sentence incorrectly "spliced together" using a comma, you were right!

By now you have probably figured out what a comma splice is:

> A comma splice is a type of run-on sentence in which two independent clauses (complete thoughts) are joined by just a comma.

You can use the same five strategies to correct a comma splice that you can use to correct a standard run-on:

1) A period.

   I started working for Pizza Hut. **T**he management only tested me for drugs once.

2) A <u>semicolon</u>.

   I started working for Pizza Hut; the management only tested me for drugs once.

3) A comma + a coordinating conjunction (FANBOYS). | for, and, nor, but, or, yet, so |

   I started working for Pizza Hut, **and** the management only tested me for drugs once.

4) A subordinating conjunction (dependent word).

DEPENDENT WORDS/SUBORDINATING CONJUNCTIONS

after	although	as	as if
because	before	even if	even though
if	in order to	once	since
that	though	unless	until
whatever	when	whenever	where
wherever	whether	which	while

After I started working for Pizza Hut, the management only tested me for drugs once.

I can work the hours I want to work **since** the time or day does not matter.

5) A colon (This is less common and only works to set up for an explanation, illustration, affirmation, or elaboration that comes in the second clause.).

   I can work the hours I want to work**:** the time or day does not matter.

Exercise 7:

Correct these comma splices adapted from student essays by replacing the comma with a period and capitalizing where necessary between the two independent clauses.

1) Bob parks his car next to the railroad tracks and gets out to take a walk, he sees a run-away train speeding down the tracks heading towards a child off in the distance.

2) Her patients would not get the best care from her, her family and social life would also be damaged.

3) These noble ideals leave no margin of error for life's mishaps, for example, in 2010 my mother took ill and had to be hospitalized.

Exercise 8:

Correct these comma splices adapted from student essays by replacing the comma with a semicolon between the two independent clauses.

1) I have heard of Children International, a nonprofit organization that helps children escape poverty, they give people the chance to sponsor a child for only $25 a month to help provide emergency food as needed, medical and dental care, educational support, clothes, and more.

2) My brother was driving and crashed into three parked cars, the damages were very expensive in total since there were three separate vehicles to cover.

3) The boy was homeless, people should donate money to places like the boy's home country to eliminate these social problems.

Exercise 9:

Correct these comma splices adapted from student essays by adding a coordinating conjunction (FANBOYS) between the two independent clauses.

1) Peter Singer makes a compelling case for wealthy and middle class people to sacrifice their luxuries and save the lives of impoverished children overseas, people still disagree with him.

2) Peter Unger gave his readers an exact number, $200, he reassured the reader that was enough to pay for all the grunt work and still save that child.

3) I depended on small donations of clothes and food from many different families, all the help I received was more than enough to hold me over until my parents could provide for me on their own.

Exercise 10:

Correct these comma splices adapted from student essays by inserting a subordinating conjunction (dependent word) between the two independent clauses **or** at the very beginning of the sentence and keeping a comma between the two independent clauses.

DEPENDENT WORDS/SUBORDINATING CONJUNCTIONS			
after	although	as	as if
because	before	even if	even though
if	in order to	once	since
that	though	unless	until
whatever	when	whenever	where
wherever	whether	which	while

1) My aunt does not take vacations, her patients suffer.

2) People earn their money, they want to buy their dream car, buy a new house, or take a vacation.

3) I was in a car accident, I had medical bills, an insurance deductible, and my car was totaled.

Exercise 11:

Correct these comma splices adapted from student essays by replacing the comma with a colon between the two independent clauses.

1) Many nations donate very little to reduce poverty, Singer states that "the United States government is not going to meet even the very modest United Nations-recommended target of .7 percent."

2) People donating some of their extra money would create a win-win situation, the people who are starving would receive some help, and the person donating the money would spend the rest of his/her extra money on luxuries.

3) A question arises regarding this situation, should Dora feel bad about upgrading her television or is her first responsibility to herself?

SENTENCE FRAGMENTS

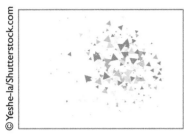

© Yeshe-la/Shutterstock.com

When you think of a fragment, what do you envision? Maybe you think of a fragment of glass or stone or pottery. As you can see in the images, a fragment is a piece of something larger. It is not the complete bottle or stone or pot, only a portion of it. The same goes for a sentence fragment.

Imagine if you gave someone the fragment of glass in the image to the left and expected him to drink from it. Ouch! That would never work because the fragment is not a complete bottle, so it cannot be used like a bottle. The same goes for a sentence fragment. Students include sentence fragments in their writing and expect them to work as complete sentences, but they don't.

> A sentence fragment is a group of words that lacks one or more elements of a complete sentence but tries to pass itself off as one anyway.

Most of the time, you will find that the best way to correct a sentence fragment you've written is to attach it to another sentence to make a complete thought.

DEPENDENT CLAUSE FRAGMENTS

As you learned earlier, a dependent clause cannot stand alone. It must be attached to an independent clause to work. However, one common type of sentence fragment is one where students try to force dependent clauses to stand alone. Below the fragmented dependent clause is in bold. What should we do to correct it?

Incorrect:

I still like to eat at McDonalds and Burger King. **Even though those restaurants sell processed foods.**

It's simple. We can just join the dependent clause with the independent clause:

Correct:

I still like to eat at McDonalds and Burger King even though those restaurants sell processed foods.

ADDED INFORMATION FRAGMENTS

In many cases, a student might write a sentence, end the sentence with a period, and then add more information or an example in the form of a sentence fragment.

Incorrect:

(The added information fragment is in bold below).

Michael Pollan recommends that people eat foods that contain a lot of nutrients. **For instance, vegetables such as lettuce and cabbage and also fruits such as apples, oranges, pears, and strawberries.**

Again, to correct this error, we can combine the complete sentence with the fragment:

Correct Option 1:

Michael Pollan recommends that people eat foods that contain a lot of nutrients, for instance, vegetables such as lettuce and cabbage and also fruits such as apples, oranges, pears, and strawberries.

We can also add to the fragment to turn it into its own complete sentence:

Correct Option 2:

Pollan recommends that people eat foods that contain a lot of nutrients. For instance, vegetables such as lettuce and cabbage and also fruits such as apples, oranges, pears, and strawberries all contain nutrients necessary for good health.

PHRASE FRAGMENTS

A phrase cannot stand alone because it does not contain a subject and a verb. However, students often try to pass phrases off as complete sentences. As a result, they end up with phrase fragments.

Gerund Phrase (-ing Phrase) Fragment

Incorrect:

(The gerund phrase fragment is in bold below.)

Eating healthy is the right thing to do, but every once in a while, it is okay for people to treat themselves to something unhealthy. **Like going to a fast food restaurant and eating processed foods.**

The best way to correct this fragment is by joining it with a complete sentence:

Correct:

Eating healthy is the right thing to do, but every once in a while, it is okay for people to treat themselves to something unhealthy like going to a fast food restaurant and eating processed foods.

Prepositional Phrase Fragment

Though prepositional phrases sometimes get long and may include a noun, a prepositional phrase is still a phrase, not a complete sentence and cannot stand alone.

Incorrect:

After dinner every night. My mom let me eat dessert.

Correct:

After dinner every night, my mom let me eat dessert.

Infinitive Verb Phrase Fragment

While infinitive verbs are verbs, they do not act as the main verbs of their sentences, and their phrases cannot stand alone.

Incorrect:

I eat fresh fruits and vegetables at every meal. **To decrease my chances of getting the Western diseases Pollan mentions in his book.**

Correct:

I eat fresh fruits and vegetables at every meal to decrease my chances of getting the Western diseases Pollan mentions in his book.

Exercise 1:

Correct the fragments in the following sentences.

1) I do not like to cook for myself because I tend to make large portions, and I find it wasteful. Which only convinces me more that I should really take some of the food rules and use them in my daily life.

2) For dinner I heat a frozen dinner or a Hot Pocket in the microwave. Rather than cooking a meal with real food like fruit, veggies, meat, dairy, etc.

3) Unless I stop eating so much of my favorite fast food meals from Taco Bell, Jack in the Box, and Arby's. I am likely to develop heart disease.

4) Michael Pollan recommends that we avoid eating too much processed food. Like the food that is housed in the center aisles of the supermarket.

5) To protect yourself from diabetes and heart disease. You should, as Pollan recommends, "Eat your colors" (57).

Review Exercise:

The student paragraph below contains <u>three sentence fragments</u>, <u>two run-on sentences</u> and <u>two comma splices</u>. Circle each sentence fragment, underline each run-on sentence, and double underline the comma splices. Then, rewrite the paragraph on a separate sheet of paper correcting the sentence fragments, run-on sentences, and comma splices.

In Ishmael Beah's book, *A Long Way Gone*. Ishmael tells his story about his experiences in Sierra Leone's civil war. The book shows how different Ishmael and I are from each other. Ishmael is very patient I am not patient at all. In the book, Ishmael waits with his friends for his family to come from his home village, he says, "We hadn't heard any news about our families and didn't know what else to do except wait and hope they were well" (21). Unlike Ishmael, I am impatient I do not like to wait for anything. Especially my sister. For example, once, my sister was late picking me up to go to my parents' house, I decided to just go by myself. Maybe I could benefit from learning to be more patient. Just like Ishmael.

Note: *Ishmael Beah is referred to by his first name in this student assignment because he is functioning as a literary character in his own memoir. In all other circumstances, you must refer to authors by their last names.*

COMMONLY CONFUSED WORDS

Linking words with associated spellings may help you remember these commonly confused words.

> **Loose** and **Lose** are frequently confused.
>
> A m<u>oose</u>   /   Don't **l<u>ose</u>**
> got **l<u>oose</u>**.   the r<u>ose</u>.
>
> *A moose got loose and is wandering in the road!*
> Notice the "oose" in both "moose" and "loose."
> "Loose" is an adjective used to describe a noun.
> *Don't lose the rose I gave you.*
> Notice the "ose" in both "lose" and "rose."
> "Lose" is a verb used with a subject or an object.

Piece and **Peace** are frequently confused.

Piece / **Pe**ace

of Pi**e**. on **E**arth.

Please give me a piece of pie.

Notice the "ie" in both "piece" and "pie."

Let there be peace on earth.

Notice the "ea" in both "peace" and "earth."

Plain and **Plane** are frequently confused.

Plai**n** / **Pl**ane

H**ai**r **att**endant

I have very plain hair.

Notice the "ai" in both "plain" and "hair."

"Plain" is an adjective that describes a noun.

A flight attendant works on a plane.

Notice the "a_e" in both "attendant" and "plane."

"Plane" is a noun; either the plane that flies in the sky, or a plane in geometry or woodworking.

Then and **Than** are frequently confused.

Th<u>e</u>n / **Th<u>a</u>n**

tim<u>e</u> comp<u>a</u>re

Th<u>e</u>n it will be tim<u>e</u> to go.

Notice the "e" in both "then" and "time."

We use "then" to indicate what we will do next in time.

My d<u>a</u>d is stronger th<u>a</u>n your d<u>a</u>d.

Notice the "a" in both "th<u>a</u>n" and "comp<u>a</u>re."

We use "than" to compare any two things, like two dads.

Weather and **Whether** are frequently confused.

W<u>ea</u>ther / **Wh<u>et</u>her**

is b<u>ea</u>utiful. we g<u>et</u>

w<u>et</u>

The w<u>ea</u>ther is b<u>ea</u>utiful today.

Notice the "ea" in both "w<u>ea</u>ther" and "b<u>ea</u>utiful."

"Weather" is a noun.

Do you know wh<u>et</u>her we will g<u>et</u> w<u>et</u> at Sea World?

Notice the "et" in "wh<u>et</u>her", "g<u>et</u>" and "w<u>et</u>."

"Whether" is a subordinating conjunction (or dependent word).

OTHER COMMONLY CONFUSED WORDS

Below find some other commonly confused words. Add your own into the empty boxes. Then create your own memory charts, like those above, for the words below that you often confuse.

Choose / Chose	Dessert / Desert
Effect / Affect	Passed / Past
Quiet / Quite	Site / Sight / Cite
Their / There / They're	Through / Threw
To / Too / Two	Whose / Who's
Your / You're	Are / Our
Woman / Women	Deaf / Death
Its / It's	

CHAPTER CHAPTER CHAPTER 7

ADVANCED GRAMMAR AND STYLE

MORE RUN-ON AND FRAGMENT SOLUTIONS:

What would you say if we told you that we have a trick that can help you avoid many of your run-ons and sentence fragments? Read on.

You must know whether a clause is independent or dependent before you can fix a fragment or a run on. Many students are able to identify simple run-ons and sentence fragments, but when compound sentences are involved, this can get a little trickier. We would like to provide you with two "cheat sheets" to memorize conjunctive adverbs (transitional expressions) and subordinating conjunctions (dependent words) that are responsible for many of the run-ons and sentence fragments in student writing because they affect whether or not a clause is dependent. Once students understand these, their run-on and sentence fragment woes are often over.

RUN-ON BUSTERS

We recommend keeping the following lists handy when writing so that you can use any of these words properly. See below.

When you use any of the following words, you must remember that they do not make the clause that follows them dependent. They do not affect the clause the way using coordinating conjunctions (FANBOYS) would. These are the words that tend to make run-ons because students **incorrectly** assume they make dependent clauses.

CONJUNCTIVE ADVERBS/TRANSITIONAL EXPRESSIONS

These words do NOT make a clause dependent.

also	in addition	now
as a result	indeed	of course
besides	in fact	on the other hand
consequently	in other words	otherwise
finally	in the first place	similarly
for example	meanwhile	still
furthermore	moreover	then
hence	nevertheless	therefore
however	next	thus

FRAGMENT BUSTERS

On the other side of the spectrum are the following subordinating conjunctions or dependent words (see the chart below). These words are responsible for most of the sentence fragments students write because they do make clauses dependent. Once a clause is dependent, it cannot stand alone. If a student punctuates a clause beginning with the dependent word the same way as an independent clause that begins with a conjunctive adverb (transitional expression), this creates a dependent clause and thus a fragment.

DEPENDENT WORDS/SUBORDINATING CONJUNCTIONS

after	although	as	as if
because	before	even if	even though
if	in order to	once	since
that	though	unless	until
whatever	when	whenever	where
wherever	whether	which	while

COORDINATING CONJUNCTIONS, FANBOYS:

for	and
nor	but
or	yet
so	

There is some debate about starting sentences with coordinating conjunctions (FANBOYS). Advanced writers do this occasionally for style. The official rule has long been not to start sentences with coordinating conjunctions. Use sparingly.

Thus, if a student uses the dependent word "although" the same way as "however," this creates a dependent clause and thus a fragment.

Let's see through examples how the choice of words from these lists can affect grammar.

Let's compare two sentences that mean exactly the same thing. However, one of them is correct and one is a run-on/comma splice:

Correct:

I love cats, but they make me sneeze.

The sentence above is a correct, compound sentence that uses one of the coordinating conjunctions, FANBOYS (for, and, nor, but, or, yet, so), to connect it. No problem.

However, if we replace "but" with "however," even though the meaning remains exactly the same, we have created a run-on/comma splice:

Incorrect:

I love cats, however they make me sneeze.   (Run-on)

We would have to fix the run-on by using a semi-colon or a period instead of a comma. For example,

Correct:

I love cats; however, they make me sneeze.

I love cats. However, they make me sneeze.

Now, what if you decide to substitute the word "although" for "however?" After all, the two sentences mean the same thing. Then what? If you're not careful, you might be setting yourself up for a sentence fragment:

Incorrect:

I love cats; although I am allergic to them. (Sentence Fragment)

I love cats. Although I am allergic to them. (Sentence Fragment)

Correct:

I love cats although they make me sneeze.

Although they make me sneeze, I love cats.

You would have to know that "although" works like "but" and not like "however" because it makes the clause that follows dependent. (Dependent clauses cannot stand alone).

Note: the words on these two lists are terrific words that add variety and a professional tone to your prose, but they can be difficult to punctuate correctly if you don't know how they affect the clauses. Keep the above lists handy and consult them when in doubt.

Exercise 1:

Correct the following run-ons and sentence fragments by referring to the lists above.

1) The stapler was broken furthermore it was rusty and old. Therefore, Lashonda wanted to throw it away.

2) Jennifer turned off the television; although she loved that show.

3) Happy is the man; who never knows hunger.

4) Tim was confused because he loved football, however he also loved baseball and his dad made him choose between the two.

5) Whether to be or not to be. That is the question.

6) Grandma loves shopping at Ralph's, moreover she has a preferred shopper card. Which gives her discounts.

7) My lemon tree kept growing and growing, however I never watered it.

8) Because I love my mother; I bake her famous chocolate chip cookies. Whenever she's on vacation, to remind myself of her.

Exercise 2:

Find the run-ons and fragments in the following paragraph.

While they are the victims of many stereotypes, Nuns are amazing and admirable women. They were the world's first professional women and feminists, as early as the Middle Ages, they found a way to get an education when it was unheard of for women, furthermore, they avoided having to marry the men their parents chose for them. As managers of hospitals, schools, and powerful convents, they were the first female CEOs. Mother Angelica was the first nun to run her own television network EWTN. Despite the stereotype of the ruler-toting disciplinarian, Nuns do excellent work and support communities in crisis while they also stand up and defend those who are too weak to defend themselves. Before I got married to a wonderful man, I considered joining a convent; however, I wanted to have children. Otherwise, I might be wearing a nun's habit and going by the name of "Sister" today. I don't regret my choice, Although I look very good in black and white.

ACTIVE VOICE AND ACTION VERBS

Once your writing is conceptually and grammatically sound, that is, the ideas and writing are solid, you can start thinking about ways to improve your style. One of the most effective ways to attain a more polished style is to limit your use of passive voice and the verb "to be."

PASSIVE VOICE

In any sentence, if the "doer" is not the subject of the sentence, we call that sentence "passive." Passive construction always requires some form of the verb "to be."

> The sandwich was eaten by Alex.

> The race was won by Penelope.

The problem with passive voice is that it takes the action away from the "doer." In the examples above, the race and the sandwich are the subjects of the sentences, but they didn't actually do anything; Penelope and Alex did.

To change the passive voice, we must rewrite the sentence with the doer as subject.

> ~~The race was won by Penelope.~~ (passive) then becomes:

> Penelope won the race. (active and better)

In this version, the emphasis is on Penelope as subject where it belongs. Because it is more dynamic, active voice is preferable. Using active voice also tightens the prose and avoids unnecessary prepositional phrases.

In some select cases, you may choose to use passive voice because you want to emphasize someone's victimhood or that something is being done to someone or something. For instance,

> My grandmother was attacked in broad daylight.

Here the writer may use passive voice to accentuate the fact that the grandmother is a passive victim.

Passive voice is also acceptable when the doer is general or nonspecific (you don't know exactly who is doing the action) and/or when you wish to keep your attention on something or someone other than the doer. For example,

> Random acts of kindness are always appreciated.

Here the writer wishes to focus on the random acts of kindness, not the people who appreciate them.

Exercise 1:

Convert the following sentences from passive voice to active if you think it is necessary. (Hint: You may choose to leave one or two passive).

Example:

> ~~The sandwich was eaten by Alex~~. (passive) becomes:

> Alex ate the sandwich.

1) The car was given a clean bill of health by the mechanic along with a new radiator.
2) The doll was played with by the little girl for hours.
3) Reservations were made by me at noon.
4) Howard Stern is reviled by feminists everywhere.
5) "Hooray!" was shouted by the graduating seniors.
6) The students were allowed to wear jeans for National Denim Day.

ACTION VERBS

Replacing the verb "to be" with dynamic action verbs can take your prose to the next level. Look at the differences in these sentences.

Weak:

> There are a lot of bears in the Pacific Northwest.

Better:

> Bears populate the woods in the Pacific Northwest.

Weak:

> Cigarettes butts are everywhere.

Better:

> Cigarette butts pollute our streets and threaten our wildlife.

Do a "search" in your papers for "is," "are" and other forms of the verb "to be." See how you can replace those tired verbs with fresh and evocative action verbs. You'll see a big difference in your writing.

Exercise 2:

Rewrite the following sentences to eliminate the verb "to be" and make them more dynamic. Feel free to add words and change them in any way you choose, but retain the original meaning.

1) There are many reasons why we should impeach the current fan club president.

2) Greeting cards are in a lot of stores on Mother's Day.

3) It is important to make an effort to be pleasant during an interview.

4) Halle Berry is great because of her acting.

5) Is he going to be accepting the award tonight?

ANALYTICAL ACTION VERBS

The analytical action verb chart below includes many verbs that can be useful when trying to replace "to be" or "there is/are" in your writing. These terms are elegant and when used properly can elevate your paper to the next level. Be sure to know the meanings of the words so that you use them appropriately.

ANALYTICAL ACTION VERBS:

acknowledge	analyze	argue	assert	assess	attribute	believe
calculate	challenge	characterize	clarify	classify	compare	consider
construct	construe	deduce	define	delineate	depict	derive
designate	detail	determine	devise	disagree	distinguish	estimate
evaluate	extrapolate	generalize	guide	hypothesize	imply	indicate
infer	inform	insist	interpret	introduce	investigate	invoke
maintain	measure	narrate	note	predict	organize	point out
postulate	present	propose	prove	provide	reiterate	report
represent	restrict	set forth	simplify	specify	speculate	state
sum up	summarize	support	synthesize			

Exercise 3:

Plug the following words from the list above into the correct sentence below. Look up the meanings of any unfamiliar words.

Words: *characterize, attribute, maintain, determine, extrapolate,* and *acknowledge*

1) It is difficult to _____ whether or not she is guilty, based on the evidence.

2) I _____ his lack of enthusiasm to the fact that he hasn't slept in two nights.

3) The author _____ that there should be a cap on campaign spending because it is unfair.

4) I do _____ the fact that my opponent brings up excellent points; nevertheless, I stand by my position.

5) When the professor heard Adela _____ the new quizzes as "short, sweet, and easy to cheat," he immediately wrote a difficult two-page question.

USING AN ACADEMIC TONE

You have probably noticed that people speak differently in different settings: home vs. school, work vs. football practice, church vs. nightclubs, doctor's office vs. dog park. Most of us adjust our style of communication depending on our audience. The same applies to writing. An email to your boyfriend will probably be very different from an email to your grandma. So of course, college writing requires an appropriate style of communication, sometimes referred to as its "tone". You might use a flirtatious tone when writing to your boyfriend and an appreciative tone to your grandma if you're thanking her for a gift. You might use a sarcastic tone when writing to your best friend, but you will surely use a professional tone in an e-mail to your boss or professor.

Generally, the purpose of college writing is for you to contribute to an academic "conversation" on a certain topic. You are engaging with other scholars on the topic, including your professor. Thus, all of your college writing assignments should be written with an appropriately academic or scholarly tone.

When you write to your friends and family members, you usually address them informally. However, when you write for college, you address your fellow scholars in a formal way. Think of it as the difference between sweats and a business suit or a handshake and a fist bump. Your professors expect a formal academic tone in any college writing assignment.

INFORMAL LANGUAGE

Proper Usage of the First Person

Writing in the first or second person is not appropriate for academic writing. The first person plural pronoun "we" can be unclear and should also be avoided. Writing essays in the third person ("he/she," "they," "researchers," "students") is an academic convention that may be unfamiliar at first, but ultimately empowers one's writing.

You don't need to say "I think" to voice an opinion. Your name is on the essay, after all. "Smoking is dangerous" sounds more formal and persuasive than saying, "I think smoking is dangerous." Persuade your readers by using solid writing, support from evidence, and formal tone.

Here are some terms to avoid that connote a tone too informal for academic writing:

Slang	crappy, swag, drama (as in "I stopped talking to her because she had too much drama."), issues (as in "He's got issues."), sucks, pissed, back in the day, down with, homie, man up, my bad, got my back
Contractions	aren't, can't, don't, haven't, I'm, I'll, won't, wouldn't, wasn't, could've, shouldn't, should've

Text speak	gonna, u, i, LOL, imma, kinda, WTF?, b4
Abbreviations	appt., apt., asap, Jan., ft, min, sec
Exaggerated Terms	awesome, love, impossible, fabulous, incredible, unbelievable, really
Informal Terms	dude, stuff, you/your/yours/yourself, okay, creepy, weird, thing, great, yeah
Profanity	****, ****, ****, ****
Exclamations	What?!, Oh no!, Hey! Uh oh!

More Tips for Maintaining an Academic Tone

- Use declarative statements to make your points. Avoid asking questions in the body of your essays.
- Use concise language. Avoid using more words than necessary to make a point.
- Use fresh, direct language. Avoid clichés and other overused expressions.

Wordy Phrases	Clichés	Overused Expressions
due to the fact that	last but not least	nowadays
being that	easier said than done	needless to say
which is/are	on the same page	in today's society
who is/are	time and time again	all in all
there is/are	above and beyond	

Show yourself to be a scholar by demonstrating a scholarly tone in all of your college writing.

CHAPTER CHAPTER CHAPTER 8

FOR ENGLISH LANGUAGE LEARNERS

ARTICLES ("A," "AN," "THE")

Hands down, the proper use of articles is one of the most challenging issues for English language learners. Who knew these little words could be so difficult? Native speakers use articles without thinking about them and they themselves may have a very hard time explaining to you why they use "a" or "the" and why they don't. They just "know" it's right or wrong. This can be maddening for non-native speakers, particularly those who come from languages in which articles don't exist. Be patient with yourself. You will get used to the sound of articles through hearing and practicing English. In

the meantime, what follows are a few guidelines to help you use articles properly.

Nouns that are not specific and can be counted use the indefinite articles "a" or "an."

Note: Use "an" in front of a noun that begins with a vowel: a, e, i, o, u.

> I want **an** ice cream cone! I want **a** football.

The speaker is being nonspecific; she could mean *any* ice cream cone or any football from any shop. Because she is speaking in general terms, she uses an indefinite pronoun.

However, **use the definite article "the" when you are being specific.**

> I want the ice cream cone on the poster. I want the ice cream cone over there! I want the most delicious ice cream cone in the world.

The speaker says exactly which one she wants.

Use "the" when you use a superlative: "the most delicious," **"the fastest** car," **"the best** seats."

In addition to being specific, **use "the" when you want to discuss a broad category.**

> Braille is an invention that helps the blind.

> Here "the blind" refers to a category of people.

Some nouns are used in a general sense and you cannot count them. We call these **non-count nouns. Omit "a" and "an" with noncount nouns:**

> Please pour me some wine. (Not *a* wine).

> I pray for world peace. (Not *a* world peace).

You can, however, use "the" in front of these noncount nouns when you are referring to a specific example because "the" is used for specific nouns.

> Please pass the sugar.

> The beer is in the fridge.   BUT:

> Too much sugar is bad for you. (Nonspecific use does not use any article.)

EXAMPLES OF NONCOUNT NOUNS

MATERIALS:	FOODS:	ACTIVITIES & STUDY AREAS:	OTHER:
wood	water	reading	luggage
cloth	milk	boating	technology
ice	wine	smoking	equipment
plastic	beer	dancing	furniture
wool	cake	hockey	experience
steel	sugar	weather	applause
metal	rice	heat	news

glass	meat	sunshine	photography
leather	cheese	electricity	traffic
hair	flour	electricity	harm
dust	salt	biology	media
air		history	homework
oxygen		mathematics	advice
		economics	
		poetry	

Exercise 1:

Choose the best article, "a," "an," or "the," or omit the article if it is not needed.

1) _____ only hat I want is that one.

2) _____ cats see well in the dark.

3) Bring _____ coffee to the table.

4) Please go take _____ bath.

5) _____ happy boy is a delight to see.

6) _____ happy boy who lives next door is a delight to see.

7) Hauling _____ firewood always hurts my back.

8) Have you heard _____ news? Justina is pregnant!

9) Don't forget to take _____ umbrella on your trip.

10) That is _____ great book!

▌VERB TENSES

The nuances of verb tenses can be tricky for nonnative speakers. Use this chart to review the tenses and the formulas for recreating them on your own. Descriptions of the tenses follow the chart below. These are not all the verb tenses, but rather the fundamental ones.

Tense	Verb	Tense	Verb
Present	base form	Present Progressive	Am, is, are + present participle (-ing)
	I **laugh** every time I see that movie.		He **is laughing** now.
Past	base + ed (or irregular)	Future Progressive	Will be + present participle (-ing)
	I **laughed** yesterday.		He **will be laughing** until the sad part comes on screen.
Future	will + base	Past Progressive	Was, were + present participle (-ing)
	If he drops that tray, I **will laugh**.		They **were laughing** when they passed the note.
Present Perfect	Has, have + past participle	Present Perfect Progressive	Has, have been + present participle (-ing)
	They **have laughed** often throughout their marriage.		We **have been laughing** for fifteen minutes. My sides hurt!
Past Perfect	Had + past participle	Past Perfect Progressive	Had been + present participle (-ing)
	By the time the baby was a year old, she **had laughed** only once.		When I entered the room, I could see that the children **had been laughing**.
Future Perfect	Will have + (past participle)	Future Perfect Progressive	Will have been + present participle (-ing)
	By the time he's eighteen, Hakim **will have laughed** thousands of times.		When the clock strikes ten, we **will have been laughing** for thirty minutes straight!

- Present tense is for general situations that occur repeatedly.

  I laugh *every time* I see that movie.

- Past tense is for an isolated incident that happened at a specific time.

  I laughed yesterday when John slipped on a banana peel.

- Past tense can also indicate an action performed repeatedly that no longer happens.

  I laughed a lot as a baby.

- We use future tense to show what will happen in the future.

  If he drops that tray, I will laugh.

- Present perfect indicates actions that started in the past and continue to happen in the present.

  They have laughed often throughout their marriage.

- Past perfect shows an event that happens in the past before another time in the past.

  <u>By the time the baby was a year old</u>, she had only laughed once.

The baby turning a year old is the first event in the past. The event that occurred before that time was that she laughed once.

- Future perfect indicates that something will be done by a certain time.

  By the time he's eighteen, Hakim will have laughed thousands of times.

- Present progressive indicates something that's happening right now and that will eventually stop.

  He is laughing now, but tomorrow when his homework is due, it will be a different story.

- Past progressive tense shows an action that was ongoing, but got interrupted or ended.

  They were laughing when they passed the note.

- Future progressive tense shows that a continuing action will happen in the future.

  When he watches the movie tonight, he will be laughing until the sad part comes on screen.

- Present perfect progressive is used to show actions that started in the past, but continue on into the present.

    We have been laughing for fifteen minutes. My sides hurt!

- Past perfect progressive is a tense that shows past ongoing actions that ended before another past event.

    When I entered the room, I could see that the children had been laughing.

- Future perfect progressive tense indicates an action that will still be happening when another certain future event occurs.

    When the clock strikes ten, we will have been laughing for thirty minutes straight!

Exercise 2:

On a separate sheet of paper, put the verbs "to wait" and "to think" in all twelve tenses. Write meaningful sentences that indicate proper usage.

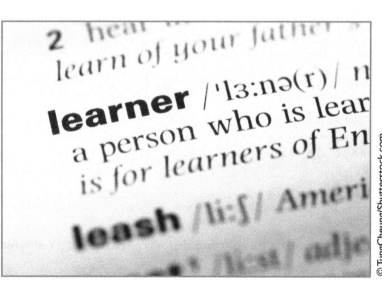

© TungCheung/Shutterstock.com

MODALS

Modal verbs are helping verbs that imply certain conditions about a situation; sometimes they suggest possibilities or imperatives, expectations, or speculation. We have tried to demystify them for you below.

should, must, can, will, would, could, may, might, ought to, shall

Remember:

Modal verbs never change.

Only one modal verb is used in the verb phrase.

Modal verbs are followed by the base form of the verb.

Modal Verbs: Eight Common Usages

Demand, Certainty, or Necessity: You **must** wear shoes inside the restaurant. The inside of an active volcano **must** be hot.

Assumption: You **must** be tired after your long flight.

Ability: My son **can** dunk the basketball on a ten-foot hoop. He **could** dribble when he was three.

Possibility: My daughter **might** be a chef when she grows up. She **may** like it.

Permission: You **may** leave when you have finished your exam.

Recommendation: You **should** finish your homework right away.

Expectation: You **should** do well on your test since you studied so hard.

Conditional: If they had studied, they **would** have gotten a better grade.

Exercise 3:

Complete the following blanks with an appropriate modal verb.

1) I heard a loud crack. Something _____ have broken.

2) You _____ wash your hands before you eat.

3) I'm sure James _____ like Paris since he loves visiting museums.

4) Max _____ never eat a tomato unless it was cooked.

5) The car _____ be full of sand since the kids took it to the beach.

6) You _____ be dreaming! That never happened.

7) Fatima _____ enjoy herself on her vacation. She's waited a long time.

8) Shelly and I _____ be the same astrological sign; we both like to argue.

9) The teacher said the students _____ not turn in their assignments late.

10) _____ we be excused?

SUBJECT/VERB AGREEMENT

Subjects and verbs must "agree" in number. A plural subject must take a plural verb and a singular subject must take a singular verb. This becomes important in the present tense.

> ### DON'T BE CONFUSED
>
> In the present tense,
>
> We **add an "s"** to nouns to make them plural;
> however we **take the "s" away** to make the *verb* plural.
>
> Girls dance. One girl dances.
>
> Plural: Noun + s; verb − s
>
> Singular: Noun −s; verb +s

Please see "Subject/Verb Agreement" in Chapter 5 for further exercises and explanation.

Exercise 4:

Make the following subject/verbs agree by circling the correct verb choice.

1) Couples often take/takes dancing lessons before their wedding day.

2) Francisco wash/washes his car every day.

3) *The Hours* is/are a great book.

4) Children ask/asks for candy all the time.

5) The kids has/have been asking to go outside.

6) Katrina and I enjoy/enjoys shopping for the baby.

7) Daisy and Omar go/goes to the store every day.

8) The women is/are going into town with their mothers.

GERUNDS AND INFINITIVES

Because the use of gerunds and infinitives is very different in other languages, English language learners are often confused about them. Let's define them and then establish some tips on how best to decide which one to use.

A gerund is the –ing form of a verb, such as laughing, playing, yawning, eating. When it is in this form, it is no longer a verb. Rather, it is acting as a noun.

> **Yawning** is rude. It is impolite.

Notice that "yawning" can be replaced by the pronoun "it." This is a sure sign that it is a gerund (noun form of the verb). It also happens to be the subject of the sentence.

Most importantly, **the gerund form is the form most commonly used for the subject of a sentence in English**. There are notable exceptions in famous quotes: "To err is human, to forgive, divine" but this is an exception. We tend not to talk like that anymore. More commonly you will hear "Studying is smart" or "Stealing is wrong." Notice that many Romance languages use the infinitive as the subject. This causes further confusion. Remind yourself that English favors the gerund as subject.

An infinitive is the "to-" form of the verb. The infinitive of "yawn" or "yawning" would be "to yawn."

The infinitive always means "to do something": to yawn, to play, to laugh, etc.

> It is impolite to yawn.

> It is impolite "to do something," in this case to yawn.

VERBS OFTEN FOLLOWED BY GERUNDS

appreciate	avoid	deny	enjoy	finish
miss	postpone	practice	quit	recall
resist	stand	suggest	tolerate	

Finish eating your dinner before you go out to play.

I can't stand going to the dentist.

VERBS OFTEN FOLLOWED BY INFINITIVES

agree	ask	claim	decide	expect
have	hope	manage	offer	plan
pretend	promise	refuse	wait	want
wish				

She claims to like him, but she won't answer his calls.

I hope to transfer to U.C., Berkeley in the spring.

VERBS THAT CAN BE FOLLOWED BY EITHER AN INFINITIVE OR A GERUND

begin	continue	hate	like	love	start

I love shopping for new school supplies!

I love to shop for school supplies.

(Both of these options are correct).

Exercise 5:

Fill in the blank with the appropriate form of the verb in parentheses, using the gerund or infinitive forms.

1) The plant will continue _____ (grow) if you water it.

2) Vegetarians refuse _____ (eat) meat.

3) I would avoid _____ (sleep) too late. You might miss the exam!

4) Start _____ (save) for your school books during the summer.

5) I expect _____ (have) the project completed by next Tuesday.

6) I decided _____ (go) on the trip even though I'm broke.

7) They suggest _____ (buy) food from local farmers in the community.

8) She would appreciate _____ (hear) your apology in person.

9) We love opera so we asked _____ (go) on the next filed trip to the Met.

10) You hate _____ (sunbathe). That's why we didn't invite you.

IDIOMS

Idioms also present challenges for anyone learning a new language. They are non-literal expressions. Often they rely on metaphors. Getting them wrong can make all the difference in making yourself understood. For example, to "back down" means something very different from to "back out."

It is impossible to memorize all idioms, but try to familiarize yourself with the meanings of idioms you come into contact with in conversation or in reading. Ask native speakers what the expressions mean and check out some of the idiom dictionaries available online and in print. Watching television and movies can also help you learn expressions you might not have learned in a formal English language class.

Take a look at some of the following and ask your instructor or a native speaker what they mean. Then try using them in a sentence.

Common Idioms Exercise:

Write a sentence using the following idioms correctly in a sentence.

1) chicken feed

2) call it a day

3) get carried away

4) catch on

5) a bit

6) about time

7) after my own heart

8) bear in mind

9) beef up

10) below the belt

Exercise 6:

Look up idioms on the internet and add five more to the above list.

PREPOSITIONS OF TIME AND PLACE ("AT," "ON," "IN")

"At," "on," and "in" seem to give English language learners a lot of difficulty and it's not your fault! There isn't a lot of logic here. You might just have to memorize that:

> You go to the movies **at** 7:00 **in** the evening **on** Third Street Promenade **at** the new movie theater **in** Santa Monica.

Refer to the example above for the following rules:

> For **specific time** we write "at" ("at 7:00").
>
> For **general time** of day we write "in" ("in the evening").
>
> For **specific streets or roads** we write "on" ("on Third Street").
>
> For **general places** we write "at" ("At the movie theater," "at the state fair").
>
> For **cities, states and countries**, we write "in" ("in Santa Monica").

Exercise 7:

Choose whether to use "at," "in," or "on" in the following examples.

1) I go to bed _____ midnight every night.

2) _____ the morning, I brush my teeth and wash my face.

3) Sprinkles Cupcake boutique is _____ Santa Monica Boulevard.

4) _____ Monday, we have Chemistry class.

5) You can see movie stars _____ Beverly Hills.

6) English class starts promptly _____ 11:10.

7) Under certain circumstances, marijuana is legal _____ California.

8) They have five new stores _____ the mall.

9) The English drink tea _____ the afternoon.

10) They sell oranges _____ the grocery store.

Finally, nothing improves your English more quickly than getting out and socializing with English speakers. Practice makes perfect. Watch television and movies and read everything you can, including advertisements on buses and benches! Immerse yourself in English, and your reading and writing will improve dramatically.

Please see Chapter 8 for helpful advice on pronouncing and reading unfamiliar words and improving reading fluency.

III

APPLY THE WRITING PROCESS

CHAPTERS

CHAPTER 9

PREWRITING

Good writing requires a process. You must take a number of steps to produce a document that will make you proud. We suggest a set of steps below that will guide you through this process and help you produce an outstanding document.

The first step in The Writing Process comes before you do any writing at all. It is called "Prewriting" because it comes *before* the actual writing. Prewriting helps you formulate ideas on your topic so you can avoid just sitting and staring at a blank page or computer screen.

A number of prewriting strategies are typically covered in English composition texts. You may be familiar with some of them: Brainstorming/Listing, Clustering/Mapping/Webbing, Freewriting, and Questioning are some popular strategies. We will get to those superstars of prewriting, but we will start with a few strategies less frequently recommended.

1. READING

You might be thinking, "Hey—I thought this chapter was about writing!" And it is; however, reading and writing go hand in hand, and we guarantee that with some targeted reading before you start on your writing assignment, you will get better results.

a. Read the assignment sheet carefully, highlight key information, and ask questions about anything that is not clear.

b. Reread the essay, article, chapter, book, and/or notes on which your writing assignment is based. If you don't go back and reread the entire book, at least read over your notes or skim through your highlighted passages to remind yourself of the text. Jotting down ideas as you reread can be very productive as a way of getting your thoughts flowing.

c. Notice patterns. If you underline texts, as you go back to your marked book and reread the passages you found important, flag any that seem to circle around your theme or topic. Often a pattern will establish itself and your evidence will become clear as the passages you have continually chosen speak to you. Once you have some compelling quotations, even if you're not yet sure how the puzzle pieces will fit together, try looking for ways to connect the evidence and order it in importance to your topic.

d. If your assignment is a research assignment, read your sources. There is nothing worse than starting a research essay only to find that your sources do not really work to support your points.

2. THINKING

This is one of our favorite prewriting strategies, which is often overlooked. Thinking about your essay topics away from the classroom or computer can sometimes produce your best ideas. For example, let's say you are asked to write an essay about whether the United States has been more a force for good or ill in the world. Your instructor gives you the assignment but gives you a day to just think about it before you do any writing. Consider how you might use this opportunity to think:

a. Watch or listen to the news listening for stories that might give you some insights in response to the essay prompt.

b. Think about the harmful things you know the US has engaged in.

c. Think about the valuable things you know the US has engaged in.

Notice you have not written a single word, but you have already begun the writing process.

3. TALKING

This strategy may be the most fun way to fit in some prewriting. Consider the scenario above again. Your own thoughts about the subject provides a great place to start. However, bringing your brother, cousin, roommate, grandma, boyfriend, wife, friend, teammate, or coworker into the conversation will expand your capacity for ideas. Most people love to be asked their opinions, and substantive conversation is good for any relationship. Take advantage of the people around you, and let them help you discover some new viewpoints. Here are some ways to start the conversation:

a. I'm writing an essay for my English class about whether the US has been a good or more harmful force in the world. What do you think?

b. What harmful things do you know about that the US has done in the world?

c. What helpful things do you know about that the US has done in the world?

4. BRAINSTORMING/MAKING A LIST OR T-CHART

This strategy works well in conjunction with the last two strategies, "Thinking" and "Talking" about your topic. In order to keep track of the brilliant ideas you develop from your thinking and from talking to your friends and family, you can make a list. If you don't have a piece of paper with you when you're thinking or talking, be creative. Use a napkin or a flyer or even a notes app on your phone. Just make sure you don't lose any ideas you might use in your essay. Here is an example of a list for the prompt, "Has the US been more a force for good than for ill in the world?"

US More a Force for Good	US More a Force for Ill
• US was the world's first democracy • US intervened in World War II and saved millions of lives • US contributes to pop culture, especially the motion picture industry • US contributes technology and innovation • US contributes humanitarian aid	• US perpetuated cruel and awful slave trade for centuries • US maintained slavery for centuries • US further destabilized the middle east with the Iraq war • Relationships with many nations were ruined as a result of US activity in the Cold War • Fear of communism led the US to fund guerrilla groups and militias around the world

5. CLUSTERING/MAPPING/WEBBING

Whatever you choose to call it, this style of prewriting gives you a visual connection between concepts and helps to express relationships between your ideas. To get started, draw a circle or a box in the middle of a page and write your basic topic inside of it. Then draw lines to connect that topic to related ideas that could be used to build your essay. This process might help you come up with new ideas for your writing assignment. It also may help you figure out how to organize the main points of your paper. Here is an example using our "Is the US a force for good or ill?" prompt.

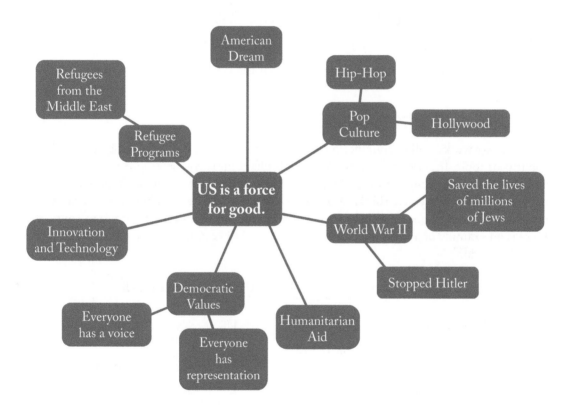

6. FREEWRITING

The purpose of freewriting is to simply get your ideas down on paper. It is a great technique if you are prone to getting stuck. In freewriting you don't worry about correct grammar, spelling, punctuation, or sentence structure; you just write down ideas about your topic as they pop into your head. The trick to freewriting is to set a timer, and then not stop writing until it rings. We recommend that you start with ten minutes. If you get stuck, keep writing. Try asking yourself questions about the topic and then answering them. Make a list of words that you associate with the topic. Try writing anything even if it's just something like this: "I don't know what to write about this topic." Just don't stop writing! See a sample of prewriting on the topic of overcoming an obstacle below.

Overcoming an obstacle.

Let's see when have I overcome an obstacle? I am here in college that took something to get here. I didn't like high school and I had to work n high school to help my mom pay the rent. She needed my help. I guess having to work would be an obstacle. I have been out of school for five years working and now I am trying to come back, but everyone is 18 and I feel kind of old. I am still working and its hard to do good in school having to work all the time. But im here. I could have not come back. Hmmmm what should I write now? Other obstacles. . . . Another thing that could have got in my way was when I got sick when I was in middle school. I was running track and one day I woke up and my stomach hurt. I thought it was food poisoning. I kept throwing up for a whole day. Then the next day I was still throwing up. And it wouldn't go away I went to the doctor. I was so sick I could not run and I missed a track meet. My coach was mad but I was too sick. When I want to the doctor, the doctor did tests but didn't find what was wrong. I was still feeling sick and could not run. But I was determined to run track so I went back to the doctor. The doctor finally tried another test it turned out I had Crohn's disease. Once I found that out I wanted to know what medicine I could take or what else I could do. The doctor gave me a prescription for medicine and told me to pay attention to what I ate. He said not to eat stuff that made me feel worse. I really wanted to run track again. He said I could but I had to start slow. I took the medicine and started to feel better. I went back to practice. My coach was glad to see me but it took a while for me to build my strength back to where it was. Plus I had to take my prescription really regularly or I would feel bad again. But then by the end of the year I had won 2 races. That's overcoming an obstacle!!

7. QUESTIONING

In questioning, you ask yourself questions about your topic and **answer those questions** to generate ideas about your topic. You might ask the familiar "Who? What? When? Where? Why?" questions to facilitate this process. Here is an example of a list of questions for the prompt, "Has the US been more a force for good or for ill in the world?"

Who is affected by American culture, government, laws, etc.?

> Americans, US immigrants, citizens of occupied nations, people worldwide (because of globalization)

What has the US done to affect people around the world?

> The US military has invaded and occupied other nations; American pop icons have performed around the world; The US has accepted immigrants from around the world; US policy has supported violent actions in many countries; US policy supports Israeli occupation of Palestine

When have Americans' actions served as good examples for others?

> When the US military intervened in World War II and liberated the concentration camps; When African-Americans stood up for their rights during the Civil Rights Movement; When Americans protested against the Vietnam War

Where has US policy had a major impact?

> In the Middle East as a result of US intervention, invasion, and occupation; in Central America where the US supported Guerrilla fighters; in Libya where the US military toppled the regime of Muammar Gaddafi.

Why do some people criticize the United States?

> The US sees itself as the "world police"; the US has hypocritical policies; American capitalism has a negative impact on outside cultures; Americans elected Donald Trump for president

8. OUTLINING

Writing an outline is a great way to organize your essay before you actually start writing your draft. You can gather the information you have generated in your prewriting and start to organize it into an outline. Read through your initial prewriting carefully and highlight or circle your most useful ideas. Some of you may have learned formal outlining with many layers and levels, but we find that informal outlines are perfectly adequate. Here's an example:

> **Introduction** (Introduce the text and use one of the strategies from our "Introductions" chapter.)

Thesis: Although the US has many flaws, the US is more a force for good than for ill in the world because the US sets an example of democratic values, everyone living in the United States has access to affordable education, and the US accepts thousands of refugees annually from around the world.

Topic Sentence 1: The US does have many flaws.

> Ex 1: Negative impact of American pop culture

> Ex 2: Election of Donald Trump

Topic Sentence 2: Fortunately, despite its flaws, the US provides the world with an example of democratic values.

> Ex 1: Equal representation in government

> Ex 2: Equal voice through voting

Topic Sentence 3: The US also offers access to affordable education.

> Ex 1: Public K-12 education for all

> Ex 2: Affordable higher education through community colleges

Topic Sentence 4: Finally, the US accepts thousands of refugees annually.

> Ex 1: Offer data about US refugee program

> Ex 2: Offer specific examples of refugees living in the US

Conclusion: I feel very fortunate to have grown up in the United States.

CHAPTER CHAPTER CHAPTER

10

DRAFTING THE ESSAY: ESSENTIAL ELEMENTS

▍THE THESIS STATEMENT

You've probably heard the term "thesis statement" in previous English classes. But maybe you still haven't fully grasped what the term means. You've heard that a thesis statement represents an essay's "main point," right? But what does that *mean*? Our goal here is to clear that up for good!

First, a thesis statement is the main point of your essay. This means that your thesis statement will state the opinion that you want to prove about your essay's topic. We know that some students have the misconception that they should avoid expressing their opinions in their college essays. That may come from the fact that teachers discourage you from using the words "I think" or "in my opinion" in your essay. However, you MUST express your opinion in almost any well-written essay. Plus, you can easily express that opinion without using the words "I think" or "in my opinion." Let us show you how.

Consider this. Let's say your instructor presents you with the following essay assignment:

Sample Essay Assignment

You have read the prologue of President Barack Obama's book, *The Audacity of Hope: Thoughts on Reclaiming the American Dream* in which he says, "America has more often been a force for good than for ill in the world" (11). In this essay you will **support** or **refute** President Obama's point.

In response to this assignment, your essay would express your opinion by making a point about America, just as President Obama has done.

You might say something like this:

Strong Sample Thesis Statement:

President Obama is mistaken in his statement that "America has more often been a force for good than for ill in the world" (11). In fact, the United States has been a destructive force in the world since its founding in 1776.

Notice that this writer did not say "I think" or "in my opinion" anywhere in his thesis. That would be unnecessary, yet the writer has expressed a clear opinion.

Even in a discipline like history, scholars do not just sit around and type lists of facts all day. They draw conclusions about history and express their opinions. For example, a presidential historian might study and write about the similarities between Barack Obama and Abraham Lincoln, and the thesis would be based on the historian's opinion. It might look something like this:

Strong Sample Thesis Statement

While many have emphasized similarities between Obama and Lincoln, the two men, in fact, maintain striking philosophical differences.

Is that statement a fact? No. That statement is the historian's opinion. Notice that the historian did not say "I think Lincoln and Obama are different." Instead, he just made his point without those unnecessary words.

CHARACTERISTICS OF AN EFFECTIVE THESIS STATEMENT

1. A strong thesis names the topic and makes a debatable point about that topic.

2. A good thesis never simply states an indisputable fact.

3. A strong thesis does not mention you or your essay.

4. An effective thesis responds directly to the essay prompt.

1) **A strong thesis names the topic and makes a point about that topic.** It is not just an idea. For example, we have ideas all the time. You might say this to yourself: "I have an idea! I'll keep a calendar this year to help me manage my time." Could that idea be a thesis statement? Does it make a point? No. However, you could transform your idea into this:

> In order to be successful, college students should keep calendars to keep track of their college, family, and work responsibilities.

Now you're making a point. So what's the difference between an idea and a point? This is something that may not be clear to some students. Here's the key: **a point is always debatable**. It's something you or someone else can agree or disagree with.

Here's another example. After reading an article about Black History Month, you might have an idea. You might decide to read works of classic African-American literature every February. What a great idea! Is that a thesis statement? No. There is no debatable opinion presented. Now consider this as a possible thesis statement:

> All Americans should take responsibility to commemorate African-American History Month every year by doing something to honor African-American history at home and in their communities.

Could someone disagree with that? Of course! It makes a point.

Let's return to President Obama's point about America. Here is the prompt again:

Sample Essay Assignment:

You have read the prologue of President Barack Obama's book, *The Audacity of Hope: Thoughts on Reclaiming the American Dream*. In that prologue, he says, "America has more often been a force for good than for ill in the world" (11). In this essay you **support** or **refute** President Obama's point.

Some students might want to say something like this for a thesis statement:

> I agree with President Obama's point that "America has more often been a force for good than for ill in the world" (11).

Based on what you've just read, what is the flaw in this thesis?

Here's a hint: **A point is always debatable.**

The flaw is that the thesis is not debatable. Nobody can dispute that you *agree* with Obama because that is not your **point**. Your **point** is that he's right, that the United States *has* been a more positive than negative force in the world (11). So instead of saying that you "agree," make your point that he's right or correct or that his statement is accurate. That way, someone can agree or disagree with you.

2) Not only is a thesis statement not simply an idea, **a good thesis never simply states an indisputable fact**. For your history class, you may be asked to write an essay comparing World War I and World War II. After you read about the two wars, you might decide on this thesis:

World War I started about thirty years before World War II.

The problem is that this is **not a thesis statement** at all. It states an indisputable fact and does not make a point. You might convert it to this actual thesis statement:

Because of the three decades between the two wars, advanced technology and progressing attitudes led to vast differences in soldiers' experiences in the two World Wars.

This statement is debatable and makes a point. Another scholar might argue that soldiers in the two wars had very similar experiences, or that the change in technology didn't really make much difference, or that some other factor or factors let to soldiers' different experiences in the two World Wars.

In another example, you may be asked to write an essay in response to Zora Neale Hurston's short story "The Gilded Six Bits" about Joe and Missy Mae's relationship. You think about it, and you come up with this thesis statement:

In "The Gilded Six Bits" Joe and Missy-Mae, a young, married African-American couple, live in small-town Florida.

Again, this is **not actually a thesis statement** at all. It states an indisputable fact and does not make a point. You might convert it to something like this:

Despite the couple's isolation from material wealth and cultural diversity in their small Florida town, Missy Mae and Joe's relationship teaches a valuable lesson about love and forgiveness.

Now that's a debatable thesis statement.

3) **A strong thesis does not mention you or your essay.** An effective thesis does not make an announcement. Especially for your English classes, avoid saying something like one of these:

~~This essay will explain how~~ America has done more harm than good in the world.

~~In this essay I will prove that~~ Missy Mae and Joe's relationship teaches a valuable lesson about love and forgiveness.

4) **The thesis statement should respond directly to the essay prompt.** Here is a sample essay prompt that ends with a question.

Sample Essay Assignment:

You have read the *Facts on File* article "Black History Month." For this assignment, you will type an essay that summarizes and responds to that article. Your essay will respond to this question:

Should people in the United States continue to observe African-American History Month?

You might start with a thesis statement that looks like this.

Weak Thesis Statement:

African-American History Month is important because it honors important figures in American history who are often ignored, it gives African-American people a sense of pride about their ancestors, and it exposes people to aspects of American history that may be unfamiliar to them.

That thesis makes a point, is debatable and does not announce the topic. But is it an acceptable thesis? No. It does not answer the question. The question does not ask whether or not African-American History Month is important. This shows how critical it is for you to **read the essay prompt or question carefully**. That is the only way you can be sure you are answering it directly. Here is the question again:

Should people in the United States continue to observe African-American History Month?

For this thesis statement to work with the prompt, it has to be revised to say something like this:

Revised Thesis Statement:

People in the United States should continue to observe African-American History Month because it honors important figures in American history that are often ignored, it gives African-Americans a sense of pride about their ancestors, and it exposes people to aspects of American history that may be unfamiliar to them.

Now that thesis statement answers the question! Your essay's thesis statement is the foundation of an outstanding essay. Once you master writing effective thesis statements, you will be on your way to being an expert college writer.

Exercise:

Rewrite and strengthen the following weak thesis statements in response to this essay question: **Should wealthy and middle class people donate the money they normally spend on luxuries to save the lives of needy children?** Then explain what you changed and why.

1) I agree with Peter Singer's point that wealthy and middle class people should donate the money they normally spend on luxuries to save the lives of poor children.

   Revised thesis:

   Explanation:

2) People can spend money on whatever they want, so if they want to buy luxuries, they can buy them.

   Revised thesis:

   Explanation:

3) There are many poor people around the world suffering and dying from diseases; a number of wealthy and middle class people donate money regularly to help.

   Revised thesis:

   Explanation:

4) My essay will explain why wealthy and middle class people should donate the money they usually spend on luxuries to save lives.

   Revised thesis:

   Explanation:

5) According to Peter Singer, wealthy and middle class people should donate any money they usually spend on luxuries to save lives.

   Revised thesis:

   Explanation:

TOPIC SENTENCES

A topic sentence is similar to a thesis statement. However, instead of stating the main point of an entire essay like a thesis statement, a topic sentence states the main point of one paragraph and connects that paragraph back to the thesis statement.

Remember the essay we discussed in the "Thesis Statement" section about observing Black History Month? Here's that thesis statement again:

> **People in the United States should continue to observe African-American History Month.**

Notice that the thesis statement states the writer's opinion (without saying "I think" or "in my opinion").

Then, the writer can list *supporting points*, or reasons, the writer is arguing for the continued observance of Black History Month:

> **People in the United States should continue to observe African-American History Month** because it honors important figures in American history who are often ignored, it gives African-Americans a sense of pride about their ancestors, and it exposes all people to aspects of American history that may be unfamiliar to them.

The writer has set up his thesis so that he can write one paragraph explaining each supporting point. Let's look at each one.

Here is the writer's first supporting point as it is stated in the thesis:

> **it honors important figures in American history who are often ignored**

The essay's first body paragraph will explain this point and support it with evidence and examples. This paragraph will begin with a topic sentence restating that point. Let's consider the three components of a good topic sentence before we begin writing one.

1) An effective topic sentence **transitions from one point to another.**

Here are some transitional words and phrases useful in transitioning between major points in your essay (See "Transitions" in the next section for a comprehensive list):

Transitions to Introduce Your Essay's First Point:

| First, | First of all, | One |

Transitions to Introduce Your Essay's Additional Points:

Additionally,	Secondly,	Also,
Furthermore,	Next,	In addition,
Moreover,	Another	

Transitions to Introduce Your Essay's Last Point:

| Finally, | Lastly, |

Many topic sentences will begin with one of these transitional words or phrases.

2) An effective topic sentence often **restates the topic**. Students are sometimes concerned about being redundant in their writing, but repeating key terms and points is useful in keeping your reader on track and reminding her of your points and ideas.

3) Like an effective thesis statement, an effective topic sentence **makes a point**.

Again, here is our thesis statement:

> People in the United States should continue to observe African-American History Month because **it honors important figures in American history who are often ignored**, it gives African-Americans a sense of pride about their ancestors, and it exposes all people to aspects of American history that may be unfamiliar to them.

The writer's first supporting point is in bold.

Now, let's turn that point into a topic sentence. Since it is the writer's first point, we will use one of the **transitions** offered to signal to the reader that this is the writer's first support point:

> First,

Then we must **restate the topic**:

> First, Black History Month

Then, we **make the point**:

> First, Black History Month honors important figures in American history who are often ignored.

Some writers opt to restate the essay's main point in the topic sentences:

> First, people in the United States should continue to observe African-American History Month because it honors important figures in American history who are often ignored.

Then, you will follow each topic sentence with evidence and examples to prove its point.

Now let's work on the second topic sentence for this thesis statement. Here is the thesis statement again:

> People in the United States should continue to observe African-American History Month because it honors important figures in American history who are often ignored, **it gives African-Americans a sense of pride about their ancestors**, and it exposes all people to aspects of American history that may be unfamiliar to them.

Now the writer's *second* supporting point is in bold.

To turn this point into a topic sentence we need to transition, and we need to include the topic. Since this is the essay's second supporting point, we will use a **transition** that indicates we are adding an additional point to the first one:

> In addition,

Then the **topic** and the **point**:

> In addition, Black History Month gives African-American people a sense of pride about their ancestors.

Again, the writer could opt to restate the essay's main point in the topic sentences:

> In addition, people in the United States should continue to observe African-American History Month because it gives African-American people a sense of pride about their ancestors.

Now let's build the third topic sentence for this thesis statement.

Here's the thesis statement one last time:

> People in the United States should continue to observe African-American History Month because it honors important figures in American history who are often ignored, it gives African-Americans a sense of pride about their ancestors, and **it exposes all people to aspects of American history that may be unfamiliar to them.**

The third point in the thesis statement is in bold. We need to **transition** into this last point of the essay:

> Finally,

Then, we need the **topic** and to **make a point**:

> Finally, Black History Month exposes people to aspects of American history that may be unfamiliar to them.

Once again, the writer could opt to restate the essay's main point in the topic sentences:

> Finally, people in the United States should continue to observe African-American History Month because it exposes people to aspects of American history that may be unfamiliar to them.

Now that we have built three topic sentences from our thesis statement, let's look at them all together as a skeleton outline:

Sample Outline

Essay Introduction (Introduce the text and use one of the strategies in Chapter 12, "Writing Introductions.")

Thesis: People in the United States should continue to observe African-American History Month because it honors important figures in American history who are often ignored, it gives African-American people a sense of pride about their ancestors, and it exposes all people to aspects of American history that may be unfamiliar to them.

Topic Sentence 1: First, Black History Month honors important figures in American history who are often ignored.

Support/Evidence/Examples

Topic Sentence 2: In addition, people in the United States should continue to observe African-American History Month because it gives African-American people a sense of pride about their ancestors.

Support/Evidence/Examples

Topic Sentence 3: Finally, people in the United States should continue to observe African-American History Month because it exposes people to aspects of American history that may be unfamiliar to them.

Support/Evidence/Examples

Essay Conclusion (Use one of the strategies from Chapter 14, "Writing Conclusions")

Now it's your turn to build topic sentences using the same steps we used above. Write a sample outline using this model thesis statement:

> **Americans should have universal, government (or state-run) healthcare** because preventative care costs less than the cost of illness, private companies should not be able to gauge sick people to fill their own pockets, and the healthier citizens are, the more taxes they can contribute to the economy.

WRITING TRANSITIONS

Students sometimes get so involved in the great paragraph work they are doing that they forget to transition between one idea and another. This is a mistake. Transitions are vital to the smooth flow of a strong essay and they remind the reader of the thesis. Luckily, we have two methods to help get you started.

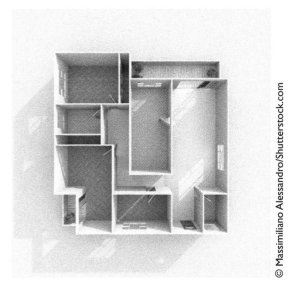

Writing an essay is a lot like giving a house tour. Each room of the house serves a different function, but they all belong in the same structure. Similarly, each paragraph is a further development of the thesis and covers new territory. Houses have hallways to get you from one part of the house to the other. In the same way, transitions provide the link between your paragraphs in the essay.

We often don't give hallways much thought, but without them, we'd have a hard time getting around. Imagine how disorienting it would be to be in the bedroom and to suddenly find yourself standing in the basement. This is the same feeling that readers have when you neglect transitions. Your job is to prepare the reader for the shift in idea so that he or she can fully appreciate your next point.

Just as you want to avoid jumping from one idea to another, you also want to avoid circling back before you have explored the whole room. In showing your house, you wouldn't start in the kitchen, go to the attic, and then go back to the kitchen again. In the same way, transitions can help keep your points moving in a logical progression that flows while also helping to keep your topics organized and contained in the appropriate paragraphs.

© Massimiliano Alessandro/Shutterstock.com

METHOD 1: STANDARD TRANSITIONAL EXPRESSIONS

Below is a list of standard transitions students use to move from one point to another in their essays.

TRANSITIONAL EXPRESSIONS

also	as a result	besides
consequently	finally	first
first of all	for example	for starters
furthermore	hence	however
in addition	indeed	in fact
in other words	in the first place	meanwhile
moreover	nevertheless	next
now	of course	on the other hand
otherwise	secondly	similarly
still	then	therefore
thus	to begin with	

While some students may worry that using these transitions will make their essays sound "too basic," professional writers and even presidents use these expressions to transition from point to point. Below are several sequential topic sentences from President Barack Obama's *The Audacity of Hope: Thoughts on Reclaiming the American Dream.* In these topic sentences he uses some of the transitional expressions we recommend. We have bolded these expressions so you can easily identify them.

Examples:

"**To begin with,** we should understand and that any return to isolationism—or a foreign policy approach that denies the occasional need to deploy US troops—will not work" (303).

"The **second** thing we need to recognize is that the security environment we face today is fundamentally different than the one that existed fifty, twenty-five, or even ten years ago" (304).

"**On the other hand**, it's time we acknowledge that a defense budget and force structure built principally around the prospect of World War III makes little strategic sense" (306-7).

"**Finally**, by engaging our allies, we give them joint ownership over the difficult, methodical, vital, and necessarily collaborative work of limiting the terrorists' capacity to inflict harm" (311).

METHOD 2: SUBORDINATING CONJUNCTION TRANSITIONS

While you can use transitional expressions as above, there's another very simple trick that involves subordinate clauses. Once you learn it, you will never find yourself at a loss for a transition. Pay special attention here if your professor has written "Transition needed" on your papers in the past.

SUBORDINATING CLAUSE TRANSITIONS

The subordinate clause portion of your sentence refers to the paragraph that has come **before**, reminding the reader of where he or she has been. Then the independent clause, or second half of the sentence, points the reader to where the essay is going.

Begin with a subordinate clause. Subordinate clauses are dependent clauses that cannot stand alone. They start with words like these:

DEPENDENT WORDS/SUBORDINATING CONJUNCTIONS

after	although	as	as if	because	before
even if	even though	if	in order to	once	since
that	though	unless	until	whatever	when
whenever	where	whereever	whether	which	while

For clarity, we have underlined the subordinate clauses in the following examples.

Transitional Sentence:

Although Virginia Woolf believes that women can be gifted writers, she fears that 'gender consciousness' can spoil the female writer who tries too hard to overcome the 'disadvantages' of her sex.

The subordinate clause portion of your sentence (underlined) refers to the paragraph that has come <u>before</u>, reminding the reader of where he or she has been:

> <u>Although Virginia Woolf believes that women can be gifted writers,</u>

(The previous paragraph discussed women being gifted writers.)

The independent clause, or second half of the sentence, points the reader to where the essay is going:

> she fears that "gender consciousness" can spoil the female writer who tries too hard to overcome the "disadvantages" of her sex.

(The next paragraph will discuss female writers whose work is "spoiled" by too much gender awareness.)

Example:

> <u>While Martin Luther King believes that 'negotiation' is an important second step in a nonviolent direct action campaign,</u> the third step of 'self-purification' is equally, if not more, vital in assuring success.

(The essay's previous paragraph discussed "negotiation" as the second step. The paragraph to come will explore the third step, "self-purification.")

When the subordinate clause comes first and describes the previous paragraph, it mimics the order of points in the essay and helps keep the essay on track. Notice, this transitional sentence can appear either at the end of the preceding paragraph, or as the first sentence of the next paragraph.

A published example of an elegant transition (underlined here) comes from Martin Luther King Jr.'s "Letter from a Birmingham Jail."

Example:

> ...I commend you, Reverend Stallings, for your Christian stand on this past Sunday, in welcoming Negroes to your worship service on a non-segregated basis. I commend the Catholic leaders of this state for integrating Spring Hill College several years ago.

> <u>But despite these notable exceptions,</u> I must honestly reiterate that I have been disappointed with the church. I do not say this as one of those negative critics who can always find something wrong with the church. I say this as a minister of the Gospel, who loves the Church; who was nurtured in its bosom; who has been sustained by its spiritual blessings and who will remain true to it as long as the cord of life shall lengthen.

Notice the previous paragraph applauds particular church members who have supported the Civil Rights Movement, but the subsequent paragraph discusses King's disappointment with the Church's stance overall. Both of these ideas are present in the transitional sentence King uses.

Finally, here is an example from the same published letter that uses two sentences to achieve the same effect:

> I have tried to stand between these two forces, saying that we need emulate neither the "do nothingism" of the complacent nor the hatred and despair of the black nationalist. For there is the more excellent way of love and nonviolent protest.

Notice that the "two forces" (complacency and hatred) were discussed in the previous paragraph. The coming paragraph will explore "love and nonviolent protest."

In essay writing as in life, it's good to remember where you've been and where you are going.

Exercise

The films *Gone with the Wind* and *Glory* both take place during the Civil War.

_____ the points of views of the different main characters illustrate very different experiences of the war. *Gone with the Wind* focuses on life in the South during the Civil War from the point of view of a wealthy, young woman named Scarlett O'Hara. Scarlett lives on her family plantation, Tara, and is in love with a man named Ashley Wilkes. _____ *Gone with the Wind* is a movie about resilience and perseverance from a wealthy Southern woman's perspective. *Glory* shows a Northern soldier's determination to end racial inequality.

_____ the theme of *Gone with the Wind* is that destruction can cause reinvention of the self. Scarlett never gives up and always finds the will to keep on going because her family's survival depends on her strength. _____ after the burning of Atlanta, Scarlett forges on and helps Melanie give birth and get back to Tara safely. _____ robbers ransack Tara and there is no food; Scarlett rebuilds the plantation and grows crops to feed herself and her family.

_____ the theme of *Glory* is that African-American soldiers had to fight for equality in the army for themselves at the same time that they were fighting for equality for slaves in the South. They are denied both trust and supplies; _____ they do everything they can to fight for their country's freedom. _____ they were not given the same pay as white soldiers, they fought for their equality in the army while still willing to fight for freedom in the South.

_____ *Gone with the Wind* and *Glory* share both similar and different characteristics. Both movies are very heavily impacted by the Civil War and its effect on the people who supported slavery and those who opposed it. _____ the films come from vastly different perspectives, one from the point of view of a Southern woman and one of a Northern man.

CHAPTER CHAPTER CHAPTER

11

PROVE IT!
THE FIVE TYPES OF EVIDENCE

▌USING EVIDENCE EFFECTIVELY

Now that you have learned tips to write introductions and thesis statements, it's

time to think about what goes into the body paragraphs of an essay.

> One of the skills required in critical thinking is for students to differentiate fact from opinion.

FACT VS. OPINION

One of the most important student learning outcomes for most English classes is critical thinking. One of the skills required in critical thinking is for students to differentiate fact from opinion. As a critical thinker, you need to be able to tell when someone is spouting his or her uninformed opinion and trying to pass it off as fact. Opinions become problematic when they are not well-reasoned, are illogical, or are biased because the person expressing them does not fully understand the topic. The important take away here is that <u>opinions must be substantiated by evidence</u>. Evidence is what gives your opinion weight and value.

While separating fact from opinion is an important distinction to be able to make, it sometimes paralyzes students when it comes time to write their own papers. We want to set you free: You can have an opinion! (In fact, you must have an opinion in order to write a thesis statement). Let us explain. Often students are taught that they shouldn't have opinions when they are writing, under the false assumption that all opinions are somehow biased or will lead to an unbalanced, subjective paper. Nothing could be further from the truth. As we stated in the "Thesis Statement" section of Chapter 11, whether we acknowledge it or not, <u>every</u> argument paper starts with an opinion. The words "I think.." are implied, but never stated. If a student writes a paper advocating the legalization of same-sex marriages, that is opinion-based. So how do we get away with it? Simple. Evidence.

What distinguishes a biased paper from an objective one is not the absence of opinion, but the presence of evidence. Evidence is the most important element of your paper and what will back up your opinions and make them persuasive. Ultimately, when you write a persuasive essay, you are trying to convince readers to agree with your opinion by showing them all the compelling evidence in favor of your view. So where do you get this evidence?

THE FIVE TYPES OF EVIDENCE

© Prath/Shutterstock.com

Evidence can be broken down into five main categories. First familiarize yourself with the five types by reading the descriptions below. As a next step, we recommend looking at published articles and noticing the types of evidence used by the authors. When it comes time to write, include some forms of evidence you may never have tried before. Ideally, use as many of the five as you can.

I. DATA AND STATISTICS

Data and statistics have become the gold standard of objective proof. If you are able to find reliable research that backs up your point, that research can go a long way in bullet-proofing your essay. Be sure to include reliable statistics and to cite very clearly where these statistics come from so that your readers can determine for themselves whether or not this is good scholarship. "Four out of five dentists recommend Crest" is less convincing when printed on an advertisement trying to get you to buy toothpaste and when the statistics come from Crest's own laboratory. On the other hand, a university study of volunteer subjects that shows 24.4% of male heavy smokers are likely to get lung cancer is more persuasive because no one stands to gain any money or "perks" from reporting these facts. University studies are very reliable in general because professors' salaries do not depend on the results of their findings. (In fact, that's why we have a tenure system, so that professors can feel free to speak the truth without fear of losing their jobs). Use scholarly journals. Look for websites with .edu (universities), .gov (government), and .org (non-profits) first. Note that nonprofits can still have a bias. Finally, remember always to cite your sources through in-text citations and on a Works Cited page. (See the "Documenting Your Sources" section). **Establishing your sources' credibility ensures your own.**

Using Visuals

Adding visual details like illustrations or graphs or charts can add a lot to your presentation and clarify points. Many people learn and absorb information visually, so this can be a great asset to your paper.

1) Choose whether to have the visual embedded inside the body of your paper (This is labeled: "Figure 1," etc.) or whether you will add it to an Appendix section at the end of your paper. You would then label the visual "Appendix 1," "Appendix 2," etc., depending on how many appendices you have to add. In the body of your paper, you would indicate this by merely adding a parenthetical: (See Appendix 1).

   Use an appendix when a graphic is too large or distracting to insert in the body of the text. You don't want to disrupt the flow of your paper or to have readers lose track of your argument.

2) Finally, don't use graphics or illustrations to dress up a poorly-researched paper. Your professor will see through this trick. Use graphs and illustrations that make your points more clear and easier for a reader to understand. Also, be sure that the graphics you use are directly relevant to the points you are making. When you insert a figure or an appendix, make sure it fits.

Example:

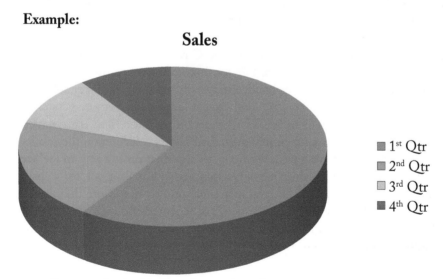

Figure 1 (embedded) or Appendix 1 (at the end of the paper)

2. EXPERT OPINION

If you were assigned a research paper on the causes of heart disease, you probably wouldn't start by enrolling in medical school. (You might, but your paper would take ten years to complete and you might miss the deadline!). Instead, you would benefit from the research of those who have gone to medical school. The purpose of research and the reason that scholarly journals publish research findings is so that individuals can use that information to further their own arguments. In the same way that you assess the reliability of the data and statistics sources, you must establish some criteria for judging your "experts." You should ask if this person is being paid to say what he or she is saying. Do the experts stand to gain financially from your following their advice? If so, they may not be as objective or reliable as you would like. Again, university websites that end in ".edu" can be a good place to start. Also, look at the credentials of the person whose advice you are quoting. If quoting a medical doctor, has he or she attended a recognized medical school, practiced medicine, done research? These are important questions to ask before you quote.

Once you find your sources, how do you get their words into your paper?

You have a choice of either quoting experts directly or paraphrasing their words. In either case, we recommend following the format for in-text citation. Briefly introduce your source's credentials in the body of your paper before adding the quote. This way, your audience can decide right away whether or not the source is reliable. For example, you might quote directly:

> Dr. James Schwab, Director of Family Medicine at the Mayo Clinic, recommends a proactive approach to patient care. He advises patients to "bring a series of questions and interview a physician before signing on as a patient" (40).

In this example, the writer has introduced the source (Dr. Schwab) and his qualifications (Director of Family Medicine at the famous Mayo Clinic) right in the body of the essay itself.

If you choose instead to paraphrase, you might state:

> Dr. James Schwab, Director of Family Medicine at the Mayo Clinic, recommends a proactive approach to patient care. He believes patients should not be afraid to conduct an extensive "interview" of their doctors before committing to the patient/doctor relationship (40).

3. ANECDOTE OR PERSONAL EXPERIENCE

Let's imagine that you are a journalist assigned to write an article about parents sending their children off to war. If you had never had that experience yourself, your first logical step might be to call the local army base and find some families who had, and then interview them. This can be a very persuasive method of illustrating a point. In fact, you might want to interview several families to show a variety of opinions and/or to give some statistical power to your generalizations. One family experiencing something doesn't mean that every family has, and could be dismissed as anecdotal evidence. Five families who all share an experience becomes more persuasive and looks like a trend.

The way to use personal experience in your essay is to include direct quotes or describe an individual's situation or point of view. "Meet the Sanchezes. Last Thanksgiving, they sent their daughter, Julia, off to Afghanistan…" This puts a personal face on an abstract issue and makes it concrete. If you have had relevant personal experience you may talk about it: "After my first tour of duty, I never looked at home the same way again."

Before you include personal evidence, be sure that the person's experience is indeed relevant to what you are discussing. Has he or she had firsthand experience with the issue? You don't want someone who says "I had a neighbor once who…" because he or she would be too far-removed from the emotional impact and the details. The immediacy of the experience is what makes it valuable (and quotable) evidence.

4. MORAL VALUES

This category might surprise some of you, but in deductively-reasoned arguments, commonly-held values can be very compelling as evidence. The key to effectively using this strategy is to be sure the audience already shares the moral value in question. If they do not, they will not find your argument based upon that value persuasive. For example, everyone agrees that the death of an innocent child is tragic. Because this is such a widely-held moral belief, you could base many argument essays upon this premise: promoting swimming pool safety or gun control, eliminating environmental hazards or world poverty, etc. Notice that many times, the value is so obvious it doesn't need to be stated. For example, if you want to write a paper on gun control laws, you might write that:

> According to the Children's Defense Fund, "In a single year, 3,012 children and teens were killed by gunfire in the United States. And every year, at least 4 to 5 times as many kids and teens suffer from non-fatal firearm injuries."

Because this value is self-evident, you would not need to write: "and we all know innocent children dying is bad…" This is assumed.

A very famous American document, The Declaration of Independence, is also based on a commonly-held value as evidence: "We hold these truths to be self-evident, that all men are created equal." "We hold these truths to be self-evident" means these truths are so obvious and widely-shared, we don't have to explain why they are values. The value stated is equality among men (at least white men. In 1776, the Founding Fathers didn't worry too much about the equality of African-Americans or women, but that's another topic!). The Declaration of Independence then proceeds to argue why America must declare war. Revolution was inevitable because colonialism trampled the value of "equality among men." Martin Luther King, Jr. shapes his argument to end segregation in "Letter from a Birmingham Jail" on exactly the same value. What is so powerful about reasoning with values, is that if your audience agrees with that value, they cannot possibly deny that its infringement is problematic. All of King's audience of white American clergymen considered themselves patriots. Therefore, when King appeals to the value of equality among men as written in one of the foundational documents of the United States of America (The Declaration of Independence), he is appealing to a belief he knows they will share. This is very shrewd. Similarly, King appeals to the values of Christian kindness and standing up for what is right. Those clergymen had to recognize that segregation was wrong because it denies men equal rights and is counter to the teachings of Christian doctrine. Because King knew his audience very well, he knew that they would share the values inherent in his "Letter." Therefore, to deny the basis of his argument was to deny their foundational beliefs. He had them!

5. HYPOTHETICALS

Hypotheticals are examples that you invent. You want to make them believable scenarios in order to be persuasive. If you were writing a paper about a proposed law that required all citizens to carry a national identification card with them at all times, you would want to use hypothetical situations to illustrate how different people would be affected by that law. Some might see it as another excuse to harrass immigrants; some who have been unfairly targeted as "illegals" might welcome it as a justification of their status. You might use expressions such as "Imagine if-", "What if-", or " X might happen if…".

> When used well, hypotheticals can help a reader see alternate points of view or the extremes of a position.

BEING SPECIFIC

You must use evidence to make your opinions persuasive, and the more concrete and specific your evidence, the more persuasive it will be. Take the time to do the research and get your facts from reliable sources. Be specific when citing the conclusions of an expert or statistics. Instead of saying "A lot of smokers get lung cancer," write "24.4% of male heavy smokers contract lung cancer." Substituting the actual percentage number for "a lot" makes it clear to the reader that you have done your research and know what you are talking about.

When quoting from a reading, be sure to quote *exactly* as it appears in the original. Also, when mentioning a character or a person in a book or article, be specific about the things they do, say, or the exact plot points and things that happen that prove your argument. If invoking a moral value, make sure it's clear which one. Remember, evidence pushes your opinion into the realm of persuasive argument.

Avoid using the following words in your essays:

- "they", "we", or "us" with no antecedent or referent
- "society"
- "nowadays"
- "these days"

All of the above refer to groups, people, and time periods that need to be specified (for example: doctors, baby boomers, students, the middle class, the 1890s, the late twenty-first century, etc.). Sometimes it takes a minute to identify the specific item you mean, since it's so common to speak in generalities. You may even have to look it up or ask someone. It's worth it to create more powerful sentences! Take a look at these examples.

Typical Usage	Specific Usage
They say salmon is good for the brain.	*Doctors say* salmon is good for the brain. *Researchers* suggest that salmon is good for the brain.
We don't like tax cheats because they increase everyone else's tax bill.	*Americans* don't like tax cheats because they increase everyone else's tax bill.
Society is a corrupting influence on children.	*Television and the news media* are a corrupting influence on children.
Nowadays swearing is more common in the workplace *than ever before*.	In the *early twenty-first century*, swearing is more common in the workplace *than fifty years ago*.
These days it's hard to find someone who isn't on Facebook.	*In the 2010s*, it's hard to find someone who isn't on Facebook.

Think about it: a lot of us speak in general terms much of the time because we don't have the facts at hand, or, because it takes an extra thirty seconds to be more specific. Conversely, people who speak specifically usually make an impression on us; they sound authoritative and knowledgeable.

It's also important to use specific, appropriate pronouns. Chances are you're using incorrect pronouns all the time and you have no idea. Play along with me for a moment.

Everyone loves their mother, right? Don't you?

It sure sounds reasonable! But it's grammatically wrong. "Everyone" is a singular pronoun and "their" is a plural, possessive pronoun. No doubt, most people think that the pronoun "everyone" is plural, but it's not. To make it grammatically correct, we have two options: use a singular pronoun, or a plural subject.

> **Both of these are correct:**
>
> <u>Everyone</u> loves <u>his/her</u> mother. (both singular)
>
> <u>All people</u> love <u>their</u> mothers. (both plural)

Developing the skill of specificity is a lot like developing a new muscle in your body that you haven't worked with before; it may seem unfamiliar at first, but then it gets easier and quickly pays off. For more on pronoun agreement and reference, see Chapter 5.

Exercise 1:

Read Sascha de Gersdorff's article, "Fresh Faces," found in the Appendix, and write down the types of evidence the authors use. Is their evidence effective? Explain.

CHAPTER CHAPTER CHAPTER 12

WRITING INTRODUCTIONS

As a writer, you cannot underestimate the importance of getting off to a great start. You'll have to back up your terrific introduction with solid evidence and persuasive points, of course, but rarely do papers with weak, sloppy (or nonexistent) introductions dazzle their readers the way they should. This is a skill set you will want to have.

How many times have you skimmed the first one or two paragraphs of a magazine article or a book before fully committing to reading it? Writing strong introductions makes sense for the same reason that making a good first impression does: it gives you an edge. A strong first impression buys you time to make your case. Most students know they need to introduce their papers, but surprisingly, many ignore their introductions because they've never been taught foolproof ways of making them work. We're going to change that today.

The entertainment industry understands well the importance of a solid and catchy opening, and many of its strategies apply to us. Who says college essays can't be entertaining? Like the quick teaser to your favorite television program, the ideal essay introduction hooks the audience members and makes them want to keep reading. You don't want your readers getting up to get a snack, or worse, changing the channel/page on you. You want them glued to their seats during the commercial break. That's why television teasers are called "teasers." They promise good things to come and spark our interest. These critical first three to five minutes of the show (or three to five sentences of your paper) serve a couple of vital functions:

1) **Introductions define the world to be explored.** They give the reader a sense of what to expect. The teaser for a television program tells the audience whether they're watching a sitcom, sci-fi, or a police procedural. Even if you had never seen them before, you would never mistake the first few minutes of *Law and Order* for *SpongeBob SquarePants*. In the same way, your paper establishes the key areas it will discuss. From reading your introduction, the audience should be able to answer the following questions: What is this paper's topic? What is the tone? And what is the topic of interest?

2) **Good introductions create curiosity in their readers.** They pose a provocative central question, but they leave it unanswered *for now*. The teaser to *NCIS* might show you the crime, but it will leave one or more elements initially unsolved so the viewer will be curious and follow key developments in the case. *How* did the killer pull it off? *Why* did the killer do it? Will the killer get away with it? Or will justice be served? Is this to frustrate you? No! It's to engage you. It is the same for college essay writers. Seek to engage your audience early. Engaged readers care about the outcome and will allow the writer to make his or her case. This is what you want. Let's face it. There are a lot of sensational news items vying for our attention these days. Professors read a lot of papers. Make yours a standout that piques your professor's interest and keeps him or her hooked until the Works Cited roll.

SEVEN INTRODUCTION STRATEGIES

1) GENERAL TO SPECIFIC

This is a darling of high school English teachers everywhere because it is a reliable method of launching into a paper. Chances are this method is already in your writer's toolbox and you have tried it yourself at one time or another. It usually takes a few sentences.

Example:

> War takes an enormous toll on society. During a war, the US military loses thousands of soldiers each year. Last Christmas, my brother was called to serve his country, and he never came back.

Notice that the progression of ideas here goes from the macro to the micro level. It starts with an abstract statement of an idea, and then gets progressively more specific until it targets the concerns of this particular paper. War taking a toll on society could work equally well as the first sentence of papers about the Peloponnesian War, the Civil War, or Vietnam; however, these would all be developed variously. The subsequent sentences refine the topic and limit each particular paper's scope.

2) SUMMARY

Most of your writing in college will be in response to something that you read (a text). Even if your assignment is not a research paper, you might be responding to an essay, article, or book you read for your English class or a section of your textbook for a different class. One way to start this type of essay is by summarizing that text for your reader so that he has the background information needed to understand the points in your paper. (Some assignments might even require you to summarize the text.) Go to our "Writing a Summary" section in Chapter 8 and follow the step-by-step instructions there to develop a summary to introduce your essay.

Example:

> In her provocative book *Are Prisons Obsolete?*, Angela Davis explores the efficiency of the prison system, its historical influences, and the need for reform.

3) THOUGHT-PROVOKING QUESTION

In this strategy, you begin your paper by asking the question you wish the paper to explore.

Examples:

"Do you know where your child is?!"

Or,

"What are the fundamental causes of racism in society?"

This question promises that the paper will discuss the different causes. After the causes are explored, the paper's conclusion would do well to take the idea further and discuss whether any of these causes can be eradicated. In the conclusion of a paper established this way, the reader wants to understand the "so what?" factor or how understanding these causes can give the reader useful information he or she can use to think about the world in a new way. Note: this is one of the unique circumstances in which you can use the second person pronoun "you" and a question in your essay. In general, we recommend limiting both, but this is an exception.

4) STRONG OPINION

This is one of the most fun and successful strategies, once students overcome their initial fears of expressing their opinions. Notice that this can be the student's strong opinion or someone else's. We professors spend a lot of time telling students to distinguish between fact and opinion because papers argued solely on the basis of opinions are not persuasive or rigorous in their argumentation. Unfortunately, as a result, students tend to shy away from expressing *any* opinions in their papers. We'd like to set the record straight here. Opinions are catchy ways to start a paper because when expressed strongly, they are provocative. The important thing to remember is that at some point in the paper (immediately), you will have to back-up every opinion with substantial and solid evidence. This is not a license to rant. Your paper will be every bit as rigorous in its argumentation as any other carefully constructed paper. For example, you might start off your paper with a bold claim (yours or someone else's).

> **Examples:**
>
> When Virginia Woolf claimed that "in one hundred years women would cease to be the protected sex," she was sorely mistaken;
>
> **or**
>
> Though few know his name, Philo Farnsworth has influenced American politics more than any other human being in American history.

Then you have the burden of proof. Once you have your audience's attention (Who's Philo Farnsworth??), you quickly explain that he was the inventor of the television and your paper explores the profound impact television has had on the voting public. (Or, you look at women's rights over the last century in the Virginia Woolf example). Ideally, when stating a strong opinion, the reaction you elicit from your reader is "Okay, show me!" And that's exactly what you will do with your evidence.

5) OPPOSING VIEW/OP-ED

In Op-Ed or Opinion Editorial columns found in newspapers, writers first introduce their opponent's position and then proceed to rip it to shreds.

Example:

> While television has certainly had an impact on American politics, historians have overstated its influence.

This strategy devotes precious real estate early on to establishing the opponent's position. You may wonder why writers would give their competition so much airtime. They have a good reason. Doing so establishes that the writer truly understands the opponent's points and *disagrees anyway*. This is an incredibly effective strategy to use when writing about controversial issues like gay marriage or the legalization of drugs. It makes the writer more credible because he or she can't be accused of misstatement or misunderstanding. It also goes a long way in getting an audience who might not agree to listen. If the writer appears to understand and even sympathize with some of the opponent's ideas and opinions, the opponent will be less defensive and more likely to read further. (If a paper starts with an insult or a rant, everyone's first impulse will be to put it down without reading. No one likes being attacked.) Intuitively, you might imagine that your goal would be to give your opponents less play, not more, but starting with their view also shows that you are an ethical writer who is not trying to sweep good, healthy debate under the rug.

6) SHOCKING FACT OR STATISTIC

This strategy functions the same way "Strong Opinion" does except you cite a fact rather than an opinion. The fact should be surprising enough to create wonder in the reader.

Examples:

> The 1918 flu pandemic was one of the deadliest natural disasters in human history, killing between 50 and 100 million people. Almost one third of the world's population was infected (Smithsonian).

or

> According to studies done by anti-slavery groups, there are currently more than 27 million slaves today, more than at any time in history (Tatlow).

You must get your facts from credible, cited sources and, hopefully it goes without saying, they must be accurate!

7) ANECDOTE

Using this method, the writer starts the essay by telling a brief story of a person whose experience is relevant to the topic at hand and the thesis. This story could be the writer's own personal experience or someone else's. Using a personal story is an effective way to introduce the larger piece because it "puts a face" on a larger issue that otherwise might feel abstract and impersonal. If you were a journalist assigned to write an essay on the experience of sending a child off to war, you would start by interviewing families who had undergone such an ordeal as part of your research. You then might start with a particular family's story (identifying the family members by name if you had their permission). This addresses the "so what?" or engagement issue head on, because while readers may not respond to an abstract idea like "injustice" or "grief," putting a human face on a problem by personalizing it can do wonders for making a reader care.

The advertising industry is full of experts at this strategy who use real-life stories and characters to get readers to understand the urgency of an issue. Public service campaigns to encourage blood donation will feature photographs of children in car accidents and concerned fathers. (For some reason, fathers often elicit more sympathy than mothers!). We all know it's a good thing to donate blood, but "Little Maria has three minutes to live. She needs blood NOW!" can get you to pull over at the next bloodmobile and roll up your shirtsleeve faster than a boring statistic can.

Notice the suspense strategy also applies here. As you recount part of an individual's personal experience in your introduction, leave part of it untold so that the reader is curious about how the story will end. Be sure then to come back to the personal anecdote by the end of the paper and let your reader know what happened. This will give you a nice conclusion and allow you to "bookend" your paper, coming full circle with the brief personal story. Thus the reader has the feeling of closure and the satisfaction of hearing an individual's experience as a topic is explored through its several facets. The key is to extrapolate from your specific example to the bigger picture. The rest of your paper will address the story's broader implications and its relevance to the world at large.

Note: A brief story may take one to three paragraphs to introduce, and that's okay, as long as your thesis statement appears at the end of the introduction, in this case, the end of paragraph three. You will have to add additional body paragraphs to your body paragraphs and you may exceed the assigned page length. Be sure to respect your professors' page limits and to choose a story length that allows you enough time to develop your own argument. Use the story to help your argument; don't let it take over your paper.

A published example of this strategy is the following found in "Fresh Faces" by Sascha de Gersdorff:

Example:

Kristin wanted a new nose. A better nose. A resculpted, slightly smaller version of the original, with no bump on its bridge and a shorter, perkier tip. It wasn't that she was ugly, or that her nose was so terrible: Kristin just wanted her features to be symmetrical. But doctors said she would have to wait at least a year before considering cosmetic surgery. After all, she was only 14. —*Boston Magazine*, 2005

Notice, sometimes the strategies blend. This is both anecdote (Kristin's story) and a shocking fact: Kristin is only 14.

Finally, be aware that with most of these introduction strategies you may have to provide background information after you have made your shocking statements, expressed bold opinions, or told an anecdote so that you can catch the reader up, and then proceed merrily on to proving your points. Try the strategies. Mix it up in different papers and have fun. Your reader will, too. Most importantly, ask yourself if your introduction makes you want to read on. If the answer is no, try a different strategy until you feel comfortable with all of them and can pull them out of your writer's toolbox at will.

EXERCISE 12

Please identify the introduction strategies used below. Choose from the seven strategies discussed in this chapter: General to Specific, Summary, Thought-provoking Question, Strong Opinion, Opposing View/Op-Ed, Shocking Fact or Statistic, Anecdote.

1) "What if your only means of viable income was completely predicated on marrying off your daughter? During the early nineteenth century, a mother such as *Pride and Prejudice's* Mrs. Bennet, is easily viewed as obsessed by her daughter's marriage prospects; however, after critically analyzing her motivation, we can see that as a mother she is justified, as marriage would determine a more stable future for her daughters as well as a means of social security for herself." *Excerpted from Sylvia Spielman-Vaught's essay in Chapter 23.*

2) "When Sharon Duchesneau gave birth on Thanksgiving Day to a deaf son, she was delighted. Duchesneau and her lesbian partner, Candice McCullough, had done everything they could to ensure that their son Gauvin would be born without hearing." *Excerpted from Wendy McElroy's essay "Victims from Birth" in the Appendix.*

3) "Father's Day no longer arrives without the national media highlighting Mr. Moms. The year before last, for example, Lisa Belkin of *The New York Times*, described the life of one Michael Zorek, whose only job was taking care of his 14-month-old son Jeremy. Zorek, whose wife brought home a good salary as a corporate lawyer, felt he had become 'remarkably good' at shopping, cooking, and at entertaining his energetic toddler...

Brace yourselves for an onslaught of such features this week, even though, in the real world, there are still 58 moms staying home with minor children for every dad who does so. This is not just an accidental social arrangement to be overcome once the media have sufficiently raised our consciousness about the joys of stay-at-home fatherhood." *Excerpted from Stephen Rhoads's article "What Fathers Do Best" in the Appendix.*

4) "In February 2012, notoriously provocative conservative talk show host, Rush Limbaugh, called a private citizen a "slut" for testifying before Congress about the importance of funding for contraceptive pills to treat her ovarian cysts." *Excerpted from Eunice Burns's essay "Reproductive Rights Protect Us All" in Chapter 17.*

CHAPTER 13

WRITING CONCLUSIONS

Conclusions can be thought of as simply the end of something, the finish, or in a more active sense as, "I conclude this speech with the thought that…" or "Based on these data, I conclude (infer) that…" In an essay, a conclusion is meant to sum up, or conclude, the arguments you've made and proven, based on whatever criteria you introduced. For instance, if in an introduction you tell the audience what your essay will be about, in a conclusion you remind them what you just told them. This is never more important than today, in the early twenty-first century, a time dominated by electronic communication and entertainment devices which reduce our already short attention spans to nearly nil! Readers don't have the patience they once did, so you have to guide them, and continually reiterate your points in key moments such as the introduction, topic sentences, transitional sentences, and the conclusion.

Conclusions provide your last chance to "touch" a reader on an issue. It's the moment at which you send him or her back out into the world of ideas either disposed to take your point or leave it. Although you may not feel the importance of this in a class setting, when writing from an assigned essay topic you may not care much about, the time will come when you are writing something you do care about when this will matter to you very much, such as asking for a job promotion or negotiating a child custody battle.

Here are a number of techniques that you can mix and match as you like to conclude essays in power and style. Many of these techniques can be used interchangeably between your introduction and conclusion. Every conclusion should reference the thesis statement.

PREDICT THE FUTURE

One way to close an essay is to offer your reader the future consequences of what you are supporting or opposing in your essay. For example, if you're arguing in support of the observance of Black History Month, you might offer a bleak image of a future without it.

> **Example:**
>
> If Americans abandon Black History Month, we may miss scores of opportunities to celebrate the accomplishments of African-Americans who have inhabited this land for the last 400 years...

If you are supporting the idea that all wealthy and middle class people donate all of their extra money to save the lives of the extremely poor, close your essay with a view of what the world would look like if wealthy and middle class people gave enough to end extreme poverty.

> **Example:**
>
> If everyone in industrialized nations would give up their luxuries for just one year and donate that money to help the poor, we could surely end extreme poverty in the world in no time.

Key terms when you predict the future: "If", "Hopefully," and "Unless."

SOCIO-HISTORICAL CONTEXT

Just as it likely took you awhile to arrive at your essay's position, so you must direct your readers to the essay's broader significance. In other words, where is your essay located in the world of ideas? Does it arrive at the end of a continuum?—say, the journey of women in the Western world to earn equality, beginning with the vote, extending to the explosive Feminist movement in the 1970's and the struggle in the following decades to win and maintain reproductive freedom and wage equality? Then say so! A contextual approach frames the essay in its natural context—how it fits into the world around it. You can use a wide lens— the scope of history—to contextualize the essay's issues with a specific time period or "place" such as a movement, a social class, or a culture group (gays in San Francisco, migrant workers in Southern California, Puritans in New England, etc.)

Socio-historical context is also a useful technique in introductions. In an introduction context helps us zoom in to the "moment" of the essay while in a conclusion it helps us zoom back out.

As academic and professional situations lead us ever more into a "global village" community, you'll need to consider the implications of writing for that wider audience. For example, you might be taking an online class with classmates in four different time zones, all with different frames of reference. In such situations context is vital.

ANECDOTE

A useful technique at any point throughout an essay, a short story or anecdote can be just the thing to leave readers with a picture of how your essay's issue impacts the world at large. Although true-to-life anecdotes often show up as "evidence" or personal testimony that "prove" a writer's specific point within a body paragraph, in an introduction or conclusion, an anecdote can inspire hope or fear and all shades in between as you draw readers a picture in black and white. For instance, in an essay on daycare, you might open or close an essay with a story of unsupervised children who light the place on fire, or something much worse—children in daycare who are given overmuch—inappropriate—attention by workers who were not properly screened before they were hired. You might think of the anecdote as a television commercial—it can carry influence and impact long beyond its airtime by planting unforgettable images or scenarios in people's minds.

There are several ways to use the anecdote. You can use extremely small ones at any place in the essay to illustrate your points.

Example:

One California man was actually imprisoned for stealing a pizza.

However, if you open your essay with a specific, substantive anecdote in your introduction, don't leave us hanging. Come back in the conclusion and finish the story.

Example:

Although Carmen had once felt powerless to protect her children, with the help of authorities and new legislation initiated by Senator Williams, she has become the victor.

If in your introduction, Julia Sanchez went off to war, tell us by the conclusion what happened to her.

HYPOTHETICAL

A hypothetical is very similar to an anecdote. It's a scenario that hasn't happened before, but [you argue that it] could. The hypothetical is meant to impact readers in precisely the same way an anecdote does. The difference is that sometimes hypotheticals can be dismissed as far-fetched. While anecdotes are recognizable to us as things that often happen, have happened before, and will happen again, hypotheticals are usually more abstract and thus can be intellectually dismissed. It's your job to make them seem real.

Example:

Suppose a woman defendant enters the courthouse to see a predominantly male jury. Would she be confident of receiving justice?

Key terms in a hypothetical are "What if," and Imagine that…"

MAKING AN APPEAL

Perhaps the most familiar conclusion technique is the final appeal. You might not recognize it by that, or any, name, but if you've ever said something like, "In conclusion, readers should use their turn signals because that's the law," then you've made an appeal. For our purposes there are roughly three categories of appeals: logos, ethos, and pathos. (You can read about these at length in our section on logic in Chapter 17. **Logos is an appeal to logic, ethos an appeal to ethics, and pathos an appeal to pity.** Therefore, if you are appealing to readers to do something because that's the law, you are appealing to their sense of ethics—what they should do. If you conclude with data—"The statistical link between smoking and heart disease is too compelling to ignore"—you are making an appeal to logic. If you conclude by inspiring pity or compassion—"In conclusion, only quick action can save abandoned animals from a cruel fate"—you are making an appeal to pity.

CALL TO ACTION

You might also choose to take your appeal a step further in your essay's conclusion and call your readers to action. You might make a request that your reader do something in response to your argument or even insist on it. Let's see how you might use the appeal above and turn it into a call to action:

Example:

Only quick action can save abandoned animals from a cruel fate. If your own pet got lost and someday became one of them, you would want to know advocacy services are in place. Therefore, consider making a monthly, tax-free donation to an animal shelter so that these resources exist for the animals that need them.

Key terms to use in a Call to Action: "Be sure," "Remember to," "Always," and "Please."

© Andy Dean Photography/Shutterstock.com

EXERCISE EXERCISE EXERCISE

13

For practice, identify which conclusion technique is used in each of the following conclusions. Choose from the strategies discussed in this chapter: Predict the Future, Socio-Historical Context, Anecdote, Hypothetical, Making an Appeal, and Call to Action.

1. "*Vogue* attempted to 'destroy the brute' by portraying James as aggressive and beast like. The editors next attempted to 'stir up' controversy by recreating a deeply-rooted racial image of a black brute carrying off the white woman. However, *Vogue* failed to stir up the kind of controversy that sells. The issue sold just over 300,000 copies, the second worst-selling April issue of the decade, and the second-lowest selling issue of 2008. The fact that *Vogue* attempted to profit from such a sensitive issue as race exposes that the deep-seated racial feelings that were a major part of this country in the past are not behind us, but alive and well. Advertising is an integral part of our society, but using hate of any kind to generate profits has no place in our society." *Excerpted from David Spielman's essay in Chapter 16.*

2. "Asked if she would consider having additional cosmetic procedures, Kristin nods enthusiastically. 'Yeah, definitely,' she says. She says there's nothing wrong with wanting to feel better about yourself. 'I'm not going out searching for things to do, but if there was something I wanted to change, wanted to be different, I would do it.'" *Excerpted Sascha de Gersdorff's "Fresh Faces" essay in the Appendix.*

3. "But if deafness is to be considered a cultural choice, let it be the choice of the child, and not the parents. Let a child with five senses decide to renounce or relinquish one of them in order to embrace what may be a richer life. If a child is rendered incapable of deciding 'yes' or 'no,' then in what manner is it a choice?" *Excerpted from Wendy McElroy's "Victims from Birth" essay in the Appendix.*

4. "When Bob first grasped the dilemma that faced him as he stood by that railroad switch, he must have thought how extraordinarily unlucky he was to be placed in a situation in which he must choose between the life of an innocent child and the sacrifice of most of his savings. But he was not unlucky at all. We are all in that situation." *Excerpted from Peter Singer's essay "The Singer Solution to World Poverty" in the Appendix.*

CHAPTER CHAPTER CHAPTER 14

REVISING AND POLISHING

The best essays require time, careful planning, and several revisions. Every student knows this, but few actually complete the process to their (or their instructor's!) satisfaction. Planning ahead can drastically alter your learning and final product, and consequently your grade. Start this revising and polishing process by giving your essay a title.

GIVE YOUR ESSAY A TITLE

After you spend time and energy composing any college writing assignment, of course, it deserves a title. Remember that your essay's title should get a reader's attention and communicate your essay's topic.

Follow these tips for writing an effective essay title:

TITLE TIPS

- The title should not restate the essay question or the thesis statement.
- The title should generally not be a complete sentence.
- The title should mention your topic.
- The title might suggest what point you're making about the topic.

Be creative and experiment with different types of titles as you practice and master college-level writing. Ask for your instructor's feedback as you try different titles. Pay attention to the titles of essays and articles you read for your classes, and let those examples inform your own trial and error process.

REVISING

Once you have given your essay a title, it is time to reread and revise. Often students get into the bad habit of printing and submitting the first (and only) draft of the essay they have written. This is not a way to set yourself up for success. While you may have been able to get away with this in grade school, standards are now higher. Plan to review several drafts before you submit a perfected one. This is another one of many reasons to begin work on your assignment as soon as possible and not wait until the night before.

Revising your essay requires you to revisit elements of the essay you might prefer to avoid. If you know your second body paragraph doesn't really focus on the thesis, you may prefer to just ignore it. However, this process gives you the opportunity to strengthen your essay by addressing that inconsistency. As you revise, look for similar problems in your essay. Start by reviewing the assignment, and reread your essay's thesis. Make sure it responds directly to the assignment. Then, go through your entire essay to make sure it contains the required components. Check that you transition between points and that you provide adequate evidence to support your argument throughout the body of your essay. Look at previous instructor comments and identify patterns in your writing that may be improved. Take your time going through, and you will likely transform a merely adequate essay into a great one. See below for checklists designed to assist you in this process.

PROOFREADING

One draft should always be printed simply for proofreading purposes. If you have been looking at an essay for several hours, your brain will fill in the words you think are there. Word-processing programs don't always catch every error in grammar or spelling. Thus, use any or all of the following techniques to effectively proofread your essay draft.

- Read the essay backwards paragraph by paragraph, and/or sentence by sentence. For example, read the last sentence first, then the second-to-last sentence next, then the third-to-last sentence, and so on. This will disrupt your brain's intentions—the words you intended to write—and cause you to see what words are actually there (or not there.)

- Read the essay aloud to yourself. Again, if a word is not there, chances are you will notice.

- Read the essay out loud to another person. If something isn't clear, he/she might notice.

- Look at previous instructor comments and check to see if you've made the same errors in this essay.

The following are resources students have found useful in revising and proofreading their drafts. Check *The West Guide* web site for printable versions of these peer or self-review documents.

A few things to remember:

Replace "being that" with "since."

Almost always delete "that is/are," "who is/are," and "which is/are" from your sentences, for example, Richard, ~~who is~~ a poet about to receive a lifetime achievement award, suffers from a terminal illness.

Quote exactly.

Italicize *Book Titles* and put "Article Titles" in quotation marks.

When writing about articles or literature, always use the present tense.

Call authors by their last names (unless you know them personally). This goes for film directors, too. Write "Woolf suggests…" *not* "Virginia suggests…"

Avoid exclamation points.

Avoid "Yes," "No," and repeated questions rather than declarations. Rewrite sentences that are formulated as questions if there are too many.

© zmkstudio/Shutterstock.com

Rubric for Peer or Self-Review

Name: **Due Date:**

Criteria	Comments
Assignment Fulfillment Does the essay fulfill the required criteria? Does it have an appropriate original title? Did the writer show every required step in the writing process? Is the essay in MLA format? (Chapters 10 and 16)	
Introduction/Thesis	
Thesis Does the writer include a clear thesis statement that states the topic of the essay and makes a point about that topic? (Chapter 11)	
Introduction Does the introductory paragraph include the title and author of the text? Does the writer introduce the essay with adequate background information in a full paragraph that leads the reader to the thesis statement? Does the writer use some version of one or more of the following techniques: Shocking Fact or Statistic Thought Provoking Question Strong Opinion Opposing View / Op-Ed General to Specific Anecdote Summary of Text (Chapter 13)	
Support/Body Paragraphs	
Organization Does the writer use a clear, logical pattern of organization? Does the writer use **topic sentences** that relate back to and support the thesis statement? Does the writer stay focused on proving the thesis statement throughout the essay using appropriate, relevant evidence? Does the writer use transitions when moving from idea to idea? (Chapter 11)	

Evidence/Support Does the writer synthesize information from the text(s) and his/her knowledge and experience to prove his/her points? Are the body paragraphs fully developed using **the five types of evidence**? 1. Data and Statistics 4. Moral Values 2. Expert Opinion 5. Hypotheticals 3. Anecdote or (Chapter 12) Personal Experience	
Conclusion	

Conclusion
 	
Does the writer avoid bringing up a new point in his/her conclusion?
 	
Does the writer wrap up his/her essay using one or more of the following techniques in an effective way?
 	
Predict the Future   Socio-Historical
                            Context
Anecdote   Hypothetical
Making an Appeal   Call to Action
                            (Chapter 14)	

Research	
Works Cited If this is a research essay, does the essay include a Works Cited page in MLA Format? (Chapter 22)	
Research If this is a research essay, does the writer cite sources according to MLA format? Does the writer integrate and synthesize relevant quotations, paraphrases, and summaries from reliable outside sources into his/her essay? (Chapter 22)	

General/Full Essay	
Critical Thinking Does the writer demonstrate an understanding of the text by explaining and analyzing its meaning? Does the writer clearly communicate well-thought-out reasons based on evidence from the text, personal experience, and/or research? Does the writer acknowledge opposing views in the essay? (Chapter 12)	
Sentence Craft Is the writing fluent, clear, and easy to understand? Does the writer use an appropriate academic tone? Does the writer use declarative sentences and avoid asking questions to prove points? Does the writer avoid using vague pronouns like the second person "you" or unclear "we" or "they?" Does the writer use a variety of sentences? (Chapters 5 and 7)	
Proofreading Does the writer use standard English throughout the essay and use correct grammar, punctuation, and spelling? (Chapters 3-7)	
Add your instructor's additional criteria to the cells below:	

SUBMITTING DRAFTS

Ask at a first class meeting whether or not your instructor accepts drafts of papers. If so, this is potentially a gold mine of "free" information. Once you have spent time refining your essay, take it to your professor for feedback. Discussing drafts can be helpful in two ways. First, hashing over ideas even in outline form is productive; a good conversation can point you to library sources for your paper and can help you to see that a topic is either too broad or too narrow. Your instructor or a tutor can also alert you to the difficulties you might encounter in the writing of your paper. For example, a term you take as self-explanatory may actually require additional explanation to come across the way you intended. Secondly, handing in a draft will help you with the nuts-and-bolts writing of the essay. How can you construct the arguments in the most persuasive way possible? Are the transitions working? Are the quotations effective? To make the most of your meeting, you should come armed with questions for your instructor or tutor. Does the introduction work? Etc.

Keep your eye on the calendar. Be sure to verify the deadline for the submission of paper drafts. Handing in a draft only the day before the paper is due will be much less productive than giving both your reader and yourself a few days to effect any necessary changes. More-over, try to make the draft as polished and close to submission-ready as possible. The closer you are to a finished product, the more useful and helpful the advice you receive will be. (See Chapter 2 for further ideas on getting feedback before you submit).

POLISHING

Once you have feedback, be prepared to throw away some of your original draft if necessary. If only minor changes are required, great. But if your instructor suggests changes in your thesis, be prepared to do significant rewriting. Although painful, rewriting is sometimes vital to the coherence and elegance of a paper. It is obvious when a writer has clung to a favorite paragraph out of love, and not with the best interests of composition logic at heart. Clearly, this process requires time. Allow yourself sufficient time in planning, submitting drafts, and completing your revision before the paper is due. (See Chapter 1 for further help with time management.)

MLA FORMATTING

In your English and other humanities courses, your professor will probably require that your paper be submitted in **MLA format**. (Other disciplines use different formats. Check with your professor.)

MLA stands for the Modern Language Association, an organization of linguistic and literary scholars who agree on paper format and style in which writers should format their papers and document their sources. Follow the basic format for a paper written in MLA style using these guidelines (unless otherwise instructed by your professor):

MLA PAPER FORMATTING CHECKLIST

1) Set your document's top, bottom, left, and right margins at one inch.

2) Set your document's spacing for double (2.0) throughout (including the document's heading).

3) Use 12 point standard professional font (Times New Roman, Cambria, Calibri, etc.)

4) Type your last name and insert the page number in the top right corner of your document as a header to appear on every page of the paper.

5) Type your first and last name, instructor's name, course title, and date in the top left corner of the first page of your document.

6) The paper's title should appear centered in the line below the date in the document's heading. (No title page is necessary, and the title's font should match the rest of the paper: no bold, italics, or quotation marks around your title.)

7) Indent each paragraph in the document one half inch from the left margin. One way to achieve this is by pressing the tab key before you begin each paragraph.

8) Italicize the titles of any books, magazines, newspapers, or other longer works in your document.

9) Place in quotation marks the titles of any articles, essays, poems, short stories, or other short works in your document.

10) Place one space after each period, comma, and other punctuation marks.

11) Print your document on standard, white, 8 ½ × 11-inch paper.

Below is a sample first and second page of a college essay typed using MLA style.

Visual Argument Sample Student Essay:

David Spielman   Spielman 1

Dr. Katherine Boutry

English 103

14 Oct. 2012

Destroy the Brute, Stir the Pot, Make a Profit: *Vogue*'s Recipe to Sell

Racial Controversy

In March of 2008, *Vogue* announced that its April 2008 cover would feature basketball superstar LeBron James and supermodel Gisele Bündchen. LeBron James would be the first African-American male and only the third male ever to grace the cover of the magazine. Touted by *Vogue* as a historical issue, the editors chose famed photographer Annie Leibovitz to shoot the cover photo. Upon release of the issue, however, many cried foul as LeBron James appeared to be posed along with Gisele Bündchen in a racially insensitive manner. *Vogue* denied the allegations of racism, but upon close examination of the photo, one might conclude that the cover was not only racially insensitive, but also a purposefully constructed controversy created by *Vogue* with the intent to boost sales.

The cover photo displays a fierce looking LeBron James, crouched down, bouncing a basketball with his right hand and clutching Gisele Bündchen in his left hand. He is wearing a black basketball uniform, looking directly into the lens, and appears to be releasing a primal scream. Gisele Bündchen is wearing a strapless, aqua green dress and looks directly into the lens with a huge smile on her face and her long blonde hair blows back. The lettering on the cover is predominantly white, with some notable red exceptions: the title *Vogue* at the top of the cover, the number 87, and the words "Secrets of the Best Bodies" at the bottom of the page between LeBron's legs. LeBron's head is directly covering the bottom and the middle of the letters O and G in the word *Vogue.* The top of the red O and G letters curve away perfectly from LeBron's head, evoking the image of large beastly horns protruding from the top of his head.

    The photo brings to mind the image of a beast-like, crazed savage clutching the innocent white woman in his arms. This is an image haunting black males since the Reconstruction Era of the United States. Dr. David Pilgrim, Professor of Sociology at Ferris State University writes, "The brute caricature portrays Black men as innately savage, animalistic, destructive, and criminal… terrifying predators who target helpless victims, especially white women." The photo was heavily criticized and compared to a 1933 King Kong poster which depicted the giant ape clutching actress Faye Wray in his hand, baring his teeth and hunched over in a menacing stance. It drew further criticism when placed side by side with a World War I propaganda recruitment poster featuring a cartoon caricature of a giant ape posed in the same stance as LeBron James on the *Vogue* cover. The similarities are too many to ignore. The ape clutches a bare-breasted white woman with an aqua green dress in his left arm, very similar in appearance to the dress Gisele Bündchen wears. On the top of the recruitment poster in bold letters are the words, "Destroy This Mad Brute." Moreover, the similarities were not lost on the public and critics. In an article in *USA Today*, magazine analyst Samir Husni is quoted saying that the *Vogue*

In "Chapter 22: Documenting Your Sources," you will learn more about citing sources in a research paper using MLA format or style.

SECTION SECTION SECTION

IV

SELECT AN ESSAY TYPE

CHAPTERS

CHAPTER CHAPTER CHAPTER

15

FOUNDATIONAL MODES OF ARGUMENTATION

In college you will likely be assigned different types of essays to help you prove different points. Your professor might ask you to explain what caused something, to compare two things, define a term, or describe a process. This chapter will introduce you to some of those types of essays and prepare you to take on any of those tasks.

CAUSAL ANALYSIS

In college, you will almost certainly at some point have to explain and prove in writing what caused (or causes) something to happen:

What caused World War I?

Why do Americans continue to eat unhealthy foods in vast quantities?

You will also likely be asked to explain and prove the effects of something:

What effects did World War I have on world politics?

How did the recent housing crisis affect the Los Angeles economy?

This type of writing is called causal analysis or a cause-and-effect essay. In some cases you will have to research the causes or effects of the phenomenon (see the examples above), but if your essay has a personal or local topic, discovering its causes and/or effects will simply call for in-depth thought.

In some cases, you will focus on causes in your writing. When an essay prompt asks "Why?" it is asking you to explain the causes of something. Below is a diagram that uses an arrow to show the causal relationship.

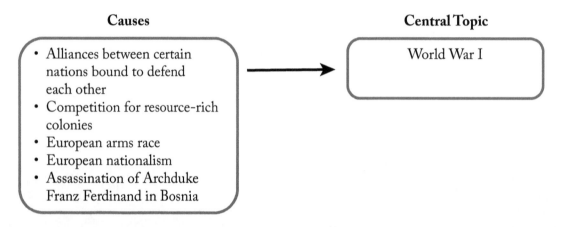

In other cases, you will be asked to write about the effects of something.

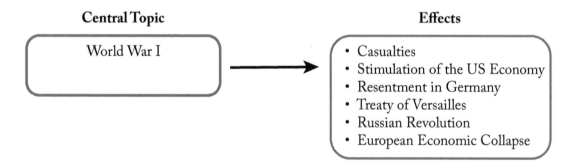

Some assignments may even ask you to examine both causes and effects. You also might have to do research to link causes and/or effects to your topic.

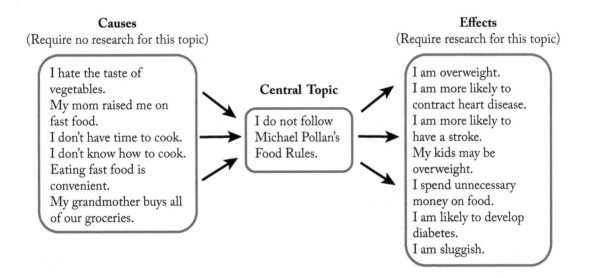

Decide how many causes and/or effects your essay will cover. Then, your thesis statement in your cause-and-effect essay should indicate your essay's central topic and indicate whether your essay will explain its causes, effects, or both.

Sometimes your thesis statement will indicate the causes or effects:

> Alliances between certain nations, competition for resource-rich colonies, a European arms race, European nationalism, and ultimately the assassination of Archduke Franz Ferdinand all led to the outbreak of World War I.

> World War I had an enormous impact on the world. It led to thousands of casualties, a boom in the US economy, the signing of the Treaty of Versailles, a Russian revolt, and German resentment against the allied forces.

However, if the list of causes is this long, your thesis may become unwieldy. You may then opt to make your thesis statement more broad and save the specific causes and/or effects for the essay's body paragraphs:

> Several factors led to the outbreak of World War I.

> World War I had a significant impact on the world.

Once you have composed your thesis, you must consider how to organize your essay. If you write about both causes and effects, you have a number of options. Here is one model based on the example in the boxes above.

Start the body of your essay explaining two reasons you don't follow Pollan's rules. For example, here is the sample thesis:

> I do not follow the rules in Michael Pollan's book *Food Rules: An Eater's Manual* because <u>I ate a lot of fast food growing up, and I do not have time to cook</u>. As a result of my eating habits, I am at high risk for diabetes and obesity.

In this sample thesis, the **causes** are underlined. The writer will start the essay's body elaborating on those two causes like this:

Body Paragraph 1: First of all, I do not follow Pollan's Food Rules because I am used to eating fast food; I ate it all the time growing up.

    Example/Detail/Explanation from experience

    Example/Detail/Explanation from experience

Body Paragraph 2: I also do not follow Pollan's rules because I do not have time to cook.

    Example/Detail/Explanation from experience

    Example/Detail/Explanation from experience

*In your essay's body paragraphs, the most important thing to remember is to connect the cause to the topic. So, in this case, the writer will describe his/her experience eating fast food growing up, and **he/she will also connect that experience to his/her <u>current</u> eating habits, which do not follow Pollan's rules.***

Then, for this assignment, once you have explained what causes your behavior, you will explain the effects. Here is the sample thesis again:

> I do not follow the rules in Michael Pollan's book *Food Rules: An Eater's Manual* because I ate a lot of fast food growing up, and I do not have time to cook. As a result of my eating habits, <u>I am at high risk for diabetes and obesity</u>.

This time, the **effects** are underlined. The writer will develop those effects this way:

Body Paragraph 3: Unfortunately, because I don't follow Pollan's rules, I am likely to develop diabetes.

    Example/ Detail/Explanation from <u>research</u> and/or experience

    Example/ Detail/Explanation from <u>research</u> and/or experience

Body Paragraph 4: I am also likely to develop obesity because I do not follow Pollan's rules.

    Example/ Detail from <u>research</u> and/or experience

    Example/ Detail from <u>research</u> and/or experience

Finally, the writer would compose a conclusion paragraph using one of the strategies in our "Conclusion" chapter.

*In your essay's body paragraphs, the most important thing to remember is to connect the effect to the topic. So, in this case, the writer will clearly explain using research **how his/her eating habits, which do not follow Pollan's rules, make him/her more likely to develop diabetes.** Avoid just talking all about diabetes.*

*Remember that **the most important element of this type of writing is to connect the causes with the topic and prove that relationship**. In the World War I essay, you would not simply* describe *the European arms race; you would convince your reader that it caused* World War I. *For the eating habits essay, don't just describe how busy you are, show that your busy* schedule *prevents* you from following Pollan's rules. ***The same applies to effects.*** *Make every effort to prove the connection between your topic and its effects.*

Analyzing why things happen and their consequences is a crucial college-level critical thinking skill. This essay format will give you access to show off that skill with grace and ease.

Use the bubbles below to develop some prewriting for your own causal analysis.

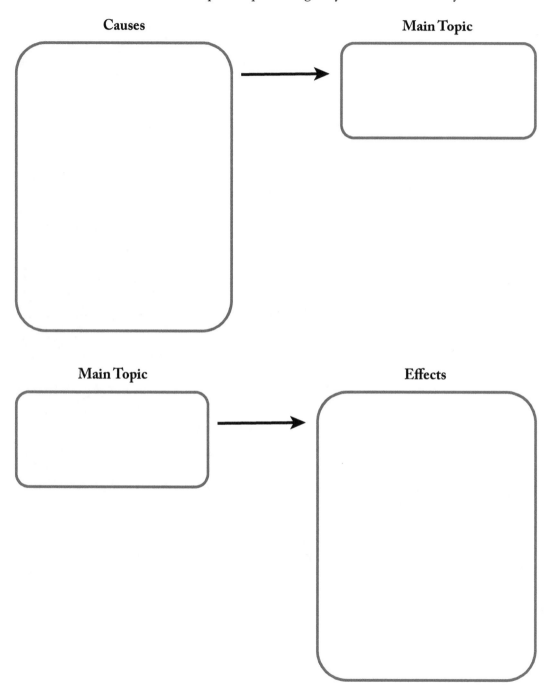

Causes

Main Topic

Main Topic

Effects

CLASSIFICATION

Everywhere we go in our society, items are divided into categories or classes. For example, in a bookstore, books are organized based on different categories: novels, nonfiction, humor, textbooks, mystery, self-help, graphic novels, fantasy, etc. You might have your files on your computer divided into different folders based on categories, and your friends on Facebook may be divided into categories too. You group into categories based on common characteristics, and this skill is one you will use in your college writing.

The type of essay you might write to practice using this skill is an essay of classification. In this type of writing, you categorize items to make a larger point. You might write about types of students, types of professors, types of nail salons, types of jobs, types of Republicans, or types of Democrats. Taking a larger topic and dividing it into categories gives you an opportunity to explore it in depth. It also gives you an opportunity to demonstrate your understanding of that topic or help your reader understand it.

You can approach this type of writing from two perspectives:

1) **You can approach it from dividing the larger topic into categories.** Perhaps your essay topic for biology class is apes. You decide to look at how apes are divided into two main groups: the great apes and the lesser apes. You write about those two classifications of apes and make this basic point: Apes come in two different categories: lesser apes and great apes.

2) **You can also approach this type of writing from starting the individual items and grouping them into each category.** Let's say your essay topic is friendship. To tackle this topic, you make a list of the names of all your friends. As you look at your list, you see that you can divide your friends into five categories: new friends, enduring friends, fading friends, peripheral friends, and fluctuating friends. You might settle on this point based on your categorization of your friendships: My friendships are in a continuous state of transition.

Here are some sample thesis statements dividing various topics into categories.

> Although Republicans sometimes represent themselves as a monolithic united front, there are different types of Republicans like conservative Republicans, moderate Republicans, Libertarians, and liberal Republicans.

> To be truly successful, one must achieve all four types of success: financial success, personal success, spiritual success, and professional success.

> The food I eat seems to fit into one of these categories: wholesome food, comfort food, convenient food, and social food.

Here is a graphic organizer of an extended definition that classifies Democrats into three categories:

Democrats								
Liberal Democrats			**Disadvantaged Democrats**			**Conservative Democrats**		
Support government spending on social programs and environmental regulations	Oppose excessive military spending	Support universal healthcare, same sex marriage, and gun control	Come from a low-income and/or historically underrepresented group	Tend to be socially conservative	Favor government spending on social programs	Support more gun rights	Tend to be conservative on social issues like gay marriage	Support spending on social programs, just not what they would see as wasteful spending

Sample Outline

Introduction: Give background information on the history of the Democratic Party. Also, provide a standard list of characteristics that all Democrats have in common.

Thesis statement: Democrats are actually quite diverse. There are three major groups of Democrats: liberals, conservative Democrats, and disadvantaged Democrats.

Body Paragraph 1:   Explain what makes a liberal a Democrat and what characteristics liberals have in common.

List three major characteristics of liberal Democrats.

Provide one or two specific examples of liberals and their characteristics that make them fit into this category.

Body Paragraph 2:   Explain what makes a disadvantaged Democrat a Democrat and what characteristics disadvantaged Democrats have in common.

List three major characteristics of disadvantaged Democrats.

Provide one or two specific examples of disadvantaged Democrats and their characteristics that make them fit into this category.

Body Paragraph 3:   Explain what makes a conservative Democrat a Democrat and what characteristics conservative Democrats have in common.

List three major characteristics of conservative Democrats.

Provide one or two specific examples of conservative Democrats and their characteristics that make them fit into this category.

Conclusion: Use one of the strategies from our "Conclusions" chapter.

This essay will likely contain some elements of comparison/contrast. You will observe differences and similarities between the categories. This type of essay will also define the broad topic and the categories within.

Use a graphic organizer like this one to organize categories for your classification essay assignment:

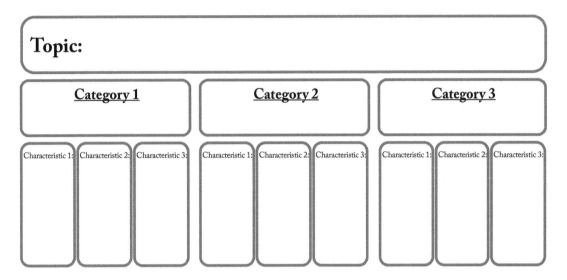

COMPARING AND CONTRASTING

Another strategy you may use to prove a point in a college writing assignment is comparing or contrasting two subjects. You have surely bickered with friends about which basketball player, movie, pop icon, or restaurant is better. You have argued to prove your point, that your favorite is the best one, and you have used evidence (scoring averages, plot twists, song lyrics, or fish tacos) to prove your point. You can do the same thing in your college essays. Think about how you might prove that your college is a great college. You might compare it to another college to highlight its virtues. The same might apply to a candidate for president, a type of job, a style of dress, or a character in a movie or book. For example, one way you might prove that your circumstances at your job at Jim's Deli are dire is to compare your experiences at Jim's to Barbara Ehrenreich's experiences working at Jerry's in her book *Nickel and Dimed: On Not Getting By in America*. Comparing or contrasting is a strategy that comes naturally to most students because it is so familiar. Here we give you a chance to fine-tune those skills for an academic setting.

First you want to make sure the two things you're comparing are worth comparing. So, you'll do some prewriting to see what points the two subjects have in common that can be compared or contrasted. You might first make a list of characteristics of one of the items you are comparing:

Ehrenreich's experience at Jerry's

- *No breaks*
- *Terrible uniforms*
- *Busy shifts*
- *Unfriendly coworkers*
- *Cruel manager (BJ)*
- *Filthy environment*
- *Rude customers*
- *Unpredictable schedule*

Then, write a list of comparable characteristics of the second subject:

Ehrenreich's experience at Jerry's

- *No breaks*
- *Terrible uniforms*
- *Busy shifts*
- *Unfriendly coworkers*
- *Cruel manager (BJ)*
- *Filthy environment*
- *Rude customers*
- *Unpredictable schedule*

My experience at Jim's

- *Breaks*
- *Terrible uniforms*
- *Busy shifts*
- *Unfriendly coworkers*
- *Some nice some cruel managers*
- *Dirty environment*
- *Some rude customers*
- *Unpredictable schedule*

Once you have completed your lists, choose the points of comparison you want to focus on and compose your thesis statement. You may or may not choose to list those points in your thesis statement. In this essay, the writer wants to prove that his job situation is dire, so he will focus on the similarities between Ehrenreich's job at Jerry's and his job at Jim's. Here is a possible thesis without the points of comparison:

Sample Thesis:

Even more than a decade after Ehrenreich's project, low-wage workers in food service like me still have to endure circumstances similar to what Ehrenreich describes in her book.

You might use a table like this one to ensure that you have support for the areas you have selected to compare.

Comparison/Contrast Table

Tentative thesis statement: Even more than a decade after Ehrenreich's project, low-wage workers in food service like me still have to endure circumstances similar to what Ehrenreich describes in her book.

Points of Comparison	Management	Physical Environment	Customers
Subject 1 Ehrenreich's job at Jerry's	Unprofessional	Dirty/Unsanitary	Rude/Demanding
	Examples: "B.J. the bitch" (34)	Examples:	Examples:
Subject 2 My job at Jim's	Unprofessional	Dirty/Unsanitary	Rude/Demanding
	Examples: My manager Marc tries to turn my coworkers and me against each other.	Examples:	Examples:

As you can see in the table, the writer identified three relevant points of comparison when comparing his job at Jim's to Ehrenreich's experience at Jerry's: the management, the physical environments, and the customers. You might identify more than three depending on the length and scope of your paper.

Once you identify the points of comparison, you might add them to your thesis statement. Here is a revised version of the writer's thesis statement that includes the points:

Sample Thesis (with points of comparison):

Even more than a decade after Ehrenreich's project, low-wage workers in food service like me still have to endure circumstances similar to what Ehrenreich describes in her book like unprofessional managers, an unsanitary physical environment, and demanding customers.

Remember that your essay is not just comparing or contrasting the two subjects, it is making a point. Another strategy you might use to strengthen your thesis statement is acknowledging the opposing viewpoint. In this case, some readers might think that a job at Jim's deli is great since, unlike Jerry's employees, Jim's employees get breaks. Thus, the writer might revise the thesis to say this:

Sample Thesis (with opposing view):

Although there are some advantages to working at Jim's over Jerry's, low-wage workers in food service like me still have to endure circumstances similar to what Ehrenreich describes in her book, like unprofessional managers, an unsanitary physical environment, and demanding customers.

Then the writer could also opt to remove the points of comparison and save them for the essay's topic sentences:

Sample Thesis:

Although there are some advantages to working at Jim's over Jerry's, low-wage workers in food service like me still have to endure circumstances similar to what Ehrenreich describes in her book.

As you can see, you have many options when it comes to a comparison/contrast essay thesis statement. However, there are some basic components that your thesis should contain:

1) An effective comparison/contrast essay thesis should name the subjects being compared or contrasted.

2) An effective comparison/contrast essay thesis should indicate whether the writer will focus on similarities, differences, or both between the two subjects.

3) Of course, an effective comparison/contrast essay thesis should make a point.

ORGANIZATION

When you write an entire essay that focuses on making a point by comparing and/or contrasting two things, there are two standard ways to construct that comparison. You can organize the essay by the points, focusing on one point at a time, or you might organize the essay by subjects, articulating all points about each subject separately. Here is an example based on the sample topic above:

POINT BY POINT CONSTRUCTION

Introduction (Use one of the strategies from our "Introductions" chapter and end with your thesis.)

> Thesis: Although there are some advantages of working at Jim's over Jerry's, low-wage workers in food service like me still have to endure circumstances similar to what Ehrenreich describes in her book.

Body Paragraph 1: First, Ehrenreich and I both experienced unprofessional managers at Jerry's and Jim's.

> Examples of unprofessional managers at Jerry's and Jim's

Body Paragraph 2: Also, Ehrenreich and I were both subjected to unsanitary working conditions at Jerry's and Jim's.

> Examples of unsanitary working conditions at Jerry's and Jim's

Body Paragraph 3: Finally, Ehrenreich dealt with demanding customers at Jerry's just like I do at Jim's.

> Examples of demanding customers at Jerry's and Jim's

Conclusion (Use one of the strategies from our "Conclusions" chapter.)

SUBJECT BY SUBJECT CONSTRUCTION

Introduction (Use one of the strategies from our "Introductions" chapter and end with your thesis. Be sure to introduce the author and title of the book.)

> Thesis: Although there are some advantages of working at Jim's over Jerry's, low-wage workers in food service like me still have to endure circumstances similar to what Ehrenreich describes in her book.

Section 1: At Jerry's Ehrenreich experienced unprofessional managers, an unsanitary environment, and demanding customers.

> Offer examples of unprofessional managers, an unsanitary environment, and demanding customers at Jerry's.

Section 2: Like Ehrenreich, I experience unprofessional managers, an unsanitary environment, and demanding customers at Jim's

> Offer examples of unprofessional managers, the unsanitary environment, and demanding customers at Jim's

Conclusion (Use one of the strategies from our "Conclusions" chapter.)

*The subject by subject construction will not fit into the conventional five-paragraph format. Depending on your essay's length and number of points, it may be just four paragraphs or more.

As you can see, you can easily plug the same content into either construction and see which one suits your topic best. You can also see in the example above how crucial transitions are to effective comparisons.

If you are focusing on differences between two subjects, use transitions like these:

| On the other hand | Unlike | While |

If you are focusing on similarities, use transitions like these:

| Similarly | Like | Likewise | Also |

Sometimes you might write an entire essay comparing and/or contrasting two things like the example above. Other times, you might use this strategy in addition to other strategies to make and prove a point. Either way, effectively comparing or contrasting two subjects in writing is a valuable skill for effective college writing. Use the table and outline forms on the following pages to help you develop your next comparison/contrast assignment.

Comparison/Contrast Table

Thesis statement: _____

_____

Points of Comparison			
Subject 1			
	Examples:	Examples:	Examples:
Subject 2			
	Examples:	Examples:	Examples:

Point by Point Construction

Introduction and Thesis:

BODY PARAGRAPH 1: Point one about your two subjects
Topic Sentence:

Point 1:

Details/Support/Examples

Point 1:

Details/Support/Examples

BODY PARAGRAPH 2: Point two about your two subjects.
Topic Sentence:

Point 2:

Details/Support/Examples

Point 2:

Details/Support/Examples

BODY PARAGRAPH 3: Point three about your two subjects.
Topic Sentence:

Point 3:

Details/Support/Examples

Point 3:

Details/Support/Examples

Conclusion: **(Summary and/or Closing Remarks)**

Subject by Subject Construction

Introduction and Thesis:

Section 1: All three points about one subject
Topic Sentence:

Point 1:

Details/Support

Point 2:

Details/Support

Point 3:

Details/Support

Section 2: All three points about the other subject
Topic Sentence:

Point 1:

Details/Support

Point 2:

Details/Support

Point 3:

Details/Support

Conclusion: **(Summary and/or Closing Remarks)**

EXTENDED DEFINITION

What is success? What is a good mother? What is a necessity? What is a Republican? What is love?

Defining a term or concept is another strategy you might use to make a point in a college writing assignment. This is a valuable skill and can be implemented in many different ways. You probably have answers to the questions above, but you'll notice that in many cases, your answers will be different from your classmates' answers. Thus, defining a term with your own unique definition and supporting that definition with evidence is a great way to argue a point in a college essay.

You may encounter an entire essay assignment in which you must define a term. It will likely be a term that different people define in different ways like "success." By offering your unique definition of success, your essay will make a unique point *about* success. You might also define a term associated with many misconceptions or misunderstandings like the political terms "Republican" and "Democrat." Many people have assumptions and beliefs about the political parties, but those are often not based on facts. Your extended definition gives you an opportunity to spell out the definition of a term or concept and clarify any misunderstandings or misconceptions. Here are some strategies for you to employ when you write an extended definition of a term:

1) Identify the term or concept's category.

2) Describe the term's general characteristics.

3) List categories within the term or concept. (See "Classification" for more on this.)

4) Provide specific examples and their related characteristics.

5) Offer characteristics that distinguish the concept from similar concepts.

6) Acknowledge complexities.

1) **Identify the term or concept's category.**

   A Republican is **a person** who . . .

   Success is **a state** in which . . .

   A necessity is **an item** which . . .

   An ape is **an animal** that . . .

   Love is **a feeling** that . . .

Any concept you seek to define will fall into a category, and it will likely be useful to your reader for you to name that category early in your definition.

2) **Describe the term's general characteristics.**

In addition to stating the category of your term, you must provide its general characteristics. A sentence stating the general characteristics of your concept or term may serve as your essay's thesis statement:

> In the United States, a Republican is a person who **supports keeping the government's power minimal and allowing the free market economy to dictate the nation's priorities. Republicans generally support business interests and oppose government spending on social services except the country's defense system.**

> Success is a state in which **a person has achieved his/her financial, spiritual, professional, and personal goals.**

> A good mother is a mother who **accepts her children, communicates with them, and helps them.**

These definitions are useful and provide characteristics of each concept, but an extended definition paints so vivid a picture that, even if the reader never heard of the term before reading your essay, he or she has a full grasp of it by the end of the essay. Thus, you will need to provide more information than just the general characteristics.

3) **List categories within the term or concept. (See "Classification" for more on this.)**

Are there different types of Republicans? Foods? Successes? Good mothers? Necessities? Apes? Love? Within most concepts, you can find some categories. When you want someone to really understand the concept, identifying those categories is useful.

> Some different types of Republicans are conservative Republicans, moderate Republicans, libertarians, and liberal Republicans.

> Apes come in two different categories: lesser apes and great apes.

> There are different types of success: financial success, personal success, spiritual success, and professional success.

> Romantic love, familial love, and plutonic love are three different types of love.

4) **Provide specific examples and their related characteristics.**

One of the most crucial elements of an extended definition is the providing of examples. You must provide specific examples of your concept and characteristics of each example that show what ties all of your examples together.

> Paul Ryan, Stacey Dash, Ted Cruz, and Donald Trump are all Republicans.

Orangutans, chimpanzees, gibbons, and gorillas are all apes.

I will be financially successful when I am out of debt and have a full time job that covers all of my bills every month with enough left over for me to enjoy social outings, save for the future, and donate to charity.

The love between Missy Mae and Joe in Zora Neale Hurston's short story "The Gilded Six Bits" is a perfect example of romantic love.

Food, water, and shelter are all necessities.

5) **Offer characteristics that distinguish the concept from similar concepts.**

A way to ensure that your reader could identify an ape or Republican after reading your essay is to contrast your concept or term with something similar and show how they are different. That way, your reader is sure not to confuse your concept with the similar concept. You might start that explanation with a sentence like one of these. Then you would continue with further examples and support.

Not all Republicans are conservatives.

Unlike Republicans, Democrats favor government spending on social services.

Many people confuse monkeys with apes, but the two are quite different from one another.

Success is not the same as wealth. Someone might be wealthy, but not successful.

Loving someone is different from just liking her.

Although people may eat Twinkies, Pringles, and Hot Pockets every day, those items are not really food.

6) **Acknowledge complexities.**

If a term or concept warrants an extended definition, it likely is a concept whose definition is not obvious or simple. There may be overlap between categories. Definitions may vary across populations or fields of study. You must acknowledge these complexities in your essay.

People may disagree about whether a Republican can ever actually be liberal.

Was Whitney Houston really successful?

Some readers may argue that the character Mrs. MacTeer in Toni Morrison's *The Bluest Eye* needs to be more loving and affectionate to be a good mother.

Many people would agree that education and healthcare are necessities, but art and beauty are more controversial examples.

You might focus and organize an extended definition in a number of ways. Here is a sample outline of an extended definition that focuses on three characteristics of a good mother and uses the above strategies:

Sample Outline:

Introduction: Introduce the text and acknowledge that different people have different definitions of a good mother. You might also mention how a good mother is distinct from a merely adequate mother.

Thesis: A good mother helps her children, communicates with them, and accepts them.

    Body Paragraph 1: First, a good mother is helpful.

        Ex 1: Daisy (Alvaro's mom in *After the Fire*)

            She took care of Alvaro when he returned home. She helped him bathe and dress. She did everything for him.

        Ex 2: My friend, Jennifer

            She helps her son with his homework. She helps him by driving him to basketball practice and games.

    Body Paragraph 2: A good mother is also communicative.

        Ex 1: Christine (Shawn's mom in *After the Fire*)

            Quotation showing Christine's level of communication with Shawn and how her mothering goes beyond what an adequate mother would do.

        Ex 2: My best friend's mom.

            She talks to my friend about everything. I learned about sex from her since my mom didn't want to talk about it.

    Body Paragraph 3: Finally, a good mother accepts her children.

        Ex 1: Christine (Shawn's mom) in *After the Fire*

            Quotation showing Christine's level of acceptance of Shawn.

        Ex 2: My grandma

            She accepted me even though my dad was upset when I shaved my head and got a tattoo on my neck.

Conclusion: If I am ever a mother, I will follow these great examples to be the best mother I can be.

We define terms and concepts or explain what things are all the time in our daily lives. Doing this effectively in writing will help you demonstrate your understanding of concepts in future college classes and will even help you propose a new idea or product to your colleagues, supervisors, or investors. Master using these strategies in your college writing classes, and be ready to explain what anything is at a moment's notice.

▌NARRATIVE

A narrative essay is generally an essay in which you tell a story based on your own experience in order to make a point. Narrative essays often focus on one specific life-altering or highly impactful event like one of these:

> your first day of college
>
> a breakup
>
> the day you decided to turn your life around
>
> your first day on the job
>
> an experience of great loss
>
> the day you met someone
>
> your most embarrassing moment
>
> your first experience using a life-altering technology

You might be assigned a narrative essay in response to a reading assignment. For example, *After the Fire: A True Story of Friendship and Survival* is a book about two college students who overcome a serious obstacle. In response to that book, your professor may ask you to write a narrative about a time when you overcame an obstacle. Your narrative should fulfill these basic guidelines:

1) **Write your narrative from a clear point of view.** Many narratives are written from the writer's (first person) point of view. Remember that you may explore a variety of options when it comes to your essay's point of view. An essay told through the point of view of a family pet or an antique wedding ring could be powerful. Don't be afraid to get creative and try something new.

2) **Include sensory details** that contribute to your essay's point and to your reader's experience reading. As you write describe what you saw, smelled, heard, tasted, and felt at the moment of your story. Use words to appeal to all five of your reader's senses: bright, sweet, pop, orange, sticky, smooth, round, breeze, muffled, rotten, cry, sharp, etc.

3) For a powerful narrative essay, **focus on one specific event**. For example, instead of describing your entire high school experience to make a point about life transitions and growing up, you might just write about your graduation day.

4) Avoid broad adjectives in your writing. Instead, **use nouns and verbs** to show your reader what occurred instead of telling your reader what occurred: light shone, students squirmed, hat pinched, sweat dripped, eyes stung, speaker droned, smile invited, etc.

5) **Include conflict.** Like in literature and film, conflict is what will give the essay energy and forward momentum. Talk about what obstacles were in your way in relationship to the event you chose. Then, a surprise resolution to the conflict is an effective way to keep your reader engaged and keep the essay from being predictable.

A great way to come up with ideas for a narrative essay is by doing some freewriting. Here is a sample of a student's ten-minute freewriting about overcoming an obstacle.

Overcoming an obstacle.

Let's see when have I overcome an obstacle? I am here in college that took something to get here. I didn't like high school and I had to work in high school to help my mom pay the rent. She needed my help. I guess having to work would be an obstacle. I have been out of school for five years working and now I am trying to come back, but everyone is 18 and I feel kind of old. I am still working and it's hard to do good in school having to work all the time. But I'm here. I could have not come back. Hmmmm what should I write now? Other obstacles. . . . Another thing that could have got in my way was when I got sick when I was in middle school. I was running track and one day I woke up and my stomach hurt. I thought it was food poisoning. I kept throwing up for a whole day. Then the next day I was still throwing up. And it wouldn't go away I went to the doctor. I was so sick I could not run and I missed a track meet. My coach was mad but I was too sick. When I want to the doctor, the doctor did tests but didn't find what was wrong. I was still feeling sick and could not run. But I was determined to run track so I went back to the doctor. The doctor finally tried another test it turned out I had Crohn's disease. Once I found that out I wanted to know what medicine I could take or what else I could do. The doctor gave me a prescription for medicine and told me to pay attention to what I ate. He said not to eat stuff that made me feel worse. I really wanted to run track again. He said I could but I had to start slow. I took the medicine and started to feel better. I went back to practice. My coach was glad to see me but it took a while for me to build my strength back to where it was. Plus I had to take my prescription really regularly or I would feel bad again. But then by the end of the year I had won 2 races and passed my previous record. That's overcoming an obstacle!!

Once you have completed a page of freewriting about your topic, think about what point your story makes. Then, develop a thesis statement. The student above settled on this:

> When people use good judgment and honor their limitations, they can overcome obstacles and achieve their dreams.

Then, construct an outline based on your freewriting to support your thesis.

Sample Outline

Introduction:

If your essay is in response to a text, introduce the text with its title and author's name and include background information for your essay:

Just as Shawn and Alvaro encountered a major obstacle to accomplishing their goals in Robin Gaby Fisher's book *After the Fire,* my goal was in jeopardy when I discovered I had Crohn's disease.

Use your prewriting to start your story in the introduction, which may be more than one paragraph.

Thesis:

When people use good judgment and honor their limitations, they can overcome obstacles and achieve their dreams.

Topic Sentence 1:

I took my doctor's advice by taking the drugs he prescribed and paying attention to what I ate.

Provide details (including sensory details) and support in the body paragraph.

Topic Sentence 2:

I was patient and honored my body by gradually resuming my track regimen.

Provide details (including sensory details) and support in the body paragraph.

Topic Sentence 3:

Despite the physical challenge of recovering from the disease and regaining my strength, I exceeded my previous track record.

Provide details (including sensory details) and support in the body paragraph.

Conclusion: Refer to your thesis, and employ one of our strategies from the "Conclusions" chapter.

Like this student, you have stories to tell. Writing a narrative essay will give you a chance to practice sharing your own experiences and telling your stories in order to make a point.

PROCESS ANALYSIS

Process analysis is writing that explains the steps of a process for your reader. As with the other types of essays, you will likely do this to prove a point. You might be proving how difficult or easy a certain process is. You might also show off your knowledge of a certain process integral to a particular discipline, like the process by which a bill becomes a law in the United States for a political science class or the process of human gestation for biology.

If you are writing so that your reader can implement the process, your essay will be written directly to your reader, and as a result, you will address the reader with the second person pronoun "you." For example, you might write a process essay describing the best way to get over a broken heart, how to ace a job interview, the steps necessary to transform one's eating habits, or what someone needs to do to break into the entertainment industry. You might also write about steps necessary to overcome a major obstacle to academic success. Any of those essays might be written based only on your experience or based partly or exclusively on a reading assignment. Let's look at the last one about overcoming obstacles to academic success. Here's a possible thesis statement:

> Although overcoming obstacles in the way of your academic success may seem impossible, you can do it by following these few simple steps.

Notice the use of the second person pronoun "you" in the thesis. This is a unique case because the writer is directing his words directly to his reader. Addressing your reader directly is the only case when using that pronoun is appropriate in an academic essay.

To start some prewriting for a process analysis, you might just make a list of all the possible steps in the process. That way, you can go back later to reorganize the steps and eliminate any that seem redundant or unnecessary. A student could write this essay in response to the book *After the Fire: A True Story of Friendship and Survival* by Robin Gaby Fisher and in that case would include steps the boys took to overcome their obstacles.

Sample Prewriting List: **Steps in Overcoming an Obstacle**	Narrowed List: **Steps in Overcoming an Obstacle**
appeal to your community for help engage in positive self-talk maintain a positive attitude acknowledge your obstacle ~~choose your friends wisely~~ ~~maintain perspective~~ ~~be determined~~ make a verbal commitment ~~support others~~ keep your commitment share your experience	1. acknowledge your obstacle 2. appeal to your community for help 3. make a verbal commitment 4. maintain a positive attitude a. engage in positive self-talk 5. keep your commitment 6. share your experience

Next, depending on the scope of the assignment, decide on what steps you will cover and in how much detail. Generally, you will dedicate a paragraph to each major step. Be sure to cover all of the major steps in the process. Then organize those steps in the appropriate order.

Here's the thesis statement, once more followed by a graphic organizer showing the steps in a different format:

> Although overcoming obstacles in the way of your academic success may seem impossible, you can do it by following these few simple steps.

Sample Prewriting in a Graphic Organizer

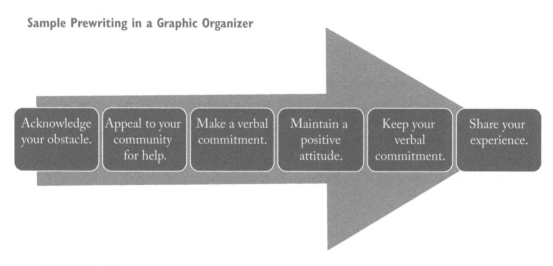

A process analysis essay is generally organized in chronological (time) order. You will start the body of the essay with what needs to be done or what happens first in the process, and you'll finish the body of the essay with what needs to be done or occurs last. As a result of this order, you must transition effectively between steps so that your reader is clear when you transition from one step to the next. Use these transitions between steps in your process analysis:

TRANSITIONS FOR CHRONOLOGICAL (TIME) ORDER				
after	at the same time	before	during	finally
first	last	later	next	now
secondly	soon	then	when	while

Now we will outline and use the transitions in our topic sentences:

Introduction (Use one or more of the strategies listed in Chapter 12, "Writing Introductions".)

Thesis: Although overcoming obstacles in the way of your academic success may seem impossible, you can do it by following these few simple steps.

Topic Sentence 1: First, in order to overcome an academic obstacle, you must acknowledge the obstacle.

Explain what you mean.

Offer one or more examples from your experience and/or a text.

Topic Sentence 2: The next step is to appeal to your community for help.

Explain what you mean.

Offer one or more examples from your experience and/or a text.

Topic Sentence 3: Then, you will need to make a verbal commitment.

Explain what you mean.

Offer one or more examples from your experience and/or a text.

Topic Sentence 4: Once you have made a commitment, you must maintain a positive attitude.

Explain what you mean.

Offer one or more examples from your experience and/or a text.

Topic Sentence 5: Along with your positive attitude, be sure to keep your verbal commitment.

    Explain what you mean.

    Offer one or more examples from your experience and/or a text.

Topic Sentence 6: Finally, share your experience.

    Explain what you mean.

    Offer one or more examples from your experience and/or a text.

Conclusion (Use one of the recommended strategies in Chapter 13, "Writing Conclusions".)

Notice that some transitions might refer back to the previous step. Within the essay's body paragraphs, you will describe the step in detail, and you can also provide examples of how the step may be executed. You might use your own personal experience or examples from a text or texts.

Close your essay with a conclusion that refers back to your essay's main point and uses one or more of the techniques from our "Conclusions" chapter.

Practicing the logical, linear, descriptive thinking it takes to lay out a process step by step in writing is certain to benefit you as you continue your college education and in your personal and professional pursuits.

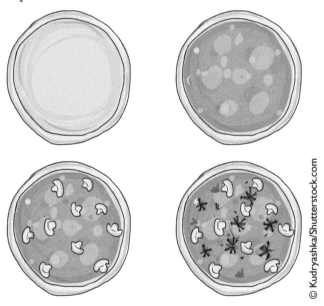

© Kudryashka/Shutterstock.com

16

ANALYZING VISUAL ARGUMENTS

Essays that analyze visual media are commonly assigned in composition classes, and with good reason. Analyzing visual media gives you the opportunity to engage in active critical thinking and cultural analysis.

What do flowers, chocolate, or the size of a diamond have to do with really loving someone? The advertisement industry has gotten most Americans to accept these symbols of love without question. We all know on a logical level that the size of the diamond in the engagement ring has nothing to do with how long a marriage will last. Kim Kardashian is ample proof of that. Nevertheless, DeBeers launched a brilliant ad campaign that convinced most Americans that no matter what their salaries, if

they really loved their fiancées, men would shell out two months' salary for the diamond. Anything less wasn't real love. And most Americans accepted that as truth! This is the opposite of critical thinking, and we want to make you aware of what we take for granted because advertisers tell us it is so. Visual arguments can be very compelling, but we need to exercise critical thinking. If we still pull out the plastic, fine, but let it be our choice, not the advertisers'.

Analyzing an advertisement on paper is a lot of fun. Many students discover a love for this type of analysis. It is a rewarding challenge to decipher how the ad executives make their case with visuals. We have included pointers below to consider when analyzing advertisements, but the same principles apply to all visual media. Every semester, students write wonderful papers about vintage advertisements, modern-day ads, photographs, paintings, graffiti, and public murals. The common denominator in the works students choose is that they have subtext and a thesis.

It might surprise you to discover that just like in essays, all advertisements have a thesis. Oftentimes, the thesis attempts to convince you to part with your money by buying whatever it is the advertiser is selling, whether it be the latest handbag or a charitable cause. However, the ad doesn't usually come right out and tell you to open your wallet. Most consumers would resent such a direct approach and refuse. Instead, advertisements **persuade** you to purchase something by presenting visual **evidence** that it's in your best interest to buy the product, that you should "just do it," that you'd feel better, look better, and be happier if you did. Does the evidence-based persuasive argument sound familiar? It should. This is the same strategy a persuasive argument essay employs. However, unlike writers, advertisers get away with using a lot of logical fallacies in their argumentation. Have your list of logical fallacies handy (See Chapter 17) as you flip through a magazine looking at ads. You will be amazed to see logical fallacies in almost every ad. There are a few steps to follow and we'll show you how to make the most of this type of assignment so you can shine as a critical thinker.

First, let's flex your critical thinking muscles. Each of the following advertisements makes an argument.

Visual Argument Exercise:

State in a sentence or two what you think the arguments or theses are in the following ads.

The "Corporate Flag" and the following three ads are spoof ads from *Adbusters.org*. *Adbusters* contains many spoof ads that attempt to change our perceptions of the society in which we live. Being familiar with the original ad campaigns they are imitating would be crucial to appreciating the spoof ads and recognizing their dark humor.

ACLU versus God

Corporate Flag

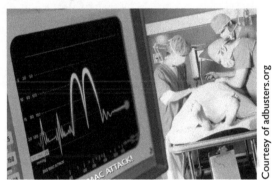

Big Mac Attack

Joe Chemo

BP Vietnam

Now that you've found the thesis, consider these points when writing an essay.

Below is a standard paper assignment used in one of our English classes.

Choose your ad wisely. When leafing through a magazine, be sure to choose an advertisement that has subtext. **Subtext is the layer of meaning beneath the obvious literal meaning on the surface.** Subtext is what we mean when we say "reading between the lines." For example, Newport cigarette's "Newport pleasure!" ads never show people smoking. Instead, their latest campaign shows young, happy couples engaging in outdoor physical activities like biking on a bright green background. It doesn't say so anywhere in the ad, but the subtext suggests that cigarette smoking can be part of a healthy, "green" lifestyle. When you read that sentence, you know it is absurd, but when you see what appears to be visual "proof" of that statement, you might be willing to shelve your rational reservations about smoking enough to buy a pack, figuring, if you are a smoker, that this is a better, healthier alternative to your brand. If you are a young kid who has never heard that smoking is unhealthy, you might actually be tempted to think by looking at the picture that cigarette smoking would actually make you healthier and happier. This is a logical fallacy, of course. The cigarettes did not cause the couple to be athletic (or happy), but the co-existence of these two ideas in the same ad leads us to the faulty conclusion that there is a relationship between the two. What many consumers fail to remember as they are having an emotional reaction is that they are looking at models and a carefully-staged situation; these are not real people or real situations.

Because of the prevalence of subtext (and logical fallacy) in them, cigarette, alcohol, and fragrance ads are strong choices to analyze. Why do you think that is? Think about why ads for these products in particular would have to use logical fallacies to convince their viewers. In an advertisement for women's perfume, you are likely to find a beautiful naked woman with a man in the background. The surface text is "buy this perfume." The subtext is that if you buy the perfume, you will be as attractive as a model and that you will have great sex with people who also look like models. We all know that spraying on expensive perfume does not affect the way we look or have sex, but the ad suggests that it does. (Fabric softener also makes your clothes smell good, but we never see ads of sweaty, scantily-clad launderers). The viewer accepts the fallacy on a subconscious level because he or she wants to believe, and because it upholds a value, stereotype, or an ideal that the target audience shares.

WHAT IS A TARGET AUDIENCE?

The target audience is the ideal consumer for the product, and hence the specific category of people the marketer wants to attract. The target audience for sports cars is men, ages 18–45. The target audience for fabric softener is middle-aged women. These two demographics are attracted to ads for different reasons, and the product itself affects the role the viewer wants to play in the "story." Women buying fabric softener want to feel like good homemakers who provide the best for their families. The same women buying "Obsession" perfume want to feel sexy on a hot date. What makes advertisements so powerful, is that the viewer actually inserts him or herself psychologically into the ad. Notice that often faces are obscured to facilitate this process. (Think of all the silhouettes in the iPod advertisements.). The fragrance subtext suggests that if you are a woman, you will be the center of a man's attention, thus appealing to a consumer's desire for acceptance and love. In male fragrance ads, these roles are reversed. Likewise, alcohol and cigarette print ads often suggest that their products will make you the life of a party filled with gorgeous people fascinated by your body and everything you have to say. They promise instant cool. The subtext in these ads has been so seductive that alcohol and cigarette ads are no longer permitted to air as television commercials. Studies show that their effect on consumers, particularly young consumers whose sense of self may not be fully developed, is too great, and thus too dangerous.

In general, consumers are very susceptible to ads that address issues of self-image. Marketers know this and play on our insecurities when devising subtext. The societal markers of a person's sense of self-worth are predominantly superficial, external qualities such as youth, beauty, and wealth. Indeed, you can learn a lot about a culture's values by looking at its advertisements.

Because these ideals and values are embedded in the message, an ad with subtext might mean you will have to sit with it for a few moments before you "get it." This is normal. Advertisers want to make you work to understand meaning because then you are more curious and more invested in the advertisement. If you flip through and understand the thesis too quickly, you are likely to forget it just as quickly.

Note: Although a quickly understood ad seems like a safer bet, choosing ads that are too obvious to analyze is a mistake. The Fat Pill 1000 with a page full of text and a box devoted to side effects will be pretty straightforward and low on visuals. Similarly, clothing catalog photos also have limited subtext, and you will run out of things to say in the first paragraph. Though it may initially seem more challenging, if you choose an advertisement or painting rich with subtext, you will have a lot more layers to talk about in your paper.

HOW DO I START?

Like you would for any research paper, do some prewriting in the form of lists and observations. Answer as many of these questions as you can:

1) **What's the idea being put forth?** What's the political agenda or argument being expressed by the image? **This will be your thesis.**

2) Where did you find the ad? **Who is the intended audience?** How do you think the intended audience is meant to feel?

3) What is the picture's **context**? History? The picture didn't just turn up in a vacuum. Advertisements and products after 9/11 were literally draped in American flags (Ralph Lauren, Tommy Hilfiger, etc). What kind of context or contemporary moment is your ad/picture a product of?

4) What are the **visual details** of the picture? Start with a brief orientation to the image as if your reader can't see it. Notice all details—framing, color choice, background, mood, atmosphere, tone, shape, connotations, and emphasis. This is your paper's **evidence**. Be specific and thorough.

5) **Examine text**, font, etc. Analyze any written words (if there are any) and their meanings.

6) If you are writing about an ad, think about or research the company's demographic/target consumers. If your subject is a painting, research the artist or photographer. This could be a great excuse to spend a few hours at a local art museum or gallery.

HOW DO I WRITE AN ESSAY ABOUT THE VISUAL?

Start with a snappy introduction style from the seven we gave you. (See Ch. 13, "Writing Introductions"). Then, give a brief description of the ad's visuals as if the reader hadn't seen the photo, "The latest Newport Menthol cigarette advertisement shows a young, happy African-American couple biking outside on a bright green background."

Now launch into the analysis. Through your prewriting, you should have developed a thesis such as, "The visual elements of Newport's latest ad campaign suggest to the viewer that smoking is part of a healthy lifestyle."

Now emphasize all details that support that thesis —framing, color choice, background, mood, atmosphere, tone, shape, connotations, and visual emphasis. How do the written words reinforce the picture's argument? Look at the font style used and determine why it was chosen. How does "go army!!" feel different from "**GO ARMY!**"? This is your paper's **visual evidence**. Be specific and thorough. This will take up a lot of your paper. The order in which you put the visual and textual elements is entirely up to you, but usually, the evidence is grouped thematically. Just remember to discuss all of them as an aspect of your thesis.

Visuals and text are not the only types of evidence you have, however. **Now you must research.** When you write a paper analyzing an ad, incorporate as many of the six kinds of evidence as you can. **You will use this research to give your advertisement <u>context</u>.** If writing about a cigarette ad, you might research, and add to your argument, statistics about the effects of smoking or the age and habits of smokers; you might add personal experience with the brand or conduct a survey of your classmates, asking them to respond to the ad. Does it make them want to buy the cigarettes? What emotion does it make them feel? You should also research both the product and the magazine in which you find the ad. This can often be done by visiting the product and magazine's own websites. The goal of company websites is to give a company profile or personality; click on the "About Us" tabs for a great source of quotes and data that shows how the companies think of themselves and the image they are trying to project and to whom. If the advertiser has done his or her homework, the demographic (target audience) for both the magazine and the product should be the same. We wouldn't expect the same advertisements in *Vibe* as we would in *Martha Stewart Living*, or *Sports Illustrated* and *The New Yorker*. Where you find the ad will tell you who is likely to buy the product. If Newport cigarettes have a majority of African-American female customers, it would make sense for them to advertise in *Ebony* and feature African-American female models as the center of male attention. **Be sure to link your research to your thesis**.

Finally, after you have made your case for the advertisement's argument and put it in context, you might conclude with a brief discussion of whether or not the ad effectively communicates its message or whether it misses the mark, and how this reveals certain values that we hold as a society.

Remember to **submit a photocopy** of your ad/painting to your instructor along with your paper, so that he or she can easily refer to it.

VISUAL MEDIA PAPER ANALYSIS PEER OR SELF REVIEW WORKSHEET

Before you submit your paper in-class, take a moment to go through this checklist of ten items and be sure that you have covered your bases. You can use this on your own paper or on a friend's. Whoever wrote the paper is the "author/writer."

1. Does the paper look professional? Is the paper properly formatted? 3-4 pages, double-spaced, paragraphs indented? Are there typos or proofreading mistakes? Run-ons and/or sentence fragments?

2. What kind of introduction does the paper have? What strategy did the author use? Factual shocker, bold statement, mapping, personal experience, etc.? Is it effective? Does it make you want to read more? Could it be improved upon? If so, how?

3. Does the writer orient the reader by giving a very brief summary of the ad? "This Suave deodorant ad depicts a woman dangling over a lagoon of crocodiles."

4. What is the paper's thesis? What is the ad or artwork's argument? What behavior is it trying to encourage or discourage in the consumer?

5. Does every paragraph support a different aspect of that thesis?

6. What kind of evidence has the writer used? Data and statistics, personal experience, shared values, authority (sources)? Are quotes properly marked off with quotation marks?

7. Do you feel that the author researched the paper enough? Do you still have questions about the **product** (or organization paying for the ad) or the **periodical** (magazine)? Have the media's demographic and the targeted consumer been discussed and researched?

8. Have the **visual components** of the ad been addressed fully, or have important details been left out?

9. What about the conclusion? Does it restate the major points? (It doesn't have to, to be good.) Does it bring us back to the issues raised in the introduction? (It doesn't have to, but this is often effective.) Does the paper end on a strong, well-written statement? (Remember, unlike Eliot, it's nice to end with a bang, not a whimper.)

10. Has the paper made you see things you might not have noticed initially in the ad? In other words, has the writer discussed both the text and the subtext of the ad? The subtext involves the audience's associations and the subliminal, sometimes out of focus, elements in the ad or photograph.

The sample student essay that follows discusses the racial implications of the April 2008 cover of *Vogue*. Please visit: http://watchingthewatchers.org/news/1378/annie-lei-bovitz-monkeys-around-lebron to see the *Vogue* cover alongside a World War I recruitment ad. The cover spurred a lot of controversy. You decide: Is this a racially-insensitive photo meant to remind us of a shameful past, or is it a positive cover intended to show how far African-Americans have come? One student gives his theory below.

Visual Argument Sample Student Essay:

David Spielman
Spielman 1

Dr. Katherine Boutry

English 103

14 Oct. 2012

Destroy the Brute, Stir the Pot, Make a Profit: *Vogue*'s Recipe to Sell
Racial Controversy

In March of 2008, *Vogue* announced that its April 2008 cover would feature
basketball superstar LeBron James and supermodel Gisele Bündchen. LeBron
James would be the first African-American male and only the third male ever
to grace the cover of the magazine. Touted by *Vogue* as a historical issue, the
editors chose famed photographer Annie Leibovitz to shoot the cover photo.
Upon release of the issue, however, many cried foul as LeBron James appeared
to be posed along with Gisele Bündchen in a racially insensitive manner. *Vogue*
denied the allegations of racism, but upon close examination of the photo,
one might conclude that the cover was not only racially insensitive, but also a
purposefully constructed controversy created by *Vogue* with the intent to boost
sales.

The cover photo displays a fierce looking LeBron James, crouched down,
bouncing a basketball with his right hand and clutching Gisele Bündchen
in his left hand. He is wearing a black basketball uniform, looking directly
into the lens, and appears to be releasing a primal scream. Gisele Bündchen
is wearing a strapless, aqua green dress and looks directly into the lens with
a huge smile on her face and her long blonde hair blows back. The lettering
on the cover is predominantly white, with some notable red exceptions: the

title *Vogue* at the top of the cover, the number 87, and the words "Secrets of the Best Bodies" at the bottom of the page between LeBron's legs. LeBron's head is directly covering the bottom and the middle of the letters O and G in the word *Vogue*. The top of the red O and G letters curve away perfectly from LeBron's head, evoking the image of large beastly horns protruding from the top of his head.

The photo brings to mind the image of a beast-like, crazed savage clutching the innocent white woman in his arms. This is an image haunting black males since the Reconstruction Era of the United States. Dr. David Pilgrim, Professor of Sociology at Ferris State University writes, "The brute caricature portrays Black men as innately savage, animalistic, destructive, and criminal… terrifying predators who target helpless victims, especially white women." The photo was heavily criticized and compared to a 1933 King Kong poster which depicted the giant ape clutching actress Faye Wray in his hand, baring his teeth and hunched over in a menacing stance. It drew further criticism when placed side by side with a World War I propaganda recruitment poster featuring a cartoon caricature of a giant ape posed in the same stance as LeBron James on the *Vogue* cover. The similarities are too many to ignore. The ape clutches a bare-breasted white woman with an aqua green dress in his left arm, very similar in appearance to the dress Gisele Bündchen wears. On the top of the recruitment poster in bold letters are the words, "Destroy This Mad Brute." Moreover, the similarities were not lost on the public and critics. In an article in *USA Today*, magazine analyst Samir Husni is quoted saying that the *Vogue* cover "screams King Kong" (LeBron James). He went on to say that "given *Vogue*'s influential history, covers are not something that the magazine does in a rush… So when you have a cover that reminds people of King Kong and brings those stereotypes to the front, black man wanting white woman, it's not innocent."

When confronted with this information one might ask, would *Vogue* magazine purposefully release such a controversial issue? Given the evidence from past pictures and magazine analysts, we must come to the conclusion yes. Further proof lies in the photographer responsible for this picture. Annie Leibovitz is a world-renowned photographer, famous for her influential advertising campaign photos and her work with *Rolling Stone*, *Vanity Fair*, and *Vogue* magazines. Leibovitz is also known for her photos recreating historical art, and her ability to stir up controversy with some of her more provocative photos. Leibovitz created controversy with her 1980 *Rolling Stone* cover which featured a naked John Lennon cuddled next to a clothed Yoko Ono. She further stirred the pot with her 1991 cover of *Vanity Fair* featuring a naked and pregnant Demi Moore, and again in 1992, with Moore naked and a suit painted on her body. A few months after the release of the *Vogue* cover in June 2008, Leibovitz came under fire again for her provocative photos of what appeared to be a semi-nude, underage Miley Cyrus with her father, Billie Ray Cyrus.

Clearly, *Vogue* specifically chose Annie Leibovitz to take this photo with the intent to boost sales. One might ask what the editors hope to achieve by releasing such a racially insensitive image and what they are attempting to sell. The answer is simple. Stirring the pot of controversy creates dialogue about the magazine and can in turn generate higher sales. Magazine analyst Husni suggests, "The controversy could increase sales as people rush out to get a collectors edition." Furthermore, in a 2008 *Business Insider* article, Hilary Lewis writes about the *Vanity Fair* issue featuring Miley Cyrus, "Controversial *Vanity Fair* photos might have hurt her career but they certainly helped the mag, which sold 435,000 copies of the issue." The article further quotes *Portfolio's Mixed Media Blog*, "Annie Leibovitz's outrage-baiting didn't do much for *Vogue*, but it helped give *Vanity Fair* its best-selling issue of the year."

Although *Vogue*'s target demographic is women between the ages of 18 and 34, the magazine undoubtedly used a recipe to create a controversy with the hope of generating interest and opening up opportunity for sales in a broader market. This is a known business strategy; "any publicity is good publicity." Business and marketing motivational speaker George Torok advises, "Take a controversial position. Offend someone and attract your target market. . . . Controversy can be a powerful branding technique."

Vogue attempted to "destroy the brute" by portraying James as aggressive and beast like. The editors next attempted to "stir up" controversy by recreating a deeply-rooted racial image of a black brute carrying off the white woman. However, they failed to stir up the kind of controversy that sells. The issue sold just over 300,000 copies which is the second-worst selling April issue of the decade, and the second-lowest selling issue of 2008. The fact that *Vogue* attempted to profit from such a sensitive issue as race exposes that the deep-seated racial feelings that were a major part of this country in the past are not behind us, but alive and well. Advertising is an integral part of our society, but using hate of any kind to generate profits has no place in our society.

Works Cited

"LeBron James Vogue Cover Called Racially Insensitive." *USA Today,* The Associated Press, 24 Mar. 2008, www.usatoday30.usatoday.com/life/people/2008-03-24-vogue-controversy_N.htm. Accessed 17 Oct. 2011.

Lewis, Hilary. "Nude Miley Cyrus Pics Blew Vanity Fair Sales Through Roof." *Business Insider,* 18 Jul. 2008, www.businessinsider.com/2008/7/nude-miley-cyrus-pics-blew-vanity-fair-newsstand-sales-through-roof. Accessed 17 Oct. 2011.

Pilgrim, David. "The Brute Caricature." *Jim Crow Museum of Racist Memorabilia,* Ferris State University, Nov. 2000, www.ferris.edu/jimcrow/brute//. Accessed 17 Oct. 2011.

Responts, Mike. "LeBron Cover Was a Flop." *Mike Responts: The Blog: Fear and Blogging from the Pacific Northwest,* WorldPress.com, 7 July 2008, www.mikeresponts.wordpress.com/page/43/. Accessed 17 Oct. 2011.

Torok, George. "Branding Secret: Controversy Sells." *Articles for Business Professionals,* 6 Sep. 2010, www.torok.com/articles/marketing/Controversy Sells.html. Accessed 17 Oct. 2011.

Sample Student Essay:

Kathryn Hansen   Hansen 1

Dr. Katherine Boutry

English 103

25 Oct. 2012

A Clothing Company Marketing Tactic: Keeping Up with the Joneses

In 1913, a cartoonist by the name of Arthur R. Momand created a cartoon strip entitled "Keeping up with the Joneses." The title of this cartoon strip has become a well-known phrase which means roughly "to keep up appearances equal to your affluent neighbors." The clothing company, Jones New York, uses this popular phrase as a marketing tool to sell their products. On the surface this may appear to be a clever play on words. But there is a destructive underlying message. The ad would have us believe that in order to be successful, beautiful, and even happy, we must look outside ourselves. Jones New York is telling us in their advertisement that we must keep up appearances and compete with those we see as our betters. Jones New York wants us to believe that if we wear their jeans, we will be "keeping up with the Joneses" and our desires will come to fruition.

In a recent *Glamour* magazine, Jones New York placed a two-page ad to sell their Jones Jeans Brand. The left page of the ad features a yellow cab whose license plate number is the address of Jones New York executive offices in New York City. Under the license plate frame are the words in big, bold white lettering, "Jones New York Jeans, with secret slimming features." On the right page, two beautiful models walk down a New York City street sandwiched between two yellow cabs. The blonde, super slim models, who are wearing Jones Jeans with slimming features, would look no different in jeans without the slimming feature. On this page the words "keeping up with the Jones" takes center stage with white italic lettering. The models look like they just stepped out of a cab and have somewhere fun and exciting to go. The reader gets the impression that these women live an exhilarating lifestyle, one that would certainly be appealing to the career woman.

Glamour magazine targets an audience of fashion-forward women between the ages of 18 to 49. Additionally, the focus of *Glamour* is luxury consumer items that appeal to women. So it is no accident that Jones New York placed this ad in *Glamour* magazine. According to the Jones New York website, Jones New York is "dressing the modern American woman." Most of their women's clothing is designed for the working woman, so we can say that Jones New York's target audience is the modern, career woman.

There is nothing wrong with wanting to look and feel one's best. Fashion is one way in which we express ourselves. Women especially love to wear clothing that makes them feel good. However, the underlying suggestion we get from Jones New York is that just being ourselves is not good enough. The company wants us to believe that we have to keep up with the arbitrary Joneses who may have more money, more beauty, and more success than we do. The phrase "to keep up" assumes a constant reaching for something but never quite catching it. Granted, it is good to have something great to aspire to. We all want to achieve something great and be the best we can be. However, Jones New York would have us believe that we can achieve greatness simply by wearing their jeans.

In 1913 when Momand created his cartoon, "Keeping up with the Joneses," the Joneses were very literally the neighbors in the house down the street. It's logical to assume that the income level of different people in the same neighborhood would be reasonably comparable. Juliet Schor PhD, professor of sociology at Boston College, writes in her book, *The Overspent American*, that in today's society, because of television, internet and other media sources such as newspapers and magazines, we have a much broader base with which to compare ourselves. The Joneses don't just live next door anymore; they live everywhere. Today's women are comparing themselves to actresses they see on television and in the movies. What celebrities wear, how they look, and the lifestyles they lead are widely coveted. However, the average American woman's income does not compare to the extravagant incomes of actresses and other women of means she admires. During an interview with *Multinational Monitor*, Schor contends that status plays a significant role in consumer spending. Schor asserts those things which are visible to the public, what you own, what you wear, and what you drive, are all major factors in being able to "keep up." Moreover, she says that,

> Companies play an important role in keeping this going. They spend a lot of time and effort through advertising and promotion to get people to play the game, to get people to participate, to keep us upscaling, to keep us buying… to keep us desperate to keep up in the game.

Advertisements are designed to make us want "desperately" what they are selling. Advertisers use our emotions as a tool in this process.

There is a price to pay for trying to obtain an outer appearance for the sake of status. "Keeping up with the Joneses" can be brutal on one's wallet. The idea that we can and should have everything we want is more common today than ever before. According to data found on CreditCards.com, as of August 2012, Americans owe $854.9 billion dollars in revolving credit, and most of that is from credit card debt (Dilworth). We are a nation of living beyond our means.

The "keeping up with the Joneses" attitude may even have contributed to the most recent housing crisis. We are being led to believe by advertising and the media that we should have the biggest and the best of everything, that nothing is out of our reach. Credit card companies make it easy for us to obtain what we desire. We must ask ourselves, why are we so swayed by the media and outside forces? The driving factor that would persuade people to spend beyond their means for the sake of "keeping up" lies in our emotions.

For everything that we put on the outside, there is motive that can be found on the inside. Susan Matt, author of *Keeping up with the Joneses: Envy in American Consumer Society, 1890-1930*, believes that the emotion triggered in advertising is envy. In her book, Matt explains that during the years between 1890 and 1930 values changed. Specifically, in regards to middle class urban women, she explains that during those years, there was a shift in thinking from believing that dressing above their station in life or above their means was a form of dishonesty and was looked down upon. But by the following generation of women, the shift in thinking changed dramatically; the better you dressed, the more appealing you became. Matt asserts that men and women envied that which other people had more than ever before in history, mainly because of the introduction of magazines and catalogues during that time (Clendinning).

Jones New York is shamefully using envy as a tool to persuade women to buy its clothes. But Jones New York also knows that career women want and need support from each other. Again, cleverly, they have used this knowledge to launch yet a different sort of marketing campaign. In contrast to the "keeping up with the Jones[es]" marketing tactic, Jones New York launched a marketing campaign that supports and encourages strong-willed and confident women. Jones New York chose political analyst Dee Dee Myers to be the national ambassador for the "Empowering your Confidence" campaign. Myers knows what it takes to be a leader. She was the first woman ever to hold the position of White House Press Secretary (Myers). One of Myers duties as Ambassador is to mentor JNY empowerment fund winners. The grants were given to women to help them reach their personal and professional goals. Jones New York's 2011 Annual report states that "Jones New York sought out women to feature in this campaign who have built, created, and nurtured businesses, ideas, and people – the embodiment of empowerment and confidence" (Jones New York). Clearly, a woman who is empowered and confident is a leader, an innovative thinker, a woman who paves her own path.

Jones New York indeed uses clever marketing, appealing to our emotions, knowing the desire all women have to look and feel their best. While it is commonly accepted that companies often play on our emotions to sell their products, we need to be able to recognize it when we see it, and not get suck[er]ed in. Instead of believing the lie that we must be "keeping up with the Joneses," women should be reminded that being themselves is enough. An empowered woman is not a follower; she does not need to keep up with anyone except herself. An empowered woman paves her own way. We could say that Jones New York should think twice about the implications of its slogans, but more importantly, women should have enough confidence in their own unique beauty, talent, and gifts to walk right by jeans they don't need.

Works Cited

Clendinning, Anne. "Keeping Up with the Joneses: Envy in American Consumer Society, 1890-1930." *Urban History Review,* vol. 34, no. 2, 2006, pp. 58-60, *ProQuest Research Library.* search-proquest-com.library.wlac.edu/docview/216506174/1D9196E59654006PQ/1?accountid=38212. Accessed 8 Oct. 2012.

Dilworth, Kelly. "Consumer Credit Card Balances Rise." *CreditCards.com,* 5 Oct. 2012, www.creditcards.com/credit-card-news/g19-federal_reserve-consumer_credit-card-balances-rise-100512-1276.php. Accessed 2012.

Jones New York. *The Jones Group 2011 Annual Report.* Last10k.com, www.last10k.com/sec-filings/jny/0000874016-11-000010.htm. Accessed 8 Oct. 2012.

"Keeping up with the Jones" by Jones New York. Advertisement. *Glamour,* Oct. 2012, p. 115.

Myers, Dee Dee. "About Dee Dee Myers." 2008. Accessed 8 Oct. 2012.

Schor, Juliet B. "The Overspent American Upscaling, Downshifting, and the New Consumer." *The New York Times Books,* 1998, archive.nytimes.com/www.nytimes.com/books/first/s/schor-overspent.html?_r=1. Accessed 8 Oct. 2012.

"The Overspent American: An Interview with Juliet Schor." *Multinational Monitor,* vol. 19, no. 9, 1998, pp. 21-4, www.multinationalmonitor.org/mm1998/98sept/interview-schor.pdf. Accessed 8 Oct. 2012.

CHAPTER CHAPTER CHAPTER 17

ADVANCED MODES OF ARGUMENTATION

INTRODUCTION TO LOGICAL ARGUMENT

Does the word "argument" make you think of fighting or disagreeing with someone? That might be because sometimes what we disagree with others about is a difference in opinions. An opinion is a "position" (perspective) that a person takes on a specific issue. You probably have positions on a million different things, like which is the best restaurant in town, or whether or not it is important to go to college.

Often we get into disagreements because our opinions differ. But between two reasonable adults, the "winner" (for lack of a better term) of a difference in opin-

ions is the person who has the most solid reasoning. The root of the word "reasoning" emphasizes this. The person who wins any argument often has the most convincing evidence. When constructing a formal, logical argument, we need to support our position with strong evidence. From this point on we will refer to "reasons" as "support." As humans we can't walk around without legs! In the same way, an argument needs something to stand on—it needs support.

To construct an argument, you must formally state an opinion as an assertion. A formal assertion is called a **premise**. In logical reasoning, a conclusion is derived from a number of premises, often two. Logical arguments can allow us to consider the possibilities of things which differ from actual reality. Philosophers, scientists, and mathematicians can draw conclusions from premises which, if true, can take us in powerful new directions. Therefore, philosophers make a distinction between what is true and what is valid. Something that is **true** corresponds to reality. **Valid** follows from the premises. This allows us to make inferences about things which may not yet exist—in other words, logic allows us to think hypothetically.

For example, let's say I have a wet shoe I need dry by morning. I'm not sure what to do, but I will construct an argument to reason out a possible solution to my dilemma. My argument is built from two possible premises which contribute to the possible conclusion.

> Heat dries wet things.
>
> Heat rises.
>
> Therefore, if I hang my shoe near the ceiling, it might dry by morning.

The ancient Greek philosophers standardized a system for writing out an argument, called a **syllogism**. This formal argument structure is drawn graphically as two sentences above a line, with the conclusion below it (similar to a mathematical proof.) In a syllogism with two premises, the first premise is called the **major premise** and the second premise is called the **minor premise**. Below follows an example of a classic Greek syllogism.

SAMPLE SYLLOGISM

All Greeks are humans.	**Major Premise**
All humans are mortal.	**Minor Premise**
Therefore all Greeks are mortal.	**Conclusion**

Notice that the conclusion is derived from the two premises and depends on them for support. The minor premise is built on the major premise. If both are valid, the conclusion is valid.

Classical and contemporary philosophers have not only defined the elements of argument, but categorized the logical processes we use to reason out arguments. These are known as **deductive and inductive reasoning**.

DEDUCTIVE REASONING

It is often said that **deductive reasoning** is a "top-down" process, meaning that if the premises are true, the conclusion should follow from the premises. This is the process that can be used by detectives. Premises are determined from the scene of the crime. For example, two premises might be:

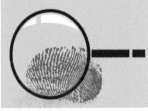
© abeadev/Shutterstock.com

> The victim has a bullet in his neck, which measures five feet from the ground when the body is perpendicular to the ground.

> Additional bullets hit the door [behind where he apparently stood] in a horizontal trajectory.

The conclusion derives from the premises:

> Only a person at least six feet tall could have shot the victim, for a shorter shooter's bullets would have been shot at an upward angle.

In many respects, deductive arguments reason from general premises (which depend on established principles or values) to a specific conclusion.

Furthermore, deductive arguments often locate their premises in established principles or "facts" if possible, for if the premises are valid, the conclusion will be valid as well, making the entire argument **sound**. Consider the following deductive argument.

> The professor stated on the syllabus that late papers will have penalty points subtracted.

> My paper is three days late.

> Therefore, my paper cannot earn a perfect score.

This argument is based on a principle established by the professor. The argument cannot assume that the rules will change for any reason.

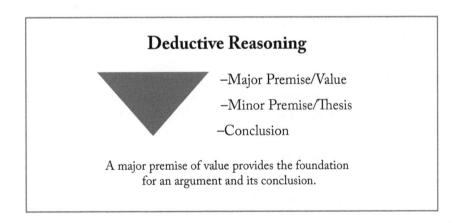

Deductive Reasoning

–Major Premise/Value

–Minor Premise/Thesis

–Conclusion

A major premise of value provides the foundation
for an argument and its conclusion.

Inductive Reasoning

A + B + C → Conclusion

Evidence leads to a likely conclusion.

Inductive arguments are based on observation and statistical probability, and are inferential in nature. Inductive reasoning argues from specific (experience or observation) to general (principle or value.) For an inductive argument, if the premises are probably true, then the chances are good that the conclusion might be true. The strength of an inductive argument depends on the size of the evidence sample and how the evidence was collected (over how long a time period, for example, and in what circumstances). Consider this inductive argument.

> Every morning this week, the bus has come at 8 a.m. Therefore, it will come this morning (Saturday morning) at 8 a.m.

This argument is based on one premise, the observation of an emerging pattern. However, in reality, patterns are not always consistent. This person has seen the bus at 8 a.m. Monday through Friday mornings, but Saturday it might be on a weekend schedule. It might come at 9 a.m. Saturday and Sunday mornings, and then revert back to the 8 a.m. business day schedule. If this is true, the observer has not observed the *entire* pattern, and there's the rub: one cannot be *sure* what will happen until it actually does (or does not). This is the weakness of inductive arguments; they are simply not conclusive.

The strongest inductive argument is built with a large evidence sample. Probability that the conclusion is true grows in direct proportion to the size of the sample. For example, if the observer had seen the bus come every day at 8 a.m. every day for an entire year, the argument would become more convincing.

As you learn to develop strong, evidence-based arguments, you will want to choose careful logic. You may build a deductive argument from a series of linked premises, or you may infer the probability of an outcome with a pattern-based inductive argument.

AVOIDING LOGICAL FALLACIES

"Logical Fallacies" is a term we use to label the kinds of logic potholes that thinkers can step into when they argue a point. Fallacies (or "errors") in logical reasoning are so common that thinkers have actually categorized them. What this means is that although an argument may look and sound logical, it's not--any error in the logic weakens the argument and leaves it open to attack by opponents.

Let's be very clear: fallacies are to be avoided at all costs in your own arguments. Not only do they create holes in your argument, thereby making your paper unpersuasive, they also undermine your credibility. The reader can't possibly know whether you committed a logical fallacy in your paper because you made a mistake in your own reasoning (an undesirable impression to give your opposition), or you used it on purpose to manipulate the audience. Notice we use the verb "to commit" a logical fallacy the same way you "commit" a crime. That should tell you something!

Logical fallacies are not just committed by mustache-twirling villains. They appear all the time. The advertisement industry makes billions of dollars every year and convinces you to buy all kinds of products by using logical fallacies. Being able to identify them for yourself will prevent them from appearing in your own writing and will develop your skills as a critical thinker. Once you identify the logical fallacies in an advertisement or an argument (and let's be honest, advertisements are argument "papers" themselves. Their thesis is almost always "Spend your money on this product now!"), you will be able to judge for yourself whether or not you need that product or want to agree with the writer's thesis. But at least you will have a conscious choice in the matter and not be acting out of habit or because you were being manipulated. Critical thinking is conscious choice. Forewarned is forearmed!

By learning these common argument fallacies, you can learn to recognize false logic. This knowledge is very empowering. From now on, everything that is thrown at you—whether by the media, politicians, or even your friends and neighbors—can be evaluated for its logic. If you learn these well, never again will you feel captive to a compelling argument that you cannot refute.

The following are logical fallacies commonly found in persuasive arguments.

> Note: If you do an internet search for "logical fallacies" you may find slightly different fallacies, or they may have different names, but this is the list from which we teach. The other names are also acceptable.

APPEALING TO PITY, OR PATHOS

This is making the reader agree because they feel sorry for you or someone else rather than because they agree with your logic. How many times have you driven by a billboard with an appeal to donate blood? This is, of course, a very noble and good thing to do. However, the next time you see such an ad, notice who figures in the picture and the narrative accompanying the ad. Often, you will see a picture of a father with their young child at the scene of a car accident. Let's think for a moment about why such "characters" were chosen to represent the population in need of blood. Many people need blood for many reasons, but many of us

wrong only if that's the only reason why.

might feel more pity for a young, innocent child than we would for a gangbanger fresh from a drive-by shooting. He may need blood just as badly as young Maria, but some may be less inclined to pull off the highway and roll up their sleeves for him. The Red Cross knows this, and wants to invoke our pity so that we act.

Notice, pity is not always a bad thing to inspire in your audience. Sometimes tragedies occur and we are right to feel sad and want to help. Pity becomes a problem when it is the *only* reason to agree with the writer or to motivate an action. You want to convince your audience on the argument's merits, not guilt them into action.

APPEALING TO PREJUDICE, OR HASTY GENERALIZATION

Appealing to Prejudice or Hasty Generalization assumes that, because something is true for one member of a sample group, it will be true for all. This is the logical error on which stereotypes are built. Just as it sounds, this fallacy is basing your argument on a race, gender, sexual orientation, age, or ethnic prejudice: "All women are bad drivers; therefore women shouldn't be given licenses." This fallacy is never persuasive except to those people who already share your bias. Appealing to Prejudice also makes you look unethical and weak as a writer. Good arguments stand on their own merits. They don't have to appeal to prejudices.

You might think that if a stereotype is positive, that it is okay. It's not. (*"Those people... are good at math, can really dance, are better cooks, etc..."*). Every individual deserves to be evaluated on his/her individual characteristics. It is intellectually irresponsible to extend conclusions about one person to another (similar person). Bottom line: regardless of whether it's 'nice' or not, it's still bad logic.

GUILT BY ASSOCIATION

Like Appealing to Prejudice, this is unfairly grouping people. If an "A" student always sits in a group of rowdy, disrespectful failing students, the professor might make wrong assumptions about the "A" student's attitude and abilities based on the fact that he or she is "hanging with the wrong crowd." This would be unfair. During his first presidential campaign, President Obama was similarly criticized for "having the wrong friends."

APPEALING TO TRADITION

This is arguing that because something has always been done a certain way, it should continue as is: "We've never had a woman president; therefore we should never have one." It is surprising how many times writers rely on this strategy when they are trying to keep things the way they are. Sometimes change is good, and it is merely habit that keeps us repeating our actions. As critical thinkers, it's important to analyze why we do the things we do, and whether our habits still work.

FALSE ANALOGY

A False Analogy is a construct that assumes that because two objects have one quality in common, they are the same (and have all qualities in common.) Comparing the hearing-impaired to quadriplegics because of their challenges would be one such example. Think of the Herbal Essences commercial that likens a woman's experience of shampooing her hair to something orgasmic. We know that the two experiences are not the same at all. But it's enough of a tease to motivate some women to buy that brand of shampoo! Many advertisements use the False Analogy. See if you can find any next time you are leafing through a magazine.

AD HOMINEM, OR ATTACKING CHARACTER

From the Latin words meaning, "against the person," *Ad Hominem* is a logical fallacy that occurs when you focus on the character of an opponent rather than upon his or her ideas. When all other arguments have been exhausted, or when we are outwitted or outranked, we might resort to a personal attack. This often will have the desired effect of humiliating the other party into silence, but it is not ethical, nor is it good logic.

Ad Hominem is everywhere in negative political ads. One candidate (or his political party) will attack the other on personal grounds that have nothing to do with the candidate's potential for serving the public: That politician was a bad husband; therefore all his political policies are wrong. You may still have personal reservations about voting for that person, but you would have to analyze his policies on their own merits. His committing adultery has nothing to do with his healthcare bill.

During campaign seasons, we are inundated with examples of this "mudslinging." Regardless of the bad logic, the smear tactic will still produce bad press for the opponent and might convince uneducated or undiscerning voters who might react more emotionally than intellectually.

STRAW MAN

The Straw Man fallacy is when you misrepresent your opponent's argument just so you can tear it down. You might falsely suggest that people who support gay rights do not respect the sanctity of marriage, when it is possible that the opposite is true. The proponents of legalizing gay marriage might actually revere the institution more than other citizens who take the right for granted.

FALSE CAUSES

This fallacy uses the wrong cause to explain something that happened. "The teacher didn't call on me today; therefore she doesn't like me." This fallacy assumes that correlation implies causation. Just because two conditions exist simultaneously does not mean that one caused the other. California has a lot of illegal immigrants and a lot of earthquakes, but illegal immigrants do not cause earthquakes.

POST HOC ERGO PROPTER HOC

Post hoc ergo propter hoc means in Latin "after this, therefore because of this."

This fallacy implicates A as the cause of B because A preceded B. For example, "It rained today because I washed my car yesterday." Although it's understood that no one particularly believes the car example in anything other than a superstitious way, many people suggest in utmost seriousness that the current president or governor is responsible for the economic woes that started a few years into his administration. This is so common, in fact, that each political party makes this type of argument about the other party's president during each new presidential administration. Just because an economic downturn happened after Governor Brown took office does not mean he caused it—if only it were that easy! Rather *all* possible causes and factors must be examined before blame can be placed anywhere.

BEGGING THE QUESTION OR CIRCULAR REASONING

This is a circular argument where the answer is just a restatement of the question without answering it. For example, "Students cannot park in the Faculty Lot because the Faculty Lot is not for students." It does not explain why students cannot park there. Circular Reasoning is often the language of bureaucratic procedure. This logical fallacy is committed every time a parent answers a child's question with: "Because I said so!"

EQUIVOCATING

This is playing fast and loose with a word's definition to suit your side: i.e., "victim," "justice," or "freedom." One might call a murderer a "victim of his environment," but many might argue whether this entitles him or her to the same sympathy as a murder victim.

IGNORING THE QUESTION

Watch any political debate; any time a political candidate wants to avoid answering a question, he or she simply changes the subject. If I said, "How can we think about saving dolphins when so many human babies are going hungry?" I am not actually answering the issue of whether or not saving dolphins is important, but rather complicating the issue to distract my audience or opponent. You might be tempted to commit such a fallacy when you are not prepared for an essay exam question or essay topic. Chances are pretty high that your professor will notice.

JUMPING TO CONCLUSIONS OR NON SEQUITUR

A *Non Sequitur* (from the Latin meaning "does not follow") makes an unwarranted jump to a conclusion. For example, just because someone is a good player does not mean he/she will make a good coach. To argue, "Tom is a good father, so he will be a good educator" is a Non Sequitur. The two are not necessarily related.

This logical fallacy is strong on opinion but weak on evidence. Often it overstates the significance of one piece of evidence as irrefutable proof. Therefore it leads faulty thinkers to make assumptions that aren't true. For example, if you see your boyfriend in a jewelry store, he may ask you to marry him. Or he may be buying a Mother's Day gift for his mom. Jumping to conclusions can be embarrassing. Get your facts before you act.

SLIPPERY SLOPE

This fallacy exaggerates the consequences of an action to an unreasonable degree. It is called "Slippery Slope," because if you take one step off the edge, you'll end up at the bottom the hill. What makes it "slippery" is that it concludes that A causes F without proving each step along the way, i.e., that A causes B which causes C, etc.

It is often used unfairly to cause alarm in the reader (or listener if you are watching local news: "Is your kitchen sponge killing you?! Tune in at eleven!") The premise here is that one step will lead to a terrible end. "If you take a puff of a cigarette, you will become a drug addict." The consequences are neither as dire nor as automatic as the writer suggests.

PRESENTING A FALSE DILEMMA OR "EITHER/OR"

This fallacy reduces an issue to only two alternatives when there are typically many options. "You are either with us, or against us." You might actually be neutral. Or "You are either a vegan, or you hate animals." We all know that real life contains many shades of gray. This fallacy ignores nuance. In reality, there is a lot of middle ground.

False dilemmas truck in extremes ("black and white" thinking) and create alarm, reducing the possibility of compromise and rational discussion. Rationality is vital to any well-reasoned argument.

BANDWAGON

Bandwagon is perhaps the least logical of any of the logical fallacies in the sense that at least the others look and sound logical, even though they in fact are not. However, the Bandwagon argument is based completely on an appeal to the majority. It is straight-up peer pressure at its worst. If you are told that "everybody is doing it," you might be more inclined to do it yourself. If you are told that everybody who is doing it is now a millionaire, you are even more convinced. The hook of the Bandwagon "argument" (if you can even call it argument) is in the implicit promise it offers of fitting in and being "acceptable."

Here are two examples:

Everyone knows pizza; is fattening, so don't eat pizza.

Nobody who is anybody is wearing trucker hats anymore, so don't wear trucker hats.

In the first example, the argument is wrapped up in the "hook," which is that you will get fat if you eat pizza; therefore you should not eat it. In the second example, the argument is that since nobody "who is anybody"—in other words, no one fashionable or cultured—is wearing trucker hats anymore, you shouldn't either. The hook here is that if you persist in doing what fashionable people do not do, you will be unfashionable—horrors! Notice that although the first Bandwagon argument uses a variation of the "everyone" phrase, the second does not. Even so, the second communicates the same thing: that you should do what everyone else is doing; in other words, you should jump on the bandwagon. This is a popular tool of advertisers.

ARGUMENT TO IGNORANCE

An Argument to Ignorance "argues" that because no one has proof about an issue, his/her premise must be true. For example, "No one can prove that God doesn't exist, so God must exist." This is not a logical argument; a lack of proof does not prove anything. Notice, this works both ways: you cannot conclude that something is true because you don't know it is false, and you cannot conclude that something is false because you don't know it's true.

LOGICAL FALLACY SAMPLE ASSIGNMENT AND WARM-UP

Write a formal assignment on the logical fallacies in Wendy McElroy's "Victims from Birth" to be handed in. You will list all of the fallacies you find in the article, where you find them, and you will EXPLAIN why they are fallacies. This will be a list with short paragraphs of explanation.

As a warm-up to that assignment, work with two partners to identify the logical fallacies in Steven Rhoads' "What Fathers Do Best." Report your findings to the class. Both articles can be found in the Appendix.

THREE TRADITIONAL MODES OF ARGUMENTATION: CLASSICAL, TOULMIN, AND ROGERIAN

Three of the most standard styles for the writing of persuasive arguments are the three rhetorical modes of the Classical style, patterned on the ancient Greek rhetorical style; Toulmin argument style, created by philosopher Stephen G. Toulmin; and Rogerian style, created by American psychotherapist Carl Rogers. Though not the only models for argumentation, these are the ones most often taught at the college and university levels, and prove ever useful to essay writers.

It's important for students to realize that these styles are not radically divergent. In the same way that a Honda, a Mustang, and a Mercedes are all styles of a car, so the Classical, Toulmin, and Rogerian modes of argumentation are all styles of persuasive writing. Although each has the same goal of convincing readers to agree with the author's argument, they all accomplish that goal with slightly different features and flourishes.

CLASSICAL ARGUMENT: BACKGROUND AND CHARACTERISTICS

The Classical argument style is short and sweet compared to the more contemporary styles that will be discussed next. In writing a classical argument, the writer must identify the reasons for his/her main claim, evidence to support those reasons, reasons for the opponent's position, and evidence that the opponent's reason is faulty. The classical argument writer must be careful not to misrepresent the opponent's position, which would be considered the Straw Man fallacy (as per "Avoiding Logical Fallacies" section earlier in chapter). Rather the evidence must prove that the opponent's actual position (correctly and fairly stated) is wrong.

The familiar, often-taught five paragraph essay model comprises the first two elements of the Classical argument style: the main claim and evidence proving the reasons the claim is true. Sometimes instructors also advise students to include a paragraph or two before the conclusion which considers (but dismisses) opposing views. However, it's a stretch to fit the entire Classical argument style into the Five Paragraph essay template; rather, the five paragraph essay model would have to grow to accommodate the additional paragraphs needed.

In a speech, a Classical argument has two distinct parts: the **introduction**, in which the writer establishes rapport with the audience and "warms up," and the **narration**, in which the speaker introduces the issue at hand with a brief description and perhaps context. In writing, the writer can blend these two together into the introduction (which can comprise as many paragraphs as necessary.) Again, most students are already taught to introduce the matter at hand, the circumstances and context in which the issue is important, and to use some rhetorical device such as a question, quote, or a representative case (we call this an "anecdote" in our "Writing Introductions" and "Writing Conclusions" chapters) to focus the issue for readers. All of these devices are derived from the Classical mode of rhetorical strategy.

The next element of the Classical style after the introduction/narration is the **confirmation**. This is where the speaker/reader presents his/her main claim (or thesis) and reasons and evidence to support it. (Note: Many instructors teach that a good thesis statement is comprised of both items: the main claim and the reasons the claim is true. This is sometimes called a "Map Thesis." This is another point of familiarity.) The confirmation will last as long as is necessary, but is usually the "body" or main part of the entire speech or essay.

After the confirmation is complete, the next element in the Classical argument style is the **refutation** (and concession.) In this portion, the writer considers possible opposing views and explains why they are wrong or inapplicable. The writer can make a small concession for "special circumstances," but traditionally in the Classical argument style, the less often concessions are made, the stronger the argument looks and the more confident and uncompromising the speaker/writer appears.

The final element of the Classical argument is the conclusion, and here again, students are in familiar territory. This is the point at which the speaker/writer restates the main claim, its reasons, and perhaps offers a final emotional or ethical appeal to persuade audiences. (Any of the techniques described in Chapter 13 would be appropriate here.)

TOULMIN ARGUMENT: BACKGROUND AND CHARACTERISTICS

In his groundbreaking 1958 book, *The Uses of Arguments*, British philosopher and educator, Stephen Toulmin (1922–2009), introduced a new form of persuasive argument that added several additional elements to the more traditional (Classical) argument style based on forward-thinking philosophical paradigms. The elements of a Toulmin argument are the **claim**, the **qualifier**, the **grounds** for the claim, the **warrant**, (the assumption on which the claim and grounds are based) the **data** or **backing** (support) and finally (the familiar) **rebuttal**. These elements need not follow a strict order; although the claim, the grounds, and the backing usually precede the rebuttal, the qualifier and the warrant can "float" to the most appropriate spot.

While the Classical argument rhetorical style is as much about arguing from a place of authority and absolutely- held high ground, the Toulmin argument style's uniqueness is in its willingness to acknowledge a bit of flexibility in one's argument. This reflects the twentieth century's philosophical shift away from "master narratives" and absolutes to a more negotiable exchange of ideas. If I am willing to admit that my **claim** may not hold in "all" cases but only in "most," (these are typical Toulmin **qualifiers**) or in specific, defined cases, my audience may be more likely to agree with me. To increase my credibility even more, I explicitly state the shared assumption or value—the **warrant**—on which my claim rests. This is probably the most distinctive and innovative feature of the Toulmin style, for which it is primarily known.

The logic of the Toulmin argument structure rests on identifying assumptions (called warrants) on which we base our claim, to either gain agreement from an audience that shares it, or if necessary, to refine or correct a weak warrant so as to strengthen the argument (the claim.) By acknowledging the readers' possible unstated (or unknown) assumptions, and stating it directly, the essay writer can avoid losing readers and perhaps even keep them interested long enough to convince them of his/her point of view. In order to be most effective, the warrant should be a universally shared value or assumption.

Example of a Weak Warrant:

Claim: She is a bad mother.

Reason: She yells at her daughter.

Warrant: Only a bad parent yells at her children.

Most people would agree that there are situations in which yelling might be appropriate; perhaps the woman's daughter was about to step out into the street.

Example of a Stronger Warrant:

Claim: She is *probably* a bad mother.   ("Probably" = qualifier)

Reason: She yells at her daughter *all the time*. ("All the time" qualifies the claim.)

Warrant: *Sometimes* yelling indicates bad parenting.

In the second example, the use of the Toulmin qualifiers, as well as a qualified assumption that can be more readily shared, strengthens the entire argument and makes it more persuasive to readers.

ROGERIAN ARGUMENT: BACKGROUND AND CHARACTERISTICS

The Rogerian style of argumentation is named for influential American psychologist Carl R. Rogers (1902–1987). As one would expect from one of the founders of the Humanistic approach to psychology, his argumentation method de-emphasizes confrontation while prioritizing cooperation and dialogue. This style is extremely similar to the Toulmin argument mode, distinguishable from it mainly by its intentional steps to reduce any perceivable threats to the audience and set them at ease to "participate" in the "conversation." This brings us full circle from the Classical argument style that opened this chapter. Scaffolded on his understanding of psychology, Rogers' argument style recognizes that people are sensitive to the perception of being judged, and thus quick to react emotionally to arguments/statements they find off-putting or unfamiliar if such statements are outside their frame of reference or belief systems. Therefore, the writer of the Rogerian argument must carefully scrutinize his/ her language for any possible terms of offensiveness or exclusivity which might betray the least hint of sexism, misogyny, ethnocentrism, classicism, or condescension. Simultaneously, the writer must directly validate the audience's existing positions or beliefs before (Rogers reasoned) audience members can feel free to actually listen/ consider the presented claim(s).

For example, let's say Juan wants to argue that Los Angeles households should be limited by law to one car each in order to reduce oil dependency and pollution, alleviate traffic, and encourage the use of public transportation. Anyone with a large household will react immediately on the defensive. "Why discriminate against large families? How will we get to work in different parts of the city? How can we live if we can't get to work?" Someone in a smaller household of two or three might not feel as personally affronted, but may ask, reasonably, "How will this impact small businesses like gas stations and vehicle repair shops? Isn't anyone on the side of the small businessperson?" These issues are all valid and must be acknowledged by Juan before he discusses any merits, grounds, or backing for his claim, or he might lose the majority of his readers. Thus, immediately after his statement of the problem, he might say something like, "Los Angeles needs a traffic solution that will not place an undue burden on drivers or small businesses." This makes any of those mentioned feel "heard" and mentioned before he even states his main claim. Now they are listening (or at least more of them than would have been!) Thus, the beauty of the Rogerian approach is the increased chance that your readers will actually consider your argument. Both the Toulmin and the Rogerian modes are great choices for particularly controversial topics since each structure allows the essay writer to emphasize common ground and shared values.

The following charts, Tables I,II, and III, offer three skeleton outlines for Juan's essay, one outline in Classical Argument style, one in Toulmin style, and one in Rogerian style. Note the similarities and the differences.

Table I: Classical Argument Outline

Introduction & Narration	**Hook:** Mention excessive travel times, clogged freeways, choking exhaust, lungs black from pollution, etc.

Confirmation	**Thesis:**
	
	L.A. households should be limited to one car each in order to reduce oil dependency, alleviate traffic, and encourage the use of public transportation.
	
	    + Evidence and explanation
	
	    + Evidence and explanation
	
	            (etc.)

Refutation	Most people will react to this proposal saying, "People can't do it." But forced to, they will. Necessity is the mother of invention.
	
	    + Historical examples (war-torn Europe, etc.)
	
	    + Explanation of birth of car culture in SoCal, elimination of public transport

Conclusion	Change is needed now… *(Closing context and appeal)*

Table II: Toulmin Argument Outline

Topic	**Hook:**
	Our state and country is facing a crisis and we must come together. (Mention excessive travel times, clogged freeways, choking exhaust, lungs black from pollution, etc.)
Claim, Qualifier, and **Data** (Support)	*Some* L.A. households should be limited to one car each in order to reduce oil dependency, alleviate traffic, and encourage the use of public transportation.
	+ Evidence and explanation
	+ Evidence and explanation
	(etc.)
Warrant (s)	California, indeed the whole U.S., cannot continue to thrive if status quo levels of oil dependency, exhaust pollution, and traffic issues continue / increase at such rate.
Rebuttal	Most people will react to this proposal saying, "People can't do it." But forced to, they will. Necessity is the mother of invention.
	+ Historical examples (war-torn Europe, etc.)
	+ Explanation of birth of car culture in SoCal, elimination of public transport
Conclusion	Change is needed now…
	(Closing context and appeal)

Table III: Rogerian Argument Outline

Introduction	Hook:
Keep the audience from becoming alienated with inclusive, sensitive language. ***Allay their fears.***	Mention excessive travel times, clogged freeways, choking exhaust, lungs black from pollution, etc. *Change can be uncomfortable, but can lead to unexpected opportunities such as new friendships with fellow carpoolers and financial savings. We can all have a say in finding solutions to increase the health and happiness of California drivers!*

State your <u>position</u>, **and show circumstances in which it is valid.**	**Main position:**
	
	 L.A. households should be limited to one car each in order to reduce oil dependency, alleviate traffic, and encourage the use of public transportation.
	
	 Claim 1> If oil dries up, no one will have cars. We'll have to deal with the situation then, and we will. Why not now?
	
	     + Evidence (Facts, projections)
	
	     + Historical example: before the family car!
	
	     + Status quo= Metro in NYC, Philly, DC, etc.
	
	 (Add additional claims and support…)

State <u>opponent's</u> positions, and **show circumstances in which they are valid.**	It's true that this regulation might unduly burden large families; therefore large households might qualify for an extra car.
Statement of Benefits in Conclusion	The sooner we act, the sooner we can begin to enjoy clean air, cost savings, and an expanded sense of community as people take to public transportation and explore carpool opportunities. (Closing context and appeal)

Eunice Burns
Burns 1
Professor Cordova
English 103
May 13, 2012

Reproductive Rights Protect Us All

In February 2012, notoriously provocative conservative talk show host, Rush Limbaugh, called a private citizen a "slut" for testifying before Congress about the importance of funding for contraceptive pills to treat her ovarian cysts. Ignoring the context of Fluke's testimony, Limbaugh suggested that if women want to have "so much sex" they should bankroll it themselves (Geiger). Limbaugh appeared not to be as troubled by the existing healthcare subsidy of performance-enhancing drugs for men. A month later, a similar issue erupted again among candidates in the Republican primary when Senator Rick Santorum, a Republican from Pennsylvania, suggested raped women should accept a[n unwanted] child as a gift from God ("Rick Santorum on Opposition to Abortion...")

Such talk should raise serious alarm in a nation often inaccurately referred to as "post-feminist." Studies show that although women are employed in increasing numbers in the workplace, a woman still earns only 75% of a man's wage for the same position, and still does most of the chores at home (Sweet; McVeigh). Women are still working "the second shift" (Hochschild). Furthermore, when a man and a woman have intercourse, the woman still risks disproportionally more, as either her body must bear the pregnancy, or her psyche the termination (along with the economic costs of either one, without the father's financial support). Should a woman be raped, she might be judged not only for her alleged role in precipitating the act, but for her decision about any ensuing pregnancy. While a woman's pregnant body is impossible to hide, the man's participation remains invisible. If we hope to define our nation as "modern" or "feminist" with straight faces, we must actively support the laws that exist to compensate for this biological inequity. It is inconsistent to subsidize Viagra without subsidizing birth control.

Reproductive rights are not just an issue for women or feminists. Most men (Limbaugh aside) recognize this; they have sisters, daughters, and mothers. Both genders benefit from growing up in families with two or three siblings, instead of fifteen (not to say, of course, that larger families can't be happy and healthy). Men also benefit from having penalty-free sex with their partners and should be able to recognize the inestimable financial benefit in not producing a child every time they enjoy sex. However, apparently these benefits are taken so much for granted that they bear emphatic mention until every US citizen recognizes that reproductive rights protect us all and the quality of life for everyone living within our borders.

Moreover, women's reproductive freedoms directly protect all workers in the long term. With industry mostly fled or outsourced to other countries, the United States is increasingly hard-pressed to employ its own citizens. The 2008 recession in the United States foregrounded the burgeoning unemployment of Americans. A significant increase in population can increase the chances of economic competition. According to projections by the Pew Research Center: "If current trends continue, the population of the United States will rise to 438 million in 2050, from 296 million in 2005" (Passel and Cohn). It doesn't take an economist to detect the benefit of existing contraceptive opportunities; it is just common sense that if all American workers alive today had double their existing competitors for a job, it would tremendously complicate their chances for economic success. Since it is in the economic interests of our entire nation that as many of our citizens as possible be employed, the continuing availability of affordable contraception is a benefit to us all, male and female.

Unemployment and disenfranchisement can often lead to crime, as research in both the United States and abroad has consistently demonstrated. Bruce Weinberg at Ohio State University puts it the most succinctly: "A bad labor market has a profound impact on the crime rates"(Grabmeier). For example, according to *The Review of Economics and Statistics*, the decrease in wages for "less skilled, less educated men" between 1979 and 1992 corresponded with an increase in crime; likewise when the wages for these workers increased between 1993 and 1997, the crime rate correspondingly dropped (Sloane). Add to that the human cost of the lives of crime victims, and the price tag grows. It seems simpler to spend tax dollars now to cover the low cost of family planning rather than the much steeper cost of unemployment benefits and/ or court and prison costs twenty years from now.

It's hard to imagine that any American, whether pro-choice or pro-life, wants to see the abortion rate grow. Most of us would agree that any prospective life lost, in any circumstance, is one too many. Making family planning and reproductive freedom as widely available to as many women as possible will prevent more abortions in the long run. In a 2009 article for *The Huffington Post*, Dr. Peter Klatsky uses statistics from the state of California to prove it:

> While I respect the opinions of those who oppose abortions, I do not
> understand why those same leaders would oppose policies proven to

reduce abortions. Modest estimates put the number of undesired pregnancies averted in California at over 108,000, with over 41,000 abortions prevented within the first four years after expanding access to contraceptive options.

It is vital to open a national dialogue about how we can strike a balance between the right of US citizens to their own religious practices and the necessity of the nation to "do business" as a secular nation-state. Just as we do not wish to disenfranchise our women, we do not wish to disenfranchise people of religious faiths who define contraception as abortion. Americans are intelligent and creative enough to arrive at a solution that maintains the constitutional separation of church and state while preserving the sanctity of life (via contraception) and protecting religious rights. Misogyny and name-calling have no place in the national conversation. We love and respect each other too much for that.

We can all agree that reducing the need for abortions is a worthy goal. Most importantly, and a point apparently lost on opponents, contraception prevents abortion. Therefore, even staunch conservatives can and should actively support available, affordable contraception.

Works Cited

Geiger, Kim. "Rush Limbaugh's 'Slut' Comment Draws Rebukes from All Sides." *Los Angeles Times,* 2 March 2012, articles.latimes.com/2012/mar/02/news/la-pn-rush-limbaugh-draws-rebukes from-all-sides-20120302. Accessed 28 Mar. 2018.

Grabmeier, Jeff. "Higher Crime Rate Linked to Low Wages and Unemployment, Study Finds." *Research News,* Ohio State University, 10 Apr. 2002, news.osu.edu/news/2002/04/10/crimwage/. Accessed 13 Apr. 2018.

Klatsky, Peter. "Why Contraception Saves Money and Prevents Abortion: A Doctor's Take on the Stimulus Package." *The Huffington Post,* The HuffingtonPost.com, 30 Jan. 2009, www.huffingtonpost.com/dr-pete-klatsky/why-contraception-saves-m_b_162520.html7. Accessed May 2018.

McVeigh, Tracy. "Forty Years of Feminism--But Women Still Do Most of the Housework." *The Gaurdian,* 10 March 2012, www.theguardian.com/society/2012/mar/10/housework-gender-equality-women. Accessed 3 Apr. 2018.

Passel, Jeffrey S., and D'Vera Cohn. "U.S. Population Projections: 2005–2050." *Pew Research Center,* 11 Feb. 2008, www.pewhispanic.org/2008/02/11/us-population-projections-2005-2050/. Accessed 3 Apr. 2018.

"Rick Santorum on Opposition to Abortion in Cases of Rape: 'Make the Best out of a Bad Situation.'" *The Huffington Post,* TheHuffingtonPost.com, 23 Jan. 2012, www.huffingtonpost.com/2012/01/23 /rick-santorum-abortion-rape_n_1224624.html. Accessed 3 Apr. 2018.

Sloane, Christina. "The Effects That Unemployment Has on the Crime Rate." *eHow Money*, www.ehow.co.uk/list_7414520_effects-unemployment-crime-rate.html. Accessed 12 May 2012.

Sweet, Lynn. "Women Still Earn Less Than Men: New Obama White House Report on Status of Women." *Chicago Sun-Times*, 1 Mar. 2011, chicago.suntimes.com/section/lynn-sweet-politics/. Accessed 3 Apr. 2018.

EXERCISE EXERCISE EXERCISE

17

Review the elements of a Toulmin essay and identify those elements in the sample essay "Reproductive Rights Protect Us All" above. Then answer: how does the choice of the Toulmin argumentation model help the author engage those who disagree with her ideologically? Was it an effective choice?

CHAPTER CHAPTER CHAPTER

18

In-Class Essay Exam Strategies

Timed writing exams are standard practice in most colleges and universities. You may not believe this at first, but essay exams (any exams) can be enjoyable when you are well-prepared. If you study, you will be excited to demonstrate what you have learned so far in class. This section contains a number of strategies for many types of in-class essay exams to prepare you for success.

The key to success on in-class essay exams (and exams in general) is to master all the factors you can control in order to increase your success in facing the factors you cannot control (like what's on the test, or how hard it will be.)

FACTORS YOU *CAN* CONTROL:

Know the test's parameters as soon as the teacher will disclose them: How long is it? How many topics to choose from? How much time will you have? Can you use scrap paper? Can you use a laptop? Can you use one bluebook page for each paragraph? What size bluebook should you use? Pen or pencil? Should you skip lines? Can you use a dictionary? Can you use notes? Etc.

BE PREPARED TO USE YOUR TIME WISELY.

Based on what you know of the test's parameters, craft a preliminary time plan before the test. (For example, I may know I have to discuss three topics in three hours; that gives me roughly one hour per topic. The teacher wants a five paragraph essay for each one; that gives me roughly ten minutes per paragraph, with ten minutes left over to review my work. This is something I can practice beforehand with a study partner, with sample topics we generate for each other). If you have little or no idea of the test's composition, schedule time at the beginning, perhaps five to ten minutes, to create a time plan on a scrap piece of paper or in the back of your blue book.

Example:

> 11:10 - 11:20: Read the prompt.
> 11:20 - 11:30: Draft a thesis.
> 11:30 - 11:40: Write the introduction.
> 11:40 - 11:50: First body paragraph.
> 11:50 - 12:00: Second body paragraph.
> 12:00 - 12:10: Third body paragraph.
> 12:10 - 12:20: Conclusion.
> 12:20 - 12:35: Reread, revise, and edit.

These minutes spent budgeting time before even getting started can help you in the long run; it's better to get most of the way through three different topics than it is to complete one topic and leave the other two blank. If some questions are weighted with more points, do those first. Then, if you see that you are running out of time towards the end of the test, list the topics or phrases you had hoped to discuss rather than leaving that topic completely blank. This shows instructors that time management was more of a problem for you than content knowledge, and might allow them to throw one or two points your way (which they cannot do for a blank space).

Do not leave the exam early. If you are finished much earlier than all of the other students, double-check that you have read and followed all of the instructions completely. Perhaps you were required to answer two questions and you only did one. Professors usually ask questions suited to the length of the exam. Even if you have completed everything, reread your answer. Be sure that you have included all of the persuasive evidence you can to make your points. Proofread your essay for careless errors.

BE AS PREPARED AS YOU CAN BE PHYSICALLY.

Get enough sleep. Eat a meal beforehand, and take a few nuts or candies in your pocket. Know beforehand if you will be able to leave the room during the test to use the restroom. Arrive early to choose a seat that will be comfortable for you and to get settled and centered so that you can concentrate on your exam. If you come in late, your stress affects your performance and may also distract other students.

BE AS PREPARED AS YOU CAN BE ON A CONTENT LEVEL.

Know the textbook chapters, handouts, and lecture material. Practice these with a study partner if possible. Review any prior tests or quizzes for key terms and themes. Meet with a tutor or attend any study session held by the instructor or the teaching assistant.

BE AS PREPARED AS YOU CAN BE MENTALLY.

Try deep breathing exercises or affirmations before the test, or during, if your mind wanders or if negative messages come up for you while you are trying to work. If you are as prepared as you can be with the content, as mentioned above, it doesn't hurt to remind yourself of this if at any point you start to panic. "I know I can do this," you might tell yourself, "I've got this." Write down something you do well just before you start writing your essay. Research shows students who do this do better on exams.

Students who have a history of bad test-taking experiences may have to spend time journaling "historical" negative feelings which originated in a legitimate experience at some point in the past, but which are now impeding performance, in order to work through these feelings before they can come up on test day. Sometimes it also helps to calculate how much the exam can possibly hurt your grade, so you do not worry overmuch. Telling yourself, "This is only a portion of my grade, and my take-home essay scores are very high" might help calm you down from the start.

If negative messages are coming up for you, talk back to them by writing down affirmations on a scrap page, like, "This is going really well" or "I am right on schedule" (You may not feel like it's going really well, but telling yourself that anyway is encouraging and affirming. Why not think the best, instead of the worst?). Remind yourself how much you've already gotten done.

Consider approaching each of your tests as athletes approach a game. We can all think of history-making games in which players conquered their opponents against all odds. You can bet they didn't do it by talking down to themselves beforehand. They did it by encouraging one another, putting on their lucky shoes or shirts or whatever talismans made them feel strong, painting their faces, and going into battle. It might sound silly to think about creating a test-taking ritual, but why not? Attitude is everything!

Always keep writing. If you hit a wall, try to avoid picking your pen off the page—it might be very difficult to get it back down there! Instead, go back to your outline or thesis and check off the items you have already covered, or list items that you've realized you can add. It's important to keep focused on the subject matter, or you may lose your concentration. Avoid thinking about what you have to do later, or any other thoughts that will take you outside of the present experience.

Note: Don't spend time recopying your essay unless the instructor has specified that you are accountable for neat handwriting and presentation, which would be unusual for an in-class essay. Many students spend valuable time recopying sloppily-written work when they could spend more time writing and simply number the paragraphs at the end. Make sure you are clear on the instructor's grading priorities before you even begin in case you are spending time on a step that is completely unnecessary.

However, if, when you are rereading your essay, you realize with a jolt that you have forgotten to include a very important point or a whole paragraph, don't panic. Draw an asterisk * and write "please insert paragraph A here." Then, at the end of your essay, write paragraph A and put the * sign again next to it with a margin instruction to "Please insert this paragraph into p. 2."

Every time you take an in-class essay test, no matter how well you do on a content level, you are getting valuable practice in test-taking, and your skills will grow. Start paying attention to what works for you in this process and what doesn't. Follow up with the instructor whenever possible to debrief and ask what you could have done differently, or how you could have better spent your time. Although there can be a range of instructor expectations and priorities for in-class essays, commonalities will emerge.

If getting stuck is a common experience for you, it would benefit you to explore this outside of the in-class testing situation, so that you can determine the root of the problem and learn strategies to disrupt this harmful pattern. This might be something to explore with a professor or academic counselor. Some of your professors may have had similar difficulties themselves as students, and might be willing to share some of their own test-taking strategies.

Test-taking is a challenge for so many students that many colleges offer test-taking strategy workshops and/or courses through the Library, Tutoring, or Counseling Divisions. This is a skill that can be learned.

IN-CLASS ESSAY EXAM STRATEGIES

Know the test's parameters.

What is expected of you?

Be prepared to use your time wisely.

Budget your time.

Be as prepared as you can be physically.

Fortify yourself with sleep and food.

Be as prepared as you can be on a content level.

Study!

Be as prepared as you can be mentally.

Think positively!

Always keep writing.

Keep your attention on the task.

THE ESSAY EXAM WITH A CHOICE OF PROMPTS

The instructions for your in-class essay might look like this:

> "Choose **ONE** of the essay questions below and write your answers in your blue book. You will have the class period to complete the exam."

Even simple instructions like the ones above, are meant to be followed to the letter and can help you excel.

© LStockStudio/Shutterstock.com

- If given a choice, be sure to **read all of the questions fully before making your decision** which to answer.

- **Read the question you will answer three times. Breathe.** Many times, when we read an essay question for the first time, we panic. The quote and question may feel out of context and surprising. This is a normal first reaction and will pass! As you reread and start to relax, **take notes and underline important words in the question** as you prepare your answer.

- The best question is not the shortest one! It is the one about which you will have the most to say. Oftentimes, longer questions give you a lot more material to work with and to discuss. This will help you to write a thorough and interesting essay chock full of information you have learned so far in the class. Shorter questions may seem like an "easier" choice, but they are not necessarily simpler. The professor will be expecting you to provide the same length essay as the longer question, but is giving you fewer hints or a shorter quote to discuss. This means more material must come from you.

WRITING AN ESSAY EXAM IN ENGLISH CLASS

- Remember that when writing an essay exam for an English class, your professor will expect you to follow the conventions of essay writing. This means:

  1. Include an introduction.

  2. Each essay must have a clear thesis statement.

  3. Each body paragraph must have a topic sentence that transitions and recalls your thesis statement.

  4. Remember a brief conclusion to sum up your points.

- Demonstrate knowledge of the texts you have read during the term by using one to three examples from the reading for each point you make.

- Be specific when using examples. Details show that you have read and have been listening in class.

THE ESSAY EXAM WITH A QUOTATION

A common essay exam question is one in which you are provided with a quotation (often from the reading assigned in class). Sometimes this generates a series of questions from the professor that you will incorporate into your essay. Sometimes, however, you will merely be asked to "explicate" it. This is just a fancy way of saying that the professor is asking you to demonstrate **three** skills surrounding the quotation:

1) **Paraphrase the quotation.** (Put it in your own words).

2) **Close read the quotation.** (What's interesting in the details?)

3) **Contextualize the quotation.** (Tell how it fits into the overall text. Discuss the significant themes you see. Explain why it is important to or a good example of the rest of the book. Include other examples from the text.)

Now let's explore each of these steps in a little more detail.

1) To paraphrase the quotation, means you will put the quote in your own words. Simply explain what is happening on a literal level. After you have written a topic sentence, this is often a strong way to start because it gets you over the fear of facing the blank page, and it lets the professor know you have understood the quotation. (This is similar to showing your work when you solve a math problem. It allows the math professor to see how you are reading and where the train may have gone off the rails). Paraphrasing lets the professor know you know what's going on.

2) Now you must roll up your sleeves and go about "close reading" the quote. Close reading is exactly as its name suggests, a method of reading for details. This is what we practice in class when we go over a passage either through group work or together as a class. We explain what's going on and what's interesting about the passage. This time, <u>you</u> will be pointing out the interesting and significant details for your professor to see. Close reading looks for recurrent images, use of particular language, tone, subtext, and irony. Subtext is when a character or the author says one thing on a literal level, but means something else underneath. When we read for subtext, we "read between the lines." For example, in *Mrs. Dalloway*, a pompous character Hugh Whitbred, after making Clarissa feel self-conscious about her hat, tells her that "Of course he'll come to her party tonight," he just has to go to a small function at Court first. On a textual, literal level, he's telling her he will attend her party. On a subtextual level, he's telling her "I'm important" because he's needed at Court and will speak with more famous people than Clarissa. Irony is when a character or situation ends up the opposite of what you expect. The character Peter who always crowds Clarissa and invades her personal space, is himself very annoyed when his personal space is invaded. This is irony, and wonderful to point out in an essay.

3) Finally, contextualizing the quote means that you put it in "context" or explain why it's important to the entire book, what's happened before this passage, and, if you know it, what happens after the quote appears. This is where you would discuss how this quote has an impact on the whole and what it reveals about the larger work. You might also discuss how it foreshadows or anticipates events to come. Usually professors choose a quote because it contains some specific language or themes that have been discussed in class that are important to the book or poem. This is your chance to pull out all the stops and show what you have learned. Don't be shy.

Remember, an essay exam is not the time to be subtle. You want to impress your professors with how much you have learned in the lectures and class discussions, how well you have read and understood, and how you are able to identify these components in the larger work. Try hard to find the meaning and significance of the quote. Chances are good that if you think something is important, it is.

SAMPLE LITERATURE ESSAY PROMPT:

"Quiet descended on her, calm, content, as her needle, drawing the silk smoothly to its gentle pause, collected the green folds together and attached them, very lightly, to the belt. So on a summer's day waves collect, overbalance, and fall; collect and fall; and the whole world seems to be saying "that is all" more and more ponderously, until even the heart in the body which lies in the sun on the beach says too, That is all. Fear no more, says the heart. Fear no more, says the heart, committing its burden to some sea, which sighs collectively for all sorrows, and renews, begins, collects, lets fall. And the body alone listens to the passing bee; the wave breaking; the dog barking, far away barking and barking," (39-40).

Characters throughout Virginia Woolf's *Mrs. Dalloway* are aware of their mortality to varying degrees throughout the novel. Discuss how the passage above incorporates imagery that relates to mortality. Compare several characters' responses to the passage of time and their inevitable deaths.

TIPS:

1) Paraphrase who is being discussed here and what she's doing. Note that this is Clarissa Dalloway. Note how she feels: calm. This is consistent with the quote "Fear no more." "As Clarissa sits sewing her evening dress for her party, her thoughts lead to her own mortality. But rather than panic or fear, the imagery in the quote shows that Clarissa feels calm and collected about her mortality."

2) Mention that "Fear no more" is a quote that recurs throughout the novel, and that it is itself a quote from Shakespeare's *Cymbeline* that the character Clarissa reads in a bookshop window on her way to buy flowers for her party. (Flowers are themselves symbols of mortality and how short our lives often feel).

3) Pay special attention to the imagery that appears in the quote above: waves. Not only does Woolf write the words "waves" very specifically, but the other imagery and action in the quote evokes waves as well. Discuss how the gesture of Clarissa sewing the folds on her dress replicates the up and down fluid movement of waves. Notice the verbs and how they also express the motion of waves: "collect, overbalance, and fall; collect and fall;" and "renews, begins, collects, lets fall." Moreover, the repetition mimics the cyclical nature of waves. Discuss the places in the novel where Woolf uses imagery that evokes "mortality," and mark down which characters think about their own mortality and when.

4) Clarissa also seems to be having an "out of body" experience where "only the body" hears the barking dog (the annoyances and chaos of life) and only from far away. Her soul seems to be preparing to separate from her physical body. To add further context, you might note that the character Septimus, who mirrors Clarissa throughout the novel, has a very similar passage including the waves and "barking dogs" at the sea, a moment of calm acceptance of death, just before he leaps from a window to escape being taken to a mental hospital.

5) If you knew about it, you might add the information in your conclusion that the author, Virginia Woolf, herself committed suicide by filling her pockets with rocks and drowning herself in the Ouse River. Clearly, water represented a soothing relief from life's cares to her, just as Shakespeare's quote tells us to "fear no more" (and right before Clarissa reads that quote, she comes to the conclusion that the end of life doesn't have to be awful. It could be a relief from life's worries).

PREPARING FOR AN ENGLISH ESSAY EXAM

1) Reread your class notes. Decide from your professor's comments in class what's important from lecture and the readings. Show in your essay that you have been attending and listening carefully to your professor.

2) Study your reading notes and review. Know what has happened in the reading. Professors are not sympathetic to students who don't read carefully.

3) Reread any passages in the text that you found difficult.

4) Review characters' and authors' names and how to spell them. Mistakes on this order look sloppy and cost you points.

5) Review your notes right before coming into the exam.

SAMPLE NONFICTION QUOTE ESSAY PROMPT:

1. In "Dorm Brothel" Vigen Guroian asserts that:

   "The sexual revolution . . . was not won with guns but with genital groping aided and abetted by colleges that forfeited the responsibilities of in loco parentis and have gone into the pimping and brothel business."

   Do you agree that colleges have gone into the "pimping and brothel business"? What role should a college play in parenting students who live away from home? Assess what you think the college administration's responsibilities are or should be. Discuss the quote first. Then answer the questions.

In the question above, since the quote comes from an assigned reading, students would likely have heard the term "*in loco parentis*" and remember it from class discussion. As in the example above, start with a paraphrase of the quote to explain the central thesis behind the article and demonstrate a thorough knowledge of the reading material. Then set about answering the questions posed by the instructor in the question. This is a good time to incorporate any of the class discussions into your answers as well.

Don't recopy the questions or list them. The questions are there to give you ideas to put into your essay. They may even suggest a structure in which you give a paragraph to each one.

Follow These Steps:

1) Paraphrase the quote provided.

2) Define the exaggeration "pimping and brothel business." What do you remember about Vigen Guroian, the author, from class discussion? Is he the parent of a college-aged daughter? Explain his possible bias. (This doesn't mean he's wrong about his argument. You can still agree if you choose).

3) Agree or disagree that colleges have gone into the "pimping and brothel business." Make your answer nuanced. It doesn't have to be either/or. Give examples.

4) Discuss what role you think a college should play in parenting students who live away from home. Assess what you think the college administration's responsibilities are or should be.

5) Write conclusion.

SECTION SECTION SECTION

V

Be a Researcher

CHAPTERS

CHAPTER CHAPTER CHAPTER 19

CONDUCTING RESEARCH

Research papers are a staple in most classes regardless of the discipline. You may not believe it yet, but they can be the high-point of your semester. The trick to making research papers enjoyable is to go about them in the way that research was originally intended: to address a question or a problem that needs to be solved. Research papers are very exciting when approached in this way because there is suspense involved. Research involves using outside sources rather than simply writing from opinion or personal experience. You pose a question and, like a detective, you set about uncovering the solution. Research papers only become boring when you ask questions to which you know the answer.

CHOOSING A TOPIC

The litmus test to choosing a good research topic is this: if you know what your thesis statement will say *before* you do your research, you have not chosen a real question that requires research. For example, everyone knows that eating only junk food is bad for your health. Therefore, writing a paper that proves that is a waste of everybody's time. Your reader and you both already know that unhealthy food will not be good for you, and everyone will be going through the motions of research and learning without actually doing either. The same applies to the dangers of smoking, air pollution, taking drugs, etc., unless you have something specific or surprising to add to the conversation.

No surprise = BORING. A paper with a foregone (obvious) conclusion will be deadly to research and you will sleep through the writing of it. I guarantee also, that your instructor will not be excited to read your findings. If, however, you choose a legitimate question that is fresh, interests you personally, and isn't already obvious to everyone who hasn't been living under a rock for the past ten years, then you will learn something in the process of doing the research and you will be carrying out *true research*, the way it was meant to be undertaken. Often this is by digging deeper into the "obvious" question; for example, "What is the environmental impact of fast food? What is the best healthy option in fast food?"

> Note: It's okay to think you *might* know the answer. Great scientists often have a working hypothesis before they start their experiments, but they are open to the possibility that they are wrong, and they allow their research findings to give them the ultimate answer or conclusion. You must maintain the same open-mindedness when conducting your own research. Only draw a conclusion once the results are in.

Your findings may even have the power to change your life.

When Dr. Boutry first started teaching at West Los Angeles College, she had a baby at home. She thought she already knew everything there was to know about raising babies since this was her third child. Boy, was she wrong, and it was a student research paper that changed her mind. She assigned an environmental research paper to her class and left the topic open for students to explore a subject of their interest. One young woman we'll call Chantel, who did a lot of babysitting to pay for her books, researched and wrote a paper about the dangers of BPA (a chemical) commonly found then in plastic baby bottles. This chemical was dangerous when the bottles were heated, and the research was just starting to appear. Dr. Boutry found Chantel's research informative, her evidence persuasive, and the conclusion downright scary. As soon as she had slapped a big "A" on Chantel's paper, she threw away all of her daughter's plastic baby bottles and purchased glass ones.

Moreover, the effects of Chantel's findings didn't stop with Dr. Boutry. Chantel informed the families for whom she was babysitting of her conclusion, and they also rid their cabinets of their old BPA bottles. Furthermore, Chantel shared her research with the rest of the class, many of whom were concerned mothers, fathers, and older siblings. These days, there is labeling on baby bottles that contain BPA.

The best papers change the way you and your readers see the world, and could even have an effect on someone's health. Now that's power!

PRIMARY AND SECONDARY RESEARCH

So once you have a great question, you have to go about locating your sources. Research sources can take two forms: primary and secondary. We're going to walk you through both.

PRIMARY SOURCES

As its name suggests, primary source research goes directly to the original historical source. This includes original documents or artifacts from the time period you are researching. For example, you might examine the Declaration of Independence written in 1776, or a hand-written letter from Napoleon to his wife, Josephine. Primary sources also include interviews you might conduct with individuals whose personal experience relates to your topic. For example, if you were writing a research paper on noise pollution, you might interview a local resident whose home is near the airport. (See "Conducting Surveys" and "Conducting an Interview" later in this chapter). Or if you were writing about ex-soldiers adjusting to civilian life after combat and you served in Iraq, you could include your own relevant personal experiences. You can also examine physical objects like the cave paintings from Lascaux or a piece of pottery with a design that tells you something about the culture or time in which it was made.

Examples of primary sources include speeches, letters, interviews, film footage, court records, journal or diary entries, accounts of personal experience, works of art, advertisements, even architecture. (You might use a Soviet building's strong lines, equally-sized offices, and lack of ornamentation to illustrate the principles of Communism at work). For primary research, Dr. Boutry's student Chantel looked at an original lab report on BPA seepage from heated plastic.

Original primary sources are powerful additions to your evidence. Notice, these documents don't tell you how or what to think about an issue. You must do the interpretation yourself. However, if you had to write a research paper on the American Revolution using only primary sources, it would take a very long time to track down and interpret all of those materials. This is why researchers often rely upon secondary sources as well. Instead of reinventing the wheel each time, we build on solid research that has already been conducted to augment our primary source research.

SECONDARY SOURCES

Secondary sources are analyses or interpretations of original events or primary sources. If an historian writes *about* the Declaration of Independence, that article is considered a secondary source because it is a step removed from the original, primary source. You as a researcher will be trusting that the historian's interpretation of facts is accurate. This is why it is so important to use secondary materials that come from reputable, trustworthy sources or experts. Examples of secondary sources include journal and magazine articles, histories, encyclopedias, news commentary, newspaper articles, reviews, and textbooks.

For secondary sources, Chantel read scientific journal articles that analyzed the original findings published about BPA and its effect on human health when ingested. These articles confirmed or refuted the original conclusions.

FINDING SOURCES

To set about finding primary and secondary sources, you have two immediate options. You can go to your school or local library and you can go online. Much of the research that used to be conducted only in person at a library can now be undertaken in the comfort of your own home. Libraries have online databases that make it easy to find what you are looking for.

© goodluz/Shutterstock.com

LIBRARY DATABASES

It is much better to start your research using a library database or Google Scholar than it is to conduct a standard Google search. Your responses will be too many, and much of the material you will have to sift through will not all be relevant. There will also be advertisements distracting you, and the last thing you need when you're setting out on a research paper is distractions!

Library databases would be very costly if you tried to access them as a private individual. Happily, these commonly-used databases are paid for by your library and are available to you free of cost as a patron or student. You may need your student I.D. number or another form of password and username to access them. Your librarian will be happy to assist you with accessing their sites.

COMMONLY-USED SUBSCRIPTION JOURNALS AND PERIODICALS

- *CQ Researcher:* Comprehensive reporting and analysis on current political and social issues.

- *EBSCOhost:* Academic Search Premier, American History and Life full text, ERIC, Health Source Consumer and Nursing, Newspaper Source Plus, Psychology and Behavioral Sciences, Regional Business News, Religion and Philosophy Collection, Medline, Military and Government collection.

- *Facts on File:* Includes Facts on File World News Digest (1940–Present), provides comprehensive reporting and analysis on current political, social, and scientific themes. *Gale Literary Databases - CA, CLC, DLB:* Access three of the world's premier literature resources with a single search.

- *Gale Virtual Reference Library:* Encyclopedias, dictionaries, and specialized reference sources for multidisciplinary research.

- *JSTOR:* Arts & Sciences I: includes core journals in economics, history, political science, and sociology, as well as in other key fields in the humanities and social sciences. This collection also contains titles in ecology, mathematics, and statistics.

- *LexisNexis:* Full-text articles from world, US regional, trade and professional, news, business, legal, medical, and reference sources.

- *Literature Resource Center:* LRC is your most current, comprehensive, and reliable online resource for research on literary topics, authors, and their works. Its coverage includes all literary genres, all time periods, and all regions of the world.

- *Opposing Viewpoint Resource Center:* Pro and con viewpoint articles on current social issues, topic overviews, statistics, primary documents, links to web sites, and full-text journal articles.

- *Oxford English Dictionary – OED Online:* The Oxford English Dictionary is the accepted authority on the evolution of the English language over the last millennium.

- *ProQuest:* Articles from over 4,000 academic and popular magazines and journals.

OPEN ACCESS JOURNALS AND PUBLICATIONS

- *BioMed Central:* STM (Science, Technology and Medicine) Publisher of 223 peer-reviewed open access journals.

- *Directory of Open Access Journals (DOAJ):* Free, full text, quality controlled scientific and scholarly journals, covering all subjects and many languages.

- *Education Resources Information Center (ERIC):* World's largest digital library of educational literature.

- *PubMed:* PubMed comprises more than 21 million citations for biomedical literature from MEDLINE, life science journals, and online books. Citations may include links to full-text content from PubMed Central and publisher web sites.

GOVERNMENT DOCUMENTS, PUBLICATIONS, STATISTICS

- *Federal Digital System (FDSYS):* US Government Printing Office (GPO) search for government publications

- *FedStats:* Centralized statistics search across multiple US.government agencies.

- *Library of Congress*

- *National Archives*
- *Science.gov:* Science.gov searches over 50 databases and over 2100 selected websites from 14 federal agencies, offering 200 million pages of authoritative US government science information including research and development results.

BEGINNING RESEARCH

Once you have your topic and a question, you can type a keyword search into any of the databases above. Try a few. Allow yourself enough time to refine your search words in case you get too many or too few hits. Students almost always underestimate the amount of time it takes to find good articles. A little extra time spent at this stage will give you quality quotes and material to work with in your paper. Your research paper can only be as good as the research and sources you have to work with. Quality research will take many hours. Here are some time-saving strategies for getting started.

Beginning Research Time Savers

1) Narrow your search terms.

2) Use the "Advanced Search" options.

3) Read article abstracts.

4) Read the articles' works cited pages.

5) Write down or highlight complete, correct publication information for your Works Cited page before you navigate away from the article's internet page.

6) Email the articles to yourself if the database gives you the option.

7) Take advantage of the "Cite this" database buttons that will put a citation in MLA, *Chicago*, or APA format for you. Double-check for accuracy.

8) Choose an extra article for insurance.

---

1) **Narrow your search terms** if you get too many hits. Instead of typing in "bad health," try "fast food" AND "heart disease." If that is still too broad, try "French fries" AND "cholesterol." Using the perfect search terms is an art mixed with an increasing knowledge of your topic.

2) **Use the "Advanced Search" options.** Advanced Searches will allow you to narrow down the results by many factors.

Time Period

Sometimes professors request that all research—especially scientific—be taken from articles published in the past five years to keep the data up to date. You can weed out older articles by performing an advanced search.

Full Text

It can be disappointing to find the perfect-sounding article only to discover that it's only available in hardcopy at the University of Chicago when you are in Los Angeles and your paper is due tomorrow. Select "full text" articles that allow you to read the entire article online from your computer. You can also print the entire article.

Type of Journal

In an advanced search, the "Peer Review" button allows you to refine your search to "peer-reviewed" journals. These are often preferable. "Peer-reviewed" means that specialists in the fields read each article to determine that it meets the standards in that discipline and that the author knows what he or she is talking about. This ensures that you are reading a "vetted," quality article written by an expert. Reading a poor-quality article is a waste of your time.

3) Once you have narrowed your search results to a workable list, **read the abstracts** attached to articles from databases or printed at the beginning of articles. Abstracts are paragraph-long summaries of the article. Quickly scanning abstracts will save valuable time. You may have narrowed down some promising-sounding titles, but titles can be misleading. An article entitled "The Iron Lady" could be about Margaret Thatcher, or it could be about the Eiffel Tower (both shared the same famous nickname), or it could be about a female bodybuilder. By reading the abstract, you will quickly see which iron lady your article discusses and whether it is relevant to your paper about British politics, the World Exposition in Paris, or steroid use in athletes.

4) **Read the Works Cited lists of the articles you find helpful.** If you find an article or part of an article relevant to your topic, check that article's Works Cited for further sources that pertain to your topic. This is like getting research advice from a trusted source and can save you loads of time.

5) **Write down or highlight complete CORRECT publication information for your Works Cited page before you navigate away from the article's internet page.** Time and again, students find great articles and then, because they mistake the spelling of the author's name or the title, they are unable to find the article again. Searching for an article you have lost wastes time and is heart-breaking. You cannot use a quote from an article you cannot cite fully. No article information means no quote.

6) **E-mail the articles to yourself if the database gives you the option.** By e-mailing yourself the article, you have a backup in case you have difficulty finding it again. Still, take down the citation information elsewhere as well so that if the attachment doesn't work or the e-mail message doesn't go through, you haven't lost the information and a way to find the article again.

7) **Take advantage of the "Cite this" database buttons that will put a citation in MLA, *Chicago*, or APA format for you.** But be careful! These databases almost always make mistakes in citation. They are a great start, but it is your responsibility to verify that the citation appears in the proper format at the end of your paper. Common database mistakes include errors in capitalization and not putting the author's last name first. These mistakes will cost you points, so double-check. Saying the computer made the mistakes is not a valid excuse! (Please see Chapter 20 for guidelines on proper citation format.)

8) **Choose an extra article.** If the professor's minimum is four sources, print six for extra backup. Sometimes when you begin reading, you find out too late that the article isn't really as useful to your paper as you had hoped. Moreover, sometimes your thesis will change as you learn more about the topic. Cover your bases by having more research than you need and a variety of it.

READING SOURCES EFFICIENTLY

Once you have your articles selected, you'll have to read them! Follow these guidelines to develop good study habits and save time when it comes time to write.

How to Read Sources Efficiently

- Take neat, informative notes as you read. If you print the article, you can take notes in the margins and highlight important ideas.

- Include citation information with your notes.

- Paraphrase long quotes and summarize the entire article for yourself. (Please see "Writing a Summary" in Chapter 8 if you are unclear on how to summarize).

- Remember not to insert any of your own biases or opinions (no matter how brilliant) into your notes on the articles at this point. Have a separate paper for that. The reason is very simple: after you have read four articles, you won't remember exactly who said what. When it comes time to write your paper, you might be confused whether that elegant sentence you wrote down is the author's idea or your own. When you aren't sure, you'll have to reread the entire article to find out. Save yourself time by taking good notes from the start.

- If you print the article, highlight or write down—on paper, in a Word document, or on your phone—any useful quotes that stand out to you, *even if you aren't sure yet how you will use them*. Oftentimes, our instincts will point us towards our topic and we will be drawn to specific quotes. After writing them all down, you can take a look and see that a pattern and a thesis are developing. This is an exciting process that happens if you keep an open mind about your conclusion and see where your research leads you.

NOW CHOOSE THE ESSAY MODEL BEST-SUITED TO YOUR TOPIC.

Before you begin writing your research, consider which structure is best suited to your material. If you are integrating secondary research sources with your own assertions, you have many options. For example, a Comparison/Contrast essay is ideal to showcase two opposing views. If you've found your own mind changed by your research findings, you may feel strongly enough to craft a Classical Argument essay. For many possible essay models, see Chapter 15. If your research essay consists entirely of primary research, see "Special Case: Writing the Primary Research Essay" at the end of this chapter.

▌WRITING WITH RESEARCH: "QUOTATIONS"

Great quotes are the must-have ingredient for any research essay. Here is a recipe for concocting a finished product that will earn you credibility and persuade your readers: use quote sandwiches!

CREATE A QUOTE SANDWICH

© baibaz/Shutterstock.com

1) First introduce the quote in one sentence.

2) Then, insert the quote exactly as it appears in the original.

3) Finally, add a sentence that explains why the quote is important to your argument. Too often students drop in quotes from out of nowhere with no introduction or discussion afterwards.

Exercise:

Write your research essay's thesis statement:
Write your paragraph's topic sentence:

Transition and introduce the source (author, date, publication, article title) in a full sentence:
Quote the text exactly with a sentence or two that support your topic sentence:
Explain what the quotation means and how it supports your topic sentence and thesis:

USE IN-TEXT CITATION

In-text citations make research papers easy to navigate by naming the author right inside the body of the paper. All of the information your reader needs to find this source on the Works Cited page is already present in the sentence. In-text citation does not use footnotes or end-notes to cite sources and no superscript numbers above the examples. Look at this example.

In-Text Citation Example:

According to Virginia Woolf in *A Room of One's Own*, "In one hundred years, women will have ceased to be the protected sex" (40).

The readers can now refer to the Works Cited page and find the book if they want to learn more. The sentence in the essay tells us that the quote appears on page 40. Notice that only the page numbers appear in the parenthesis. There is no "p." "pg." or "pp." If the quote stretches over into the next page in the original source, the appropriate parenthetical would be (40-1).

In-Text Citation Example:

Maxine Hong Kingston evokes tenderness when she imagines, "The words stenciled on the box mean 'Fragile,' but literally say 'Use a little heart,'" (62).

Notice in this example the quotes within a quote get single quotation marks. If they appear at the end, there are actually three quotation marks: one single and a double as in the example above.

A "signal phrase" signals the reader a quote is coming. In the previous example, the signal phrase was "According to Virginia Woolf in *A Room of One's Own…*". You could also have a signal phrase with a verb. For example, "Woolf <u>states</u>, 'In one hundred years…'" Other common versions of the signaling verb are "writes" or "says".

Signal phrases are important. When quotes aren't properly integrated, they don't do what you want them to do: support your points.

Incorrect Quotation (*without* a signal phrase)

Every year, children are injured or killed by a handgun in an unintentional shooting or a suicide attempt. "In 2007, 3,067 children and teens ages 0-19 were killed by firearms in the United States."

Correct Quotation (*with* a signal phrase)

Every year, children are injured or killed by a handgun in an unintentional shooting or a suicide attempt. <u>According to The Brady Campaign to Prevent Gun Violence</u>, "In 2007, 3,067 children and teens ages 0-19 were killed by firearms in the United States." [Signal phrase is underlined.]

This quote is properly introduced and allows the readers to evaluate the source for themselves.

NOTE: Never use "quotes" as the verb of a signal phrase. An author can never "quote" him or herself.

Incorrect:

Virginia Woolf quotes, "In a hundred years…"

"Quotes" is not accurate unless she is quoting someone other than herself.

Correct:

Critic Kathy Newton quotes Woolf when she predicts "Women will have ceased to be the protected sex."

To get out of the doldrums with your verbs and spice things up, here is a list of verbs that work well in signal phrases so that you don't get stuck in a rut with "writes" and "says." Using a different verb instantly elevates your paper. Notice that each verb has a slightly different meaning, so choose the one that fits best with what you believe the author is trying to say with the quote, or how the quote fits into your argument.

SIGNAL VERB LIST

acknowledges	declares	opposes	reports
agrees	disagrees	points to	responds
argues	explains	posits	reveals
asserts	emphasizes	proposes	states
assumes	expresses	predicts	supports
believes	implies	suggests	wishes
charges	maintains	recognizes	wonders
claims	objects	regards	
considers	observes	remarks	
criticizes	offers	replies	

Only quote passages that support your point just made. Often students like a quote and throw it in without paying attention to its relevancy. Rather than supporting your argument, inapplicable quotes just confuse your reader. Be sure to use the quotes that support your argument.

Block long quotes. When quotes get too long, that is, longer than four typed lines or three lines of poetry, we "block" them. This means we indent them one inch into the text. Introduce a block quote with a complete sentence followed by a colon.

Block Quote Example:

In *The Woman Warrior*, Maxine Hong Kingston discusses what real luxury in the life of a woman means to her:

> To shut the door at the end of the workday, which does not spill into evening. To throw away books after reading them so they don't have to be dusted. To go through boxes on New Year's Eve and throw out half of what is inside. Sometimes for extravagance to pick a bunch of flowers for the one table. Other women besides me must have this daydream about a carefree life. I've seen Communist pictures showing a contented woman sitting on her bunk sewing. Above her head is her one box on a shelf. The words stenciled on the box mean "Fragile," but literally say "Use a little heart." The woman looks very pleased. The Revolution put an end to prostitution by giving women what they wanted: a job and a room of their own. (62)

- Notice that when a parenthetical page citation appears inside the text of your paper, you must put a period at the end of it. However, when you block quote, the quote's end punctuation goes before the parentheses, which "dangles" outside the end punctuation.

- Block quotes are double-spaced, and are only appropriate in longer essays.

- When no page number is available from a website, the parenthetical is not necessary.

Special Case: In block quoting, you don't put quotation marks around the text. The indentation alone shows that it is a quote. Therefore, if there is a quote within a quote, you do not use single quotation marks. You keep it exactly as it appears in the original. (See *The Woman Warrior* block quote).

Ellipsis (…)

We use ellipses to indicate that a part of a quotation has been omitted.

Example:

Maxine Hong Kingston imagines a "carefree life" as a woman a lot like Virginia Woolf did: "The Revolution . . [gave] women what they wanted: a job and a room of their own" (62).

Example:

"I've seen Communist pictures showing a contented woman sitting on her bunk sewing. . . . The Revolution put an end to prostitution by giving women what they wanted: a job and a room of their own" (62).

Notice, when you take out sentences after a complete sentence, you will actually have four periods separated by spaces. One is the period from the previous sentence followed by the three ellipsis marks. Note also, we usually do not begin or end quotes with ellipses (…). We assume that a quote comes out of a larger work and that the work continues after it.

[Brackets]

When we put brackets [ ] we can insert our own words into the quote to clarify meaning for readers as long as we retain the quote's original meaning.

a. Brackets can identify the referent for an unclear pronoun. The original might say, "<u>They</u> need a room of their own." Since we might want to clarify who "they" is, we can write in: "[Women] need a room of their own," (62).

b. We can also use brackets to show that there is a spelling or grammatical error in the original. If when quoting from a blog, for instance, you notice that the original writer has made a mistake, you don't fix it, because you must quote exactly the way he or she wrote it, but you do want the reader to know that this is not just a case of you being sloppy or making the mistake yourself. Therefore you insert [sic] right after the mistake to show that you are aware of it, but that is indeed what the original said.

Example:

Partygirl4 maintains "Women don't needs [sic] protection from any men." The correct verb would be "need" since "women" is a plural noun.

SPECIAL CASE: WRITING THE PRIMARY RESEARCH ESSAY

Among different disciplines, "research paper" means different things. In an English literature class, it means writing about literature. In an English composition or writing class, students often write research papers entirely from secondary sources (existing commentary, scholarship, or research on something, for example, any article found in a library database, a journal, a periodical, or a book itself.) In the social sciences, you may be asked to write a paper based on your own primary research. This is sometimes presented as a project since you must first gather the research yourself by means of interviews, surveys, or observation and study. (See "Conducting Surveys, Conducting Interviews" at the end of this chapter).

It is helpful to consider the context for these assignments. All classroom writing assignments can seem confusing in the sense that they are artificial—they are created to give students the experience of practicing certain types of writing. In a real world context, in your job as a financial professional, scientist, research analyst, etc., you won't need to reach for a thesis sentence, as your work—your findings and observations—will reveal it to you. Thus, what students experience as the "research paper" or research project is in the real world the work that's done on the job to find solutions.

PRIMARY RESEARCH IN THE REAL WORLD

For example, let's say you are working for a large financial group, and you are asked to research the profile of a small start-up company and assess whether or not your company should acquire it. You would use a combination of secondary research (looking up the company's financial profile on *LexisNexis*, the Internet, etc.) and primary research (meeting with the company's staff, asking them questions, poking around their facilities, observing their work firsthand, speaking with customers, etc.) The thesis for the written document you generate will be simple: either, "We *should* acquire Company X because -----" or "We *should not* acquire Company X because ----- ."

Many nonfiction books assigned in composition classes and in the social sciences are, for the sake of our discussion, effectively published research papers. For example, the now infamous *Fast Food Nation*, which reveals the dark underbelly of the American fast food industry, was researched and written by Eric Schlosser. In *Reefer Madness*, Schlosser researches the history of marijuana legislation and use in America. In her controversial book *Are Prisons Obsolete?*, professor and activist Angela Davis examines the prison-for-profit model of American incarceration and its implications for our prisoners, our taxpayers, and our nation.

Each of these authors began with a research question: Davis's research question actually became the title of her book. Schlosser likely began with a research question like, *What are the costs of this cheap food for workers, suppliers, manufacturers, and consumers?* As you approach your own research paper, you must begin with a research question. This section is not meant to be a comprehensive guide or a substitute for a Research Methodologies class, but it's enough to get you started.

GETTING STARTED: CHOOSING A RESEARCH QUESTION

You might begin by thinking about general topics that interest you, such as politics, public policy, city planning, social networking, stereotypes, racial profiling, social class disparities, gay rights, immigration issues, and so forth. The topic should be one you will be able to spend a lot of time with, since undertaking a primary research project will require a lot of time and effort.

Another way to arrive at a research question is to consider a question you have about phenomena you've observed. Look around you. What things have you always wondered about? Is there something about which you've wondered, "Is that fair?" or "How come ---?" or "Why is that ---?" For example, you might wonder why there are so many liquor stores in poor neighborhoods, or why California spends disproportionally more tax dollars on prison than on education. Such questions can lead to some fascinating answers, which you will compile in written form.

Here are some research questions brainstormed by English students.

Sample Research Questions

- Gated communities: who's locked out?
- Who does it better? Green Dots charter schools vs. Los Angeles Unified School District
- Liquor stores in South Central: sabotage by design?
- Homeless: by choice or necessity?
- What's hot & what's not: how do young people choose their boyfriends/girlfriends?
- Is white privilege still a powerful currency?

Your instructor can help you evaluate your question to make sure it is not too general, not too specific, and not a foregone conclusion (something everyone already knows.) Your research should consider a new aspect of the subject you examine. You may not arrive at one definitive answer, but the goal of research is simply to begin the conversation. Then another researcher will someday come along where you left off.

IMPORTANT FIRST STEPS

It's important to have a **hypothesis** in mind as you begin your project, since the contrast between what you expected to find and what you actually found can be discussed in your analysis. It's not important whether you are correct or not. It is not considered a weakness of your study if you failed to predict the outcome.

As you brainstorm about where and how to gather research data, it's important to ask yourself, what do I want to know, and how can I find it? The longer your research project takes, the easier it gets to lose perspective. That's why it's valuable to make some notes that you can look at and objectively evaluate. This will keep you from investing time and effort into less relevant leads.

What I Want to Know	Ways to Find Out
Who benefits from the legalization of marijuana?	Visit marijuana collectives and dispensaries
	Interview/Survey people waiting in line at those dispensaries, if possible
	Interview patients who legitimately use marijuana for chronic illness
	Try to get interview at mayor or city councilmen's offices to get their perspective

You might even rank the items on your chart in order of importance. That way, if a friend suggests you interview a local celebrity to discuss his recreational marijuana use, you would recognize that it is more important for you to get an interview with a city councilman or councilwoman. Likewise, it might make more sense to spend time crafting a survey to administer to young people standing in line at a dispensary. It really depends entirely on what you are looking for and how best you feel you can find answers, and keeping careful notes will help you stay on task.

CONDUCTING THE PRIMARY RESEARCH PROJECT: OVERVIEW

In simplest terms, the steps of conducting the primary research project are as follows: first, ask a research question; second, research the answers to your question; third, detect and analyze the patterns found in your data; and fourth, communicate these patterns in your essay (sometimes as your thesis).

Conducting the Primary Research Project: Overview

1) Decide on a research question.

2) Research some answers (which become your data).

3) Detect and analyze the patterns formed by your answers.

4) State the pattern(s) in your thesis.

	Example
1. Research Question	Why is the Three Strikes law still on the books?
2. Your research (interviews, etc.) shows that:	The state benefits from it, the prison industrial complex benefits from it, and prisoners aren't a sympathetic audience.
3. Detect and analyze patterns	The pattern here seems to be that those who benefit monetarily from those they have power to control can do as they please.
4. State the pattern as your thesis:	*The Three Strikes Law is still law because of its economic benefits to the state of California and to private companies inside the prison industrial complex, and because prisoners have no defense against those powerful groups.*

GATHERING DATA

While you may examine some secondary research sources (for example, internet or database articles) to find context for your issue and develop your hypothesis, a primary research project is so named because you will gather as much of your own data as possible. Data can be gathered from surveys, personal interviews, and focus groups (one interviewer with a number of respondents present at once—essentially a group interview.) Once you gather and read all your responses, you can begin to compile data by adding up like responses to each of your closed questions, and by typing up the answers to open questions (see below). Here are some considerations as you begin your research.

RESEARCH PAPER FAQ

The following can be used in both primary and secondary research.

What if I can't find answers?

- Vary your search terms.
- Vary the places you are looking (books, research databases, internet, etc.)
- Vary the databases you use.
- Consult a professor or a librarian.

What if I find *too many* answers?

- Limit your scope:
  - from the nation, to just one state, to just one city, etc.
  - from all time to a specific time period (a range of dates)
- Use some of your research results, rather than all.
- Choose the most timely, compelling, representative data.

What if the answers are not obvious?

- Then detect possible patterns.
- Not finding any info at all can be a pattern (of no existing data, or of hidden data.)
- Conflicting data can be a pattern (of conflicting data!)
- Data that exists only in a certain time period,(e.g., before the 1990s, or only after the 1990s) can be a pattern: why the gap?

Is there a correct answer to a research question?

- There is only what your research shows to be true. Just support all your assertions with research, and you've done your job.

CONDUCTING SURVEYS

There are a number of considerations for writing and conducting surveys in primary research. Two types of questions that can be used in surveys, personal interviews, and focus groups are open and closed questions.

OPEN AND CLOSED QUESTIONS

Once you've decided what you want to know, think about how you can phrase your survey questions to generate the data you want. There are two different kinds of questions: open and closed. Closed questions give respondents a limited range of options and in doing so, generate the most measurable data. For example, if respondents can only answer "Yes" or "No," responses will be split between the two and easily calculated. (If anyone ignores those two options and writes in "Other," you will have to decide how you want to count that: if you want to skip it, or create a third response category called "Other," or if you want to combine it with a similar category of those who skipped the question entirely as, "Other/No Answer.")

Open questions allow respondents the freedom to respond in any possible way. While their answers will be less easily classified, they will also offer a more in-depth snapshot of the experience you hope to capture. Open questions keep the survey from entirely missing important realities that a closed question could miss entirely. For example, let's say Linda wants to survey respondents about two local colleges to find out which they like better. In order to produce data which will qualify the top choice (explain why it was chosen), she uses closed questions:

Sample Closed Survey Questions

1) Which college is better, in your opinion?

   College X_____   College Y_____   No Difference_____

2) Please rank the qualities that were important to you in making this decision. _____ Library Resources   _____ Instructional Quality   _____ Athletics Program
   _____ Night Classes

While Linda's choices are thoughtful, what if many students chose College Y because of the childcare center? Her data would not reflect that at all. Thus, her ultimate conclusion based on her data, which might be that most students who preferred College Y ranked "Library Resources" and "Night Classes" as most important, would be potentially skewed.

There is always a margin of error, and experienced researchers know how to allow for that. (That's another reason this section is no substitute for a Research Methodologies class.) But by using a mix of open and closed questions, and asking the same questions both ways, students can arrive at data that is likely to give a fuller picture.

MAKE RESPONDENTS COMFORTABLE.

Almost as important as what you ask is how you ask it. Respondents need to feel comfortable and safe, and need to be assured that their feedback is anonymous and will not affect their status in a class or a job. Make it clear that you are doing this research for a class project, that no one will see it except for you and perhaps your group partners, and that no names will be attached. Offer to provide a copy of the resulting data if it is requested. Find neutral territory to collect surveys. For example, surveying women inside (or outside) of a battered women center is not neutral territory. Personally interviewing a crisis counselor that works at the center and listening to her experiences might be a better way to arrive at essentially the same data. Likewise, asking your high school basketball coach's current players to fill out surveys about their team experience under the coach's watchful eye may make respondents feel pressured and unsafe, even if you don't plan to show the results to the coach, since he is the one facilitating the administration of the surveys. Rather, distributing surveys at your local sporting goods store, or catching students as they get off the bus back home in the neighborhood, might be a better choice.

EFFECTIVE ADMINISTRATION OF SURVEYS: TIMELINE

Before:

Tell your research subjects or "respondents" that you are doing this project for school, and that answers are private and anonymous. Smile and be friendly.

Example: "Could you fill out this survey for my school project? It's anonymous."

During:

Don't make eye-contact or "watch" your respondents while they complete the survey. You don't want them to feel they are being judged. Put their response into a box, a large envelope, or on the bottom of the pile to show you are indifferent to it.

After:

Thank the person enthusiastically and smile. Offer some affirmation or validation of their contribution. Example: "Thanks, I'm trying to get an A!" or "It's so hard to get people to help; thank you!"

CONDUCTING INTERVIEWS

One of the most valuable types of primary research is the personal interview, which generates what researchers call qualitative data. While it can't be quantified (or measured mathematically) in the same way as survey data, it can provide equally valuable information that might not have emerged at all from an analysis of numbers alone. In essence, your interview is a big open question to your interviewee, a chance for him or her to ruminate on an issue aloud. Often when you get people talking, they will express things they haven't consciously considered before.

As with survey respondents, make your interviewees comfortable. Whenever possible, offer them food or coffee at your own expense. Travel the distance to meet the person in his/her comfort zone, and/or suggest a neutral middle ground nearby (for instance, the campus café, rather than the instructor's office, where he/she might feel less comfortable speaking freely with colleagues walking by).

Before the interview begins, make pleasant small talk, avoiding controversial or uncomfortable topics. Don't spend too long on chatter because as you want to respect the person's time, even if he/she says time is no issue. Your goal is to make the interview safe, comfortable, pleasant, and *not too long*, no matter how willing the person seems.

Immediately during or after small talk, establish the parameters of the interview. This is especially important if the interviewee is a personal friend or family member, as establishing parameters is a way to invoke a certain degree of formality in this exchange. If you want to record the session, ask your interviewee for permission. If he/she consents, place the recording device (a recorder, your iPhone, etc.) close enough to catch sound, but not close enough to make the person uncomfortable. The placement of a recording device that seems harmless enough at the beginning of an interview can come to seem, at uncomfortable moments, to point at the person. (It's a good idea to test out the range of your recording device with your own voice well in advance of this situation, so you know far away, or how unobtrusively, you can position it while still catching the sound.) Although it's common for movie characters to try and record conversations with hidden devices, this is in fact illegal in the real world.

Note: Never attempt to record a person's voice without explicit verbal, or written, consent.

If the person does not wish to be recorded, ask if it's okay for you to take notes. It would be very surprising if the person does not agree to this since it would be very difficult for you to remember his or her comments exactly. The more you record, by sound or on paper, the more faithful you can be to the person's exact wording. If an interviewee is still uncomfortable, explain that your goal is to quote him or her accurately.

Parameters of the interview should also include the length, the range, and the topic of the questions. You even have the option of presenting the interviewee with a printed copy of the questions. (If you only have one copy, you might lay it on the table between you.) This helps make the person feel even more comfortable since he/she knows what to expect. You need to be fairly flexible with the questions, as you can't demand answers to questions that make the person uncomfortable. Also, some questions might emerge spontaneously in response to comments your respondents make. It is quite an art to know which questions to push and when to back away. If you are not a journalist investigating a life or death situation, it's best just to back off. You don't want the person to decide that the whole thing is off and tell you not to use anything that was said. You can always find someone else to interview who might have similar information, so therefore honor the wishes of your interviewee.

SAMPLE PRE-INTERVIEW SCRIPT: ESTABLISHING PARAMETERS

Do you mind if I record this? I want to be able to use your exact wording whenever possible.

Great, I'm going to put my [recording device] right here on the side table, does that work for you?

Now, here is a copy of the questions I have for you. Do you have any questions or comments about them? Are there any you know you don't want to answer?

Okay, I think we could get through the first six questions in about thirty minutes, what do you think? Then we can take a break. If you need anything (more coffee, etc.) or want to take a break at any time, just let me know and we can stop at any time. Let's set my cell phone timer for thirty minutes. Here we go!

Finally, and perhaps most importantly, conduct the entire interaction of the interview—before, during, and after—with as much authority and confidence as possible. When we ask people to open up and speak to us, we are asking them to be vulnerable. Unconsciously they take cues from us, our body language, our facial expressions, and even our energy. Be very mindful of all these factors. Try not to respond verbally in any way other than "thank you for that response" or just "thank you," before you move on to the next question. You don't want to give the appearance of having any opinion or judgment about what has been said. Even saying "interesting," to one response and not another can make it seem as if the second was lacking or disappointing to you. For this reason, keep your verbal and facial expressions as neutral as possible. At the same time, remain calm, confident, and businesslike so the person feels at ease. Whatever you are feeling can be all too easily transmitted to the interviewee. If you are uncomfortable because you are hungry, the interviewee could interpret your discomfort as boredom, judgment, etc. Cover your own bases (food, bathroom, parking meter, etc.) before conducting the interview so that you are just as comfortable and prepared as *you* can be. If something comes up for you, just be direct about it. Imagine how you would feel in the interview seat, but remember also that even if you are the sort of person who is comfortable in most situations, not everyone is. Therefore follow these instructions whether you think they are necessary or not. You are showing respect, and the person—especially a friend or family member—will be flattered.

In terms of interview content, decide what you want to know and how you can get that information from the interviewee. Brainstorm both open and closed questions (as discussed in "Conducting a Survey"). Open questions are more ideal for interviews, as closed questions can be considered "leading." When you ask a person, "How damaging would you say this was to your son's education?" you are *suggesting* that it was damaging, and allowing the person to state only the range of (what you've decided was) damage. Rather, ask open, neutral questions ("How did this affect your son's education?") which allow the respondents to provide their own words to describe the breadth of their experiences. "It made a significant impact on my son's education, in both good and bad ways."

Don't bring a list of twenty-five questions when five revised questions will do. Your goal, as always, is to make this process as time-efficient, comfortable, and easy as possible for your respondents; you want them to leave you having had a good experience. As with essay writing, writing multiple drafts of interview questions is essential. Scribbling the questions on the back of an envelope on the car ride over is not the way to prepare for a successful interview! Taking time to review your questions will allow you to remove redundant questions or questions you can get answered elsewhere. However, it's always a good idea to have a few "warm up" or "softball" questions ready in case the interviewee is initially nervous and/or some back up questions in case he or she very brief in his/her responses. Creating these on the spot as necessary is a skill you will develop over time.

Like any outside source, surveys and interviews will need to be documented on your Works Cited page. (See Chapter 20 to find out how.)

Tabulating Survey (Quantitative) Data

Although there are some online services available, such as Surveymonkey.com, which administer surveys and calculate data automatically, the services offered to the free user are minimal. Users must register and pay to access the programs' full utilities. Therefore, this section will walk students through the traditional, offline process.

1) Use a copy of your survey to tabulate your data. (You can either use a physical copy and score it by hand, or open an electronic document in Microsoft Word or Excel and record the data electronically.) Make sure to save a copy of your original, unscored survey to include at the end of your paper, if desired.

2) Before you begin tabulating your data, count the number of surveys completed and write this down for reference as "Total Responses" on the top of your score sheet (See Figure I). Count the pile again after you have tabulated all your data to make sure no responses went missing during the process.

3) Go through the questions one by one and for each answer option, make a small score mark to represent 1 response. You will need to count all the answers for each of the question's answer options. For example, if one question has four possible responses, you will need to count all the answers for each of the options before you go on to tabulate the responses to another question. Take a look at the sample question in Figure I.

Figure I: Sample Tabulation of Survey Question

Total Responses: __7__

1) Were you able to attend this year's event?

III Yes, all or some portion of it   _IIII_ No

1b) If NO, what kept you from attending? (Check all that apply.)

_II_ work   ____ a class I couldn't miss

_I_ transportation issue   _I_ personal emergency

____ other _____

In the tabulation example in Figure I, Question 1 got a total of 7 responses (3 Yes's and 4 No's.) Therefore, the tabulator put 3 score marks by the "Yes" option and 4 score marks by the "No" option.

If a respondent leaves a question blank and does not select any of the possible options, that should not be counted as either a "Yes" or "No" response. It is a "No Answer" (you can either overlook these, or keep a "No Response" count for each question).

Likewise, treat "write-in" answers (Figure II) in the same fashion. When respondents write in their own answer(s), you can decide if there are enough write-ins to be counted and listed.

Figure II: Sample Write-In Response

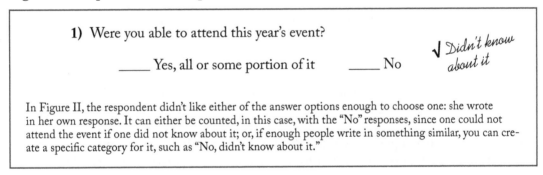

1) Were you able to attend this year's event?

_____ Yes, all or some portion of it   _____ No   ✓ Didn't know about it

In Figure II, the respondent didn't like either of the answer options enough to choose one: she wrote in her own response. It can either be counted, in this case, with the "No" responses, since one could not attend the event if one did not know about it; or, if enough people write in something similar, you can create a specific category for it, such as "No, didn't know about it."

Continue this process with all of the questions on the survey until all responses are recorded. For the sake of organization, it's a good idea to check off each question (or even each answer choice within a question) so that you know what you have already tabulated. on your score sheet, in case you are interrupted at any point in this process. Consider placing tabulated surveys face down or fold them over in one corner to indicate that they have been recorded.

4) Once you have tabulated all responses, convert your score marks to numbers to reflect the totals for each answer option. See Figure III for an example.

Figure III: Sample Survey Question Tabulation : Convert Score Marks to Numbers

Total Responses: <u>7</u>

1) Were you able to attend this year's event?

   <u>3</u> Yes, all or some portion of it   <u>4</u> No

   1b) If NO, what kept you from attending? (Check all that apply.)

   <u>2</u> work   <u>0</u> a class I couldn't miss

   <u>1</u> transportation issue   <u>1</u> personal emergency

   <u>   </u> other <u>   </u>

In Figure III, the score marks were summarized as numbers for easy reference.

In questions with an option to select "other" and record an individual response, you will need to tabulate such responses by writing/typing up these responses (see Figure IV).

Figure IV: Sample Survey Question Tabulation : Tabulate "Other" answers as applicable

Total Responses: <u>10</u>

1) Were you able to attend this year's event?

   <u>3</u> Yes, all or some portion of it   <u>7</u> No

   1b) If NO, what kept you from attending? (Check all that apply.)

   <u>2</u> work   <u>0</u> a class I couldn't miss

   <u>1</u> transportation issue   <u>1</u> personal emergency

   <u>3</u> other <u>"lack of childcare" (2), "couldn't afford it" (1)   </u>

In Figure IV, the 3 "other" responses were listed.

Figure V: Sample Chart for Tabulation of Percentages

Total Responses=10	#	%
Number that attended this year's event	3/10	30%
Number that did not attend this year's event	7/10	70%
Number reported they did not attend due to work	2/7	28%
Number reported they did not attend due to class	0/7	0%
Number reported they did not attend due to transportation issue	1/7	14%
Number reported they did not attend due to a personal emergency	1/7	14%
Number reported they did not attend due to "other" reason	3/7	42%

In this chart, the answer options (reasons for non-attendance) in the shaded boxes are divided by 7 since there were a total of 7 "No" responses. But since the items in the white boxes represent 10 total "Yes" *and* "No" answers, they are divided by 10.

5) To arrive at percentages, divide each number by the amount of total responses in that category. For example, 3 divided by 10 total responses equals a 30% rate of "Yes" responses, and correspondingly, a 70% rate of "No" responses. (Note that if you are not recording skipped answers, responses may not always correspond so nicely.) For convenience, you may choose to create a chart wherein you can list these calculations or have Microsoft Excel calculate the data automatically.

6) If you are so inclined, create a chart to represent the data patterns. Microsoft Power-Point is a great tool for making charts/graphs, and many services are available online (then import the image into your paper.) Not every style of chart (bar graph, pie chart, Ven diagram, etc.) is suited for every data set. Choose something that is neither unduly complicated nor too simplistic, yet highlights patterns. The chart must make sense to you in order to make sense to others.

7) When all your data is tabulated, look for trends (any highs and lows) and patterns in the data: spikes, no answers, everyone writing in a certain answer, etc. Any patterns in the data can be discussed and analyzed at length in the data analysis section of your paper.

THINGS TO LOOK FOR IN SURVEY DATA

- Are there differences or similarities in responses among demographic groups? (e.g., age, gender, ethnicity, religion, neighborhood, profession, income, etc.) What could this possibly mean?

- Other than demographic patterns, what other differences or similarities can you detect? What could they possibly mean?

- Might there be differences or similarities in responses based on the place, time, and method by which the survey was administered? What could this possibly mean?

8) Ultimately, relate your most significant data in sentence form in the Data Analysis section of your primary research paper. After you describe the data, augmented with chart(s) as applicable, discuss the possible reasons for these findings and any obstacles you encountered that might have influenced your data.

9) Describe any recommendations you have for data collection on this topic/research question in the future (e.g., time, funding, or access needed; what you had hoped to do but didn't have the time; different methodology, etc.).

Now and then, researchers find ways they erred either in the administration of the surveys or in the survey creation (the way the questions were worded, the range of choices given, the choice of open vs. closed questions, etc.). Except in extreme cases, this does not mean the data is completely useless; that's why every research project has a standard margin of error. (You can learn about this at length in Statistics and Research Methodology classes.) It does mean that you should describe the data's limitations in your analysis and extrapolate meaning as best you can. If you think you somehow influenced the data, say so. You will learn and grow as a researcher and do it differently next time. Every researcher—amateur, student, or professional—is a part of the "team" of those who create the body of research and literature on a topic. Together they pass the baton from one to another and each can pick up where the last left off, tweaking project scope, methods, etc. as necessary to gather even stronger data from which all can benefit.

COMPILING/CODING INTERVIEW (QUALITATIVE) DATA

The process of compiling interview data originates from your method of data collection.

If you recorded the interview (with the respondent's permission, of course) you will simply begin by transcribing it (writing/typing up the person's words word for word). There are many software programs available to speed this process.

If you are working from notes, you can begin by fleshing them out as much as necessary to retain meaning. Once a few days have passed after the interview, you may no longer remember what you meant when you jotted down "fnd. lky repl."

Once you have a transcript or completed notes from which to work, you can begin the process of **coding**. This is the process by which you categorize responses.

First, read over the complete text several times to detect words and topics which appear often. Then, devise a color or mark (circle, underline, etc.) to use for each distinct category.

For example, you might use a green highlighter pen every time the person mentions his/her workplace or the business environment. The words might or might not be the same each time the reference is made, but if it more or less addresses the same topic, you highlight it in green. Go through this process for all the main themes, topics, and key phrases.

Conducting this process in a word processing program allows you a range of color highlighting choices without the purchase of highlighter pens! But more importantly, word processing programs have a "Find" or search command which allows you to quickly find the occurrence of specific words. This can be a real time saver in a document of considerable length.

Once you have coded each data set (each different person's set of responses) as thoroughly as you can, look for patterns and trends among the answers: repeated/similar answers, questions all respondents seemed uncomfortable answering, those answered most confidently and readily, etc. Any patterns in the data can be discussed and analyzed at length in the data analysis section of your paper.

Things to Look for in Interview Data

- Are there differences or similarities in responses among demographic groups? (e.g., age, gender, ethnicity, religion, neighborhood, profession, income, etc.) What could this possibly mean?
- Other than demographic patterns, what other differences or similarities can you detect? What could they possibly mean?
- Might there be differences or similarities in responses based on the place, time, and method by which the survey was administered? What could this possibly mean?

Ultimately, relate your most significant data in sentence form in the Data Analysis section of your primary research paper. You may have pages and pages of coded interview data, but you won't need to use it all, just what you find most significant. After you describe the data, augmented with chart(s) as applicable, discuss the possible reasons for these findings and any obstacles you encountered that might have influenced your data.

There are several options for reporting qualitative (interview) data. You can narrate the "story" of your interview in a narrative style, such as "When I asked [Kadiri] his income, he became shy," or a more summary-like style which omits the exact questions, since they often implied by the answers: "[Kadiri] was shy about his income." Here the respondent's name is bracketed, suggesting that the researcher did not use the respondent's real name, to protect his privacy. [Make sure to ask your respondents whether or not they feel comfortable with you using their real, and/or full, names in your written work.)

Writing up the primary research essay is in many respects much like writing an essay about literature. In both contexts, we make observations about data; in literature, patterns in the text, and in primary research, patterns in our collected data.

However, while literary analysis essays tend to use a more classical style of argumentation (thesis followed by supports) the primary research essay follows a different template. The convention for writing up one's research that has been established in the humanities and the social sciences looks something like this.

STRUCTURING THE PRIMARY RESEARCH ESSAY

Note: This is a specific format for primary research essays only.

Introduction — Discusses **purpose** of the study, **research question** (what you wanted to find out) and **hypothesis** (what you thought you would find).

You might also include some **historical or sociological context** which frames your study (explains why it's pertinent or necessary).

The **length of your introduction** can be anywhere from a paragraph to a page or two, depending on the length and scope of your paper.

Methodology — Discusses the methods you used to conduct your research: surveys, focus groups, interviews, etc.

Sometimes it is pertinent to mention any secondary research that guided you in a certain direction. (e.g., "Because most statistics show that the largest group of medical marijuana users are under 40, we started with this age group.")

The **length of your methodology** section is as long as it takes to explain your methodology! It is usually substantially longer than the introduction; an average in a 10 page paper might be 3 pages. There's really no hard and fast rule.

Data	Your data are the results of your interviews, surveys, or observations. Some explanations may be in order to explain apparent discrepancies or overwhelming patterns.	The **length of your data section** is as long as it takes to explain your data. The more research you gathered, the more data you will have. It could range from 1 to 3 pages in a 10 page essay.
Data Analysis	The data quickly gives way to an analysis of the data collected. This is where you make meaning of your findings and accept or reject them as "answers" to your research question.	The **length of your data analysis section** is as long as it takes to thoroughly analyze your data. It could range from 2 to 3 pages in a 10 page essay.
Conclusion	Your conclusion is the place to summarize your project, "answer" your hypothesis with a brief summary of your findings, describe any obstacles that limited your findings, and to offer recommendations for changes in practices/policy or for further research.	The **length of your conclusion** is as long as it takes to conclude and offer final reflections and recommendations. It could range from 1 to 2 pages in a 10 page essay.
Documentation and Appendices	Tables or charts illustrating your data can be included in one or more appendices and referenced in the body of your paper. (e.g., "See Appendix I.")	Documentation pages such as Works Cited page, Bibliography, and/or Appendices do not count as pages of the essay for the sake of the required minimum.

Read the article "The Early Catastrophe" and identify its components as per the "Structure of the Primary Research Essay" chart.

http://www.aft.org/pdfs/americaneducator/spring2003/TheEarlyCatastrophe.pdf

CHAPTER CHAPTER CHAPTER 20

DOCUMENTING YOUR SOURCES

▌WHY CITE?

Students often mistakenly believe that citing sources is only a method for professors to police student work and make sure no unauthorized borrowing occurs. In reality, however, scholars began citing their sources so that other researchers could take their work further. Let's say you are writing a research paper on "green architecture." You read a terrific article on different methods of eco-friendly construction and find out what "LEED certified" means. Perhaps the article mentions permeable pavement materials or solar heating panels only briefly, but this is really what you are most interested in. Your next step should be to look at that article's

works cited page to get further sources on solar heating panels to deepen your own research. Because you have enjoyed the article and found it persuasive, you are likely to find trustworthy sources of information from its Works Cited page. Think of it like getting a recommendation from a friend.

> Citing identifies and credits sources used in a research paper, acknowledging their role in shaping your research. Properly citing also allows others to retrieve this valuable information.

AVOIDING PLAGIARISM

When you borrow from other sources to support your argument, you must give proper credit. By crediting your sources, you avoid plagiarism.

> "Plagiarism is the same as cheating or stealing. It is using someone else's words or ideas without giving them credit." Ken Lin, East Los Angeles College librarian

Plagiarism always represents a missed opportunity for the student because it robs him or her of the opportunity to learn. If you paid someone to run the Boston Marathon for you and you won, how would you feel? You might have a nice trophy, but it wouldn't mean you would know how to run around the block or that you would have the muscles or stamina to do so. Doing the work enables you to gather the life skills you need to succeed. Ultimately, these are much more valuable than the grade you won't have "earned."

But, since we brought up grades, let us point out that plagiarism inevitably wreaks havoc with the guilty student's grade and college record. It is much easier for professors to spot plagiarism than students think. Multiple computer programs exist that enable us to detect plagiarism. Once we have spotted it, colleges and universities require professors to report plagiarism and a permanent record is made on the student's file. It's just not worth the risk or the hassle. If you plan to plagiarize, don't bother coming to college. You will be robbing yourself (and that student whose seat you took) of an education.

WHEN SHOULD YOU CITE?

Simply put, **if you are using another person's idea, you must cite your source.** Many students plagiarize unintentionally. Remember, whenever you summarize, paraphrase, or quote other authors, you must properly credit your sources, even if you haven't used the exact wording they have.

To review, quotations can be direct (using quotation marks) or indirect (no quotation marks and often introduced by 'that'). Here are some sample uses.

Direct Quotation:

> A noted scientist states, "A hundred years ago, the average temperature of the earth was about 13.7°C (56.5°F); today, it is closer to 14.4°C (57.9°F)" (Silver 11).

Paraphrase:

> A noted scientist observes that the earth's current average temperature is 57.9°F compared to 56.5°F a hundred years ago (Silver 11).

HOW DO I CITE?

Following a mutually-accepted code of citation like MLA, APA, or Chicago Manual style allows fellow researchers to understand instantly where the information was found so that they can get it for themselves. Which citation style you use depends upon the discipline in which you are conducting research. English papers use MLA; social and behavioral sciences typically use APA. History often uses Chicago Manual style. When in doubt, check with your instructor.

CITING SOURCES MLA STYLE

MLA stands for the Modern Language Association. The MLA determines guidelines for preparing student research papers and projects and scholarly manuscripts in the humanities. The humanities generally means the disciplines of English, modern and classic Languages, Law, Performing arts, Philosophy, Religion. "MLA style" refers to a system of citing research sources. We all agree in the humanities to use the same format so that we know what all of the information means. For example, that: (35) means "page 35."

There are two parts to citing according to MLA style:

1) Brief in-text citations (in parentheses and in the signal phrase) appear within the body of your essay.

2) A list of full citations on the Works Cited page appears at the end of your paper.

   Note:

   • All references cited in the text must appear in the Works Cited.

   • Conversely, each entry in the Works Cited must be cited in the text.

In-text Citation

The most important thing to remember when citing is that your reasons for doing so are to establish your credibility as a researcher and to provide a clear path for another scholar to find your sources and learn from them. You want to strive for clarity at all times. If in doubt, ask yourself whether you could find the original source from the information you have provided. If the answer is "no," then you must add more information in-text. You must provide information that will allow the reader to locate exactly where you found information in your sources. Usually for print sources this is the page number (188) and sometimes, when necessary, the author's last name and page number (Gibaldi 216).

Parenthetical reference at the end of the sentence before the punctuation mark:

> The average world temperature is rising at an alarming rate of 200 degrees Celsius per year (Polar 188).

More than one page:

> Smith states some startling facts about the changing world temperature (123-25).

Multiple page locations from your source:

> Jones alludes to this premise (136-39, 145).

Two works cited:

> (Taylor 54; Thomas 327)

When you cite more than one work by the same author in your paper, indicate which work in your parenthetical citation:

> Governments can be slow to react to the threat of global warming (*Our Environment* 87).

Electronic Sources

If possible, electronic and online sources are cited just like print resources in parenthetical references. Often electronic resources will not have page numbers. In these cases omit numbers from the parenthetical reference:

> (Smith)—the author's last name

> ("Bovine Flatulence: A Major Source of Greenhouse Gases")—if no author

For all its notoriety, *Lolita*, Nabokov's novel about a middle-aged professor of literature in love and in lust with his twelve-year-old step-daughter, was never banned in the United States, though through its courts were dragged, among others, Joyce's *Ulysses* and Lawrence's *Lady Chatterley's Lover* (titles which were ultimately vindicated). Arguably, movie adaptations of the novel faced more difficult hurdles in getting approval for cinematic release (Power 101). Rejected by litigation-shy American publishers on its completion in 1954 and a year later published in France, *Lolita*, however, promptly earned a ban from the French government and was hauled into its courts to defend itself against obscenity charges—even though not a single act of sex (normal or deviant) explicitly graces its pages, nor, for that matter, is nary a vulgar four-letter word to be found (Ladenson 188). Besides being banned in the country that gave the world the Marquis de Sade and the French kiss, *Lolita* has been censored by the governments of England, Argentina, New Zealand, and South Africa ("Banned . . ."), but not in America. In other words, *Lolita*, in its "birth" country never had to pass the litmus test for obscenity—defined by one authority, Joseph Slade, as "nastiness . . . demeaning prurience . . . sheer inhumanity" (4). Despite, or because of, the federal government's official reticence regarding *Lolita's* propriety, countless local communities in America have placed the novel on its censorship lists since the novel's wildly successful domestic publication in 1958. Within a month of its publication, it was banned by the Cincinnati Public Library (Boyd 367) and as recently as 2006, the supervisors of Marion County, Florida, challenged the book as "unsuitable for minors" ("Banned . . ."). If *Lolita* were just another book of pornography among the heaving, tumescent mountains of such books, it would have been flushed down *le toilette* on the day it was published. *Lolita*, however, is not such a book.

Even though it is a novel at base about a pedophile, it is an artful book about a pedophile (or in Nabokov's more felicitous phrase, a "nympholeptic"). Just before the French government banned the book, Graham Greene named it one of the three best books of the year (Kuzmanovich 7). Over time, critical appreciation of *Lolita* has only become more positively engorged, appearing on many "best" lists: Modern Library's "100 Best Novels" of the 20th century (ranked 4th!), Le Monde's 100 Best Novels (ranked 27th), *Time's* "All Time 100 Novels" of the English-language, 1923-2005 (ranked alphabetically), Harold Bloom's "Western Canon," and on and on. While critics and scholars (though not in unanimity) praise *Lolita* for its aesthetic value, Nabokov in a letter to pre-eminent critic and friend, Edmund Wilson, cites its virtue, "When you read Lolita, please mark that it is a highly moral affair" (Boyd 227). *Essay continues but is not reprinted here.*

Works Cited

"Banned and/or Challenged Books from the Radcliffe Publishing Course Top 100 Novels of the 20th Century." *American Library Association.* 20 July 2009, http://www.ala.org/Template.cfm?Section=bbwlinks&Template=/Content Management/ContentDisplay.cfm&ContentID=136590. Accessed Nov. 2018.

Page from a Website

Boyd, Brian. *Vladimir Nabokov; The American Years.* Princeton UP, 1991.

Print Book

Kuzmanovich, Zoran. "Chronology." *Approaches to Teaching Nabokov's Lolita,* edited by Zoran Kuzmanovich and Galya Diment, Modern Language Association of America, 2008, pp. 1-12.

Essay in an Anthology

Ladenson, Elisabeth. *Dirt for Art's Sake; Books on Trial from Madame Bovary to Lolita.* Cornell UP, 2007.

Print Book

Power, Elizabeth. "The Cinematic Art of Nympholepsy: Movie Star Culture as Loser Culture in Nabokov's *Lolita.*" *Criticism,* vol. 41, no. 1, 1999, pp. 101-08. *JSTOR,* www.jstor.org/stable/23124232. Accessed 3 Nov. 2018

Journal Essay found in a Database

Slade, Joseph W. *Pornography in America: A Reference Handbook.* ABC-CLIO, 2000.

Print Book

(Excerpt reprinted with permission from Ken Lee, East Los Angeles College Librarian)

MLA CITATION MODELS

Table 1: MLA Citation

Author's Name Last, First	Publication Title	"Article Title"	Date of Publication

Power, Elizabeth. "The Cinematic Art of Nympholepsy: Movie Star Culture as Loser
Culture in Nabokov's *Lolita*." *Criticism* vol. 41. no. 1. 1999. pp. 101–08. *JSTOR*,
www.jstor.org/stable/23124232. Accessed 3 Nov. 2018.

URL	Date of Access	Volume and Issue Number	Pages	Database Title

We have reproduced for you the most common citation models. Additional models are
available in the *MLA Handbook for Writers of Research Papers*. 8th ed. and online at www.owl.
english.purdue.edu/.

According to the *MLA Handbook,* the following months are written out in full: May, June,
July, and September is abbreviated as "Sept." All other months are abbreviated to three letters, for example, "Oct." for "October."

1) **Book with One Author**

   Cunningham, Michael. *The Hours*. Picador, 1998.

2) **Book with Two or Three Authors**

   Hart, Betty, and Todd R. Risley. *Meaningful Differences in the Everyday Experience of
   Young American Children*. Paul H. Brookes Publishing, 1995.

   Boutry, Katherine, Clare Norris-Bell, and Holly Bailey-Hofmann. *The West Guide to
   Writing: Success through the Sequence from Community College to University*.
   Kendall Hunt, 2018.

3) **Book with Four or More Authors**

   Lastname, Firstname et al. *Title*. Publisher, Publication date.

Et al. is a Latin abbreviation that means "and the others." It corresponds to the abbreviation "etc.," short for *et cetera*, which means, "and the other [inanimate things]."

4) An Edited Book

Edited books follow the same pattern listed above, according to the number of editors, but with the edition of the word "editor" or "editors."

> Sugg, Richard P., editor. *Jungian Literary Criticism*. Northwestern University Press, 1992.

> Ashcroft, Bill, Gareth Griffiths, and Helen Tiffin, editors. *The Post-Colonial Reader*. Routledge, London, 1995.

5) An Authored Book with an Editor

Sometimes a book written by a poet or novelist has been edited for length or clarity by an editor. In this case, proceed as per the "one author" guidelines above, but embed the editor inside the citation, as so.

> Mill, John Stuart. *On Liberty*. edited by Currin V. Shields, Bobbs-Merrill Educational Publishing, 1956.

6) Electronic Book or eBook (Kindle, Nook, iPad, etc.)

In general, for eBooks, follow the format for print books. According to OWL, "An e-book is considered a version, so it should be listed after the title of the book, before the publication information. If you know the type of e-book you used (such as Kindle or Ebook library), be sure to specify that."

> Rowling, J. K. *Harry Potter and the Chamber of Secrets*. Kindle ed., Arthur A. Levine Books, 1999.

7) Literary Work in an Anthology

> Packer, ZZ. "Buffalo Soldiers." *LIT*, edited by Laurie G. Kirzner and Stephen R. Mandell, Wadsworth Cengage, 2012.

8) Essay in an Anthology or Chapter of an Edited Book

> DeSalvo, Louise A. "As 'Miss Jan Says': Virginia Woolf's Early Journals." *Virginia Woolf And Bloomsbury*, edited by Jane Marcus, Palgrave Macmillan, 1987, pp. 96–124.

9) Journal or Magazine Article Found in a Database

> Schiff, James. "Rewriting Woolf's Mrs. Dalloway: Homage, Sexual Identity, and the Single-Day Novel by Cunningham, Lippincott, and Lanchester." *Critique*, vol. 45 no. 4, 2004, pp. 363–82. *Proquest*, www. search.proquest.com/docview/ 212443579?accountid=38212. Accessed 23 Apr. 2018.

10) **Magazine Article from the Web**

> Anderson, Sam. "Sussex Chainsaw Massacre: The Horrification of Jane Austen." *NYmag.com,* New York Media, 6 Sept. 2009, nymag.com/arts/books/reviews/58847/. Accessed 22 Apr. 2018.

11) **Page from a Website**

> Character Spotlight: Maria Stewart." *Slavery and the Making of America: The Slave Experience,* Thirteen: Media with Impact, 2004, www.thirteen.org/wnet/slavery/experience/education/index.html. Accessed 16 Oct. 2018.

12) **Film or Book Review**

> Holden, Stephen. "Who's Afraid like Virginia Woolf ?" Review of *The Hours,* directed by Stephen Daldry. *New York Times,* 27 Dec. 2002, www.nytimes.com/2002/12/27/movies/film-review-who-s-afraid-like-virginia-woolf.html. Accessed 23 Apr. 2018.

13) **Film or DVD**

> *The Hours.* Directed by Stephen Daldry, performances by Meryl Streep, Julianne Moore, and Nicole Kidman, Paramount, 2002.

14) **Personal Interview**

> Jacobs, Betty. Personal interview. 26 June 2012.

15) **Published Interview**

> Hockensmith, Steve. "Pride and Prejudice and Prequels: Mash-Up Author Talks Austen and Zombies." *Time,* by Allie Townsend, 14 Apr. 2010, http://techland.time.com /2010/04/14/pride-prejudice-prequels-mash-up-author-talks-jane-austen-zombies/. Accessed 22 Apr. 2018.

16) **Work of Art**

If accessed in person:

> Lange, Dorothea. *Migrant Mother.* 1936. Photograph. The Getty Center, Los Angeles.

If accessed by the web:

> Rousseau, Henri. *The Sleeping Gypsy.* 1897. Museum of Modern Art, New York, *The Archive,* www.moma.org/collection/works/80172. Accessed 12 Sep. 2018.

17) **Advertisement**

> Daisy by Marc Jacobs. Advertisement. *Marie Claire.* Oct. 2012, p. 165.

18) **Entry from a Blog, Listserv, Product Review, User Comment, or Discussion Group**

Cite Web postings as you would a standard Web entry. Provide the user name, then the author of the work in brackets (if available), the title of the posting in quotation marks, the Web site name in italics, the publisher, and the posting date. Follow with the URL and the date of access.

> Screen name, real name (if available). "Posting Title." *Name of Site*, Name of organization (sponsor or publisher), posting date, URL. Date of access.

> JuliaM. "Took a chance and tried something different." *Amazon Product Reviews*, Amazon, 1 Oct. 2017, www.amazon.com/gp/customerreviews/R31LCZQ56 T819V/ref=cm_cr_dp_d_rvw_ttl?ie=UTF8&ASIN=B001KWH9H4.'?+. Accessed 12 Sept. 2018.

19) **Tweet**

Twitter handle. Entire tweet in quotation marks. 'Twitter' in italics. Date and time of posting. URL. Access date optional.

> @REALStaceyDash. "Vote for Romney. The only choice for your future." *Twitter*, 7 Oct. 2012, 11:32 a.m., twitter.com/realstaceydash/status/255012859363352576? lang=en. Accessed 20 Apr. 2018.

20) **YouTube Video**

If the author's name is different from the name of the uploader, include the name of the uploader after the name of the video. Only include the author's name once, either at the start of the citation, or after the name of the video.

> "Video name." *YouTube*, uploaded by Username, Publishing date, URL. Accessed date.

> Derby, Bruce. "Critical Readings and Approaches to Othello." *YouTube*, 21 July 2012, www.youtube.com/watch?v=05Q24Lv0z1Y. Accessed 17 Apr. 2018.

APA STYLE

APA (American Psychological Association) is most commonly used to cite sources within the behavioral and social sciences. These references appear at the end of the paper in a "Reference List."

Book:

> Cunningham, M. (1998). *The hours*. New York, NY: Picador.

Electronic or eBook (Kindle, Nook, iPad, etc):

> Hong Kingston, M. (1975). *The woman warrior*. Retrieved from http://xxxxxxxxx

Film or DVD:

> Daldry, S. (Director). (2002). *The hours* [DVD]. United States: Paramount Home Entertainment.

Journal Article Found in a Database:

> Power, E. (1999). The cinematic art of nympholepsy: Movie star culture as loser culture in Nabokov's *Lolita*. *Criticism*, 41.1, 363–82. http://go.galegroup.com.library.wlac.edu/ps/start.do?p=LitRC&u=lawest.

Magazine Article from the Web:

> Anderson, S. (2009, September 14). Sussex chainsaw massacre: The horrification of Jane Austen. *New York*. Retrieved from http://www.new-york-magazine.com/

Film or Book Review:

> Sim, L. (2005). No ordinary day: *The hours*, Virginia Woolf and everyday life [Review of the film *The Hours*, 2002]. *Hecate, 32 [1]*, 60–70.

Essay in an Anthology or Chapter of an Edited Book:

> DeSalvo, L. (1987). As 'Miss Jan Says': Virginia Woolf's early journals. In J. Marcus (Ed.), *Virginia Woolf and Bloomsbury* (96–124). Bloomington: Indiana UP.

Personal Interview:

No personal communication is included in your reference list. Instead, cite the reference in parenthesis.

> (B. Jacobs, personal communication, June 26, 2012)

Published Interview:

If an interview is not retrievable in print form, cite the interview only in the text (not in the reference list) and provide the month, day, and year in the text.

If an audio file or transcript is available online, use the following model, specifying the medium in brackets (e.g., [Interview transcript, Interview audio file]):

Townsend, A. & Hockensmith, S. (2010, April 14). *Pride and prejudice* and prequels: Mash-up author talks Austen and zombies. Retrieved from Time Magazine Web site: http://www.time.com/time/

The in-text citation includes the author and date, as with any other APA Style citation.

Please visit www.apastyle.org for additional examples and model reference pages.

CHICAGO MANUAL CITATION MODELS

The following citation formats for *The Chicago Manual of Style* include both the Foot or End Note model followed by the Bibliography model.

Book:

Note:

1. Michael Cunningham, *The Hours* (New York: Picador, 1998), 23.

Bibliography:

Cunningham, Michael. *The Hours*. New York: Picador, 1998.

Electronic or eBook (Kindle, Nook, iPad, etc):

Note:

1. Jane Austen, *Pride and Prejudice* (New York: Penguin Classics, 2007), Kindle edition.

Bibliography:

Austen, Jane. *Pride and Prejudice*. New York: Penguin Classics, 2007. Kindle edition.

Film or DVD:

Note:

2. *The Hours*, directed by Stephen Daldry (2002. Hollywood, CA: Paramount Home Entertainment, 2003), DVD.

Bibliography:

The Hours. Directed by Stephen Daldry. 2002. Hollywood, CA: Paramount Home Entertainment, 2003. DVD.

Journal Article Found in a Database

According to *The Chicago Manual of Style*,

"Include a DOI (Digital Object Identifier) if the journal lists one. A DOI is a permanent identifier that, when appended to http://dx.doi.org/ in the address bar of an Internet browser, will lead to the source. If no DOI is available, list a URL. Include an access date only if one is required by your publisher or discipline."

Model:

Note number. First name Last name, "Title of Web Page," *Publishing Organization or Name of Website in Italics*, publication date and/or access date if available, URL.

Note:

3. Elizabeth Power, "The Cinematic Art of Nympholepsy: Movie Star Culture as Loser Culture in Nabokov's *Lolita*," *Criticism*, 41.1, (1999): 101–08.

http://go.galegroup.com.library.wlac.edu/ps/retrieve

Bibliography:

Power, Elizabeth. "The Cinematic Art of Nympholepsy: Movie Star Culture as Loser Culture in Nabokov's *Lolita*." *Criticism*, 41.1 (1999): 101–08. http://go.galegroup.com.library.wlac.edu/ps/retrieve

Magazine Article from the Web:

Note:

1. Sam Anderson, "Sussex Chainsaw Massacre: The Horrification of Jane Austen," *New York*, September 14, 2009, 26.

Bibliography:

Anderson, Sam. "Sussex Chainsaw Massacre: The Horrification of Jane Austen." *New York*, September 14, 2009. http://www.new-york-magazine.com/

Article or Chapter of an Edited Book:

Note:

4. Louise A. DeSalvo. "As 'Miss Jan Says': Virginia Woolf's Early Journals," in *Virginia Woolf and Bloomsbury*, ed. Jane Marcus (Bloomington: Indiana UP, 1987), 96–124.

Bibliography:

DeSalvo, Louise A. "As 'Miss Jan Says': Virginia Woolf's Early Journals." In *Virginia Woolf and Bloomsbury*, edited by Jane Marcus, 96–124. Bloomington: Indiana UP, 1987.

Published and/or Broadcast Interview

Note:

1. Steve Hockensmith, interview by Allie Townsend, *Time*, April 14, 2010.

Bibliography:

Hockensmith, Steve. "*Pride and Prejudice* & Prequels: Mash-up Author Talks Austen and Zombies." Interview by Allie Townsend. *Time*, April 14, 2010.

Unpublished Interview

Note:

1. Betty Jacobs (Chair Language Arts Division, West Los Angeles College) in discussion with the author, June 26, 2012.

Bibliography:

The *Chicago Manual* Website specifies that informal interviews are discussed in the text, but seldom cited on the bibliography. If you wish to cite them, do so as follows:

Betty Jacobs (Chair Language Arts Division, West Los Angeles College), Interview by the author, Culver City, CA., June 26, 2012.

Additional examples of citations and model reference pages may be found at http://www. chicagomanualofstyle.org.

Tips on Writing a Correct Works Cited Page

Remember:

1) Double-space evenly throughout. No extra spaces between entries.

2) Alphabetize sources by last name of the author. If there is no last name available or a source is published online anonymously, alphabetize by the article title.

3) Use a "hanging-indent." The first line is flush left. Subsequent lines are indented. Under "Paragraph" in Word you can choose "hanging indent" under "Special" for Indentation. This will do the hanging indent for you.

4) URLs/DOIs are required. Access dates are optional, but highly recommended.

CITATION DOCUMENTS: THE WORKS CITED PAGE, BIBLIOGRAPHY, AND THE ANNOTATED BIBLIOGRAPHY

In college classes, some written assignments require a bibliography and/or Works Cited page. What's the difference between the two? **A bibliography is a general term for a list of sources or works consulted in the essay's construction.** It might include a mix of books, journal articles, electronic articles, etc., depending on what sources you used. You may have read all these items and used them to inform the direction of your research, but you may not have quoted or paraphrased each one. **The Works Cited page, a specific requirement of MLA format, includes only the sources you directly quoted, paraphrased, or summarized in the essay.**

An essay might have both a bibliography and a Works Cited page if required, and in that case there will be some duplicate entries. Occasionally, an instructor may require an **annotated bibliography, a bibliography in which a brief description of the source and its usefulness in writing your essay accompanies each citation.** This is a place to provide readers with a helpful direction for their own research on the subject.

It's important to remember that although it feels like you are producing your essays and citations documents simply for your professor, in a larger context you are practicing the skills you will use if, in a professional capacity, you publish your work in an academic conference proceedings magazine or a professional journal. In this sense, an annotated bibliography can be very useful to readers and researchers. But, in the classroom, you might choose to submit a bibliography, or even an annotated bibliography, even if not required by the instructor, in order to supplement a small Works Cited page, and give a more accurate picture of the overall effort you invested in your essay. If, as is good practice, you are keeping a list of all the sources you consult, it doesn't take that much more time to produce a bibliography in order to show all the items you combed through before you found the two gems you repeatedly quoted. This is a good habit that benefits you by serving as a record of your research—you might be able to come back to a source in another semester, in another essay—and can also help to make your essays appear professional and thorough.

Let's take a look at the following documents: a sample MLA Works Cited page, a sample bibliography, and a sample annotated bibliography.

Sample Works Cited:

Works Cited

Geiger, Kim. "Rush Limbaugh's 'Slut' Comment Draws Rebukes from All Sides." *Los Angeles Times*, 2 March 2012, http://articles.latimes.com/2012/mar/02/news/ la-pn-rush-limbaugh-draws-rebukes-from-all-sides-20120302. Accessed 28 Mar. 2018.

McVeigh, Tracy. "Forty Years of Feminism—But Women Still Do Most of the House-work." *The Gaurdian*, 10 March 2012, www.theguardian.com/society/2012/ mar/10/housework-gender-equality-women. Accessed 3 Apr. 2018.

Sweet, Lynn. "Women Still Earn Less Than Men: New Obama White House Report on Status of Women." *Chicago Sun-Times*, 1 Mar. 2011, chicago.suntimes.com/ section/lynn-sweet-politics/. Accessed 3 Apr. 2018.

"U.S. Interim Projections by Age, Sex, Race, and Hispanic Origin: 2000-2050." United States Census Bureau, Population Division, 18 Mar. 2004, census.gov/prod/1/pop/ p25-1130.pdf. Accessed 3 Apr. 2018.

Note that even though there is usually a page number in the upper right-hand corner of the works cited, neither the works cited nor the bibliography, nor any appendices, count as a "page" of writing. When your professors ask for ten pages, they mean ten pages of *writing*. We insert a header with last name and page number into our documents for the sake of identification, in case the pages become separated.

Notice in the above example that the entries are all in alphabetical order. "McVeigh" comes before "Sweet." Some entries—like the two just mentioned, for instance—begin with names. But not all citations begin with a name. Sometimes there is no listed author, and a citation thus begins with an article title, like the one that begins, "U.S. Interim Projections." No matter how a citation begins, all citations are alphabetized.

The same rules apply in the following bibliography.

Sample Bibliography:

Bibliography

Boyd, Brian. *Vladimir Nabokov; The American Years.* Princeton UP, 1991.

Fein, Sin. "Freedom." *Sin Fein*, May 1991, www.sinnfein.org/documents/freedom.html. Accessed 3 Apr. 2018.

McVeigh, Tracy. "Forty Years of Feminism—But Women Still Do Most of the House-work." *The Gaurdian*, 10 March 2012, www.theguardian.com/society/2012/mar/10/housework-gender-equality-women. Accessed 3 Apr. 2018.

Power, Elizabeth. "The Cinematic Art of Nympholepsy: Movie Star Culture as Loser Culture in Nabokov's *Lolita*." *Criticism*, vol. 41, no.1, 1999, pp. 101–08. *JSTOR*, www.jstor.org/stable/23124232. Accessed 3 Nov. 2018.

Sweet, Lynn. "Women Still Earn Less Than Men: New Obama White House Report on Status of Women." *Chicago Sun-Times*, 1 Mar. 2011, chicago.suntimes.com/section/lynn-sweet-politics/. Accessed 3 Apr. 2018.

"U.S. Interim Projections by Age, Sex, Race, and Hispanic Origin: 2000-2050." United States Census Bureau, Population Division, 18 Mar. 2004, census.gov/prod/1/pop/p25-1130.pdf. Accessed 3 Apr. 2018.

Notice that this bibliography is longer than the sample Works Cited page, since as mentioned earlier in the chapter, a bibliography lists *all* sources consulted, while the Works Cited page lists only the sources that were actually cited (in exact quote or paraphrase) in the essay.

Thus, several of the citations in the bibliography *are exactly the same as on the Works Cited page.* The essay writer can simply copy all the citations from the Works Cited page to the bibliography and build around it. This applies to an annotated bibliography as well.

Sample Annotated Bibliography:

Bibliography

Boyd, Brian. *Vladimir Nabokov: The American Years.* Princeton UP, 1991. The seminal

biographer of Nabokov gives context to Nabokov's American novels and his influ-

ences in writing them.

Fein, Sin. "Freedom." *Sin Fein,* May 1991, www.sinnfein.org/documents/freedom.html.

Accessed 3 Apr. 2018. Fein offers a statistic here that was tempting to use: that at

one time, 40% of nationalists were twice as likely as to be unemployed. However,

like many self-published documents, the article failed to provide a list of sources

for its information, so it seemed prudent to omit a figure without knowing either

the sources or the research methodology that produced such a statistic.

Kuzmanovich, Zoran. "Chronology." *Approaches to Teaching Nabokov's Lolita,* edited

by Zoran Kuzmanovich and Galya Diment, Modern Language Association of

America, 2008, pp. 1–12. This book is full of useful strategies for teaching students

the nuances of *Lolita.*

McVeigh, Tracy. "Forty Years of Feminism—But Women Still Do Most of the

Housework." *The Gaurdian*, 10 March 2012, www.theguardian.com/society/2012/

mar/10/housework-gender-equality-women. Accessed 3 Apr. 2018. Based on

UK data.

Power, Elizabeth. "The Cinematic Art of Nympholepsy: Movie Star Culture as Loser

Culture in Nabokov's *Lolita*." *Criticism*, vol. 41, no.1, 1999, pp. 101–08. *JSTOR*,

www.jstor.org/stable/23124232. Accessed 3 Nov. 2018. This article explores the

portrayal of film and film actors in *Lolita*.

Sweet, Lynn. "Women Still Earn Less Than Men: New Obama White House Report

on Status of Women." *Chicago Sun-Times*, 1 Mar. 2011, chicago.suntimes.com/

section/lynn-sweet-politics/. Accessed 3 Apr. 2018. This article includes the exact

text of the White House documents.

"U.S. Interim Projections by Age, Sex, Race, and Hispanic Origin: 2000–2050." United

States Census Bureau, Population Division, 18 Mar. 2004, census.gov/prod/1/pop/

p25-1130.pdf. Accessed 3 Apr. 2018. Very straightforward, offering the data in

several formats such as Excel spreadsheet or pdf.

We notice in the Annotated Bibliography above that the notes (or "annotations") beside each entry begin immediately beside the citation, without any additional spaces or skipped lines. Notice that annotations can address a source's credibility, its relevance, the reason a source was used or consulted (especially if it is not particularly recent), whether or not it was useful, and whether the essay writer recommends it to others. In our digital age in which electronic sources and websites change frequently, this is increasingly useful.

FIGURES, TABLES, AND APPENDICES

Often, students wonder how to include non-essential elements in an essay, such as a picture, chart, or list. Any of these items can be attached to the end of the document in an appendix. Named for the appendix in the human body, an organ considered non-essential, the appendix at the end of an essay can contain any items which you feel will illustrate your point, but which might disrupt the flow of your essay should they be inserted directly into the text. appendices (this is the plural form of the word Appendix) can be numbered or lettered and then referred to within the body of your essay like so: "See Appendix 1" or "See Appendix 2."

Likewise, each picture (called Figure) or chart (called Table) you insert into the body of your essay should be labeled "Figure 1," "Figure 2" and so forth (unless it appears in the appendices, in which case it is labeled accordingly "Appendix 1" and so forth.) If appropriate to the subject you are discussing in a paragraph or on a page, these can occasionally be embedded into the text of your essay. (Note: this will affect your page count. If the instructor has required ten pages, two charts—which together add up to an entire page—do not necessarily count as a page of written content. In this example, your document would then need to run to at least eleven pages in order to satisfy the minimum page requirement. Be sure to ask your instructors what their preferences are.)

Any chart, data, or picture not created by you, but taken from a source, should be appropriately labeled and cited on your documentation page(s). It should be attributed to the source in which you found it, with page number if applicable, unless you are prepared to give the citation information of the original document.

SECTION SECTION SECTION VI

ANALYZE LITERATURE

CHAPTERS

CHAPTER CHAPTER CHAPTER

21

INTRODUCTION TO LITERARY ELEMENTS

▍WHAT IS LITERATURE?

Literature is artistic writing that opens up worlds to us. It lets us experience life as we have never done before, and it makes us feel that we are not alone. Another character has felt as we do, has harbored the same impulses and emotions, and has nevertheless gained our sympathies. Hemingway said, "There is no friend as loyal as a book." Gustave Flaubert, author of *Madame Bovary*, describes reading in the following way:

> You forget everything. The hours slip by. You travel in your chair through centuries you seem to see before you, your thoughts are caught up in the story, dallying with the details or following the course of the plot, you enter into characters, so that it seems as if it were your own heart beating beneath their costumes.

Literature, in short, is writing that is meant to be read and valued for its ability to transport us.

We can sit back and enjoy a good book, play, or poem on the surface, but when we *study* literature, we figure out just how it does what it does. Indeed, we have a specialized vocabulary for literature's elements. We have provided here an introduction to terms that should improve your appreciation and understanding of the literature you read, and help you talk about it knowledgeably in your papers.

PLOT OR NARRATIVE

Plot is what happens in the story. However, this is not always as obvious as it sounds. The writer has several choices when recounting a story. Sometimes, authors play with chronology and put events out of order through flashbacks. Sometimes, authors lead readers to believe a certain outcome is inevitable and then reverse our expectations. O. Henry's short stories are so famous for this that his name has become synonymous with surprise endings. Beginnings and endings are usually where an author concentrates significant energy. Some authors spend weeks on their first and last lines. Students should pay special attention to these. Often opening and closing lines yield important clues about the author's theme and tone.

Telling a story in the best order is an art. As you may have learned from firsthand experience, there is also an art in knowing what details to include and what to leave out. When your friend tells a story that includes every minor detail, you might want her to cut to the best part: the conflict and how it was resolved. "So what did she *do*?!" **Conflict** is an essential element to a good plot; it is said to "turn" the story because it gives the plot forward movement and makes things happen. A story in which every character agrees and there is no obstacle to a character's desire is a boring story indeed. Notice that plot conflict almost always stems from the main character's desire for something and the obstacles preventing him or her from getting it. It is the writer's job to frustrate the protagonist with as many barriers as possible to attaining the goal. In real life, this would be cruel, but in literature it is gold. Why? Because this is where we learn about our character's true nature. When pushed to their limits, Hamlet hesitates. Macbeth kills ruthlessly, Othello kills is a jealous rage. King Lear loses his sanity. Romeo and Juliet commit suicide.

Conflict

- Through difficult or awkward circumstances, we see how characters react under pressure. These reactions show us who they are. Conflict develops character.
- Conflict also moves plot forward.

These characters react the way they do because of their personalities. Hamlet hesitates because he is philosophical and cautious by nature. Macbeth kills ruthlessly because he is ambitious. King Lear is politically powerful but banishes his beloved daughter because he is emotionally insecure. Romeo and Juliet commit suicide because they are passionate, young, and impetuous.

If we put the characters in different plays, we would get very different outcomes. Hamlet and Juliet might have tried a long distance relationship or "taken a little break." Lear might have banished Lady Macbeth for being so ambitious and forgotten all about the throne. If Othello heard his uncle murdered his father, he definitely would have killed him immediately, not hesitated for five acts like Hamlet. But if he did so, the play would be over immediately. Conflict makes for drama and story. Without it, we have nothing; we pack up and go home.

> **Note: Conflict happens because of who the characters are. Plot makes the characters' true natures emerge.** Many writers debate which comes first: the plot or the character. As you can see, both are equally important and closely tied to each other.

The plot of a well-crafted literary work also starts at a carefully chosen moment. Some works begin at the very beginning with the birth of the character. This kind of comprehensive storytelling was popular in novels in the eighteenth and nineteenth centuries. Increasingly, however, writers have eschewed this practice for a more targeted approach to the character's life. In the twentieth century, James Joyce and Virginia Woolf wrote entire novels about one June day in the life of their main characters. When reading a work, ask yourself "Why today?" Writers have a reason why they chose the day on which the plot starts. The protagonist's 18th birthday (when he or she is planning to enlist)? Her wedding day? His deathbed? We must see why *this* specific day in particular highlights the choices a character will have to make. It is in these choices and decisions that character is revealed.

In the ordering of the action, there is often a structure that looks loosely like this:

ELEMENTS OF PLOT STRUCTURE

> 1. **Introduction** of the conflict and characters' desires. *The set-up*.
> 2. **Backstory**—where these characters came from and what shaped their desires.
> 3. **Rising Actions** increase conflict. *The heat is on*.
> 4. **Climax**—does the character get what he or she wants? This is the highest point of tension in the piece. *The showdown*.
> 5. **Falling Action** brings the story full circle. *What the characters do next*.
> 6. **Denouement**—the resolution of the storylines. If we get one at all, this section is usually the shortest. *What has the main character learned?*
>
> This structure is often refered to as Freytag's Pyramid.

The structure above holds for short stories, screenplays, plays, novels, and even narrative poems. Of course, writers are never bound to this progression, but this is a common way to order the events and information in a work of literature.

POINT OF VIEW OR NARRATION

The narrator is who's telling the story. A narrator who knows everything about everyone and has access to all of the characters' interior thoughts is called **an omniscient narrator** because "omniscient" means "all-knowing." When the narrator describes characters from outside, (he did this, she did that) it's called **third person**. Sometimes, the narrator is one of the characters and uses the **first person** ("I"). In some cases, the narrator uses the **second person** "you" to address the audience directly. In "Girl," Jamaica Kincaid addresses an imagined reader directly:

> this is how to hem a dress when you see the hem coming down and so to prevent yourself from looking like the slut I know you are so bent on becoming; this is how you iron your father's khaki shirt so that it doesn't have a crease; … this is how you grow okra—far from the house, because the okra tree harbors red ants; when you are growing dasheen, make sure it gets plenty of water or else it makes your throat itch when you are eating it…

Point of view indicates through which character's consciousness we experience the book. Notice that an omniscient narrator can tell the story so that we are in the point of view of one of the characters. For example, in Maxine Hong Kingston's *The Woman Warrior*, the narrator writes, "Brave Orchid did not know whether she had fallen asleep or not when she heard a rushing coming out from under the bed. Cringes of fear seized her soles as something alive, rumbling, climbed the foot of the bed." The narrator here and Brave Orchid are not the same person, and although Brave Orchid never says "I," we are in her head and know what she is thinking.

In poetry, we use the word "speaker" or "persona" instead of "narrator." For example, you might write, "In Robert Browning's poem 'My Last Duchess,' as the speaker shows off the portrait of his deceased wife, the audience begins to wonder if he had her killed."

CHARACTER

Characters are the fictional people who perform the action in a short story, book, or play. For instance, Little Red Riding Hood is the character in the story who goes into her grandmother's house and defeats a wolf. She is not a real person. The main character we are rooting for is called the **protagonist**. The **antagonist** is the character who stands in the way of the character achieving his or her desire. Little Red Riding Hood is the protagonist who wants to visit her Grandma; the Wolf is the antagonist. Sometimes the protagonist is an obvious evil **villain** like the Wolf, but not always. In Margaret Edson's play *Wit*, the antagonist is the main character's cancer. An antagonist can even be a mother who "loves" her daughter so much, she doesn't want to see her go off and fulfill her dreams. She keeps her trapped at home with her. This is the set up for Marsha Norman's play *'Night, Mother*.

When speaking of characters, we differentiate between **primary or main characters** and **secondary characters**. Primary characters are the characters in whose plots and emotions we are most invested. This is because the author spends more time developing these characters and making them multidimensional, and if the story is not told through their points of view, it is at least told about them. Secondary characters take up less room in the narrative than main characters although they can significantly affect plot. These characters are usually less developed and may fit more easily into recognizable **archetypes** such as the wealthy miser, the lonely spinster, or the wise, old sage.

In all great literature, no matter how short, the main character has an "arc." **The character's arc is the emotional and spiritual distance the character travels during the time of the work.** What has the character learned from this experience? How has the character changed forever? The character almost always starts at one point and through the plot, ends up in a different emotional space at the end of the piece. In Toni Morrison's *The Bluest Eye*, the narrator Claudia is changed forever by having witnessed her friend Pecola Breedlove's tragic life.

SETTING

Setting is where the action takes place. This can be as big or as small as the author chooses to make it, but it often reflects the tone and theme of the work. It is no accident that plays and stories about entrapment take place in a single room: Sartre's *No Exit*, Kafka's "Metamorphosis." A story about feeling confined by gender roles is appropriately set in a single bedroom in Charlotte Perkins Gilman's "The Yellow Wallpaper." On the other hand, a story about universal love might take place over the entire galaxy, *The Little Prince*. As you can see, setting has a big impact on the tone and feeling of the work. Jonathan Safran Foer's novel *Extremely Loud and Incredibly Close* has all of New York City as its setting. The city presents challenges for the young narrator trying to solve a mystery and the big urban maze helps us feel what he's up against.

Setting can have a dramatic impact on tone. Imagine two different stories set in the settings above. How would the tone of the stories differ?

IMAGERY AND SYMBOLS

Imagery is figurative language and pictures made of words. Often, comparison is used to make images meaningful and to make the reader think in new ways. **Metaphor** is a type of comparison in which two things are said to **be** each other. For example, in "A Sonnet Is a Moment's Monument" poet Dante Gabriel Rossetti writes: "A Sonnet is a coin: its face reveals/The soul—" Probably, the reader never thought of a poem as a monument or a coin. **Similes** function like metaphors, but they use "like" or "as" to make a figurative comparison: "My love is like a summer's day."

Symbols are objects that stand for a bigger idea. For example, an American flag stands for something: patriotism, the United States, capitalism, democracy. A wedding band is a symbol of love and commitment. Literature frequently uses symbols. If a male character gives a female character flowers that wilt after they fight, we might read that as symbolic of the death of their relationship.

Finally, **personification** is the attribution of human qualities to animals or inanimate, non-human objects. Consider Homer's "Rosy-fingered dawn..." or Tennyson: "The vapors weep their burden to the ground." Dawn doesn't have fingers and vapor doesn't weep, but this paints a vivid picture for the reader and adds emotional tone.

Exercise:

Label the following passages as using **personification, simile, metaphor, or symbol** by writing in the appropriate word next to each example.

1) "O, my love's like a red, red rose," Robert Burns. _____

2) "The Wind begun to knead the Grass—" Emily Dickinson. _____

3) "An omnibus across the bridge/Crawls like a yellow butterfly," Oscar Wilde. _____

4) "That time of year thou mayst in me behold/When yellow leaves, or none, or few do hang/Upon these boughs which shake against the cold,/Bare ruined choirs, where late the sweet birds sang," William Shakespeare. _____

5) "The Dust did scoop itself like Hands—/And throw away the Road—" Emily Dickinson. _____

6) "Ships at a distance have every man's wish on board. For some they come in with the tide. For others they sail forever on the horizon, never out of sight, never landing until the Watcher turns his eyes away in resignation, his dreams mocked to death by Time. That is the life of men." Zora Neale Hurston. _____

7) "We wear the mask that grins and lies, / It hides our cheeks and shades our eyes," Paul Laurence Dunbar. _____

8) "Because I could not stop for Death/ He kindly stopped for me—" Emily Dickinson. _____

9) "Well, they are gone, and here must I remain,/This lime-tree bower my prison!" Samuel Taylor Coleridge _____

10) "The reaches opened before us and closed behind, as if the forest had stepped leisurely across the water to bar the way for our return. We penetrated deeper and deeper into the heart of darkness. It was very quiet there. At night sometimes the roll of drums behind the curtain of trees would run up the river and remain sustained faintly, as if hovering in the air high over our heads, till the first break of day." Joseph Conrad. _____ (Hint: there is more than one type of figurative language used here).

Once you are able to identify figurative language, symbols, and imagery, you can see how they contribute to the tone (or mood) and theme of a work of literature. Read on.

TONE

Tone is the mood or emotional feeling of the piece. (In fact, in poetry it is called **mood**). It can be dark and heavy, exhilarated, frenetic, nervous, foreboding. The tone is often relayed to the audience through the figurative language chosen to describe characters and setting. (See "Imagery and Symbols" above). The cumulative effect is to give us tone. In Sylvia Plath's poem to her baby, "Morning Song," we sense that this is not a pure ode to the joys of motherhood, as the mood is detached. View "Morning Song" at the link provided here: https://www.poets.org/poetsorg/poem/morning-song

Tone is also conveyed through sentence length and styles. In poetry, we call sentences "lines" and paragraphs "stanzas." (Note that lines, unlike sentences, are not always grammatical sentences and do not have to finish with end punctuation.) In poetry, short, rhyming lines can contribute to a younger, lighter mood in Emily Brontë's "I'm Happiest When Most Away": "On a windy night when the moon is bright/ And the eye can wander through worlds of light—" On the other hand, longer, flowing lines slow a poem's pace and convey a more ponderous mood. In Matthew Arnold's "Dover Beach," the pace of the lines echoed in the setting contributes to tone and mood:

> Listen! You hear the grating roar
>
> Of pebbles which the waves draw back and fling,
>
> At their return, up the high strand,
>
> Begin, and cease, and then again begin,
>
> With tremulous cadence slow, and bring
>
> The eternal note of sadness in…

We hear the waves and the relentlessness of the violence and sadness through the language Arnold uses.

THEME

Theme is an idea (expressed through mood, words, or image) that recurs throughout the work. Often, the theme is a rather general or abstract idea: "Love conquers all." However, it is the work of literature that applies that theme specifically to a set of characters in a particular time and place to illustrate it for the audience. Theme is hard to define, but you'll know when you have landed on it. In good writing, the theme is not so obvious that the reader feels as though he or she is getting a big "message" with every turn of the page. Theme is more subtle than that. For example, the theme of mortality in *Mrs. Dalloway* comes through in the wave and cut flower imagery, as well as in the frequent chiming of the tower clock Big Ben, heard throughout London.

CHAPTER 22

INTRODUCTION TO GENRE: DRAMA, FICTION, AND POETRY

▌INTRODUCTION TO DRAMA

Contemporary drama, specifically the stage play, owes much to the infrastructure of the Greek dramatic performance. Plays were usually performed on a stage in an amphitheater. This stage, called the **proscenium**, marked the division between the actors and the audience. Ancient audiences understood, as we do today, that what happened on the stage was artifice, not reality. For this reason, in the study of literature, theater, and film, the stage is referred to as **the fourth wall**. In contemporary theater, television and film, characters occasionally break the fourth wall by addressing audience members.

Greek actors, all male, tied on masks with built-in amplification. This is why the masks are a common emblem of the theater today. All citizens could enjoy the theater at a nominal cost and leave their worries aside for those precious few hours and experience a **catharsis**, or purging, of deep emotion. Ancient playwrights such as Sophocles and Euripides encoded lessons into their plays to teach the populace values such as honor, obedience, and piety (devotion to the gods). If a nobleman such as King Oedipus suffered so tragically for trying to outrun his ordained fate, a common man or woman could expect even more profound consequences for misbehavior. Thus theatergoers not only experienced theater as entertainment, but learned through the example of the characters the importance of devotion to their king, their gods, and acceptance of their (mis)fortunes.

Several recognizable forms of contemporary drama derive from ancient Greek tradition: tragedy, comedy, tragicomedy, and melodrama. As Aristotle defined **tragedy**, a tragic hero (a character of noble status) with a particular flaw (often pride) will make a mistake and, as a result of circumstances outside his control, will suffer a terrible tragedy that results in the suffering of many. He will heroically realize and repent his mistake, and accept his fate.

Ancient Greeks did not take comedy to mean "comical," as we do today. Ancient Greek **comedy** involved ordinary people making the kind of ordinary mistakes that all humans do, but learning from their errors in time to avert disaster. While ancient tragedies ended in suffering and mourning, comedies often ended with a community ritual like a wedding or a feast, to celebrate life and the eternal cycle of renewal.

A television sitcom is a good example of a modern comedy that shares many characteristics with ancient comedy. In both, average people struggle with the absurdities of everyday life. One character might make the same choice every day and expect a different result. One character might have an unusual habit or weakness that rules his life despite his best efforts to overcome it. These are struggles all humans can relate to. In modern comedy, the situations and characters are comical, and there were certainly light-hearted moments in ancient comedies as well, especially in Shakespeare. But it would be inaccurate to define ancient comedy solely as comical; that is a contemporary understanding of the term.

Contemporary theatergoers are also familiar with the melodrama and the tragicomedy. Both of these are variations of the dramatic templates born in ancient Greece. A **tragicomedy** combines elements of tragedy and comedy. For example, John Guare's *Six Degrees of Separation* juxtaposes dark humor against the tragic waste of a young man's aspirations. It pokes fun at people's tendency towards celebrity worship of actors and other very important people, while underscoring how such superficiality can have disastrous effects.

A **melodrama** offers clear-cut solutions to complex problems.

Things are black and white in a melodrama. The hero is handsome and the villain is ugly. The hero wins and the villain loses. The hero gets the girl and the villain doesn't. We know that real life isn't so black and white, and that's what makes the melodrama so entertaining: it's satisfying and gratifying. It's the way we *want* things to be, the way we think they should be.

As in ancient Greece, contemporary drama means spectacle. It is written to get your attention, to draw you in, to excite you, depress you, anger you, whatever, but in short: involve you while you are listening and watching it in person, and make you think about a larger theme, such as, *What is true loyalty and what is blind faith?*

Unlike film, which can take you to any place or moment in time, drama preserves **unity of time**; it usually does not **flash forward** (move abruptly into a future time) or **flashback** (move abruptly into the past), but rather remains continuous.

A drama, or play, is a narrative driven by a premise. A **premise** can be defined as the central question or theme that the play raises. These are ideas like "Love conquers all." In *Macbeth* the premise might be phrased: "Blind ambition is destructive."

Fun Fact: in television, "premise" is used differently than in drama. In television, "premise" means "the idea of the show." In *The Sopranos*, the premise is "a mafia mob boss enters psychotherapy." In *Mad Men*, the premise is "a 1960's period drama that unfolds in the high stakes world of advertising in Manhattan."

On the day the action of the play begins, or **the point of attack**, the characters, who have been going along in their lives, who have been brooding, loving, hating, looking for revenge, or whatever they've been doing, suddenly, for some reason, act. And the play happens. Thus, the play brings the audience in to witness a transformative moment—the moment the characters finally act and the drama unfolds.

In order to draw the audience in, in good drama, something must be at stake for the audience members. In other words, something has to matter. Perhaps a value is at stake, like love, trust, honor—something that matters to us (the audience members) in our lives, something we can understand because we experience it.

In that sense, the greatest thing about a play is this: we can watch others (the characters) take the risks, the falls, the consequences of the things they do—we can laugh, we can cry—and then we can leave, and go home! And go home a little lighter. Then the play has done its job. It has entertained us, allowed us a little escape from our own humanity—perhaps given us a little perspective on it—and we have lived vicariously through the characters. We have experienced, like the common folk who went to see a play in ancient Greece or Rome, a **catharsis**.

Drama and film share several characteristics. The following chart shows elements common to both:

Acts*: the division of the plot into units, like chapters in a novel.

Act Break: The end of an act. Audiences expect a dramatic event that turns the action at the end of every act.

Arc: both characters and plots can have arcs. This is a way of saying that the characters/plot circumstances are significantly changed by the end of the work because of the events that have occurred.

Catharsis: Greek for "purging" or processing pent-up feelings in a gratifying release.

Comedy: A dramatic term in use long before television, an ancient comedy concerned ordinary people learning lessons about their human weaknesses.

Conflict: tension caused when characters' desires are thwarted.

Description: The writer directs the characters' actions, the set design and props, the time, and the location of scenes in the description lines between passages of dialogue.

Dialogue: conversation between characters.

Fourth Wall: the line of demarcation (once physical, now metaphorical) between artifice—the world on stage—and audience.

In Medias Res: the term for a drama that opens "in the middle of things."

Motif: a recurring image, color, or idea that unifies the drama and relates to the theme.

Monologue/Soliloquy: a long speech by one character, whether or not others are present.

Opening images/scene: These set the tone. Often they raise the central question and evoke theme.

Ticking clock: a time limit to the action that increases tension and suspense. *24.*

Tragedy: In ancient Greece, a tragedy involved the death of many people as a result of the hero's tragic flaw and the outside circumstances which lead him to his Fate.

Subtext: when characters say the opposite of what they mean.

Setting, Sets: the physical space the actors inhabit when filmed or seen.

Scenes: the breakdown of acts into smaller elements.

*Acts are the major divisions in the action of the play. There are often one to five scenes per act, but that number varies. The number of acts in a play is also variable, from one-act plays, to three-, to five-act plays (which were the standard for Shakespeare).

DIALOGUE

While there is dialogue in novels, short stories, and even sometimes in poetry, dialogue is the single most important element in drama. Unlike film, which can direct a viewer's eye to a symbol or an actor's reaction, plays are held in a theater with rows and good and bad seats. In a film, the screen is so large, no one misses a move. If the director wants you to see a character rolling her eyes, you will be forced to see it. There is no equivalent way, except through dialogue, for a play director to make every audience member notice the same thing at the same time. Therefore, in a play, symbolism must be physically acted out. The object must be touched, lifted, or referred to explicitly in the dialogue. While in a film the director could **cut to** (focus the camera lens on) Yorick's skull in the graveyard, in the play, Hamlet must lift the skull and give his "Alas, poor Yorick, I knew thee well" soliloquy. Therefore, dialogue is more explicit and much more important in plays than it is in film. If you have the nosebleed seats, you still have to know what's going on. Good dialogue is how the playwright achieves his or her effects.

At home, if you rent or stream a film, you can pause it and replay any part you miss any time. The playwright, however, must ensure through clear, emphatic dialogue that everybody gets it the first time around. In live performance, there is no second chance. That is what makes drama so delicious. It is a fleeting experience that, once over, can never be experienced in the same way again. It is a metaphor for our own mortality.

We can summarize the differences between stage and screen in the following ways.

MAJOR DIFFERENCES BETWEEN DRAMA AND FILM/TELEVISION

In Drama:

- Settings are limited.
- Unity of time.
- Special effects are limited.
- No camera angles.
- Can't direct audience attention.
- Only one chance to keep people hooked; if they leave, they won't come back.

In Film:

- Settings are unlimited.
- Time is flexible.
- Wide range of special effects.
- Close-ups, extreme close-ups, "focus on," "pan to" can direct audience focus to make a point.
- Much longer opportunity to capture viewers' attention; viewers can stop and start endlessly.

Exercise:

Think about the differences between film and plays listed above. What kinds of settings and subjects lend themselves to plays? Which better exploit the medium of film? Give examples.

INTRODUCTION TO FICTION

It took centuries for literature to evolve into the genres of fiction we recognize. Most literary traditions across the world originated, like the Athenian one, in an oral and thespian (performed) tradition. In the Middle Ages, poetry and drama were sung, danced, and acted out for the benefit of an audience.

The journey of literary content is a fascinating one. In ancient times, the content for dramas came from oral legends and teachings, which were refitted or fleshed out to serve the culture's or author's purpose. Most authors of Shakespeare's day and earlier, from Marie de France and Chaucer to Marlowe, all drew upon some of the same source material: their culture's fables and tales. But with the birth of the novel, for the first time, writers invented new stories in prose. Literary historian Ian Watt suggests that this was because a growing middle class wanted to start reading literature that reflected its own existence, as opposed to the exalted poetry of the aristocracy, and why early novels are concerned with money (economic, Capitalist individualism) and the growing importance of the individual (philosophical individualism). The Declaration of Independence (1776) and The Rights of Man (1791) are emblematic of the philosophical individualism reflected in the novels.

Previously, individuals were only important in terms of their affiliation to king, country, family, church, etc. Originality of any kind—scientific, religious, political, etc., was treated with suspicion and sometimes death or exile. It was not until the birth of the English novel in the 1720's with Daniel Defoe's *Robinson Crusoe* (1719) and *Moll Flanders* (1722), that a writer might chronicle the experiences of one individual, even a "commoner" (someone with no social standing. "Moll" means "prostitute"). Vermeer's *Girl with a Pearl Earring* was scandalous at the time for Vermeer's choice to paint a young servant girl. Samuel Richardson followed soon after with *Pamela* (1740), an epistolary novel in the form of fictional letters home to the main character's parents. Henry Fielding's *Tom Jones* (1749) and Laurence Sterne's *Tristram Shandy* (1759–67) are also early novels that follow the model of the protagonist examining his or her life. *Tom Jones* is a ***picaresque***, a satirical sub-genre of fiction, in which the rebellious anti-hero tells his life story very comically. The early novels strove for **verisimilitude**, or realism so that readers would feel that the story they were reading was "true." In fact, the protagonists are preoccupied with defending themselves against accusations of lying in *Robinson Crusoe, Moll*

Flanders, *Pamela*, and *Tristram Shandy* and all tell their tales in the first person "I" in order to make their fiction feel more "real" to the reader.

The nineteenth century continued to investigate the life of the disenfranchised protagonist. Novelists felt freer, now that the art form was accepted, to create truly complex fictional gothic worlds (Austen, the Brontës, Hawthorne) and to comment upon social issues as they did so (Thomas Hardy, Dickens, George Eliot). Only slightly earlier had painters started using common people as the subjects of their paintings, instead of only religious subjects and royal or wealthy patrons.

With our American tradition of social mobility, it's hard for us to imagine how unusual it was for artists and writers to focus on ordinary people and the ordinary—and the often banal, terrible, or possibly immoral things that happen to them. Novels were often called "lies" because the events inside them were made-up—complete **fiction**. (Before the novel, no nonfiction "prose" existed. Poetry was the standard form of written literary consumption.) Aristocratic ladies and young women from upwardly mobile families were expressly forbidden to read these "lies." They were not, as with the stories narrated by Chaucer and Shakespeare, the same old tales told anew. They were also suspect because they exposed "innocent minds" to "dangerous" ideas. Novels gave readers a sense that they, too—like the characters—could choose a different life than the one prescribed for them by their society and their families. That was very threatening to the existing social structure.

Over the next few centuries, as writers experimented with fiction and novel's form, not all works were as long as a complete novel anymore—they might be significantly shorter. Therefore, the terms emerged for **novella** (substantive, but not as long as a novel) or **short story** (quite short). Therefore, today the term fiction comprises all these forms.

Various other terms have emerged to characterize the elements of fiction. Some are general terms that describe overall qualities of a work. An **allegory** is a story about a story, i.e., a story that represents a reality outside the literary work. For example, George Orwell's novel, *Animal Farm*, is an allegory for the Russian Revolution. Each of the characters corresponds to a real historical figure. Franz Kafka's short story, "The Metamorphosis," is a less specific allegory, or metaphor, for the twentieth century office worker and the anxiety that characterizes the expectations and duties of a middle-class life in an industrialized nation. **Magical Realism** is a term used to characterize stories in which the extraordinary is treated as ordinary. In Gabriel Garcia Marquez's short story, "A Very Old Man with Enormous Wings," residents of a rural fishing village find what appears to be an angel washed up on shore. Rather than taking time to explore the implausibility of such an event in the physical world, the story examines the characters' responses to this event—how they absorb it into the trajectory of their everyday lives. In this way, many stories, especially science fiction, ask us to **suspend disbelief**. In other words, readers are expected to "play along" with the story's premise and see how events will unfold in a world with different qualities than our real physical world. Ironically, what caused early audiences such distress, this believing of fictional "lies," is now an accepted (and enjoyable) convention of literary consumption).

GLOSSARY OF FICTION TERMS

Allegory—a tale or story which represents a reality outside the literary work (for example, George Orwell's novel *Animal Farm*)

Antagonist—the character (or force, or circumstance) working against the interests of the protagonist.

Archetype—a type of motif of character or situation which repeats throughout literature, like a "wise old man" or a "virgin Queen."

Character—can be primary or secondary, includes protagonist, antagonists, villains, and archetypes.

Foreshadowing—when readers are shown a glimpse of events to come later in the story.

Freytag's Pyramid: Fictional works usually include introduction and backstory in the **Exposition**, **Rising Actions** which accelerate the conflict and culminate in a **Climax** (turning point) finish out with **Falling Actions** and often some resolution in the **Denouement**.

Irony—the opposite of what is expected.

Magical Realism—the literary technique of treating the extraordinary as ordinary

Narrator—who tells the story.

Novel—A full, book-length work of fiction in which the main character(s) undergo significant challenge or change

Novella—a work longer than a short story, but shorter than a novel

Plot—what happens in a story; for structural. elements, see "Freytag's Pyramid" above in this list.

Point of View—the perspective through which the story is related to readers.

Protagonist—the character readers are rooting for.

Short Story—a short work of fiction

Suspension of Disbelief—when readers are asked to read along as if the events described could actually take place in reality

Theme—there are usually many themes, or topics, of every work; for example: anxiety, community.

Villain—a character who is evil for evil's sake; not every work has an actual villain (though antagonists are common).

INTRODUCTION TO POETRY

What are your perceptions of poetry? Where, when, and how you were exposed to it probably framed your experience of it. Do you think that poetry always rhymes? Did you realize that some stories you have read in prose form (*The Odyssey*, or Dante's *Inferno*) were originally written in verse? Poetry comprises many forms and styles; just like art, it offers something for everyone to enjoy. The following introduction to poetry offers a brief overview of the genres, terms, and functions of poetry.

Poetry is written in verse (the broken lines of poetry, rather than paragraph form). Poetry may rhyme, or it may not. Non-rhyming verse that still has a rhythm (called **meter**) is called **blank verse**. Poetry with no fixed meter and no rhyme is generally called **free verse**, and as you might expect, is the most contemporary form.

POETRY TERMS

Blank Verse—no end rhyme, but a fixed meter.

Couplet—two lines of poetry set off by themselves, a space before them and after them; sometimes they rhyme.

© finwal89/Shutterstock.com

Free Verse—no fixed meter or rhyme.

Elegy—a poem composed for the deceased.

Epic—a narrative poem telling the larger-than-life story of heroic characters or mythical tales.

End Rhyme—when the last word of a line rhymes with another line above or below it.

Line Break—the space between lines of a poem.

Haiku—short lyrical poem consisting of three lines, five syllables on the first line, seven on the second line, and five on the third line, or any other combination of seventeen syllables.

Metaphor—comparison of one thing to another.

Meter—a poem's rhythm (the amount of syllables per line).

Ode—a poem of praise to the recipient (could be a person, or an inanimate object, like John Keats' famous "Ode to a Grecian Urn").

Personification—when a poem "personifies" an inanimate object by giving it human qualities, e.g., "the mirror *stared* back at me."

Point of View—the speaker's perspective: first person, second person, or third person.

Sonnet—one of the most famous forms of lyrical poetry, consisting of fourteen lines; the two types of sonnets are Italian (Petrarchan) or English (Shakespearean).

Speaker—the voice "speaking" or narrating the poem.

Stanza—each "paragraph" of the poem; in a song, we would call it a verse.

Simile—a specific type of metaphor that uses the word "like," e.g., "the rain droplets spattered like blood."

Poems can accomplish many things: they can praise a (living) loved one in an **ode**, eulogize a deceased loved one in an **elegy**; they can declare romantic love, document a place or period in time, educate readers and agitate for social change, or simply experiment with craft, producing art for art's sake.

Like fiction, poetry can be expressed in one of three **points of view: first person, second person**, and **third person**. In poetry, we call the narrator the **speaker**. This is the voice which "speaks" the poem, not to be confused with the poet him or herself. This is a critical distinction. For example, Anne Sexton wrote a poem called "Their Kind," in which a witch speaks. But Anne Sexton, the poet, is not a witch, and it might be embarrassing to conclude that she was. Rather, Sexton wrote the poem from that character's perspective, to give a voice to the experience of a witch.

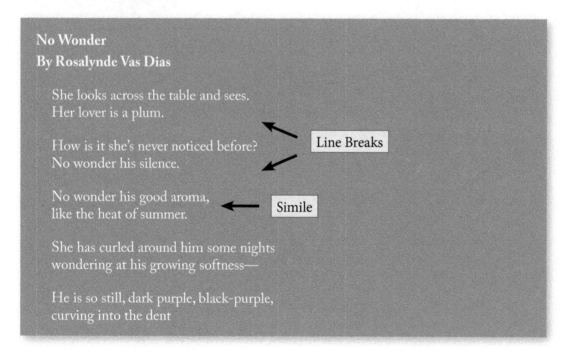

No Wonder
By Rosalynde Vas Dias

She looks across the table and sees.
Her lover is a plum.

How is it she's never noticed before?
No wonder his silence.

No wonder his good aroma,
like the heat of summer.

She has curled around him some nights
wondering at his growing softness—

He is so still, dark purple, black-purple,
curving into the dent

Line Breaks

Simile

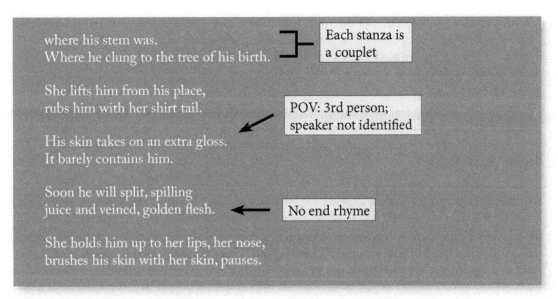

where his stem was.
Where he clung to the tree of his birth.

Each stanza is a couplet

She lifts him from his place,
rubs him with her shirt tail.

POV: 3rd person; speaker not identified

His skin takes on an extra gloss.
It barely contains him.

Soon he will split, spilling
juice and veined, golden flesh.

No end rhyme

She holds him up to her lips, her nose,
brushes his skin with her skin, pauses.

Generally speaking, there are two main types of poetry: **narrative and lyric(al)** poetry. This categorization transcends time periods and regions of world poetry, and while it's not a hard and fast rule, it is a useful guideline for learning about poetry.

Narrative poetry tells (narrates) a story, but in verse. Famous narrative poems which document famous historical or mythological and supernatural figures are called **epics**. Homer's *Odyssey*, Virgil's *Aeneid*, and Milton's *Paradise Lost* are all epic poems, although you might have read prose versions of them. Narrative and epic poems are often written in **blank verse**. It's sometimes hard to tell, when reading a poem in translation, whether it rhymed in the original language.

Narrative and epic poetry are the spinsters of poetry: they've always been around, but they're often ignored by many contemporary poetry readers. Many of our most lauded writers and poets worked in this form, such as Milton, Spencer, Pope, Byron, Shelley, Coleridge, et al., but the form is not popular anymore. Vikram Seth, a contemporary Indian-American author, has written a novel in verse called *The Golden Gate*. Give it a try if you are interested in contemporary narrative poetry—or even if you think you aren't! Readers can forget they are reading poetry because they get so swept up in the story.

Lyric, or **lyrical poetry**, comprises poems which express emotions or feelings. Most poems you have been exposed to—or write yourself—probably fall into this category. Lyrical poems often focus on a specific event or moment in time, as a snapshot does. From nursery rhymes and Shel Silverstein's poems for children to **haiku, sonnets**, or **ballads** (the structure of modern rock songs), lyric poetry often rhymes and nearly always has some kind of meter (rhythm.) These recognizable styles of lyric poetry are probably familiar to you. Then there are others, such as the **cinquain, terza rima, sestina**, and the **villanelle** (this is not a comprehensive list) with specific structures. Another, more contemporary style of lyrical poetry is confessional poetry.

Confessional poetry is one of the most recent forms of lyrical poetry, written in service of the author's personal catharsis. In this case, then, the speaker of the poem is usually the author—a rare exception to the rule explained in "Point of View," above. Sylvia Plath and Anne Sexton were famous American confessional poets. The confessional poem, written in the first or second person, declares personal, private feelings which are either culturally taboo to discuss or shocking in some way, and often does so in very graphic—some would say harsh—words and images. Find an example of of this in the poem "Daddy" by Sylvia Plath at the following link: https://www.poetryfoundation.org/poems/48999/daddy-56d22aafa45b2

As an American poet in the 1950s, Plath knows exactly what words and images her readers will find upsetting (Nazis and Jews, for instance, in a world still smarting from World War II), and uses them defiantly to elicit emotional reactions. Similarly, the sonnets of Edna St. Vincent Millay contain revelations of sexual activity which were very transgressive for a woman in the early twentieth century. However, not every poem written in the first person is confessional poetry. Most of it is not, especially if it is written before the 1950's.

Narrative	• Tells (narrates) a story, but in verse (poetry) form. • May be rhyming or blank verse (non-rhyming, but structured). • Famous (narrative) epic poems: Homer's *Odyssey*, Virgil's *Aeneid*, Milton's *Paradise Lost*, Dante's *Divine Comedy*.
Lyric	• Express emotions or feelings in a "snapshot." • Often rhyme. • Often have some kind of meter (rhythm). • Examples: haiku, sonnets, ballads.
Confessional	• Contemporary to late twentieth century (1950s and following). • Driven by author's personal catharsis. • Famous American confessional poets: Sylvia Plath and Anne Sexton. • Written in the first person ("I" voice) or second person ("you"). • May or may not rhyme.

Not every poem falls neatly into just one category. Some poems are at once both lyrical and narrative. For example, even a confessional poem which wrestles with the emotional pain of a lost lover might have many narrative qualities. Alfred Lord Tennyson's famous lyrical poem, "Ulysses," chronicles the life of the famous mythical warrior Odysseus, and has a strongly narrative quality. These are nonetheless helpful categories for students of poetry.

Let's take a look at some examples. John Milton's epic narrative poem, *Paradise Lost*, narrates the Biblical story of Satan's fall and Adam and Eve's expulsion from the Garden of Eden. It is written in blank verse, since there is a consistent meter but no end rhyme. Here are the opening lines:

Narrative Poem Excerpt: Milton's *Paradise Lost* (1674)

Of Man's First Disobedience, and the Fruit
Of that Forbidden Tree, whose mortal taste
Brought Death into the World, and all our woe,
With loss of *Eden*, till one greater Man
Restore us, and regain the blissful Seat...
(*Paradise Lost* continues on through 12 books and is book length in full.)

Shakespeare is still famous for the beautiful lyrical quality of his poems, especially his love sonnets, so much so that the English style of the sonnet, three quatrains (sets of four lines) with a final couplet, has been named for Shakespeare, and is often referred to as a "Shakespearean sonnet" (as opposed to the Italian style made famous by Petrarch: an octet—the first eight lines—beside a sestet—the last six, called a Petrarchan sonnet). Here's one of Shakespeare's sonnets that you might recognize.

Lyrical Poem Example: Shakespeare Sonnet (1609)

Shall I compare thee to a summer's day? *a*
Thou art more lovely and more temperate: *b*
Rough winds do shake the darling buds of May, *a*
And summer's lease hath all too short a date: *b*
Sometime too hot the eye of heaven shines, *c*   5
And often is his gold complexion dimm'd; *d*
And every fair from fair sometime declines, *c*
By chance or nature's changing course untrimm'd; *d*
But thy eternal summer shall not fade *e*
Nor lose possession of that fair thou owest; *f*   10
Nor shall Death brag thou wander'st in his shade, *e*
When in eternal lines to time thou growest: *f*
So long as men can breathe or eyes can see, *g*
So long lives this and this gives life to thee. *g*

To detect and identify a poem's rhyme scheme, we assign a variable to each new sound that ends a line. You will notice that because the second and fourth lines end in the same "-ate" sound, we have assigned the variable *b* to them. (If the same sound repeats again, it will also be labeled b.) Lines 6 and 8 share the same sound too: we will call it "*d*." Readers repeat the process until all sounds are labeled.

Practiced poetry readers will begin to recognize certain rhyme combinations as specific poetic structures (for example, an English sonnet's rhyme scheme is *ababcdcdefefgg*). Recognizing that a poem has a specific rhyme scheme tells us that it is not blank verse or free verse. Your instructor can guide you in a more thorough examination.

The confessional poem, "45 Mercy Street," by Anne Sexton shows Sexton's despair and dissatisfaction with her husband, children, and suburban life, a sentiment that was not acceptable to express in 1950's America. (Because we know it is written in the confessional style, we understand in this case that that the poem's speaker is in fact its author.) This particular confessional poem is written in free verse, since it has no set meter or rhyme. Read the poem here: http://www.poemhunter.com/poem/45-mercy-street/

POETRY ANALYSIS CHART

1. Define any unfamiliar words.

2. What is the topic of the poem?

3. Identify the rhyme scheme, *if there is one* (e.g.,: abab cdcd efef).

4. Who is the Speaker of the poem?

5. What genre of poetry is the poem? (Example: sonnet, elegy, ode, etc.)

6. What is the argument or "plot" of the poem? (Example: "Don't die gently.")

7. What are the dominant images and/or repeated words?

8. Identify any other poetic technique used in the poem (metaphor, simile, personification, etc.—see Poetry Terms chart above.)

9. How do these dominant images/words and techniques (#7 & 8) help to accomplish or evoke the plot or message of the poem?

10. In a few sentences, give your overall analysis of the poem's content, form, and meaning.

Now let's practice poetry analysis, using the steps detailed in the chart, with a famous elegy for Abraham Lincoln, Walt Whitman's poem, "O Captain! My Captain!." First, we will read the poem once for comprehension.

O Captain! My Captain! by Walt Whitman (1865)

O Captain! my Captain! our fearful trip is done,

The ship has weather'd every rack, the prize we sought is won,

The port is near, the bells I hear, the people all exulting,

While follow eyes the steady keel, the vessel grim and daring;   4

       But O heart! heart! heart!

         O the bleeding drops of red,

           Where on the deck my Captain lies,

             Fallen cold and dead.   8

O Captain! my Captain! rise up and hear the bells;

Rise up--for you the flag is flung—for you the bugle trills,

For you bouquets and ribbon'd wreaths—for you the shores a-crowding,

For you they call, the swaying mass, their eager faces turning;   12

       Here Captain! dear father!

         This arm beneath your head!

           It is some dream that on the deck,

             You've fallen cold and dead.   16

My Captain does not answer, his lips are pale and still,

My father does not feel my arm, he has no pulse nor will,

The ship is anchor'd safe and sound, its voyage closed and done,

From fearful trip the victor ship comes in with object won;   20

       Exult O shores, and ring O bells!

         But I with mournful tread,

           Walk the deck my Captain lies,

             Fallen cold and dead.

In the comprehension step, we **identify any unfamiliar words and phrases**. Often, poems written a significant time before the present, even in English, contain antiquated words or terms that are no longer in use. Literature textbooks will annotate such poems and provide the definitions and historical context below the poem; otherwise, look them up in the dictionary.

Since this poem uses metaphorical imagery, not every reader can guess what is meant by a "rack" ("the ship has weathered every rack", line 2). Textbook annotations can be very helpful in this regard, putting the word in its original, perhaps obsolete context. In this context, "rack" refers to being tortured "on the rack," so we can read it as a metaphor for hardship or turmoil. The "exulting" people (line 3) are rejoicing. "Keel" (line 4) is part of a boat, and importantly in this context, its entire bottom or foundation.

With these words decoded, we can now see that the poem appears to show a victorious ship being welcomed at harbor by joyful people, bugle music, flowers, and fanfare, but also the disturbing image of a fallen hero that the speaker calls "Captain." We can thus **identify the poem's topic** or theme as both celebration and lamentation (grief).

Is there a **rhyme scheme**? Yes. Checking the sounds at the end of the lines, we see that the first two lines of Stanza 1 end in the sound "un," a phonetic spelling of the sound of the words "done" and "won." We will use the variable "*a*" to represent this sound. We see that the third and fourth lines of Stanza 1 end in the "ing" sound, which we will call "*b*." So we can notate the first quatrain (or four lines) of Stanza 1's rhyme scheme, in poetic shorthand, as *aabb*.

The **speaker of the poem** is not immediately identifiable, but as he refers to the poem's object, the "Captain," as *his*, we might start by calling him a soldier of some sort. He is clearly someone that has fought beside the Captain, since he references "*our* fearful trip" and the prize "*we* sought" (lines 1, 2). Some poems might name the speaker in the title, as in Langston Hughes' poem "Mother to Son," but this Whitman poem does not do so. Let's go to our next step of analysis to see if we can gather some more clues to the poem's meaning and the identity of main characters, if possible.

You might notice the **genre of the poem** is an elegy, since it celebrates the life and achievements of the "Captain." That might explain while the people are standing near with flowers, music, and praise; perhaps this is, after all, a celebration of an important life—a funeral, even, rather than the return of an important ship. We know it's not a sonnet because it has more than fourteen lines. It could also be an ode, since it praises the Captain, but the Captain is clearly dead, which points back to an elegy.

The **plot of the poem**, inasmuch as we have to go on, is that a group of people fought some sort of battle, perhaps on the boat, but now as the boat approaches the harbor, where a joyous reception awaits, the Captain has fallen dead. The ship and its soldiers are victorious, but feel conflicted since their leader is fallen. At the conclusion of the poem, the speaker is pacing the boat's deck in mourning.

Dominant, or reoccurring, words and images in this poem are "Captain," various synonyms for boat like "vessel," "ship," and "keel;" the phrase "fallen cold and dead," which (significantly) concludes all three stanzas, "you" and "you've," and the word "heart," which is repeated twice. Is it a coincidence that the word "heart" appears three times, just like the phrase "fallen cold and dead?" We can't be sure yet, but we take note. Often things that appear to readers as coincidences are usually purposefully crafted by the poet to convey an important message.

Now we will **identify any other poetic technique used in the poem**—most commonly, metaphors, similes, or personification. The entire frame of the poem—the voyage of the ship—is a metaphor, in fact, for Abraham Lincoln's victorious fight to abolish slavery before his untimely assassination. However, as is characteristic of Whitman's trademark journalistic style, there are few metaphors or similes in the phrases; the lines themselves are very literal depictions of the scene. Your instructor might tell you one poetic technique used here is **apostrophe**, in which the poet invokes an inanimate object by name as if it is alive and present: "O heart! heart! heart!" (line 5) and "Exult O shores, and ring O bells" (line 21).

Now we ask, **how do these dominant images/words and techniques help to accomplish or evoke the plot or message of the poem?** Knowing what we now know about the poem's historical context—that the ship is a metaphor for Lincoln's political accomplishments and the poem an elegy for his death—we can see how the staccato, controlled repetition of words and phrases punctuates the shot as it must have rung out, striking Lincoln dead. Indeed, the repetition of the word "heart" in the first stanza, "O heart! heart! heart!" (line 5) evokes the last few beats of his heart. The unique fashion in which the final four lines of each stanza seem to slowly stretch out across the page might invoke the stretched, prostrate limbs of a fallen body, or the gush of the "bleeding drops of red" (line 6).

Therefore, for an **overall analysis of the poem's content, form, and meaning**, we can conclude that Whitman's deliberate spacing of lines, controlled end rhymes, and repetition of sounds help evoke the extended metaphor of a majestic ship (abolition) whose captain, Abraham Lincoln, comes to a tragic end just as the ship's journey comes to fruition. The poem's words and sounds carefully collaborate to articulate the grief of a nation in losing a great man, echoing his legacy again every time the poem is read.

While this process may seem challenging for you when you first attempt it on your own, poetry analysis is an endlessly rewarding puzzle at which you will become more skilled with frequent practice. The more poems you read, the more poetic techniques you will learn, and you will suddenly find a world of poems unfurling their petals to you.

For practice, analyze one or more of the following poems using the Poetry Analysis chart earlier in the chapter.

BILINGUAL INSTRUCTIONS (2002)

BY HARRYETTE MULLEN

Californians say No
to bilingual instruction in schools

Californians say No
to bilingual instructions on ballots

Californians say Yes
to bilingual instructions on curbside waste receptacles:

Coloque el recipiente con las flechas hacia la calle
Place container with arrow facing street

No ruede el recipiente con la tapa abierta
Do not tilt or roll container with lid open

Recortes de jardin solamente
Yard clippings only

JASPER, TEXAS, 1998

BY LUCILLE CLIFTON

i am a man's head hunched in the road.
i was chosen to speak by the members
of my body. the arm as it pulled away
pointed toward me, the hand opened once
and was gone.

why and why and why
should I call a white man brother?
who is the human in this place,
the thing that is dragged or the dragger?
what does my daughter say?

the sun is a blister overhead.
if i were alive i could not bear it.
the townsfolk sing we shall overcome
while hope drains slowly from my mouth
into the dirt which covers us all.
i am done with this dust. i am done.

ODE TO AN AVOCADO (1997)

BY MARCOS MCPEEK VILLATORRO

I eat an avocado.
They valued it at ninety eight cents.
In old days and mother countries
that meant five thousand *córdobas*.
Enough to buy six beers
or a night at a stale inn
with one large bucket of water
for two sweaty lovers.

This little green traveler
has seen too much.
Tossed by calloused hands, it
could have dropped into the sea, like
so many dead Indians from the dock.

If it were priced at twenty cents,
Old *compañeros* would laugh at me,
pricing an avocado like a
smile, or a kiss stolen deeply
within the open branches
of an orchard.

At ninety eight, they turn their eyes from me,
looking away from an ignorant *patrón*
who holds the fruit of their labor
in his soft hand.

CHAPTER CHAPTER CHAPTER 23

WRITING ESSAYS ABOUT LITERATURE

The goal of this section is to help you gain an understanding of the kind of writing expected of you in upper-level English courses and to learn what specifics distinguish English papers from writing in other disciplines.

THE GOALS OF ENGLISH

You will encounter two types of English classes: composition classes that concentrate on the craft of writing and literature classes that study literature. Certainly writing in response to an assigned reading is common to both. Thinkers have described literature as the "written record of human experience," and Flaubert has suggested we "read in order to live." However, the study of literature involves not only emotional or intellectual responses to an author's words, but also an analysis of *how* a literary work achieves its effects.

Ideally, the first literature class you take will encourage you to think about literature in new ways and challenge you to be flexible in your perceptions about it.

Literature Class Goals:

- to encourage more conscious, close reading,
- to begin to suggest ways in which other disciplines (such as history, philosophy, psychology, linguistics, etc) shed light on literary analysis,
- to teach you how to be an effective critical writer and engage in literary analysis of your own.

Although reading lists may vary widely from class to class, the practices we engage in when analyzing literature remain constant, so that whether you read Medieval poetry or modern novels, the approaches to literary analysis and the writing of papers remain constant.

Why Take a Literature Class?

The experience of discovering a unity, ambiguity, or paradox in a work of literature is always exciting, but it is also useful. Diverse assignments in literature classes will allow you to develop several skills. Most of them are highly analytical. These skills include:

- The ability to do a "close reading" of a passage; that is, to analyze for style, form, structure, and subtext;
- the ability to apply literary criticism and/or theory to a work of literature;
- the ability to use an appropriate analytical vocabulary when writing; and
- the ability to communicate your ideas clearly and elegantly through writing.

CLOSE READING, OR C.S.I. ENGLISH CLASS

*"Close reading assumes an organic unity in which one part reflects the whole. Why do it? Because, like argument for lawyers, it's the major practice of the field; because it positions the reader as listener rather than simple hearer of the words; because, done well, **it's as much fun as a detective novel**." [Emphasis added].*

Mary Ann Boelcskevy

If you are new to English literature classes, you might not believe it yet, but close reading is a lot like watching a juicy episode of CSI! Just like the forensic detectives at a crime scene, we search for the hidden clues that will tell us the full story. This is the joy of reading: it is an interactive experience and it requires your full attention. When good detectives arrive on a crime scene, they focus intently on every detail so that they miss nothing. You will do the same when you approach your reading. The best literature requires that you work a little bit to uncover nuances and meanings, and the secret is that this is the pleasure of the text. If an author spells something out too plainly or tells you what to think, you feel insulted, as if you're wasting your time. When you unlock the mysteries of a challenging passage, you'll feel like you just solved a crime. It's addictive and fun!

Close reading is the careful analysis of a passage from a larger work. It involves scrutinizing a text for paradoxes, ambiguities, tensions, complexities, and contradictions found by reading words for both their **denotative** and **connotative** meanings, that is, the obvious, and the not so obvious.

The Close Reading Process

- Pre-text (first impressions before you lock down your interpretation).
- Text (the literal and figurative meanings of the words).
- Subtext (what meaning lurks beneath the surface).
- Context (the big picture: how the passage functions as a microcosm for the whole work and its relationship to the outside world).

A. PRE-TEXT

Begin a close reading assignment with a pen in hand. Mark down words that strike you as significant without yet analyzing why. Look first at the very literal level of action and fact. What is going on here? What does the text say? Who is speaking? What do the words mean on the most basic level? Attempt to identify tone: anxious, thrilled, melancholy? This is often reflected in the rhythm of a work. Reading aloud can help you sense particular rhythms.

These first impressions are important notes to yourself.

B. TEXT

Look for particularities of language and style in the text. Are some words repeated? Which words rhyme together? Is there personification (when an object or animal is given human characteristics)? If you are reading a poem, what is the meter and rhyme? Never just observe.

Rather, explain that the rhythm or meter gives us the feeling of short, abrupt action: "Go there. Be good. Farewell."

C. SUBTEXT

Some words are difficult to paraphrase because subtext lurks beneath the literal meaning. When you have difficulty in understanding, you may be tempted to gloss over (or skip entirely) sections you do not understand. However, this is often a sign that you should pay even closer attention to them. Use these words as starting places to explore the complexities of the reading.

> Forensic detectives don't ignore mysteries, they work on them obsessively. On *CSI*, when the puzzling clue is finally explained, we all shout: "So that's how the body got in the tree!" **Understanding something that was initially a mystery is very satisfying because it restores order to our world. Close reading is the literary equivalent.**

Your efforts will always be rewarded, for often these "difficult" passages contain the most interesting material. The passage could be challenging because it uses language in different ways or out of its usual context, implying metaphors without stating them explicitly. This should always be your starting point, for if you gloss over any part of your close reading, your interpretation will be incomplete. The great news is that these nuggets will often form the basis for your paper.

> The satisfaction of unpacking a particularly troublesome phrase is not to be underestimated and will very often be key to your paper's thesis.

Even if you think you know the meaning of a word, if it seems as though the writer is using it in an unfamiliar way, look it up! There may indeed be an alternate meaning of which you were unaware.

If there are metaphors, what specifically is being compared or contrasted? What are the double meanings? In *The Merchant of Venice*, "kind" means both "thoughtful" and "type" or "kindred" and this duality is an important one to the themes of the play. Look for wordplay. What do the metaphors bring to your understanding of the work? How do they affect the tone? What does it mean to compare a womb and a tomb? Does the tone change at some point, and where specifically? What words make it change?

D. CONTEXT

The final part of your analysis should focus on relations among the items you have noticed to place their meanings in context. How do these elements work together to provide meaning? In the case of a larger work, how do these meanings relate to the whole? Are there ironies, paradoxes? How can a poem about a coat really be about plagiarism (W.B. Yeats' "A Coat")? This is your conclusion about the work. How do the themes or images work together or against each other (happy death) to make a point? You don't necessarily have to conclude that the text works towards only one meaning. It can contain ironic or multiple messages. Whatever your conclusion, this will be your thesis.

THESIS STATEMENTS FOR LITERATURE PAPERS

Your argument is the thesis of your paper and will identify the particular lens through which you view the work. One particularly effective way of developing an argument out of a close reading is to show that while on the surface a work appears to be saying *x*, it is really doing *y*. You will show *x* and prove *y* with evidence from the text, and you will make your close reading serve the purposes of your argument. For example, in "Church Going," a poem by Philip Larkin, the speaker stops and walks around inside a church. You might notice that a poem *seems* to be mocking organized religion, but the speaker is seeking *something* inside that church and maybe feeling sad that his generation doesn't have the comforts of religion to fall back on, which means despite what he says, he does find value in religion. This is a nice tension for a thesis statement:

Example:

In "Church Going," Philip Larkin's speaker seems to be devaluing organized religion, but his quest indicates a remorse for his generation's spiritual emptiness.

You can hear Philip Larkin reading his poem at the following site: http://www.youtube.com/watch?v=qTRYBKIaD30.

Example:

In the first line of W. B. Yeat's "The Coat," "I made my song a coat," perhaps the speaker is saying both that he made *a coat for his poetry* to protect it, and that he made *his poetry into a coat* to protect his own pride. His conclusion then has a double message both for poetry and for himself: Exposing yourself as you really are is a bolder gesture than hiding or "covering up."

ADDING CONTEXTUAL INFORMATION

In the example above, if you know something about W. B. Yeats, you might wish to apply that knowledge to the poem if it helps to illustrate the themes. For example, in his earlier poetry, Yeats devised a whole mythological system for describing the world. He also loved

Gaelic myths. From the context, we can surmise that "fools" refers to other poets who imitated his style. Because so many works in the Western Canon reflect the strong influence of Christianity and the Bible on culture, you might also toy with the idea that he is making reference to the Biblical Joseph, whose brothers were jealous of the beautiful coat their father gave him. Or you might think of the fable of "The Emperor's New Clothes." These considerations might enrich your reading of the poem.

A Coat

I made my song a coat
Covered with embroideries
Out of old mythologies
From heel to throat;
But the fools caught it,
Wore it in the world's eyes
As though they'd wrought it.
Song, let them take it,
For there's more enterprise
In walking naked.

William Butler Yeats (1916)

HOW LONG SHOULD QUOTATIONS BE?

It can be more helpful to use shorter in-text citation, rather than large blocks of the work. The reason is that when you try to quote large blocks first and explain later, your paper is tied to a rehash of the "plot" in the order in which it appears in your quote. Simply put, the chronology of the work need not motivate the chronology of your paper. Instead, your paper should have an organic theme and plot of its own. Sometimes, you will quote from the beginning of a work, sometimes from the end, all dependent on the points you are making and their place in YOUR argument. By choosing small phrases from the original and incorporating them into the body of your paper, you can explore the text thematically or follow a developing symbol.

> Below is an example of how to incorporate literary quotes into the body of your text:
>
> Ophelia herself is constantly associated with the need to remember. Laertes urges her to "remember well" (1.3.84) his cautions about Hamlet's untrustworthiness as a suitor, and she answers that "Tis in my memory lock'd" (85).

Notice that this quotation appears on page 85 of Marjorie Garber's *Shakespeare's Ghost Writers*, and that the act, scene, and lines from *Hamlet* are put in parentheses after the quotation marks. Also, notice that the quotes blend into the grammar and meaning of the sentence. They don't feel like they are just added on.

HOW DO I CHOOSE A PASSAGE?

Poems provide discrete units for interpretation. Usually, the close reading of a poem will make reference to most of the lines, or, if a longer poem, a set of stanzas. However, choosing a passage in a novel for close reading can be a little more challenging. Do not concentrate only on what you perceive as climactic moments in the novel in terms of plot. Oftentimes, "quieter" scenes reveal something in the novel that you might not have noticed on the first reading. In all well-written novels, every passage has a purpose and is of importance to the artistic whole. Strive to find a relatively self-contained scene with a discernible beginning and end that might serve as a microcosm of the themes of the entire work. Because the scrutiny of the text is to be detailed, passages are usually limited in length. This allows you the leisure to spend the kind of time necessary to fully unpack the meanings in the text.

© sirtravelalot/Shutterstock.com

CLOSE READING A NOVEL: AN EXTENDED EXAMPLE FROM TONI MORRISON'S *JAZZ*

This section illustrates by example how to close read a passage from a novel.

The following passage occurs one third of the way into Toni Morrison's novel *Jazz*. It is an evocative scene, but not a pivotal one in terms of plot.

> Someone fights with the Victrola; places the arm on, scratches the record, tries again, then exchanges the record for another. During the lull, the brothers notice Dorcas. Taller than most, she gazes at them over the head of her dark friend. The brothers' eyes seem wide and welcoming to her. She moves forward out of the shadow and slips through the group. The brothers turn up the wattage of their smiles. The right record is on the turntable now; she can hear its preparatory hiss as the needle slides toward its first groove. The brothers smile brilliantly; one leans a fraction of an inch toward the other and, never losing eye contact with

Dorcas, whispers something. The other looks Dorcas up and down as she moves towards them. Then, just as the music, slow and smiky, loads up the air, his smile bright as ever, he wrinkles his nose and turns away. Dorcas has been acknowledged, appraised, and dismissed, in the time it takes a needle to find its opening groove. (66–67)

Although this passage does not affect the novel's plot in an obvious way (neither Dorcas nor the reader ever sees or hears of the brothers again), it is an excellent choice for a close reading. The scene provides a self-contained episode that has inherent within it a mini-plot, that is, action that accelerates into a climax and then tapers off. Moreover, it provides strong imagery and metaphors for analysis.

A. PRE-TEXT

First, in notes to yourself, you might summarize the action:

> *A third-person narrator observes Dorcas at a party. A record (remember those?) is being put on the record player. During the change of record, Dorcas thinks that two brothers who have noticed her, like her. She starts to move towards them when the music comes on. Then one of the brothers shows his disdain by wrinkling his nose. She's been dissed! She's been cut short in her hopes.*

From writing this summary, you might notice the importance of the record to the action. File that information away for later use.

Then you might make notes and categories such as:

- "Victrola"/record imagery: "needle," "groove."
- Dark and Light: "wattage," "bright," "dark friend," "smoky," "shadow," "brilliantly."
- Violence: "fights," "scratches," "hiss."
- Judgment: "exchanges," "right record," "dismissed."
- Body: "head," "eyes," "nose," "arm,"
- ???: words that seem important, but defy immediate categorization: "seems," "loads up."

B. TEXT

Because Morrison's writing style is so deceptively clear, you might miss her craft. However, she has used language very carefully. You might mention the onomatopoetic quality of "slips," "slides," and "slow and smoky," all of which contribute to the hazy party atmosphere while mimicking Dorcas's slow movement towards the brothers, and the movement of the needle on the record groove. The forward momentum of the scene reveals Dorcas's attraction to the brothers both physically (she is crossing the room) and emotionally as she perceives them to be accepting and "welcoming" her with their "wide" smiles. The brothers' minimal action ("fraction of an inch," "whispers," and "wrinkl[ing] his nose") contrasts sharply with Dorcas's movement towards them and underscores the power imbalance in the scene. The passage reaches a climax when the action and Dorcas stop short as one of the brothers "dismisses" her. The words "[t]urns away" are as abrupt and short as the rejection. But paradoxically, while Dorcas is the active pursuer, and humiliated in her pursuit, passive verbs define her in the last line, objectifying her and illustrating grammatically her lack of agency ("acknowledged, appraised, and dismissed").

C. SUBTEXT

This is where the pretext categories and textual observations are explored more fully. As observed earlier, references to the record frame this scene, and the needle finding the record's groove defines the time of the scene's and Dorcas's action. The opening and closing scenes of judgments, first of the record, and finally of Dorcas, make the comparison between the record and Dorcas clear. We say then that the record is a metaphor for Dorcas.

One record is initially dismissed, foreshadowing and setting the tone of an atmosphere in which things are judged, exchanged, and rejected. But the initial record exchange also gives the reader the false hope that Dorcas is the "right record." We are as shocked and surprised as Dorcas is at her rejection. We follow Dorcas when the brothers "*seem* wide and welcoming." Morrison's use of the word "gazes" suggests Dorcas's naïve admiration of the brothers.

Like a moth drawn to a flame, Dorcas moves towards them automatically (just as a record must circle). She moves out of darkness (literally away from her disregarded and smaller "dark friend") and "out of the shadow" to these brothers who are described as beacons of light. Their smiles are electric and attractive to her; they "turn up the wattage of their smiles;" they "smile brilliantly," and they draw her to them with the power of their "eye contact." But this "eye contact" is not the caress it promises to be. It is with his eyes that the other "looks Dorcas up and down" and judges her. And although his smile is as "bright as ever," this light is to be mistrusted. "He wrinkles his nose and turns away." The narrator then returns to the record; and with that gesture, we learn that we were as mistaken as she was. Dorcas is not the "right record" at all; she is the one that was "scratch[ed]" and rejected. She has misjudged the scene as we think they have misjudged her. Why does Morrison make the comparison between the record and Dorcas?

D. CONTEXT

At this stage, we look at the record imagery and the themes and relate them to the whole novel. We are answering the question, how does this passage function as a microcosm of the whole?

The passage is an important illustration of Dorcas's character and her flaws. She is steeped in the Blues culture of the Harlem Renaissance (the setting for the novel) and captivated by the promises of violence and seduction in its music. The passage underscores her strong identification with the music by comparing her to the record. One of the Blues ideals she internalizes is a masochistic glorification of pain which leads her to accept judgments about herself like those of the brothers, and to allow herself to die later, when she is shot by her married lover.

Moving into the greater world of the novel, we see that from the book's first word, the introductory "Sth" of a needle finding its groove, Morrison uses recording metaphors throughout, both for the characters and for the cultural imperatives which dictate their behavior. Following the path of other images found in the scene, we might think of the importance in the novel of light and dark skin, and how the promise of light is to be mistrusted in the entire novel as it is in this passage. Favoring light over dark also illustrates the novel's portrayal of how characters and society judge on the basis of appearances (as the brothers do in this passage) and the trap into which this leads the characters.

Finally, the passage might be a metaphor for the ultimate rejection of Blues singers after the Harlem Renaissance. The Red Hot Mamas lasted until Ragtime took over as a "happier," up and coming musical style.

LITERARY CRITICISM

Literary criticism is an analysis of a specific book, poem, or play.

Did you know you are a literary critic?

Whenever you write a paper about a novel, poem, or play, you are engaging in literary criticism.

The reasons for learning how to read literary criticism in English classes are simple. First, reading literary criticism is enjoyable and rewarding if you have just finished a book or a poem. Often when we go to a movie, we are dying to talk about it with someone afterwards. Literary criticism provides the same satisfaction by allowing you to have a "conversation" with an expert on a piece of literature, and it will open up new ways of thinking and reading for you. We have all had that "aha!" experience of reading something that rings true and enlightens our previously clouded perception of a text: "Now I get it!" Or, we read something that seems completely preposterous, unfair, unfounded, and this makes us angry. It makes us want to reply to the author, to find out how in the world he or she could have come to such a conclusion. It is exciting to read and react to another's opinion of a work you care about, and it can breathe life and passion into your paper.

Secondly, you read literary criticism in English classes because, as a literature student, you are being trained as an apprentice literary critic yourself (especially if you go on to become an English major or graduate student in English). The best way to understand the discipline is to see what professionals do and analyze how they do it. Reading criticism can teach you how to write better and more effective critical essays yourself.

You may be asked to research additional articles for papers and oral reports. Many classes have mandatory library information sessions. These sessions teach you the fundamentals of researching both articles and books for your papers, skills that will serve you in every English course. (Please see Chapter 19: "Conducting Research" for more information about literary research databases.)

Literary Theory

Literary theory is about the general act of reading and writing. It even raises the question of what literature is. Theory tries to change the ways we think and read. As a result, the language can be very powerfully charged or even offensive. There are many famous schools of literary theory: New Criticism, Reader Response, Historicism and New Historicism, Psychoanalytic theories, Deconstruction, Feminist Theory, Gender and Queer Theory, Race Theory and Postcolonial Theory. Literary theorists may look at particular works of literature to provide support for their theories, but their main concerns are with the act of reading itself. The feminist film theorist Laura Mulvey argues, for instance, that a female movie-goer is forced into a double bind of identifying both with the objectified female portrait on screen <u>and</u> with the male protagonist objectifying her. Hence, although Mulvey uses specific examples, her concerns lie more with film-watching as a whole than with critiquing a particular film or director.

Literary Criticism

Literary criticism (critical articles about works of literature) is usually text-specific, a reading of a particular work or author. Certainly, a work of literary criticism is informed by a critic's own type of reading or theories. Rather than discussing how we read in general, however, a critic will persuade us to read a text in a certain way. For example, the critic Walter Cohen reads *The Merchant of Venice* as a product of Renaissance anxieties about the transition from a feudal to a capitalist society.

Literary criticism is in the work in which you will engage most as an undergraduate. Whenever you comment upon, judge, or analyze a text, you are performing the work of a literary critic. Although it may be difficult to jump into the fray of a discussion about James Joyce when you see five hundred listings on the internet library search, you can and should do just that. Depending on your experience of a text, you will invariably find critics with whom you agree wholeheartedly, and others with whom you profoundly disagree. This is the kind of dissension that makes English classes exciting and the discussions of literature charged.

Literary critics are by no means a homogeneous group. There are several types of questions that critics might ask about a text. Consequently, there are many kinds of papers you might write as an English student. Below is a list of several methods and approaches critics take when writing about literature. You do not need to "learn" this list, and it is by no means exhaustive; it is meant merely to provide you with some examples of the types most commonly encountered by students.

1) Text-Based Criticism

Of course, in all essays about literature, the arguments will be closely tied to the text for proof. In this type of analysis, the primary focus of the essay is to explore formal stylistic and thematic conventions in the work itself. Consequently, close reading is often the method of choice for this kind of analysis. Elements discussed might include: characterization, tone, metaphors, imagery, voice, beginnings and endings, structure, theme, etc. Text-based essays will be as varied as the works themselves, for instance, an exploration of absent mothers in *Jane Eyre*, a comparison of two characters as foils in a Shakespeare play, images of mortality in *Mrs. Dalloway*, garden imagery, economic metaphors, etc.

2) Reader Response

While text-based criticism often focuses its attention on the meaning inherent in a work of literature, Reader Response criticism is, as its name implies, concerned with the readers' experience of the text. It denies the primacy of authorial intention and maintains rather that it is the reader who makes meaning out of a text. A reader's reactions thus are given more importance that the author's intentions.

3) Historical

This type of criticism examines the role of history in the work, or the work in history. This can be either in terms of the historical events which produced the work, i.e., World War I imagery in Woolf's *To the Lighthouse*, OR, the critic could explore the literary work's influence on the history of its time. What was the effect of the widespread sale of Harriet Beecher Stowe's *Uncle Tom's Cabin* in 1852 on perceptions of race?

4) Cultural

Cultural criticism is very closely allied to historical criticism, for often culture and history cannot be separated. This type of criticism generally explores societal trends more than historical events, however. Marxist, Postcolonial, Feminist, Gender and Queer Theory would fall under this category. What does Charlotte Perkins Gilman's short story "The Yellow Wallpaper" reveal about the societally-imposed limitations on upper class women at the turn of the century? What statement is D.H. Lawrence making about the effect of harsh working conditions on family life in *Sons and Lovers*?

5) Psychological

This brand of criticism concerns itself with the psychology of the characters, the reader, and/or the author as revealed through the text. It is usually grounded in one of the "schools of understanding" of the human mind (Freud, Lacan, Jung, etc.). For an example of character inquiry, critics might ask about the nature of Hamlet's relationship with his mother, or why he hesitates for so long before killing Claudius. Or, they might investigate the psychological state of the writer. Is there evidence of Virginia Woolf's suicidal tendencies in her work? Or they can explore the reader's response to the text. Why do readers prefer the character of Lucifer to God in *Paradise Lost*?

6) Biographical

Biographical criticism looks closely at the circumstances surrounding the creation of a work of art and what context and experiences shaped the artist. This kind of criticism seeks to explain the existence of the text by analyzing the life, psychology, and circumstances of the writer or poet. For example, James Joyce left Dublin to write abroad because he felt that Catholic Ireland was inimical to his writing. However, Joyce wrote in painstaking detail about the city and actual people he knew. A critic might toy with this tension, or seek out the actual subjects of Joyce's allusions. Guided tours and maps of Dublin have been made based on the character Leopold Bloom's wanderings in *Ulysses*.

7) Genre or Generic

This type of criticism analyzes a work's place in the development of a genre, or uses characteristics of a genre to provide a reading context. For example, a critic might explore *Beowulf* as an example of an epic poem. What characteristics make *Robinson Crusoe* representative of the early novel? What were the criteria for novels in the eighteenth century? An essay of this sort might also see how a work transgresses the usual boundaries for a genre. Where has the writer broken the rules for his or her given genre? Is the text changing the genre? Making fun of it (Fielding's *Shamela*)? Is it the first of its kind or a brand new genre (David Foster Wallace's *Infinite Jest*)?

8) Deconstruction

Very theoretical, Deconstruction explores the "binary oppositions" inherent in language, where words are often defined by their opposites. Oversimplified, "cold" is defined as "not hot" and can never be understood independently of its opposite. Applied to literature, tensions arise despite the intentions of the author. For example, in her famous essay "Melville's Fist," Barbara Johnson discusses the short story "Billy Budd" and illustrates that while the character Claggart seems to persecute Billy, he does so because he actually loves him too much and has projected his own self-hatred onto Billy.

Please remember that these are merely illustrations to give you an idea of some of the various types of literary study. Most criticism defies such neat categorization though, and many forms of criticism overlap. For instance, a feminist critic might rely very heavily upon cultural trends, but also upon historical events, and he or she might undertake a text-based analysis to prove his or her points.

Literary critics want to change the ways readers read, to open the readers' eyes to new insights. This can be a subversive, world-changing activity. For example, a post-colonial critic's goal is to make readers see colonized subjects (whether they be characters or writers) where they have previously been missed or relegated to the background. Post-colonial critics thereby give voice to those who might have been silenced before. They might do this by noticing stereotypical descriptions of certain characters, or by introducing previously ignored writers into the canon. This "re-vision" of the past radically changes not only our view of literature, but changes our world view as well. Literary criticism can play a vital role in society, dismantling old prejudices and uncritical attitudes. After discussing post-colonial criticism in an English course, a student may emerge with a changed perception of the world, and will perhaps be more aware of who's writing and who's being forgotten in the dialogue. Marxist, feminist, gender, and race critics all have similar goals: to make readers aware of previous oversight or biased treatment of characters, writers, and readers. Creating conscious readers and disseminating a practice of critical thinking and analysis is the first step in social change. Many critics earn the label "subversive," because they really do affect the way their readers perceive the world.

HOW DO I INTEGRATE LITERARY CRITICISM OR THEORY INTO MY OWN WRITING?

LEARNING BY EXAMPLE

Just as you would never attempt to write a novel without having read one, reading widely in criticism will expose you to a wide variety of critical responses to literature and help you model your own papers. Some approaches will feel uncomfortable and others will seem to make a lot of sense. This is to be expected. We don't all read the same way or from the same perspective. What is important is to recognize and appreciate differences in reading and writing and ultimately find your own voice and critical vantage point.

Not only will reading criticism and theory cause you to question and analyze the ways in which you read, it will also illustrate different methods for writing your own criticism. From observing other critics at work, you will discover which rhetorical strategies you find persuasive, and learn from positive examples how to construct an effective argument.

Besides helping you get a feel for the types of writing-styles available to you, criticism can also help your paper writing in very concrete ways by acting as a springboard to your own discussion of the literature at hand. When you use secondary sources, you utilize one text (the critical article) to explain a second work (the novel, poem, or play). The second work is the object of your paper's analysis. It might be a primary text like a work of fiction, a poem, an essay, a play, or it might be another critical essay. The critical source you bring into the paper will look at the literary work through its own critical lens.

PREWRITING WITH CRITICISM

1) Read the article and be sure you understand it completely. Read about the critic if you can, so that you can get an overview of his or her views and scope of research.

2) Paraphrase the article's argument in your own words so that you feel you comprehend what the article argues. This can help in your formal writing when you will need to explain the theory to your reader. Then, get down to the writing of your paper

© Billion Photos/Shutterstock.com

INTEGRATING LITERARY CRITICISM INTO YOUR PAPER

1. For the reader's benefit, *briefly* summarize the article's argument, explaining key terms you will use in your paper if necessary.

2. Apply the critic's argument to the literature you are discussing. How does it shed light on the work?

3. Now express yourself. Do not allow the critic to do all of the talking in YOUR paper. Be sure that your voice is heard loud and clear and that you take the discussion even further. What are your conclusions? What does bringing these works together create? Why is that interesting? Your thesis is what makes the paper yours.

4. Do not hesitate to call attention to the limitations as well as the advantages of your critic's position. Unless your instructor explicitly asks you to defend or apply a theory and not to critique it, he or she will probably be most impressed if you show both attentive understanding of the works you discuss and critical indepen-dent-mindedness (as opposed to merely dutiful recitation).

NON-LITERARY SOURCES

Non-literary sources can provide a wealth of material for a paper. Drawing upon other disciplines often sheds light upon literature since no author ever writes in a vacuum. There are many relevant sources for discussing literature. You might draw on the Bible, historical documents or histories, musicology, psychoanalysis, philosophy, or art history to illuminate a text. Cultural documents such as advertisements, films, cartoons, or newspaper articles can also yield fascinating discoveries. For example, you might want to research Wagner's opera *Tristan and Isolde* to better understand the mythical allusions in T. S. Eliot's *The Waste Land*. Or you might read relevant passages in Herodotus's *The Histories* when reading Michael Ondaatje's *The English Patient*, since the main character treasures this book above all others.

DECODING ASSIGNED TOPICS

First, understand the topic. This is not as obvious as it sounds and some professors are better than others at explaining what they want. Often a successful answer depends upon your skillful interpretation of the question asked.

Take your time with the assignment. Rephrase it for yourself and inspect it for subtleties you might not have noticed at first. You will acquire a whole new vocabulary when interpreting such questions. "Discuss" no longer means "talk about in a general way," but rather "explore in depth." The best papers find a way to put a twist on the question in order to give it some originality, while remaining rigorous through the careful use of textual evidence.

Below are a few paper topics of the kind you might encounter in literature classes, and ways you might go about answering them.

QUESTION TYPE 1: TRACE AN IMAGE

Sample Prompt:

Many of the texts we have read this semester contain scenes of **reading**. Focusing on one text, examine how reading and 'literary' interpretation are figured within the narrative world.

Translation:

Some of your assigned reading in this course has included either descriptions of actual characters reading or scenes in which reading is represented in a metaphorical way ("literary" and "figured" indicate that metaphors for reading should form part of your discussion, as well as literal representations of reading). Including both types of reading (literal and metaphorical), structure an argument around the idea of reading in only one text. Your thesis should state why reading is significant to the overall themes of the work.

Methods for Answering "Trace an Image" Questions:

The best possible response to this type of question is to take your answer beyond the limited confines of definition. In the "reading" example above, discuss the literal act of reading, but then also see "reading" as a metaphor for larger issues. In other words, the question could be passably answered in a narrow way, but a subtler interpretation of the question will allow you to explore the overall significance of reading to the themes of the text as a whole. Usually, the instructor is asking you implicitly to make that connection. Here's how you get there:

Literal Reading

Begin by noting all the instances where a character reads. Where, how, and what do the characters read? Which characters read romance novels and which read philosophy? Do their personalities reflect that choice? Look for patterns that might lead you to a thesis. Now move to the metaphorical level.

Metaphorical Reading

Interpret the question more broadly than just characters sitting down with a book. Do characters read letters or signs? Do they read other characters' faces, motives, actions, clothing the weather, storefront signs, legal codes, social conventions, or any of the multiple "signs" that exist in the world of the text? Remember also to include the narrator or speaker's point of view since these figures often address the reading audience directly and "read" events.

Now that you have a handle on the metaphors, you must establish a thesis.

Establishing a Thesis

You will want to present more than a mere laundry list of the instances of the image you are tracing. Your paper will need a thesis to tie it together and that thesis will be tied to what the image means. "Scenes of reading in the novel exist" is not a thesis. What does reading mean to the work? This is the gold of your thesis. Perhaps you notice that "The author uses images of reading to illustrate the difficulty human beings have interpreting the world around them." Or "Scenes of reading show that every character, no matter how objective he or she seems, holds a subjective bias. The author underscores this point by having mothers and lovers be the worst mis-readers of all." You will want to use very specific examples to support your points.

As the cherry on top, you can underscore your reading theme by the language you choose. For example, you might write, "Although she finds his face inscrutable, Penelope chooses to read Harrison's silence as disapproval."

QUESTION TYPE 2: COMPARISON/CONTRAST

> Compare Virginia Woolf and Hélène Cixous in the two articles you read. How do their conceptions of feminism resemble each other or differ?

The greatest challenge in a comparison/contrast paper is in finding a thesis to tie the two elements together. Observing that they are "similar" or "different" is not enough to make for a compelling topic. The first step towards determining your thesis is to decide why these two texts should be discussed together. You can be sure that if this is an assigned topic, the choice is not random. If you are comparing two texts of your own choosing, it becomes even more important for you to identify the common basis for comparison. "Feminism" provides this in the above question by giving you focus and a starting point.

Now you can move on to the thesis. Often what the instructor is looking for is something along the lines of these two texts look similar on the surface, but a careful reading reveals that they are really different, or vice versa. For example, Cixous and Woolf are both feminists, but their styles of writing (or their views on class, etc.) differ significantly. This significant difference (one that has meaning) will give your paper its thesis. (One author being tall and the other short is not a *significant* difference). Your thesis might be that Woolf and Cixous share similar ideological goals, but their views of history differ. This is a paper topic. It might also be important to notice that Cixous wrote her essay fifty years after Woolf. Hence, the differences in history and feminism that fifty years make should be acknowledged by you in writing when considering their similarities and differences.

A common difficulty students encounter with compare/contrast papers is how to organize them. The most basic difficulty is the placement of the two texts in relation to each other and the amount of space you give to each one. This decision will depend both on your topic and upon the relationship between the two texts. If you are using Woolf as a lens through which to read Cixous, you will necessarily devote more paper time to Cixous. Such a paper might be organized with an introduction to Woolf, followed by a more complete discussion of Cixous.

If the two texts are roughly equal in importance, the organization becomes a little more complicated. While dividing your paper into two parts makes logical sense, it can create two mini-essays instead of one whole, coherent essay. Moreover, the two sections essay can often become redundant as you cover points for one author and then repeat them for the second. Instead, you might try organizing the essay on topics of commonality and difference, or a point by point structure. For instance, body paragraph one might be a discussion of both authors' view of "feminine writing" where the similarities and differences are in the same paragraph. The subsequent body paragraphs move on to other topics, such as both authors' view of feminine creativity, and so on. This way, the reader doesn't have to flip back through your paper or sit through a (possibly boring) repetition of your paper's structure.

Most importantly, make sure that the points of comparison are working towards your paper's goal: its thesis. The fact that Woolf and Cixous are both women is probably not as important a point of comparison. The fact that they are both feminists is.

Let's look at a student example of a point by point discussion in response to the above question.

Student example of a point by point answer:

Closing this passage with the presentation of another distinct feature of women's writing/speech, Cixous notes, "She draws her story into history." With this idea, Cixous seems to reflect Woolf's concept that "a woman writing thinks back through her mothers," connecting her individual story into the larger history of womankind (Woolf 97). Indeed, Cixous writes, "a woman is never far from 'mother'… There is always within her at least a little of that good mother's milk. She writes in white ink" (339). With this statement, Cixous relates woman both to her feminine history and to the continual importance of her body in written/spoken expression.

Yet when Cixous speaks of history, she does not refer only to some continuation of the past. She clarifies the important role of a woman who "inscribes" herself into history… Cixous' female history is all about the creation of the *new*.

In this example, the student demonstrates that Cixous and Woolf both believe in the importance of a woman writer inscribing herself into literary history ("Cixous seems to reflect Woolf's concept"), but she then goes on to identify a difference in their views. The student argues that while Woolf remains primarily concerned with the past, Cixous emphasizes women's roles in creating a literary future ("*Yet* when Cixous speaks of history, she does not refer *only* to some continuation of the *past*. . . Cixous' female history is all about the creation of the *new*"). One could argue (e.g., by citing Woolf's *A Room of One's Own*) that Woolf is equally concerned with the creation of the new. It is by such disagreements that arguments are refined. (See the "Comparison and Contrast" section in Chapter 15 for more on writing this type of essay.)

QUESTION TYPE 3: APPLY A QUOTE

Nabokov said in an interview during the publishing of *Pale Fire*: "You can get nearer and nearer, so to speak, to reality; but you can never get near enough because reality is an infinite succession of steps, levels of perception, false bottoms, and hence unquenchable, unattainable." How does Nabokov's sense of "reality" in this passage seem to apply to *Pale Fire* itself?

A question that begins with a quotation always requires that you first do a close reading of whatever is in quotation marks since the entire question hinges upon it. First, you define reality (a broad concept), then you find specific examples in the novel *Pale Fire*. This question is really the inverse of the "Trace an Image" question above. "Trace an Image" asks you to take a seemingly narrow topic (reading) and make it thematically relevant to the entire text. This question does the opposite. It starts with an abstract concept "reality" so you do not need to look for a broader theme. However, "reality" is too broad in and of itself to make for a manageable thesis. You must develop a thesis by taking the general down to a concrete level with examples.

Literal Words

Start by looking for instances where the novel seems actually to discuss "reality," or "truth," or "verisimilitude" (if you think these mean the same thing in the work). Does one character in particular speak more about reality? Do characters speak in different ways about it? Does a discussion of reality tend to follow a certain sequence of events, such as a death, accidents, or dreams? These questions will lead you further along the path to specificity.

Metaphors

An abstract concept is almost always linked to concrete images, characters, objects, or circumstances that ground it in some way for the reader and for the characters. "Coincidence" and all the discussions around it in Nabokov's work could be a suggestion about the human *perception* of reality and the human desire to control or find patterns to make life comprehensible. Or, an untrustworthy narrator such as Nabokov's Kinbote from *Pale Fire* might construct an alternate reality. The text should give us clues for when we are in reality or an alternate reality. In a film where someone is dreaming, we usually know that he or she has come back to reality when we hear an alarm clock buzzing and see the character waking up in bed.

Some of the concrete images that Nabokov uses to illustrate a shifting sense of reality are: mirrors, doors, hidden passages, and shadows. These recurring images taken in context with Kinbote's shaky hold on his own delusions, might lead you to a thesis about the instability of reality for this character.

Establishing a Thesis

Once you have come to a conclusion about the text, for example, "The narrator of Nabokov's *Pale Fire*, Kinbote, is delusional, and his own experience of reality is infirm," explore the idea and test it. How do other characters respond to Kinbote's rantings? Does he affect their notions of reality? How does the reader experience reality when a delusional character narrates a novel? This gives you great evidence for your paper. Finally, when you have some assertions to make about the novel's use of reality, pull out your close reading of the original quotation in the question and test your ideas about the novel against it. Does the novel support, refute, or complicate the quotation? In what ways?

All Literature Is a Conversation

> *"Writing, when properly managed, . . . is but a different name for conversation."*

Laurence Sterne, Tristram Shandy

Writers and critics never create in isolation. Each new composition builds on previous works or reacts against them. Likewise, in research and analysis every critical essay (including your own) is, in part, a response to another theorist, your professor, or a synthesis of the research essays that have come before. As a writer, you will continue this "conversation" with your own research paper.

DEVISING YOUR OWN TOPICS

In English classes, you will often be allowed to devise your own topics for papers. This process will undoubtedly provide the most rewarding writing for you because you are more invested and interested in your subject. It is much harder to do, but ultimately a wonderful learning experience, and with practice it will seem less daunting. Keep the following points in mind when devising your own topic and always consult your instructor.

- Your paper topic should be reasonable in scope. Don't try to tackle questions so sweeping as to invite a dissertation rather than a 7-page paper. "Love in Shakespeare" is too broad. "The film *Shakespeare in Love* as a commentary on *Romeo and Juliet*" is specific and manageable.

- You should be able to support your thesis. In other words, it's not enough to be inspired about a possible connection you've found. You have to be able to convince your reader with evidence from the text. Prove it!

- Show yourself to be personally excited and convinced by your own argument.

- Choosing to do a close reading is fine, but be sure your paper has a thesis (see the section on close reading). Do not merely paraphrase a text. The reader would do better to consult the original. Rather, show, for example, how the close reading of a poem uncovers the conflicted emotions of the speaker.

- If you choose a topic of comparison or contrast, be sure to have specific common threads to tie the two texts together in a meaningful way.

- If you wish to look at imagery or symbolism that weaves throughout the text do not just show it's there. Instead, illustrate how the image creates a theme in the larger work.

CLOSE READING LITERARY THEORY

Literary theory is writing about the act of reading and writing. You'd be surprised to find how many different theories there are about these two simple activities most of us have been doing every day since childhood. If you are assigned an article of literary theory, it is likely to be the most challenging reading you will ever be assigned in an English class. For that reason, literary theory is usually reserved for upper level classes. In many ways, your first exposure to literary theory may feel like sitting in on a conversation in a foreign language. Until you know and understand the terms, it can be difficult to participate. You may have a vague feeling that you're missing something, even when the language seems familiar. Close reading literary theory can be a very useful exercise as it forces you to analyze how the writer is making an argument. It also may be the only way to really "get" what the writer is saying.

One of the things that makes reading literary theory so challenging is that it often invents its own vocabulary for certain new concepts. The best place to start is in identifying the writer's particular vocabulary. Most often, the words used are informed by an ongoing dialogue that theorist is having with other theorists. While those "in the know" feel comfortable with the language, it can be extremely off-putting to students not yet familiar with it. "Différance" means something very specific to a Deconstructive critic—much more than mere "difference." "Other," to a critic, means a group of people marginalized by culture or history. These terms come from a history of conversations among theorists.

Start by identifying any difficult terms and see how the writer is using them. You might ask your professor or consult sites on literary theory for help in identifying these terms and their significance. These words will probably be central to the author's point, so should never be ignored.

TEXT

Paraphrase the writer's argument and examine areas where you find it particularly compelling or weak. Although it may be daunting at first to "judge" a theorist, go ahead. You are the article's audience. In order to judge accurately, however, you need to be objective. Merely expressing frustration at a critic's writing style or unfamiliar use of terms is not useful or fruitful. Rather, take the time to understand what the writer is really saying, and then engage in a dialogue. Can you find a counter argument? Why do you disagree if you do? As always, you will need to substantiate your opinions with textual proof. While the terms of the discussion may be abstract, your prose should not be.

HOW DOES A LITERATURE PAPER DIFFER FROM PAPERS IN OTHER DISCIPLINES?

While papers in all disciplines attempt to prove a thesis, style will also contribute to the success of your essays in English. Certain conventions or traditions are standard practice in literature papers, and you should adhere to these unless given permission by your instructor to deviate from the standard.

Rules of Thumb:

Avoid the use of the first person "I" when possible.

Avoid personal anecdotes as illustrations.

Avoid charged (but nonspecific) words like "brilliant, interesting, great, etc."

Write about literature in the present tense: "Macbeth is driven by ambition."

Write about critical articles in the present tense: "Cixous argues…"

Avoid overly detailed plot summary.

Remember that quotations support rather than make arguments.

Do not confuse the speaker or the narrator with the poet or the author.

Include an MLA "Works Cited" page and attribute ideas to their original sources. (See Chapter 20, "Documenting your Sources" and the sample papers below.)

Rebekah Brandes

11/28/2017

English 205

Boutry

Swift's Satire of the Travel Narrative and the Human Condition

Considered one of literature's greatest satirists, Jonathan Swift demonstrates his keen observations of society's absurdities through his trademark tone of irony in *Gulliver's Travels*, at once poking fun of the rising popularity of the travel narrative and the proud obliviousness of humankind in general. Swift utilizes the pretense of honesty and realism, and the literary devices of extreme understatement and situational irony to create the satirical version of a travel narrative akin to *Robinson Crusoe*, by Daniel Defoe, as well as an indictment of human nature's presentation in civilized society.

Before the start of *Gulliver's Travels*, the reader is treated to a personal letter from the "author," Lemuel Gulliver, to his cousin, Sympson. In this letter, Gulliver asserts his position that it is only due to the prodding of said cousin that he has agreed to publish his accounts of his travels. He complains that his memoirs were mishandled by the publisher- that certain facts had been omitted, and dates mistaken. This protestation is part of Swift's setup to his satire. The uber realism of a man being irked by small mistakes and omissions to his story creates a larger gap between the expected tale and the actual tale. The more the reader is set up to believe this is a serious account, the greater the irony when Gulliver introduces his readers to the procession of absurd situations that make up the work. Taking this idea even further, Swift has his protagonist insert himself into real-world England by mentioning it was he, (the fictional Gulliver) who advised his "cousin", the famous (non-fictional) author

William Dampier to publish his own accounts of his travels in 1697 (5). In their essay, "Jonathan Swift and Gulliver's Travels," Abigail Williams and Kate O'Conner point out that in reality, Swift himself was irked by the publisher's handling of his manuscript for *Gulliver's Travels*, and added this letter to the second edition of the book, blending the line between fact and fiction even more.

Daniel Defoe, a contemporary of Swift, published his fictional account of Robinson Crusoe's travels in 1719, a little under a decade before Swift published *Gulliver's Travels,* and also did so under the guise that the narrator is the actual author. The difference however, is that within a very few pages the reader understands that Gulliver's experiences are complete fantasy, whereas Crusoe's are intended to be a serious, albeit, fictional description of a man exploring the world. The direct parody of *Robinson Crusoe* is apparent from the very first line of Swift's book. Swift begins by introducing Gulliver in relation to his father and his birthplace, "My father had a small estate in Nottinghamshire; I was the third of five sons" (25). Robinson Crusoe, Gulliver's predecessor, introduces himself in an almost identical manner: "I was born in the year 1632, in the city of York, of a good family, though not of that country, my father being a foreigner of Bremen, who settled first at Hull" (2). In addition to mimicking Defoe's narrative prose in the first person, Swift mocks Defoe's plot points. Infamously pointed out by Charles Gildon in 1719, Defoe had made an error in his manuscript, by describing his main character stripping down to his britches to swim, and then immediately after, stuff his pockets with biscuits, (Gildon, 11). The mistake seemed to irk Gildon and others particularly because "Defoe here makes Crusoe perform unlikely, even absurd actions, and his attack is on the false realism in Defoe," writes J. Paul Hunter in his essay "*Gulliver's Travels* and the Novel." He goes on to state that "in Gulliver's Travels the thrust is to demonstrate what the realism and pseudofactuality of contemporary travel accounts and fictional narratives come to at last," (Hunter, 58). Hunter brings up the instance in *Travels* when Gulliver is forced to empty his pockets and have an inventory taken of them by the Lilliputians. He points out the implausibility of him having the long list of items, including two pistols, a diary, a comb, a razor, a pair of spectacles, a pouch of gunpowder, a pouch of bullets, a set of utensils, a watch, a handkerchief, a snuffbox, and a pouch of coins. He goes on to write, "to appreciate the full effect of this pocketful, we have to remember that Gulliver is supposed to have swum ashore—in dangerous stormy waves—with his pockets jammed like that, and he is also wearing a full set of clothes, a hat, and a large sword," (Hunter, 70). Taking into consideration the public joke that was made of Defoe's mistake, one can assume Swift's long and unlikely list of objects in his protagonist's pocket is intentional satire. Gulliver's journey parallels Crusoe's in the first chapters of both books, when the protagonists find themselves shipwrecked. Gulliver and his crew encounter a "violent storm" (Swift, 26), and Crusoe writes, "the storm continued with such fury that the seamen themselves acknowledged they had never seen a worse" (10). Their journeys deviate from then on, but the parallels continue.

In *Robinson Crusoe*, the protagonist and his newly acquired slave or servant, Xury, come across a portion of African coast that is inhabited by indigenous people, and he describes their encounter with his advanced Western technology - guns:

> It is impossible to express the astonishment of these poor creatures at the noise and fire of my gun: some of them were even ready to die for fear,

and fell down as dead with the very terror; but when they saw the creature

dead, and sunk in the water, and that I made signs to them to come to the

shore, they took heart and came, and began to search for the creature... and

the negroes held up their hands with admiration, to think what it was I had

killed him with (30)

The patronizing tone of Defoe's hero is hard to miss, and certainly referring to other

human beings as "creatures" speaks to the condescension with which many white

explorers regarded their far-off neighbors. Swift seizes the opportunity to satirize this

attitude in his description of the Lilliputians, first referring to them using the same

moniker, "creatures" (28), and then describing their awed reaction to Gulliver,

Two or three of the young natives had the curiosity to see how I looked

when I was asleep, they climbed up into the engines, and advancing very

softly to my face, one of them, an officer in the guards, put the sharp end of

his half-pike a good way up into my left nostril, which tickled my nose like

a straw, and made me sneeze violently (33)

Both Defoe's and Swift's representations of their protagonists' encounters with the

indigenous people paint the image of diminutive and childlike people, however in

Swift's case the "creatures" actually were diminutive, being six-inches high, and in

Defoe's they were merely dark-skinned. Swifts imitation and exaggeration of Defoe's

tales largely serve to highlight his literary device of choice: irony.

   In addition to Swift's direct allusions to Defoe's novel, his use of situational

irony and extreme understatement satirizes humanity in general. After some time

in Brobdignab (the playful names Swift gives the "remote regions" Gulliver visits belie the serious tone of the narrative, adding to the irony of the book), Gulliver finds

himself in the presence of a few women, each over 50 foot high, who begin to undress.

He is describing human beings from the point of view of someone much smaller, but

as anyone reading the book is a human being as well, the unflattering description can

only be seen as tongue-in-cheek,

> For they would strip themselves to the skin, and put on their smocks in
>
> my presence, while I was placed on their toilet directly before their naked
>
> bodies, which, I am sure, to me was very far from being a tempting sight....
>
> Their skins appeared so coarse and uneven, so variously coloured, when I
>
> saw them near, with a mole here and there as broad as a trencher, and hairs
>
> hanging from it thicker than pack-threads, to say nothing further concerning
>
> the rest of their persons.

This description evokes the idea of a human being shamelessly undressing before a cat

or dog, with no thought to modesty. The image is laughable but creates an unavoidable

self-consciousness in the reader, and underscores Swift's own repugnance for the

human body.

    This self-consciousness that Swift creates in his matter-of-fact descriptions occurs

several times throughout the book. In Part One, Gulliver recounts hearing of the long-

term division of two parties within the Lilliputian empire, the High Heels and the Low

Heels, who have been engaged in a cold war for 36 years over which side of an egg

is acceptable to break. The "primitive" way of breaking an egg, on the larger side,

had resulted in a cut on the finger of the Emperor's' son. The Emperor then passed an

edict declaring all men must break their eggs on the smaller side from then on. Swift

writes, "the people so highly resented this law, that our histories tell us their have been six rebellions raised on this account; wherein one emperor lost his life, and another his crown" (54). At no point does Gulliver remark on the absurdity of such a trifling argument costing anyone his life. Rather, at the end of the speech he is listening to, describing the troubles between the "Big-Endians" and the true believers, he declares his loyalty to the Emperor and claims "I was ready, with the hazard of my life, to defend his person and state against all invaders" (55). The irony of that statement is effective in causing the reader to address the trivialities of the conflicts in his own society, and the blind loyalty Gulliver shows satires the often irrational manner in which members of one political party grasp on to whichever set of beliefs, meaningful or not, their group decrees.

As Ashley Marshall states in her essay, "Gulliver, Gulliveriana, and the Problem of Swiftian Satire", "three key textual features seem to mark the Travels as satire: obvious irony; a combination of playful obfuscation and topicality; and the presence of alternative societies that are designed to illustrate shortcomings in the satirist's society," (214). Swift uses each of these features throughout his narrative, whether it is during Gulliver's description of "his box" being snatched up by a seagull and carried over the ocean, or his deadpan recounting of urinating on top of a house to put out a fire. His main character serves as a straight man of sorts, one without a huge degree of character or personality, but rather a vessel for Swift's mockery- creating a hilarious yet thought provoking satire of the popular travel narrative, and of the human condition.

Works Cited

Defoe, Daniel. *Robinson Crusoe.* http://www.literaturepage.com/read/

robinsoncrusoe.html. Accessed 27 Nov. 2017.

Gildon, Charles. Preface. *The Life and Strange Surprizing Adventures of Mr. D—*

De F--, of London... 1719. http://english.illinoisstate.edu/digitaldefoe/archive/

spring10/multimedia/gildon.pdf. Accessed 27 Nov. 2017

Hunter, J. Paul. "*Gulliver's Travels* and the Novel." *Children's Literature Review,*

Gale. *Literature Resource Center,* http://link.galegroup.com.library.wlac.edu/

apps/doc/H1420022311/LitRC?u=lawest&sid=LitRC&xid=195dad62. Accessed

14 Nov. 2017. Originally published in *The Genres of Gulliver's Travels*, edited

by Frederik N. Smith, University of Delaware Press, 1990, pp. 56–74.

Marshall, Ashley. "Gulliver, Gulliveriana, and the Problem of Swiftian Satire."

Philological Quarterly, vol. 84, no. 2, 2005, p. 211+. *Literature Resource Center,*

http://link.galegroup.com.library.wlac.edu/apps/doc/A178219380/LitRC?u=

lawest&sid=LitRC&xid=1cc35430. Accessed 27 Nov. 2017.

O'Connor, Kate, and Williams, Abigail. "Jonathan Swift and 'Gulliver's Travels'"

http://writersinspire.org/content/jonathan-swift-gullivers-travels. Accessed 27

Nov. 2017.

Swift, Jonathan. *Gulliver's Travels*. Barnes and Noble Classics, 2003.

EMOTION AND TONE

Different writers have different tones: some are impassioned, while some quietly present their points in a seemingly objective way. Compare Chinua Achebe and Edward Said, both post-colonial critics writing on Joseph Conrad's *Heart of Darkness*. First Achebe:

> The point of my observations should be quite clear by now, namely that Joseph Conrad was a thoroughgoing racist. That this simple truth is glossed over in criticism of his work is due to the fact that white racism against Africa is such a normal way of thinking that its manifestations go completely unremarked.
>
> Chinua Achebe, "An Image of Africa: Racism in
Conrad's Heart of Darkness"

Now Said:

> Conrad's genius allowed him to realize that the ever-present darkness could be colonized or illuminated—*Heart of Darkness* is full of references to the *mission civilatrice*, to benevolent as well as cruel schemes to bring light to the dark places and peoples of the world by acts of will and deployments of power—but that it also had to be acknowledged as independent... Conrad's tragic limitation is that even though he could see clearly that on one level imperialism was essentially pure dominance and land-grabbing, he could not then conclude that imperialism had to end so that "natives" could lead lives free from European domination.
>
> Edward Said, Culture and Imperialism

Both writers take a critical view of Conrad's attitude towards Africans, but the tones of the two works are very different. You will need to find a tone that suits your own personality and writing style on the one hand, and the requirements of the assignment on the other. For the most part, you will be encouraged to follow Said's more objective, professional manner rather than Achebe's more heated tone.

The discussion of literature almost always engenders strong responses, disagreements, and attempts to persuade. Have you ever gotten into or observed a heated debate in class about a character or a situation in a novel? The writing of papers channels this intellectual energy and exploration into objective and analytical written arguments.

Rather than recording gut reactions such as:

Incorrect, Emotional:

I didn't like Keats' poem because the speaker always talks about taking drugs or drinking alcohol.

Persuasive papers explain *how* a work achieves its powerful effects. In a well-argued paper, analytical observation like:

Correct, Analytical:

The "full-throated ease" of Keats' Nightingale contrasts sharply with the speaker's "heart" which "aches."

The second example replaces nonspecific (though strong) words such as "like" or "hate."

Writing about literature will make you a more sensitive judge and user of language. This will enable you to address the question of tone in your writing by making conscious choices about the words you use.

Sylvia Spielman-Vaught

Dr. Boutry

English 101

20 May 2012

Marriage as a Means of Social Security

What if your only means of viable income was completely predicated on marrying off your daughter? During the early nineteenth century, a mother such as *Pride and Prejudice's* Mrs. Bennet is easily viewed as obsessed by her daughter's marriage prospects; however, after critically analyzing her motivation, we can see that as a mother she is justified as marriage would determine a more stable future for her daughters as well as a means of social security for herself.

During this time period the economic plight of a widowed woman with daughters was nothing less than poverty. Due to entailment laws, she would usually be driven from her home if she had no sons. We see this in Austen's *Sense and Sensibility*. Once the father dies, these women are forced to move into a cottage and live a far simpler life than before. As we see them cut things from their expenses such as beef and sugar, one can't help but sympathize with them. It is easy to write these women off as being crazy, meddling mothers when it comes to marriage for their daughters, but it was the only way to escape a life of struggle.

In *Pride and Prejudice*, Mrs. Bennet's sole purpose is facilitating marriage for her daughters: "The business of her life was to get her daughters married" (7). We witness this from the very opening of the novel with the knowledge that a wealthy Mr. Bingley has moved into the neighborhood and a very excited conversation ensues between Mr. and Mrs. Bennet:

> Oh! Single, my dear, to be sure! A single man of large fortune; four or five thousand a year. What a fine thing for our girls! How so? How can it affect

them? My dear Mr. Bennet, replied his wife, how can you be so tiresome! You must know that I am thinking of his marrying one of them. (6)

The motivation behind this all-consuming wish to marry her daughters becomes clearer as the novel progresses and we find that Mr. Collins has sent a letter regarding the entailment of Longbourn. Mr. Bennet is now sharing this information with his wife and daughters, and Mrs. Bennet is mortified as she knows that this leaves her no security. She refers to Mr. Collins as an odious man and goes on to say, "I do think it is the hardest thing in the world that your estate should be entailed away from your own children; and I am sure if I had been you, I should have tried long ago to do something or other about it" (60–61). The implication for her own financial stability becomes clearer as the narrator goes on to say, "…Mrs. Bennet was beyond the reach of reason; and she continued to rail bitterly against the cruelty of settling an estate away from a family of five daughters" (61). In this passage one can decipher quickly that "family" means Mrs. Bennet herself.

Further into the story we find out that Mr. Collins has asked Elizabeth to marry him. This, of course, is something that greatly excites her mother, as this guarantees social security for herself. She further informs her daughter that she will never speak to her again if she doesn't accept his proposal. This is beyond reason for Elizabeth, for she is an intelligent, independent, character and in no way would ever align herself with Mr. Collins. This is fully noted in a critical analysis by Sandra MacPherson called "Rent to Own; Or, What's Entailed in *Pride and Prejudice*." "Mr. Collins wants to dispense favors like a fee-simple landlord; he wants to be the kind of agent-the agent *as such* he thinks the tenancy in tail makes him. He understands his marriage proposal to Elizabeth as a dispensation, at once moral and legal-in other words as a will" (14). This is what he associated moral action with, much like Mrs. Bennet (2). Looking towards the future and the entailment of Longbourn, Mr. Collins and Mrs. Bennet have similar agendas in mind. We find him thinking upon it as such, "…his plan of amends-of atonement-for inheriting their father's estate; and he thought it an excellent one full of eligibility and suitableness, and excessively generous and disinterested on his own part" (68). Mrs. Bennet agrees. Once she has found out what Mr. Collins' true intentions are, everything changes for her: "Mrs. Bennet treasured up the hint, trusted that she might soon have two daughters married; and the man whom she could not bear to speak of the day before, was now high in her good grace" (70).

Hand in hand with Mrs. Bennet's view of Mr. Collins is the irrational change in behavior that is elicited as soon as she hears her Lizzy is engaged to Mr. Darcy. Prior to this, she has viewed Darcy with much contempt, and even goes so far as to apologize to Elizabeth for having to walk about with him. However, upon hearing the news of their engagement, Mrs. Bennet becomes a completely changed woman. This is unequivocally the best news of her life, her Lizzy marrying Darcy and her improved prospects. One can hear her voice change and shake as she utters these words:

> Good gracious! Lord bless me! Only think! Dear me! Mr. Darcy!
> Who would have thought it! And is it really true? Oh! My sweetest
> Lizzy! How rich and how great you will be! What pin-money, what
> jewels, what carriages you will have! Jane's is nothing to it-nothing at
> all. I am so pleased—so happy. Such a charming man! —so handsome!
> So tall! Oh, my dear Lizzy! Pray apologise for my having disliked him
> so much before. I hope he will overlook it…Three daughters married!
> Ten thousand a year! Oh lord! What will become of me? I shall go
> distracted. (357)

It's hard to comprehend that this is the same woman who only hours ago was calling down evil upon Mr. Darcy when now she embraces him for what he will do to her life circumstances.

Despite her character flaws, to fully embrace all that is Mrs. Bennet is to realize that her obsession with marriage is necessary for survival. A woman looking out for the social security of herself and her daughters is justifiably passionate about how to attain it and with good reason. Any woman who loves her daughters and obsesses about a way to create a happy, long, and secure future is a warrior who should be held in high esteem, no matter how foolish she may seem.

Works Cited

Austen, Jane. *Pride and Prejudice.* 1813. Penguin, 2002.

MacPherson, Sandra. "Rent to Own: Or, What's Entailed in *Pride and Prejudice*." *University of California Press*, vol. 82, no. 1, 2003, pp. 1–23, www.rep.ucpress.edu/content/82/1/1. Accessed 27 May 2012.

Sylvia Spielman-Vaught

Dr. Boutry

English 103/1016

21 Nov. 2012

Society's Role in Excusing the Aberrant Behavior of Artists: *Lolita*, a Case in Point

If you are a patron of the arts, then you are undoubtedly familiar with great art that moves you. You may read and appreciate the works of one of the Romantic Poets such as Lord Byron. If films are a source of inspiration, then perhaps Roman Polanski films are what move you, or Michael Jackson's music. All of the aforementioned artists are men who, besides being celebrated geniuses, have also at one time or another been accused of pedophilia. However, very often the general public looks the other way when their "dalliances" come to light, excusing their behavior because of their art. This is the same defense Vladimir Nabokov's narrator in *Lolita*, Humbert Humbert, counts on in retelling us his criminal sexual exploits as he compares himself to a poet.

Humbert Humbert, a confessed pedophile, writes in such a fluid way that he manipulates us into feeling empathy for someone who would violate social *mores*. But does genius excuse criminal behavior? In *Lolita*, our "humble" narrator, Humbert Humbert, tries to convince the reader ("ladies and gentlemen of the jury") that he is simply an innocuous poet and that the captivation, control, and de-flowering of Dolores Haze was done simply as a remarkable expression of love and art, not unlike the exploits of some of history's most celebrated artists, including Edgar Allan Poe, who married his thirteen-year-old cousin, and with whom Humbert repeatedly compares himself.

Taking a look back into history, we can see why Humbert Humbert may have formed his opinions on so called "nymphology," or the sexual adoration of young prepubescent girls. Looking into the world of the Romantic Poets we find their work celebrated centuries later and remember them as great poets while their sexual proclivities seem to remain a side-note. One of the most noted poets from that movement is Lord Byron. According to critic Fiona MacCarthy, "he had an innate sexual orientation toward boys," (Matthews). These examples only support Humbert's opinion of poets as pedophiles. The gift that these artists have is to persuade us to see things in a different way. Humbert is persuasive. In a critical essay entitled, "Lolita and the Dangers of Fiction," author Matthew Winston states:

> The book's protagonist, narrator, and supposed author, Humbert Humbert, continually forces us to maintain a double perspective by calling on us to pass moral and legal judgment upon him as a man and aesthetic judgment upon him as an artist. "You can always count on a murderer for a fancy prose style," and from that point on the murderer, madman, and pedophile is balanced against the artistic creator, stylist, lover of language, and master of literary allusion.

Humbert uses this fancy prose and style to entangle us in his web of deceit. He seduces us with the romantic language of love, French. He achieves his goal, drawing us into his world in such a way that we no longer want to pass moral or legal judgment on him, we only want to know the story of the romance that came and disappeared from one "depressed dog-eyed gentleman's" life.

The contribution that great artists give to society does not excuse their aberrant behavior. Popular cliché states that artists should not be held to the same moral standards as the rest of us, and frequently this idea is used to justify trysts with young girls much as Polanski or Picasso did. But we are all accountable for the pain that we inflict upon another in society. Every culture has societal taboos on pedophilia. Taking advantage of the minds of young people to exploit them in a sexual way is only imprisoning them, and thus we the readers of *Lolita* are imprisoned the same as Dolly is. Humbert, as a self-proclaimed poet of a bourgeois old-European style, takes great care in craftily spinning his reflections on Lolita. We are duped by his self-deceit. Of this, critic

Marcus Amit states, "Self-deception is a mental state in which the subject is motivated (as opposed to harboring a conscious intention) to believe in a specific proposition or state of facts, this motivation causes the subject to enact certain mental strategies and behavioral patterns that convince him or her of the truth, despite his exposure to information that tips the scales" (188). Later in the essay, he goes on to conclude that Humbert is unable to see Lolita as an autonomous subject to whom he is morally committed, but only as an inanimate aesthetic object. As such, the reader can forget about all of the moral complications that arise from the story, and focus on the beauty as though its only measure were aesthetic.

Establishing the true nature of the artist with open eyes works to dismantle the art itself. The films, *The Pianist* and *Chinatown*, are both classic masterpieces of art for which Polanski should be praised. However, one has but only to read the undisputed testimony of how he drugged, raped, and sodomized a thirteen-year-old girl to tarnish his genius. We are what we create. Similarly, the masterpiece that Humbert has created with his prose falls to the wayside when we take off the rose-colored glasses and are willing to come to terms with who and what he is. We find a glimpse of Humbert's admission as reflected in a critical essay by Anthony Moore, which states, "He compensates in some small way for the damage inflicted as he poignantly narrates a summary of Dolores' point of view in fluent flashbacks: she soon grew aware of her deprivation and had long mourned the childhood he stole from her," (74). Indeed, Humbert admits in a moment of clarity that "even the most miserable of family lives was better than the parody of incest, which, in the long run, was the best I could offer the waif" (287).

The admission of incest as true should now cause the reader's blinders to come off and the manipulation to end. And yet it does not. The reader finds himself in a position where she or he almost feels like the charade has ended, and the narrator's simple admission is justifiably a reason to grant the pedophile empathy. Perhaps as long as it does not affect one directly, then it may be easier to get caught up in the beauty and art to which we are witness. Art's ability to move our emotions and blur the lines of decency despite our confrontation with the true nature of the creator is a societal conundrum. Because a large portion of society idealizes artistic genius, the artist becomes elevated to a higher status, thus without realizing it, society has allowed the artist to live his/her life by a different moral code from the common person. Presumably, this is the reason why society allows rock bands, and not you and me, to trash hotel rooms.

To recognize that as a society we all share a measure of responsibility in allowing the lines of morality to become blurred is a small step towards recompense. Artistic genius does not excuse criminal behavior, yet society often turns a blind eye. Because of this, the best plan of attack towards curbing the deviant behavior of those who have the power to manipulate our emotions in society would be to keep your dear loved ones close and aware. We have only to turn to the man we love and hate, our dear narrator Humbert Humbert. He finally gives us a hint of remorse as he says to a pregnant Lolita: "Do not talk to strangers. I hope you will love your baby. I hope it will be a boy" (309).

Works Cited

Amit, Marcus. "The Self-Deceptive and the Other-Deceptive Narrating Character: The Case of *Lolita*." *Style*, Summer 2005, pp. 187–204, *JSTOR*, www.jstor.org/stable/10.5325/style.39.2.187. Accessed 14 Nov. 2012.

Matthews, Charles. "The Man behind the Byronic Image." Review of Byron: Life and Legend by Fiona MacCarthy. *San Jose Mercury News*, 2002.

McKenna, Alix. "Larry Rivers, NYU, and Child Pornography." *California Literary Review*, 7 Sep. 2010, calitreview.com/10240/larry-rivers-nyu-and-child-pornography/. Accessed 28 Nov. 2012.

Moore, Anthony R. "How Unreliable Is Humbert in Lolita?" *Journal of Modern Literature*, vol. 25, no. 1, 2001, pp. 71–80, *JSTOR*, www.jstor.org/stable/3831867. Accessed 14 Nov. 2012.

Nabakov, Vladimir. *Lolita*. 1955. Vintage, 1997.

Winston, Matthew. "Lolita and the Dangers of Fiction." *Twentieth Century Literature*, vol. 21, no. 4, Dec. 1975, pp. 421–427, Duke University Press, *JSTOR*, www.jstor.org/stable/441055. Accessed 14 Nov. 2012.

VII

Go Beyond College Writing

CHAPTERS

CHAPTER CHAPTER CHAPTER 24

WRITING THE TRANSFER APPLICATION ESSAY

If you will be facing a transfer essay in the future, read on. Reading this section early on in your college career can help get you thinking about the way you spend your extracurricular time now and how you prepare for the transfer process.

College admissions officers reading your transfer essays want to see three things:

- What kind of a person you are.
- That you can write at a college level.
- That you know what field you would like to study.

Look at the transfer essay as a wonderful opportunity to discuss the things about you that aren't easily put on an application or resume and aren't reflected in the classes you've taken or the grades you've earned. You can talk about things that are unique to you, but remember to link them to a quality that is desirable in a student. Admissions officers might think it's cool that you're a champion speed-eater, but they'll think it's even cooler if you can say that you had to train long hours, show dedication, and research the smallest hot dogs in order to win your title. Dedication, long hours, and research characterize good students. Sometimes, the transfer application will ask you a very specific question, but oftentimes, the prompt is more general and a chance to discuss yourself. This leaves you free to explore several topics; some yield more convincing essays than others. The best topics for transfer essays often include hobbies and intellectual passions, specific challenges you have faced that might explain a bad semester, and volunteer work.

HOBBIES AND INTELLECTUAL PASSIONS

If you have a great passion or a hobby, this is the perfect time to talk about it and explain what it has meant to you. For example, if you have always loved jewelry making or fishing or *anything* (except maybe your boyfriend or girlfriend), this could make a great topic. You could talk about the time you combed the beach for five hours even when gale-force winds and pelting rain threatened to carry you off to sea looking for the perfect whorled seashell that would be the center of a bracelet you were creating. The hobby isn't the important factor, so never think that your hobbies aren't hip or intellectual enough. What *is* important is what your involvement in those hobbies can illustrate about you as a person. The type of student who will persevere and show patience in the pursuit of excellence (and the perfect shell) is the type of student who will be likely to stick with college, not get frustrated or discouraged easily, and who will ultimately succeed.

The same goes for intellectual passions. If you have a comic book collection about which you know everything, or you loved your first earth science class and since have read up on all kinds of gems and rocks, or volcanoes, that intellectual energy and passion for studying can define you as a serious and curious student with a passion for learning. If you love volcanoes, explain what it is about them that you find so fascinating and that you are saving up for a trip to Pompeii. Ever heard the expression, "too cool for school?" This is not the time to act detached about your scholarly interests. If you have one, express your inner geek. This will give a transfer officer a snapshot of who you are as an intellectual. All of us in education like to see passionate and interested students.

You can explain:

- What got you into your hobby or passion (your first experience).
- What you've actually done (climbed three summits, knit twelve scarves, etc.).
- What you've learned about your hobby (and yourself in the process). Perhaps explain what you have been willing to sacrifice for it.
- Why you love your hobby. Be specific.
- What your passion says about you as a person (particularly the good qualities that would make for a great student in your discipline).

EXPLAINING A BAD SEMESTER

Sometimes, life issues get in the way of a student's schooling, and unfortunately, these have a way of showing up on a transcript. If you had a traumatic or life-changing semester and it wreaked havoc with your grades, this is a good time to explain what happened. You don't want to explain away an entire transcript worth of bad grades, but even then, you can explain some of the struggles you have experienced: working full time, health issues, having a learning disability, trying to raise a child, struggling with the loss of a loved one. The important message to convey to the admissions officers is that the conditions that affected your performance in the past are no longer issues, and that you will be able to perform well at their college in the future. This explanation is most convincing when you can show that a bad semester was an exception and that as soon as you adapted to the new situation or fixed the problem, you got right back up and worked hard on your education. Remember also not to overdo it. While the admissions officers are kind people, they won't offer you a space someone else wants just as badly out of pity, especially if they feel that your life situation will not allow you to succeed.

VOLUNTEER WORK

Transfer essays are also great opportunities to talk about the community and volunteer work you do. The big caveat for discussing volunteer work is to be real. Don't make up community involvement or exaggerate your participation because you think it sounds good. If you can get a letter of recommendation from the head of the program for which you volunteered, that is a valuable addition to your portfolio. If you are planning to transfer in a year, it's not too late to get involved in a cause about which you truly care.

Once you have the experience, how do you talk about it in an essay?

You can explain:

- Your motivation to get involved,
- What you actually did,
- What you learned, and
- How you feel you affected others' lives and made a difference. Did you get your community market to ban plastic bags? Did you write a letter to the mayor that resulted in cleaning up your neighborhood playground? Did you teach three adults how to read? Organize a play for a retirement community? Be specific.
- How your volunteer work fits with your future major or your plans for continued involvement and how you might work with the program with the benefit of a college degree. This shows that you are serious about your commitment to the cause and not just trying to pad your resume for transfer.

Remember:

It's hard to write a convincing essay about your vast experience eating chips and watching *Real Housewives*, so think about your life and who you'd like to be in the future when it comes time to actually write your essay. After you have finished studying, is there time left over in your week for helping others or developing a passion of yours? It might take some reorganizing, but if you can find the time, make that a priority now.

RESEARCH YOUR MAJOR

Finally, if possible, research the university's professors who work in your discipline. It can be very impressive to state that you would love to take a class with Dr. Patricia Evans because you've read her work on evolutionary biology and that has been your lifelong dream. You can take it a step further and contact the professor whose work you admire six months to a year before you apply and even ask for an informational interview. Again, you want to keep it real. Don't fake an interest in a professor's work just to make a contact. That will backfire. If, however, you have a genuine passion for the field or a professor's work, make that known and discuss it in your essay.

COVER YOUR BASES

Finally, once you know what you want to say, make sure to allot enough time to writing a solid and eloquent essay.

- Be sure that your transfer essay is grammatically sound and free of errors.
- If applying to multiple colleges, be sure to change the headings and names in the essay!
- Sometimes because of the personal nature of the essay, students relax their standards and adopt a tone that is too casual. Don't be inappropriate. Avoid slang.
- Visit the writing lab with a draft or ask a friend to read.
- Finally, when it's in great shape, ask a professor or counselor you like to take a look at your essay for you. Listen to all suggestions politely and consider them. Sometimes because these essays are very personal, it can be hard to hear criticism without getting defensive. Remember that your professor wants the best for you and wants you to be accepted at the college of your choice. Rather than argue with the professor if you disagree with the notes you receive, get a second opinion if you are unsure.

Ultimately, this essay represents you to strangers, so make the best possible impression.

We wish you the best!

UC Personal Statement Prompt #2:

Tell us about a personal quality, talent, accomplishment, contribution, or experience that is important to you. What about this quality or accomplishment makes you proud and how does it relate to the person you are?

My three years in my high school chamber choir taught me that I should jump right into the next challenging situation, find ways to improve my own talents and craft, and demonstrate excellence in a multiplicity of ways.

I auditioned for my school's chamber choir in September 2007 as a sophomore while grieving the death of a close member of the family, and also suffering through my own serious illness. I had always been interested in singing, but was encouraged to audition by a friend who was concerned for my well-being. The night before my audition, I spent hours looking for an appropriate piece, questioning, "What song is best for my voice type?", "What is my range?", and "How could I stand out?" Despite my preparation, the choir director had prepared beforehand a madrigal, written by someone several centuries before anything I had considered or ever sung. Nevertheless, I became an alto, the "backbone" of the choir, a position I held proudly for three years.

In the next two years, my personal life flourished as much as my vocal capabilities in the choir. I was now focused on an independent study program in my district. In choir, I learned to sing from my diaphragm, sang pieces of music from various periods in English, Portuguese, French, and German, performed in formal concerts, cabaret nights, and musical showcases. I came to embrace the value of collaboration and hard work. I gained a greater sense of discipline and delight for music, and I also found I could maintain strong friendships and a normal life despite my illness.

It was not until my senior year that I saw my place in the choir differently. In September 2009, we learned that we would be performing in a music festival at Disney Hall. A year-long commitment was required from the first practice in September to our final performance at Disney Hall. Though the time required between practices and schoolwork was enormous, I was ready to make the commitment.

We began working immediately. Everyone was given special sheet music and official music folders, something reserved for few members in the past. In the beginning, there were interpretive conflicts during rehearsal and we lost members to scheduling conflicts. Nonetheless, we systematically learned every note and dynamic of each piece. A few months before the festival, four members of the LA Master Chorale joined us for a special master class, teaching us new techniques and approaches to our repertoire. That day we marched and clapped solemnly as though we were mourners in a funeral march to the Peruvian masterpiece *Hanacpachap Cussicuinin*. The power of the music we created at that moment dramatically improved our performance for the better.

The day of the event, we entered Disney Hall *en masse*, a process that took almost an hour. We ran through our vocal preparations, and were ready to begin at the conductor's first cue. Although we had been in rehearsal of similar scale before, it was the first time the complete chorus, one-thousand voices strong, joined together in song.

This experience greatly influenced the person I am today, dramatically facilitating a larger appreciation for developing and studying music. I learned how to approach and cultivate the craft that I love.

Transfer applicant prompt:

What is your intended major? Discuss how your interest in the subject developed and describe any experience you have had in the field — such as volunteer work, internships and employment, participation in student organizations and activities — and what you have gained from your involvement.

Over a number of years I have planned to pursue a career in the field of filmmaking with an emphasis on screenwriting. My perspective on life was altered after experiencing a serious illness as a young teenager, which caused me to enroll in an independent study program for two years in high school. My parents have always encouraged me in education, to seek challenges, and to apply myself in my studies and life, which has greatly inspired me.

During that time, I was able to enroll in a screenwriting class. I had always enjoyed film, attending every opening night possible. I grew up knowing people in the industry who enlightened me and helped whet my appetite for this career. Each of these encounters nurtured in me a true fondness for writing scripts.

Our professor gave us reading assignments to analyze script layout for future projects. We broke down scripts, learned the appropriate vernacular, and spoke with guests who discussed the development process. By semester's end, I had earned several A's, pitched film concepts to a producer, and begun to write my first script.

As I reentered high school, working with new instructors and counselors, I took additional film courses. I joined my classmates in shooting a short film as an assistant director. Weeks later, we were assigned a longer film. Our director wrote an 8-page script based on Hitchcock's Dial M for Murder set in our school library, and I was both the lead actress and the editor.

In college, I discovered a professional film program which further expanded my knowledge of filmmaking. My first year, I learned film set etiquette both in lectures and practical situations, operated specialized equipment and worked with others in previously unfamiliar settings. I helped build a set for a dance show with an advanced class in stagecraft, and I spent a day on a department-wide production of a scene from The Apartment. This year, I have learned the job of a film loader, loading film into cameras.

Apart from my production time on the set, I am steadfast in my commitment to screenwriting. In the spring of 2011, I took an additional screenwriting class where I wrote my second script. Our professor taught us certain concepts I had known before-hand, and also placed us into small groups to gain outside perspectives on our work. During that time, we "workshopped," orchestrating cold readings of our scripts to be read by others. Hearing my characters come to life during these workshops was amazing and increased my passion for filmmaking even more.

The courses I've taken so far are an essential foundation for my feature filmmak-ing endeavors and have assisted me in developing into a proficient student. I believe a UC education will enable me to pursue new challenges and to gain the capability for virtuosity in each.

It was not until my senior year that I saw my place in the choir differently. In September 2009, we learned that we would be performing in a music festival at Disney Hall. A year-long commitment was required from the first practice in September to

CHAPTER CHAPTER CHAPTER

25

GET A JOB!
PROFESSIONAL WRITING

When a job asks for a resume (sometimes called a c.v. for *curriculum vitae*) the employer is looking for a one-page list that highlights your educational and professional experiences to date. Your goal is to make this document attractive, professional, clear, informative, and easy to read. You also want your resume to represent you in the best possible way.

▌PRESENTATION

When you write a resume, presentation is very important. Because the interviewer does not yet know you, first impressions are critical. Along with your cover letter, this piece of paper is what will get you in the door of the company or organization for an interview. If you are sending or bringing a resume on paper, make sure that it is on clean, high quality paper, and that the ink is not spotty or faded. Change your ink cartridge if necessary. If the resume is to be e-mailed with your application, you can still choose a professional business resume template from the choices in Microsoft Word as well as an attractive and legible font. Then, save your resume as a PDF and send it in that format. That will prevent the employer's potentially different version of Word from affecting your resume's formatting. Remain professional with your choice of letterhead. You want your resume to be noticed for its professionalism and the promise it gives that you will fit into the workplace environment to which you are applying, not for the distracting dancing bears logo. In addition, it is of the utmost importance that you proofread your resume for errors. These types of errors call your education and professionalism into question.

The art of the resume is to make your accomplishments and attributes easy to spot. It is perfectly fine (indeed it is an art) to make what you did sound as impressive as possible. For instance, instead of writing under your duties that you were responsible for stocking the shelves, you could write that one of your duties included "Inventory Control." Just be sure to tell the truth.

Make the most of your accomplishments, but do not misrepresent yourself.

Most employers will follow up on any claims your resume makes. Claiming to be something you are not or inflating your experience may get you the interview, but once there, the employer is sure to ask you questions about your resume and to call former employers and references to confirm what you have said.

TIPS FOR RESUME WRITING

- Use clean, high-quality letterhead to print your resume or a nice template if electronic.

- Make clear, easy-to-read headings such as "Education" and "Work Experience."

- Describe your past jobs briefly and what tasks were expected of you. If you write "Summer Intern," briefly explain your responsibilities and duties.

- Proofread your resume to eliminate any grammar or spelling errors.

- Make the most of your accomplishments, but do not misrepresent yourself.

- Have friends look over your resume before you send it off. Find out if the tone is right. You want to be confident and friendly, not arrogant and superior. Remember that no one wants to work with a jerk, no matter how qualified.

SAVE YOUR BEST WORK

Keep a copy of your resume and remember to update it whenever you get a new job, join a new club, or acquire a new skill. This way you will keep it up-to-date and ready to go if a job opening should suddenly arise.

You may also wish to start an e-folio (or electronic portfolio) of your best work. There are several sites that offer this service for free. Your e-folio might include your best papers, projects, PowerPoint presentations, visual aids, posters, etc. This way, you will have all of your most impressive work on one centralized site so you won't lose things. When an employer asks you for a writing sample or a sample of your art or graphics, you can go to your e-folio and forward the materials to the prospective employer without having to get dusty looking under your bed or prying a yellowed paper from the magnet on the fridge.

SAMPLE RESUME

Below we have included a sample resume that you can use as a guide to writing your own. Microsoft Word has several templates you can use that will do the tough formatting for you and allow you to type in your own information. Notice that you can also change any of the headings and categories if something feels more appropriate. "Skills" could be changed to "Extracurricular Activities" if that feels like a better fit.

Claudia Williams (your name here)

9000 Overland Avenue, Culver City, CA 90230 [Your address]
Phone: [Your Phone] E-Mail: [Your email address]

Objective
In this section you would outline what you hope to learn or accomplish in applying for the position. Note that a higher salary is not an impressive objective to an employer. The best response is that you want to increase your knowledge of the field in which you are seeking employment, gain a special kind of work experience, or gain experience in the work environment of your chosen profession.

Experience
Your Current or Most Recent Job Here (Company Name)   June 2012–present
- Your Title. Responsibilities or duties included: list the skills you demonstrated and acquired in this job.

McDonald's (Your Second to Last Job)   Summer 2011
- Cashier. Responsibilities included: Serving the public, tallying receipts, keeping cashbox totals and receipts recorded and logged in for each shift. Compiling bank deposit slips for the manager. Reporting totals to the manager at the end of each shift. Inventory control.

Education
West Los Angeles College   September 2011–present
Dean's Honor Roll. G.P.A: 3.5. Honors Student for two semesters. Courses completed towards AA Degree: English 103, Math 127, Chem 212, etc. A.S.O. Student Body Treasurer.

Culver City High School
Honor Roll. G.P.A. 3.6. A.P. Classes: History, Chemistry and English. Include anything impressive here. Include Club Participations.

Skills (this could also be "Extracurricular Activities" or "Volunteer Work")

Note any skills you have that don't appear in your work experience or take the chance to highlight those that do. Be sure to get across any special talents or unique skills you possess. Change the heading to best fit the activities you will mention.

Track Team, competed in twenty meets over two seasons. Won team trophy for "Team Spirit."

Volunteer at the St. Aloysius Shelter for Women, Los Angeles,
two nights per week.   2008–present.

Performance Poetry, Performed at the WLAC Creative Writing Club "Poetry Night"

Hobby: Auto Mechanics. Restored 1967 Ford Mustang over three years. Replaced transmission, brakes and steering column.

COVER LETTERS

Many times, when you apply for jobs, you will be required to submit your resume as well as a letter of interest also known as a cover letter or application letter. Submitting this letter gives you an opportunity to introduce yourself to your potential employer, communicate your interest in the position, and highlight some things about yourself that may or may not be included in your resume. A relatively simple standard format for a cover letter gives you all the information you need to get started.

1) The letter should include your address and the employer's address. Microsoft Word includes a number of templates that guide you in creating your own letterhead or formatting a formal business letter.

2) Open the letter with a greeting or salutation to the person who will be hiring for the position. Do everything you can to get a name for that individual. Using a colon after your greeting is more formal than a comma.

Dear Mrs. Ochoa:

Dear Dr. Logan:

If you cannot find out the name of a real person, and you know a committee of people will review your application, address your letter this way:

Dear Committee Members:

To Whom It May Concern:

3) Start the content of your letter by stating the title of the position and sharing how you found out about the job. You might say this:

I am applying in response to your June 12, 2013 *Monster.com* advertisement for an opening for _____ position.

4) Next explain what interests you about the position. You could say this:

This position aligns with my goals/interests in three ways: _____, _____, and _____.

5) Then, tell what makes you the ideal candidate for the job. Make clear what you have to offer the company, and refer to your resume.

As my resume indicates, I am well-suited for this position since _____.

6) Be sure to clearly refer to anything you provided that was requested like an application or resume.

7) Finally, express your intentions to follow up with the potential employer and offer one or two ways the employer can contact you (phone number, e-mail address). Also, thank the employer or committee for their consideration.

I am eager to speak with you about this position; I will call next week to follow up. If you need to reach me, please call me at XXX-XXX-XXXX or e-mail me at formalemailaddress@---.com.

8) Read your letter several times to eliminate any errors. Ask someone you trust to read it as well.

Read the letter in response to the advertisement below.

Tobico Japanese Fusion

Date: 2012-10-30, 12:47PM PDT

Reply to: see below

Tobico Japanese Fusion Restaurant is seeking a full or part-time waitress/hostess/sushi chef/busser.

In order to qualify, you must be able to do the following:

Work in a fast-paced environment.
Be on your feet extended periods of time.
Be a team player.
Lift up to 30 lbs. as needed.
Follow directions.

You also MUST be experienced in Asian cuisine!!

Please apply in person at our Santa Monica location, Monday-Friday from 3:00pm–4:30pm.

Send your resume and cover letter to rozj@tobicorestaurant.com.
123 W. 4th St.
Santa Monica, CA 90567

Carmen Lopez
9000 Overland Avenue
Culver City, CA 90230
Phone: 323-555-1234
E-Mail: carmen.lopez@fmail.com

October 26, 2012

Tobico Japanese Fusion
123 West 4th Street
Santa Monica, CA 90567

Dear Hiring Manager:

I am applying in response to your October 30, 2012 *Craigslist* advertisement for a waitress. This position aligns well with my interests. I love excitement and fast-paced environments; plus, I love working in teams as the advertisement specifies. I am also interested in Asian cuisines.

In addition to aligning with my interests, this position aligns with my experience. As my resume indicates, I have four years' experience working in food service. I started at Tender Greens as a busser for six months. Next, I was a hostess at TGI Friday's for six months and was promoted and worked as a server for a year. Finally, I have been working for two years at Golden China restaurant in Culver City where I have learned about a variety of Asian cuisine. In all of those positions I worked on my feet for many hours, followed directions, and easily lifted trays weighing as much as 35 pounds.

I am excited about this opportunity to work at Tobico Japanese Fusion restaurant. I will call to follow up next week. Feel free to call me at 323-555-1234 or email me at carmen.lopez@fmail.com. Thank you for your consideration.

Sincerely,

Carmen Lopez

E-MAIL CORRESPONDENCE

E-mail is the predominant means of academic and professional communication. As a result, an etiquette has evolved that people are expected to follow when exchanging professional e-mails. Below is a list of rules to follow when you e-mail any professor, counselor, supervisor, colleague, or other professional or academic contact.

1) Use an appropriate e-mail address. Many students created their e-mail accounts for social purposes and then use those same accounts for professional or academic correspondence. They create an e-mail address that they think is cute or clever (sexy-bunny94@---.com, bigmikeymike@---.com, q-tee-pye123@---.com) but will come across as silly and distracting to a business contact. Instead, create another account strictly for e-mail exchanges with your boss or professors. That address might include your name or initials with no reference to a nickname or slang terminology.

2) Start the e-mail with a salutation. (Dear Mr. Freeman,; Hi, Dr. Chaing,; Professor Leonard,; etc.)

3) Include your full name in the message. Never assume your professor or supervisor recognizes your e-mail address. For your professors, include the course name and section number in your e-mails.

4) Use a professional or academic tone. (See our "Using an Academic Tone" section in Chapter 6 for more.)

5) Send formatted items as attachments. Never paste an assignment or resume into the email. In order to maintain the formatting of your document, you must attach it to the email. Convert the document to a PDF to guarantee that the formatting is maintained.

6) Always include a subject in a professional email. Give your recipient (supervisor, professor, etc.) an idea of the topic of your email by including a few words in the email's Subject line.

7) Read the e-mail carefully before you send it, and correct any errors. If you are prone to certain regular mistakes that you have difficulty spotting in your writing, have someone else read the message before you hit "Send." Having another pair of eyes review your e-mail is especially useful with an e-mail inquiring about a job or making a request.

Sometimes, people who receive your e-mails will never meet you face to face, so the only version of you they see is through your typed messages. So let your e-mail speak for you by presenting a professional, well-written self, and leave the recipient with the best possible impression.

26

FOR INTERNATIONAL STUDENTS

THE AMERICAN COLLEGE AND UNIVERSITY CLASSROOM

If you are an international student studying in the United States, there are certain cultural differences in American classrooms that you will want to be aware of so that you can fit in easily with your fellow students. Minor cultural differences might make the physical atmosphere different. For instance, unlike elsewhere in the world, in American colleges and universities there is no smoking. Americans can be very sensitive about this and there are laws preventing people from smoking near the entrances of schools.

More significant differences also exist in the way classrooms are managed and in the ways professors interact with students.

GRADES

American grading systems can be confusing for students from other countries. In the classroom, you will likely receive grades on a scale of 1–100 on tests and quizzes. On essays, you are more likely to receive letter grades. Your final grade for the term will also be communicated to you as a letter grade. In general, the numerical system breaks down like this:

GRADING SCALE

97–100	A+
94–96	A
90–93	A-
87–89	B+
84–86	B
80–83	B-
77–79	C+
74–76	C
70–73	C-
67–69	D+
64–66	D
60–63	D-
0–59	F

D and F grades are usually not "passing" grades, and if given for a semester's work, the student will be asked to retake the class. Grades of D and F indicate that the student has not acquired the skills or knowledge taught in the class. On essays, letter grades are more common than numerical grades. The letter grades on English papers may be described as follows:

LETTER GRADES

A work is often exceptional, well-organized, and demonstrates a resourceful use of language. It effectively presents details, evidence, and examples to prove its thesis. It responds to the assignment in its focus and scope. The writing uses lively, well-chosen, and precise vocabulary. It contains almost no errors in usage or spelling. Grammar, punctuation, and spelling enhance meaning, rather than make the essay hard to read.

Work receiving a B grade is superior in quality, but may be less thorough and graceful than A work. It contains few errors in usage or spelling.

Work receiving a C grade is acceptable. It is clearly organized but repeats commonplace ideas in an unexciting manner. It contains few serious errors in usage or spelling.

Work receiving a D grade is barely adequate. Although it may be confusing, it shows some effort to engage the topic. Often it fails to answer the question posed in the assignment. It is usually full of serious errors.

Work receiving an F grade is unacceptable. It is confusing, chaotic, and full of errors in thought and usage. Plagiarism (see below) is always F work, even when free of error.

GRADE POINT AVERAGE/GPA

To complicate things even more, college registrars' offices (which record your grades on your transcript) translate the letter grades and record them on a 4.0 scale, 4.0 being the highest, and 0.0 the lowest. An honors student must often have a GPA (grade point average) of 3.0 or higher.

It's a good idea to keep all assignments and their grades/points in case there is a question about the grade. If a question arises, do not hesitate to ask your professors about it politely. They should be happy to explain why you received the grade you did.

PROFESSOR/STUDENT ROLES

The relationship between American professors and students often surprises many international students. Although this is a generalization, professors in America tend to be more approachable and friendly, and perhaps a little less formal, than their foreign counterparts. In many countries a strong divide exists between the professors and the students. In the United States, professors pride themselves on their approachability. Nevertheless, there are some rules it is best to follow no matter how friendly the professor seems. Some professors may allow you to call them by their first names, but this is rare. The appropriate title for an instructor is "professor" or "doctor" until you are told otherwise. Retain a professional demeanor, and be respectful of the professor at all times. This extends to deadlines on a syllabus and course policies. Do not assume that your professor seems "so nice" that he or she probably will not mind if you turn in the paper next week instead or walk into class half an hour late. Although the professors seem informal, this friendliness is a privilege that is earned. If a professor feels that you are abusing his or her good will, the tone may change. In general, however, enjoy the professor's eagerness to help you and see it as an opportunity to be welcomed into a subject.

CLASS PARTICIPATION

While you are probably aware that you must raise your hand and be acknowledged before speaking, you might not realize that most professors in America will expect you to participate actively in class discussions. In fact, participation is often a factor of your grade. Therefore, not speaking in class may be counted against you. Be sure that you ask the professor and read the syllabus so that you understand what your professor expects of you. Many international students are reluctant to speak up, but in fact they should. Contributing to the class conversation is one of the ways that you demonstrate to the professor that you have read the assignment. Your instructor will expect you to raise your hand, speak often, and to make eye contact when you do.

If you know you must give an in-class presentation, be sure to practice on friends and to go over any language difficulties or questions you might have ahead of time. Read "Ace In-Class Presentations" in Chapter 2 for tips.

SEEKING HELP

American professors will also be happy to see you during their posted office hours, and you should take advantage of these opportunities. Professors will expect you to seek help and go to office hours if you do not understand some of the lecture or content in the course. This is your responsibility. If you are shy, visiting a professor after class or in his or her office can allow you to get clarification of a point or just let the professor hear your voice. (It is always harder for professors to remember the quiet students who never speak.) Moreover, if you develop a good rapport based on your interest in the subject and your good performance in class, you may also ask the professor for a letter of recommendation to add to your portfolio. Be sure to ask politely and with plenty of time before the recommendation is needed. In general, only ask the professors for whom you have done your best work.

If you are experiencing difficulties in a class, do not struggle alone in silence. Here are a few strategies you might try:

- Get a tutor. Often free tutoring services are available on campus.
- Go to instructor office hours (see above).
- Voice-record the lectures, with your professor's permission, so that you can replay sections you may have missed.
- Read and understand your syllabus thoroughly.
- Exchange contact information with another student who can explain any policies or assignments you might miss.
- If you have difficulty with the language, budget extra time for completing and understanding assignments. Go back and reread the original material.
- Take good written notes in class, and after class, compare your notes with other students to check your comprehension.

- "Taking English is a hard class for every international student. This class focuses a lot on writing, which is my weakest part. It takes me over six hours to write an essay, so I would remind the international students to prepare the essay a week before and go to the language lab to get help."

- "I still remember when the class first started, I couldn't get used to the workload. Sometimes, I had to read twice in order to fully understand what a reading meant."

- "For international students, we all need to put double effort into English classes. However, it is worth it because I can feel my English is getting better. So, hard work and looking up new vocabulary words in the dictionary is the key to success in English class."

CREATING ORIGINAL CONTENT

You will often be expected to write essays and research papers in English classes. In America, academics and professors feel very strongly that you create all original content for your papers. While it may be acceptable and standard practice in some cultures for students to borrow ideas and passages from published or online literature without having to cite sources, doing so in the United States will get you into a lot of trouble and may get you failed or expelled from the college. Be sure always to cite your sources. Please see Chapter 20, "Documenting Your Sources" for further information about this.

PUT YOURSELF OUT THERE!

Finally, make the most of your time in the United States. Of course, your studies should come first, but budget in some time to visit and go sightseeing in order to make the most of your time abroad and learn as much as you can about your host country. When you return home, people will be curious to hear about your experiences and you want to have more to talk about than just the college library! By traveling and interacting with as many Americans as you can, you will gain greater cultural understanding. Being a person who has experienced different cultures gives you a strong advantage as a broad-minded and culturally sophisticated student and will allow Americans to find out about your country.

A great way to get to know American students and students from other countries is to get involved in campus activities. Join in extracurricular activities such as, campus clubs, student government, social organizations, sports, and honors societies. Not only will you enhance your resume, you will also experience college life in a different way and learn about your fellow students outside of an academic setting. You will also improve your English skills in a relaxed atmosphere. After all, if you only socialize with students from your own country, you could have just stayed home!

Advice from an International Student:

"My advice is to practice English with your family. Read what you like because you can be surprised by how much you can learn just by reading. If you don't like to read, watch educational videos and listen to how they speak."

Although it can be intimidating to speak to students in a language you find challenging, it will be worthwhile. You will form friendships that last a long time and your time abroad will be personal and meaningful.

A CONVERSATION WITH ALFREDO QUIÑONES-HINOJOSA

BY CLAUDIA DREIFUS

A Surgeon's Path from Migrant Fields to Operating Room

New York Times
May 13, 2008

At the Johns Hopkins School of Medicine, Alfredo Quiñones-Hinojosa has four positions. He is a neurosurgeon who teaches oncology and neurosurgery, directs a neurosurgery clinic and heads a laboratory studying brain tumors. He also performs nearly 250 brain operations a year. Twenty years ago, Dr. Quiñones-Hinojosa, now 40, was an illegal immigrant working in the vegetable fields of the Central Valley in California. He became a citizen in 1997 while at Harvard.

Where did you grow up?

Mexicali. My father had a small gas station. The family's stability vanished when there was a devaluation of the Mexican peso in the 1980s. My father lost the gas station, and we had no money for food. For a while, I sold hot dogs on the corner to help.

As the economic crisis deepened, there seemed no possibility for any future in Mexico. I had big dreams and I wanted more education. So in 1987, when I was 19, I went up to the border between Mexicali and the United States and hopped the fence.

Some years later, I was sitting at a lunch table with colleagues at Harvard Medical School. Someone asked how I'd come to Harvard. "I hopped the fence," I said. Everyone laughed. They thought I was joking.

After you crossed the border, what kind of work did you find?

I was a farm laborer in the San Joaquin Valley, seven days a week, sunup to sundown. I lived in this little trailer I paid $300 a month for. It didn't take long to see that farm work was a dead end.

After a year of it, I moved to Stockton, where I found a job loading sulfur and fish lard onto railroad freight cars. My eyes burned from the sulfur, and my clothes smelled from fish lard, but it paid me enough so that I was able to go to night classes at San Joaquin Delta Community College. There, I met this wonderful human being, Norm Nichols, the speech and debate coach. He took me into his family and mentored me. Norm helped me apply for and get accepted to the University of California, Berkeley.

Once at Berkeley, I took a lot of math and science classes to up my G.P.A. Science and math are their own language. You didn't need to write in perfect English to do well in them. I pulled straight A's in science. In my senior year, someone told me to go see this guy, Hugo Mora, who helped Hispanics with science talent. I brought him my transcript and he said: "Wow! With grades like these, you should be at Harvard Medical School." That's how I got to Harvard. All along, I had much luck with mentors.

Did you find Harvard Tough?

Not really. Compared to working in the fields, it was easy. The question was what kind of doctor should I become? For a while, I thought I'd be a pediatric oncologist, because I wanted to help children. But then I thought, I'm good with my hands. Maybe I should do surgery.

One day, I was walking through Brigham and Women's Hospital and I saw Dr. Peter Black, the chairman of neurosurgery. I introduced myself, and he invited me that day to come to watch him do an operation. As it happened, he was doing an "awake" surgery, where the patient's brain is exposed and the patient is awake so that the surgeon can ask questions. As I watched that, I fell in love with brain surgery.

What about it spoke to you?

Imagine, the most beautiful organ of our body, the one that we know least about, the one that makes us who we are, and it was in Dr. Black's hand. It was in front of me. It was pulsating! I realized I could work with my hands and touch this incredible organ, which is what I do now. I cannot conceive of a much more intimate relationship than that. A patient grants you the gift of trusting you with their lives, and there is no room for mistakes.

Dr. Peter Black, he was a very humble person. And he took me under his wing. So here again, I was very fortunate with mentorship.

I'm told that you do something that not all surgeons do: You spend a lot of time wih patients before an operation. Why?

I meet them several times, and their families. They don't know if they are going to wake up after the operation. Not all the time am I successful. I do about 230 to 240 brain tumor operations a year. The majority make it. Some have complications. And some— 2 to 3 percent—it takes awhile for the patients to wake up. I need to meet everyone so that they know the risks. But getting to know these patients, it's the most painful part.

I was at a funeral yesterday. This was a 21-year-old man with a young wife, pregnant. Three surgeries, and the tumor kept growing and growing. And he told me, "There's no possible way I'll give up." He fought so hard. He trusted me with his life. Not once, several times. I owed him my presence.

How do you handle such losses?

One of the ways I work it out is through research, the laboratory. I'm trying to learn about the causes of these recurring tumors. The patients, they can donate tissue, which we will examine.

My hypothesis is—and there are quite a few scientists who believe this—there are within these brain tumors a small subset of cells that can keep growing, even when you think you've taken them all out. We call them brain stem cells. They can keep making themselves, and they can make "daughter cells" that can become anything else in the brain. They have the ability to go to sleep for a little bit and then wake up and do it again. So we're trying to identify this small subset of cells we may be leaving behind when we make these beautiful surgeries.

Have you actually found them?

Yes, but only in the laboratory. When we've found them, they may be a product of the experimental conditions of the laboratory. We haven't found them yet in live patients. The next challenge is to see if they truly exist in the human brain while the patient is alive.

When you hear anti-immigrant expressions on talk radio and cable television, how do you feel?

It bothers me. Because I know what it was that drove me to jump the fence. It was poverty and frustration with a system that would have never allowed me to be who I am today.

As long as there is poverty in the rest of the world and we export our culture through movies and television, people who are hungry are going to come here. There's no way to stop it.

VICTIMS FROM BIRTH

BY WENDY MCELROY

When Sharon Duchesneau gave birth on Thanksgiving Day to a deaf son, she was delighted.

Duchesneau and her lesbian partner, Candace McCullough, had done everything they could to ensure that Gauvin would be born without hearing. The two deaf women selected their sperm donor on the basis of his family history of deafness in order, as McCullough explained, "to increase our chances of having a baby who is deaf."

So they consciously attempted to create a major sensory defect in their child.

Scientists and philosophers have been debating the morality of new reproductive technologies that may allow us to design "perfect" human beings. Advocates dream of eliminating conditions such as spina bifida; critics invoke images of Nazis creating an Aryan race.

But what of prospective parents who deliberately engineer a genetic defect into their offspring?

Why? Duchesneau illustrates one motive.

She believes deafness is a culture, not a disability. A deaf lifestyle is a choice she wishes to make for her son and his older sister Jehanne. McCullough said she and her partner are merely expressing the natural tendency to want children "like them."

"You know, black people have harder lives," she said. "Why shouldn't parents be able to go ahead and pick a black donor if that's what they want?"

Passing over the problem of equating race with a genetic defect, McCullough seems to be saying that deafness is a minority birthright to be passed on proudly from parent to child. By implication, those appalled by their choice are compared to bigots. Some in the media have implicitly endorsed their view.

On March 31st, the *Washington Post Magazine* ran a sympathetic cover story entitled "A World of Their Own" with the subtitle, "In the eyes of his parents, if Gauvin Hughes McCullough turns out to be deaf, that will be just perfect." The article features Gauvin's birth and ends with the two women taking him home. There they tell family and friends that, "He is not as profoundly deaf as Jehanne, but he is quite deaf. Deaf enough." The article does not comment critically on the parents' decision not to fit Gauvin with a hearing aid and develop whatever hearing ability exists.

The Duchesneau case is particularly troubling to advocates of parental rights against governmental intrusion. The moral outrage it elicits easily can lead to bad law—laws that may hinder responsible parents from using genetic techniques to remedy conditions such as <u>cystic fibrosis</u> in embryos. Selective breeding, after all, is a form of genetic engineering. The Duchesneau case, then, brings all other forms of genetic engineering into question. *slippery slope & false cause.*

attacks character.

The championing of deafness as a cultural "good" owes much to political correctness or the politics of victimhood, which view group identity as the foundation of all political and cultural analysis. *they're not doing it to "victimize" themselves.*

appeal to tradition

Disabled people used to announce, "I am not my disability." They demanded that society look beyond the <u>withered arm, a clubbed-foot,</u> or a wheel chair and see the human being, a human who was essentially identical to everyone else. *appeal to pity.*

Now, for some, the announcement has become, "I am my deafness. That is what is special about me." *she doesn't like that people are embracing their disabilities. & she doesn't know.*

begging the question. who to? appeal to pity

Society is brutal to those who are different. I know. As a result of my grandmother contracting German measles, my mother was born with a severely deformed arm. She concealed her arm beneath sweaters with sleeves that dangled loosely, even in sweltering weather. She hid. *appeal to pity: grandma was ashamed.*

ironic lol

Embracing a physical defect, as Duchesneau and McCullough have done, may be a more healthy personal response. Certainly they should be applauded for moving beyond the painful deaf childhoods they describe.

However, I remember my mother telling me that the birth of her children—both healthy and physically unremarkable—were the two happiest moments of her life. I contrast this with Duchesneau who, knowing the pain of growing up deaf, did what she could to impose deafness upon her son. *False dilemma. not everyone should feel this way.*

Deafness is not fundamentally a cultural choice, although a culture has sprung up around it. If it were, deafness would not be included in the Americans with Disabilities Act—a source of protection and funding that deaf-culture <u>zealots</u> do not rush to renounce. *attack on character. begging question? false dilemma.*

But if deafness is to be considered a cultural choice, let it be the choice of the child, not the parents. Let a child with all five senses decide to <u>renounce</u> or <u>relinquish</u> one of them in order to embrace what may be a richer life. If a child is rendered incapable of deciding "yes" or "no," then in what manner is it a choice? *she thinks choice is good*

Wendy McElroy is the editor of <u>ifeminists.com</u>. *She is the author and editor of many books and articles, including the forthcoming anthology* Liberty for Women: Freedom and Feminism in the 21st Century *(Ivan R. Dee/Independent Institute, 2002).*

She's equivocating by using "choice" & advocating a false dilemma.

appeals to feminists. "choice" is a buzzword for feminists. However, it's not a possibility that could ever exist. Babies can't choose or make that decision later. the ironically opposite of pro-choice.

WHAT FATHERS DO BEST

Appealing to Tradition, Hasty generalization, appeal to prejudice.

BY STEVEN E. RHOADS

Demeaning / Condescending

FATHER'S DAY NO LONGER ARRIVES without the national media high-lighting Mr. Moms. The year before last, for example, Lisa Belkin of the *New York Times* described the life of one Michael Zorek, whose only job was taking care of his 14-month-old son Jeremy. Zorek, whose wife brought home a good salary as a corporate lawyer, felt he had become "remarkably good" at shopping, at cooking, and at entertaining his energetic toddler. He was angry at a parents' magazine whose essay contest was open only to mothers. "I'm the one who does the shopping, and I'm the one who does the cooking," he reasoned. "Why is it only sexist when women are excluded?"

①

attack on character

appealing to pity? attack on character OP-ED. INTRO

This year the homemaking fathers even got to horn in on Mother's Day. On May 8, the *Washington Post*'s Sunday Outlook section featured William McGee, a single dad who "couldn't help feeling excluded" by all the ads for products that "moms and kids" would both love. He mentioned, for example, the classic peanut butter ad, "Choosy Moms Choose Jif." McGee wanted advertisers to know that he is "one of many caring dads" who are choosy, too.

②

appeal to tradition, because not accepting the change.

attack on character, appeal to tradition

data/statistics

Begging the Question "I said it's not an accident but it is

Brace yourselves for an onslaught of such features this week, even though, in the real world, there are still 58 moms staying home with minor children for every dad who does so. This is not just an accidental social arrangement, to be overcome once the media have sufficiently raised our consciousness about the joys of stay-at-home fatherhood. Mothers are loaded with estrogen and oxytocin, which draw them to young children and help induce them to tend to infants. And the babies themselves make it clear that they prefer their mothers. Even in families where fathers have taken a four-month-long paid parental leave to tend to their newborns, the fathers report that the babies prefer to be comforted by their mothers.

③

Blanket Statement/ Begging Question

False cause,

appealing to tradition

False Dilemma/ Begging Question

The problem with honoring fathers who do what mothers usually do—what used to be called "mothering"—is this: It suggests that fathers who do what *most* fathers do aren't contributing to their children's well-being. Yet we know this can't be true. Children who grow up in fatherless families are poorer, less healthy, less educated. They die much earlier, commit more crimes, and give birth to more babies out of wedlock.

slippery slope Non-sequitur Has nothing to do w/ stay at home fathers.

appeal to tradition/ prejudice, gen evaluation, attacking char.

What do most real-world dads do? When the kids get old enough, they teach them how to build and fix things and how to play sports. They are better than moms at teaching children how to deal with novelty and frustration, perhaps because they are more likely than mothers to encourage children to work out problems and address challenges themselves—from putting on their shoes to operating a new toy.

Appeal to prejudice

From *The Weekly Standard*, Volume 10, No. 38, June 2005 by Steven Rhoads. Copyright c 2005 by Steven E. Rhoads. Reprinted by permission.

When the kids become older still, Dad is usually better than Mom at control-
ling unruly boys. Jennifer Roback Morse notes that all the surveys of who does what
around the house never mention one of her husband's most important functions—he is
responsible for glaring. When their son acts up, his glares just seem to have more effect
than hers do.

[margin: appeal to tradition]

[circled: 6]

Similarly, a fascinating study in the journal *Criminology* finds that female social ties
in a neighborhood—borrowing food, helping with problems, having lunch together—
are associated with much lower crime rates. Male social ties in the neighborhood have
no effect on crime rates. But the beneficial effect of female ties almost completely
disappears in communities dominated by fatherless families! You need husbands and
fathers—what the authors call "family rooted men"—if the crime-fighting female ties
are really to be effective. Perhaps mothers still say, "Just you wait until your father gets
home," or its 21st-century equivalent. *[margin right: non-sequitur]*

[circled: 7]

[annotation: Appeal to trad. / Hasty generalization]

Sometimes moms worry that their roughhousing husbands are making their boys
more aggressive. But, in fact, fathers are teaching their sons how to play fight—don't
bite, don't kick, stay away from the eyes—a form of play enjoyed by most boys around
the world. On the playground, boys without fathers in the home are unpopular
because they respond in a truly aggressive manner when other boys try to initiate
rough-and-tumble play. A committee brought together by the Board on Children,
Youth, and Families of the National Research Council has concluded that "fathers, in
effect, give children practice in regulating their own emotions and recognizing others'
emotional cues."

[circled: 8]

[annotation: FWTF]

[margin: Hasty gen. / begging the question.]

Of course, dads do a lot for their daughters as well. For example, by providing a
model of love for and fidelity to their wives, dads give teenage girls confidence that
they can expect men to be interested in them for reasons beyond sex.

[circled: 9]

[margin: appeal prej. & false cause.]

[annotation: Appeal to pity.]

We could begin to do dads justice if we realized that their nature makes it unlikely
that they will like intensive nurturing in the way that most mothers do. Testosterone
inhibits nurturing. In both men and women high levels of testosterone are associated
with less interest in babies. Low levels of testosterone are associated with a stronger
than average interest in nurturing. If you inject a monkey mother with testosterone,
she becomes less interested in her baby. And men have much more testosterone than
women. Thus, in those two-career families where husband and wife are determined to
share domestic and paid work equally, a common argument ensues because dads typically suggest that they get more paid child-care help; moms typically want less paid
help and more time with their children.

[circled: 10]

[margin right: false analogy.]

[margin left: He's saying that fathers who stay at home have less testosterone. (attack on character / manhood) also like a warning; monkeys: false analogy]

[annotation right: appealing to prejudice & attacking character]

[annotation: Begging question.]

If dads were as tormented as moms by prolonged absence from their children, we'd
have more unhappiness and more fights over who gets to spend time with the children.
By faithfully working at often boring jobs to provide for their families, dads make possible moms who can do less paid work and thereby produce less stressed and happier

[circled: 11]

[margin bottom: appeal to pity for working dads.]

false cause / appealing to pity.

households. Dads deserve a lot of credit for simply making moms' nurturing of children possible. On Father's Day we should more often notice, and then honor, typical fatherly virtues and declare *vive la difference.* ≠ *celebrate difference?*
contradiction.

Dr. Steven Rhoads is the author of Taking Sex Differences Seriously. The article reprinted below, "What Fathers Do Best," originally appeared in The Weekly Standard in 2005. He has a PhD from Cornell University and teaches politics at the University of Virginia.

THE SINGER SOLUTION TO WORLD POVERTY

BY PETER SINGER | PUBLISHED: SEPTEMBER 05, 1999

The Australian philosopher Peter Singer, who later this month begins teaching at Princeton University, is perhaps the world's most controversial ethicist. Many readers of his book "Animal Liberation" were moved to embrace vegetarianism, while others recoiled at Singer's attempt to place humans and animals on an even moral plane. Similarly, his argument that severely disabled infants should, in some cases, receive euthanasia has been praised as courageous by some—and denounced by others, including anti-abortion activists, who have protested Singer's Princeton appointment.

Singer's penchant for provocation extends to more mundane matters, like everyday charity. A recent article about Singer in The New York Times revealed that the philosopher gives one-fifth of his income to famine-relief agencies. "From when I first saw pictures in newspapers of people starving, from when people asked you to donate some of your pocket money for collections at school," he mused, "I always thought, 'Why that much—why not more?'"

Is it possible to quantify our charitable burden? In the following essay, Singer offers some unconventional thoughts about the ordinary American's obligations to the world's poor and suggests that even his own one-fifth standard may not be enough.

In the Brazilian film "Central Station," Dora is a retired schoolteacher who makes ends meet by sitting at the station writing letters for illiterate people. Suddenly she has an opportunity to pocket $1,000. All she has to do is persuade a homeless 9-year-old boy to follow her to an address she has been given. (She is told he will be adopted by wealthy foreigners.) She delivers the boy, gets the money, spends some of it on a television set and settles down to enjoy her new acquisition. Her neighbor spoils the fun, however, by telling her that the boy was too old to be adopted—he will be killed and his organs sold for transplantation. Perhaps Dora knew this all along, but after her neighbor's plain speaking, she spends a troubled night. In the morning Dora resolves to take the boy back.

Suppose Dora had told her neighbor that it is a tough world, other people have nice new TV's too, and if selling the kid is the only way she can get one, well, he was only a street kid. She would then have become, in the eyes of the audience, a monster. She redeems herself only by being prepared to bear considerable risks to save the boy.

At the end of the movie, in cinemas in the affluent nations of the world, people who would have been quick to condemn Dora if she had not rescued the boy go home to places far more comfortable than her apartment. In fact, the average family in the United States spends almost one-third of its income on things that are no more necessary to them than Dora's new TV was to her. Going out to nice restaurants, buying new clothes because the old ones are no longer stylish, vacationing at beach resorts—so much of our income is spent on things not essential to the preservation of our lives and health. Donated to one of a number of charitable agencies, that money could mean the difference between life and death for children in need.

All of which raises a question: In the end, what is the ethical distinction between a Brazilian who sells a homeless child to organ peddlers and an American who already has a TV and upgrades to a better one—knowing that the money could be donated to an organization that would use it to save the lives of kids in need?

Of course, there are several differences between the two situations that could support different moral judgments about them. For one thing, to be able to consign a child to death when he is standing right in front of you takes a chilling kind of heartlessness; it is much easier to ignore an appeal for money to help children you will never meet. Yet for a utilitarian philosopher like myself—that is, one who judges whether acts are right or wrong by their consequences—if the upshot of the American's failure to donate the money is that one more kid dies on the streets of a Brazilian city, then it is, in some sense, just as bad as selling the kid to the organ peddlers. But one doesn't need to embrace my utilitarian ethic to see that, at the very least, there is a troubling incongruity in being so quick to condemn Dora for taking the child to the organ peddlers while, at the same time, not regarding the American consumer's behavior as raising a serious moral issue.

In his 1996 book, "Living High and Letting Die," the New York University philosopher Peter Unger presented an ingenious series of imaginary examples designed to probe our intuitions about whether it is wrong to live well without giving substantial amounts of money to help people who are hungry, malnourished or dying from easily treatable illnesses like diarrhea. Here's my paraphrase of one of these examples:

Bob is close to retirement. He has invested most of his savings in a very rare and valuable old car, a Bugatti, which he has not been able to insure. The Bugatti is his pride and joy. In addition to the pleasure he gets from driving and caring for his car, Bob knows that its rising market value means that he will always be able to sell it and live comfortably after retirement. One day when Bob is out for a drive, he parks the Bugatti near the end of a railway siding and goes for a walk up the track. As he does so, he sees that a runaway train, with no one aboard, is running down the railway track. Looking farther down the track, he sees the small figure of a child very likely to be killed by the runaway train. He can't stop the train and the child is too far away to warn of the danger, but he can throw a switch that will divert the train down the siding where his Bugatti is parked. Then nobody will be killed—but the train will destroy his Bugatti. Thinking of his joy in owning the car and the financial security it represents, Bob decides not to throw the switch. The child is killed. For many years to come, Bob enjoys owning his Bugatti and the financial security it represents.

Bob's conduct, most of us will immediately respond, was gravely wrong. Unger agrees. But then he reminds us that we, too, have opportunities to save the lives of children. We can give to organizations like Unicef or Oxfam America. How much would we have to give one of these organizations to have a high probability of saving the life of a child threatened by easily preventable diseases? (I do not believe that children are more worth saving than adults, but since no one can argue that children have brought their poverty on themselves, focusing on them simplifies the issues.) Unger called up some experts and used the information they provided to offer some plausible estimates that include the cost of raising money, administrative expenses and the cost of delivering aid where it is most needed. By his calculation, $200 in donations would help a sickly 2-year-old transform into a healthy 6-year-old—offering safe passage through childhood's most dangerous years. To show how practical philosophical argument can be, Unger even tells his readers that they can easily donate funds by using their credit card and calling one of these toll-free numbers: (800) 367-5437 for Unicef; (800) 693-2687 for Oxfam America.

Now you, too, have the information you need to save a child's life. How should you judge yourself if you don't do it? Think again about Bob and his Bugatti. Unlike Dora, Bob did not have to look into the eyes of the child he was sacrificing for his own material comfort. The child was a complete stranger to him and too far away to relate to in an intimate, personal way. Unlike Dora, too, he did not mislead the child or initiate the chain of events imperiling him. In all these respects, Bob's situation resembles that of people able but unwilling to donate to overseas aid and differs from Dora's situation.

If you still think that it was very wrong of Bob not to throw the switch that would have diverted the train and saved the child's life, then it is hard to see how you could deny that it is also very wrong not to send money to one of the organizations listed above. Unless, that is, there is some morally important difference between the two situations that I have overlooked.

Is it the practical uncertainties about whether aid will really reach the people who need it? Nobody who knows the world of overseas aid can doubt that such uncertainties exist. But Unger's figure of $200 to save a child's life was reached after he had made conservative assumptions about the proportion of the money donated that will actually reach its target.

One genuine difference between Bob and those who can afford to donate to overseas aid organizations but don't is that only Bob can save the child on the tracks, whereas there are hundreds of millions of people who can give $200 to overseas aid organizations. The problem is that most of them aren't doing it. Does this mean that it is all right for you not to do it?

Suppose that there were more owners of priceless vintage cars—Carol, Dave, Emma, Fred and so on, down to Ziggy—all in exactly the same situation as Bob, with their own siding and their own switch, all sacrificing the child in order to preserve their own cherished car. Would that make it all right for Bob to do the same? To answer this question affirmatively is to endorse follow-the-crowd ethics—the kind of ethics that led many Germans to look away when the Nazi atrocities were being committed. We do not excuse them because others were behaving no better.

We seem to lack a sound basis for drawing a clear moral line between Bob's situation and that of any reader of this article with $200 to spare who does not donate it to an overseas aid agency. These readers seem to be acting at least as badly as Bob was acting when he chose to let the runaway train hurtle toward the unsuspecting child. In the light of this conclusion, I trust that many readers will reach for the phone and donate that $200. Perhaps you should do it before reading further.

Now that you have distinguished yourself morally from people who put their vintage cars ahead of a child's life, how about treating yourself and your partner to dinner at your favorite restaurant? But wait. The money you will spend at the restaurant could also help save the lives of children overseas! True, you weren't planning to blow $200 tonight, but if you were to give up dining out just for one month, you would easily save that amount. And what is one month's dining out, compared to a child's life? There's the rub. Since there are a lot of desperately needy children in the world, there will always be another child whose life you could save for another $200. Are you therefore obliged to keep giving until you have nothing left? At what point can you stop?

Hypothetical examples can easily become farcical. Consider Bob. How far past losing the Bugatti should he go? Imagine that Bob had got his foot stuck in the track of the siding, and if he diverted the train, then before it rammed the car it would also amputate his big toe. Should he still throw the switch? What if it would amputate his foot? His entire leg?

As absurd as the Bugatti scenario gets when pushed to extremes, the point it raises is a serious one: only when the sacrifices become very significant indeed would most people be prepared to say that Bob does nothing wrong when he decides not to throw the switch. Of course, most people could be wrong; we can't decide moral issues by taking opinion polls. But consider for yourself the level of sacrifice that you would demand of Bob, and then think about how much money you would have to give away in order to make a sacrifice that is roughly equal to that. It's almost certainly much, much more than $200. For most middle-class Americans, it could easily be more like $200,000.

Isn't it counterproductive to ask people to do so much? Don't we run the risk that many will shrug their shoulders and say that morality, so conceived, is fine for saints but not for them? I accept that we are unlikely to see, in the near or even medium-term future, a world in which it is normal for wealthy Americans to give the bulk of their wealth to strangers. When it comes to praising or blaming people for what they do, we tend to use a standard that is relative to some conception of normal behavior. Comfortably off Americans who give, say, 10 percent of their income to overseas aid organizations are so far ahead of most of their equally comfortable fellow citizens that I wouldn't go out of my way to chastise them for not doing more. Nevertheless, they should be doing much more, and they are in no position to criticize Bob for failing to make the much greater sacrifice of his Bugatti.

At this point various objections may crop up. Someone may say: "If every citizen living in the affluent nations contributed his or her share I wouldn't have to make such a drastic sacrifice, because long before such levels were reached, the resources would have been there to save the lives of all those children dying from lack of food or medical care. So why should I give more than my fair share?" Another, related, objection is that the Government ought to increase its overseas aid allocations, since that would spread the burden more equitably across all taxpayers.

Yet the question of how much we ought to give is a matter to be decided in the real world—and that, sadly, is a world in which we know that most people do not, and in the immediate future will not, give substantial amounts to overseas aid agencies. We know, too, that at least in the next year, the United States Government is not going to meet even the very modest United Nations-recommended target of 0.7 percent of gross national product; at the moment it lags far below that, at 0.09 percent, not even half of Japan's 0.22 percent or a tenth of Denmark's 0.97 percent. Thus, we know that the money we can give beyond that theoretical "fair share" is still going to save lives that would otherwise be lost. While the idea that no one need do more than his or her fair share is a powerful one, should it prevail if we know that others are not doing their fair share and that children will die preventable deaths unless we do more than our fair share? That would be taking fairness too far.

Thus, this ground for limiting how much we ought to give also fails. In the world as it is now, I can see no escape from the conclusion that each one of us with wealth surplus to his or her essential needs should be giving most of it to help people suffering from poverty so dire as to be life-threatening. That's right: I'm saying that you shouldn't buy that new car, take that cruise, redecorate the house or get that pricey new suit. After all, a $1,000 suit could save five children's lives.

So how does my philosophy break down in dollars and cents? An American household with an income of $50,000 spends around $30,000 annually on necessities, according to the Conference Board, a nonprofit economic research organization. Therefore, for a household bringing in $50,000 a year, donations to help the world's poor should be as close as possible to $20,000. The $30,000 required for necessities holds for higher incomes as well. So a household making $100,000 could cut a yearly check for $70,000. Again, the formula is simple: whatever money you're spending on luxuries, not necessities, should be given away.

Now, evolutionary psychologists tell us that human nature just isn't sufficiently altruistic to make it plausible that many people will sacrifice so much for strangers. On the facts of human nature, they might be right, but they would be wrong to draw a moral conclusion from those facts. If it is the case that we ought to do things that, predictably, most of us won't do, then let's face that fact head-on. Then, if we value the life of a child more than going to fancy restaurants, the next time we dine out we will know that we could have done something better with our money. If that makes living a morally decent life extremely arduous, well, then that is the way things are. If we don't do it, then we should at least know that we are failing to live a morally decent life—not because it is good to wallow in guilt but because knowing where we should be going is the first step toward heading in that direction.

When Bob first grasped the dilemma that faced him as he stood by that railway switch, he must have thought how extraordinarily unlucky he was to be placed in a situation in which he must choose between the life of an innocent child and the sacrifice of most of his savings. But he was not unlucky at all. We are all in that situation.

The following article, "Fresh Faces," originally appeared in Boston Magazine *in 2005.* **Sascha de Gersdorff** *is the Features Editor of* Women's Health *in 2009. Prior to that, she was an executive editor at* Boston Magazine *and the editor-in-chief of* New England Travel.

FRESH FACES

BY SASCHA DE GERSDORFF   *Brief story / anecdote*

The perfect nose. The perkiest breasts. For more and more teens, achieving the ideal look means scheduling time under the plastic surgeon's knife.

Kristin wanted a new nose. A better nose. A resculpted, slightly smaller version of the original, with no bump on its bridge and a shorter, perkier, tip. It wasn't that she was ugly, or that her nose was so terrible: Kristin just wanted her features to be symmetrical. But doctors said she would have to wait at least a year before considering cosmetic surgery. After all, she was only 14. *+ Bias?*

At 15, Kristin got her wish. A Boston plastic surgeon performed the long-awaited rhinoplasty during her school's spring break. The petite, blond Newton native couldn't be happier with the results. "It turned out exactly how I wanted it," Kristin, now 17, says, "I feel like my face finally fits together."

Others agreed. Most girls at her west suburban high school told her she looked pretty and praised her new look. And, influenced by a youth culture that is increasingly open to all things cosmetic, some did a little resculpting of their own. "My best friend just got her nose done last summer," says Kristin (whose name, like those of other young patients quoted in this story, has been changed). "And my other best friend is planning on doing it as soon as she can."

Plastic surgery is a national hot topic, thanks in no small part to television shows like ABC's *Extreme Makeover*, Fox's *The Swan*, MTV's *I Want a Famous Face*, and a veritable bonanza of other media attention. Everywhere they look, young Americans are bombarded with promises of planned perfection. Ads for cosmetic procedures pepper magazines and newspapers, toned Hollywood actors sport wrinkle-free figures, and celebrity rags rave over young starlets with impossible combinations of tiny waists and huge breasts.

The pressure to look young and beautiful is at an all-time high, and more and more people are picking up the phone to schedule surgical enhancements. Americans spent $12.5 billion on cosmetic procedures last year, according to the American Society for Aesthetic Plastic Surgery. Since 1997, the number of both surgical and nonsurgical procedures performed annually has increased by a whopping 465 percent.

Statistics / data from reputable sources.

"The television shows have really captured the country's imagination and attention," says Dr. James May, director of plastic surgery at Massachusetts General Hospital. "The sensationalism of those programs has brought plastic surgery to the minds of young people and their parents. It's now a dinner-table conversation."

And the nation is changing its perspective. Whereas some Americans used to keep their tummy tucks and Botox shots a secret, they're now showing them off with pride. Today, 60 percent of women approve of cosmetic surgery, while 82 percent say they would not be embarrassed by other people knowing that they'd had some. And these aren't just aging narcissists: 34 percent of 18- to 24-year-olds say they would definitely consider surgery for themselves, the highest proportion of all age groups.

Many teens like Kristin already have. The plastic surgery society notes that Americans 18 and younger had 46,198 chemical peels, 17,233 rhinoplasties, 4,211 breast augmentations, and 4,074 Botox injections last year alone. All in all, teenagers underwent nearly a quarter million cosmetic procedures last year.

"Teenagers are the new market," says Sharlene Hesse-Biber, professor of sociology at Boston College. "Magazines have pushed the envelope on what it means to be beautiful, and surgery is now a way to deal with body issues. We're a very visual and quick-fix society. Young people are now getting that quick fix, that instant body."

When he was 16, Brian started thinking about enhancing his appearance. He had breathing problems and was unhappy with his nose. So he did something about it. A surgeon performed a rhinoplasty. That same year, Brian paid for a chin implant. "What's great about cosmetic surgery," says Brian, who went on to attend Boston University, is that "you have the ability to change what couldn't otherwise be changed." He says he'd recommend surgery to other young people as a "self-esteem boost."

"All you have to do is watch any television show, and you will see relatively uncovered, young, supposedly ideal-looking Americans," says Chestnut Hill's SkinCare Physicians co-director Dr. Jeffrey Dover. "Twenty years ago, liposuction didn't even exist, but now young women are coming in for it. They're looking at all the magazines, from *People* to *Vogue* to *Seventeen*. Large breasts with skinny bodies are very popular right now. Look at Christina Aguilera. She has very large breasts in a tiny body, and teenagers want to look like her."

It's not just girls feeling the pressure. Young men, inspired by the metrosexual movement, are also taking shortcuts to better looks. Dover says his practice has seen a dramatic increase in the number of 16- to 19-year-old males who come in for laser hair removal. He says they might be prompted by *GQ* and *Men's Health*, whose cover models sport nary a hair on their bodies.

Newbury Street surgeon Dr. Ramsey Alsarraf agrees that cosmetically enhanced celebrities' looks are affecting the way teenagers view themselves. "I've had young boys bring in 10 pictures of Brad Pitt and his nose from different angles and say 'I want to look like this.' Those are unrealistic expectations. Generally if someone says they want to look like Britney Spears or J.Lo, that puts up a red flag."

Lisa sees red flags, too. Now a 21-year-old college senior at the University of Maryland, Lisa had plastic surgery as a teenager. She, too, is pleased with the results of her rhinoplasty, which she'd been contemplating since middle school. But she says she's seen the cosmetic culture shift since then. Lisa thinks more people find surgery acceptable and that invasive procedures have become "easier than the alternatives, such as making an effort to accept yourself as beautiful or physically working hard to lose weight." Teenagers who want to look like models or celebrities they see should think again, she says.

That's what many plastic surgeons say, too. But all too often, they say, teenagers brush off any long-term implications in favor of immediate results. This blasé attitude, coupled with widening acceptance, helps young people gloss over the potentially ugly details of surgical procedures. Nor do many Boston doctors outright refuse to perform most such surgery on teenagers, though some ask the kids to wait a few years.

"I want a 17-year-old to understand that if she's going to have breast implants, she might need a new procedure at age 27," May says. "Then at age 47 she might have another revision. I would say the likelihood of her needing to have these other procedures is around 50 percent. It's very important to send the message loud and clear that surgery early in life is heading the patient down the pathway of having more operations."

Some wonder if even teenagers who have smaller, noninvasive procedures such as laser hair removal or microdermabrasion might become mentally predisposed to surgery. While there is no solid research to support this theory, the notion that kids can become "addicted" to cosmetic alteration doesn't come as a surprise to sociologist Hesse-Biber.

"We're entering this cultlike status," she says. "Every time we have a little wrinkle, we want to run in for some Botox. We're becoming addicted. I'm not saying that women shouldn't look beautiful, but when surgery becomes the fix and you still don't feel good about yourself, what then?"

Alarmed parents are asking similar questions in response to a perceived nationwide increase in teenage plastic surgeries. And the media is fueling the fire. Nearly every major American newspaper and magazine has run stories on teenage breast augmentations and liposuctions, or procedures gone horribly wrong.

The attention rose to such heights that in February the American Society of Plastic Surgeons released a statement attributing the teenage cosmetic surgery "epidemic" to overblown media hype. A recent study found that only 5 percent of college-aged women have had cosmetic surgery. But that same study revealed that more than 60 percent of the same group surveyed could see themselves having at least one procedure in their lives.

Back in Boston, teenagers' cravings for physical perfection appear not quite as high as those of teens in places like Miami and Los Angeles, where breast augmentations are reported to be popular high-school graduation gifts. Despite its liberal airs, Boston remains steeped in conservative tradition and shrouded by a hush-hush mentality about cosmetic surgery. Many people here still consider cosmetic procedures déclassé. But local doctors say they have many teenagers come in for rhinoplasties, hair removal, and Botox, though requests from teens for breast augmentation are rare. Even rarer are doctors who would perform the procedure the Food and Drug Administration does not approve for girls under 18.

"You'd have to look hard in Boston for someone who's pushing breast implants on 16-year-old girls," Alsarraf says. "If you can't vote or smoke, should you really be able to have a synthetic piece of plastic put into your chest? That doesn't make much sense to me."

It doesn't make much sense to Kristin either. But while her mother says she would be shocked by a high school student having a breast augmentation, Kristin seems nonplused. "At my school, it doesn't happen enough for people not to be surprised," she says. "But it wouldn't be like 'Oh my God!'" Cosmetic procedures have simply become part of the culture, something she says her friends all talk about briefly before moving on to the next topic.

Kristin's mother admits she knows at least one parent who would let her own daughter get much-desired bigger breasts. And May says that although the media reports may be exaggerated, all the fuss does represent a fear that soon kids will be planning their dream bodies at an alarmingly young age.

Asked if she would consider having additional cosmetic procedures, Kristin nods enthusiastically. "Yeah, definitely," she says. She says there's nothing wrong with wanting to feel better about yourself. "I'm not going out searching for things to do, but if there was something I wanted to change, wanted to be different, I would do it."

INDEX

INDEX

INDEX

Ehrenreich, Barbara, 233
Ehri, Linnea, 42
Elegy, 386
E-mail
    online classes and, 18
    rules for proper etiquette, 455
Emotion, 427–428
English class
    reason to visit professor, 16–17
    study groups, 19
    time management and, 10
English language learners, 149–160
    article, 149–151
    gerund, 157, 158–159
    idiom, 159
    infinitive, 157–159
    modal verbs, 154, 155–156
    noncount nouns, 150–151
    subject/verb agreement, 156
    time and place prepositions, 160
    verb tense, 151–154
English tutor, 19
Epic, 387
Equivocating, 280
Essay, 397–437. *See also* Literature essay
Essay exam strategies, 299–308
    content knowledge, 301
    exam with quotation, 304–307
    mental preparation, 301–302
    parameters of test, 307–308
    physical preparation, 300–301
    preparation, 307–308
    with prompts, 303–304
    sample prompt, 306, 307
    time management and, 299–300
Ethos, 210
Euripides, 377
Evidence, 187–195
    anecdote or personal experience, 191–192
    data and statistics, 189–190
    expert opinion, 190–191
    fact *vs.* opinion, 187–188
    hypotheticals, 193
    moral values, 192–193
    specificity, 193–195
    specific usage examples, 194
    using effectively, 187–188
    visual, in advertisement, 254
    words to avoid, 194
Evidence-based persuasive argument, 254
Exam strategies, 299–308. *See also* Essay exam strategies
Excel, 48
Exclamation mark, 93
Expert opinion, 190–191
Extended definition essay, 242–246
    sample outline, 245

F

Fact *vs.* opinion, 187–188
Fallacies, 276–282. *See also* Logical fallacies
False analogy fallacy, 279
False causes fallacy, 279–280
FANBOYS acronym, 67, 77, 127, 130
Fences, 43
Fiction, 382–384
    allegory, 383, 384
    antagonist, 384
    archetypes, 384
    character, 384
    climax, 384
    denouement, 384
    exposition, 384
    falling actions, 384
    foreshadowing, 384
    Freytag's pyramid, 384
    history of, 382–383
    irony, 384
    Magical Realism, 383, 384
    narrator, 384
    novel, 383, 384
    novella, 383, 384
    picaresque, 382
    plot, 384
    point of view, 384
    protagonist, 384
    realism, 382–383
    rising actions, 384
    short story, 383, 384
    suspension of disbelief, 383, 384
    terms, 384

Interview
    conducting, 331–333
    data compilation, 334–339
In-text citation, 320
Introduction, 168, 180, 197–206
    anecdote in, 202–203
    exercise, 205–206
    functions of, 198
    general to specific strategy, 199
    opposing view/op-ed, 201
    shocking fact or statistic, 201
    strong opinion in, 200
    summary strategy, 199
    thought-provoking question in, 199–200

J

Jazz, 403–405
Job posting sample, 454
Jumping to conclusions fallacy, 281

K

King, Martin Luther, Jr., 97, 192–193
Kushner, Tony, 43

L

Learning Center, 19, 20
Learning differences, 24
Learning disability, 24
Learning inventory, 24
Learning outcomes, 9–10
Learning style, 22
Learning tools
    learning inventory, 24
    memorization, 22–23
    for students with learning differences, 24
    study partner, 24
"Letter from a Birmingham Jail," 97, 192
Librarian, as resource, 20
Library database, 314
Linking verb, 61
Literal reading, 413
Literary criticism, 406–410
    non-literary sources, 412

    prewriting and, 411
    reading, 410–411
Literary theory, 407
Literature
    character, 373
    defined, 369
    essay writing and, 397–437. *see also* Essay
    imagery, 374
    metaphor, 374
    narration, 372
    personification, 375
    plot, 370–371
    plot structure, 371–372
    point of view, 372–373
    setting, 373–374
    symbol, 374
    theme, 376
    tone, 376
Literature essay
    close reading a novel, 403–406
    close reading literary theory, 417–418
    close reading process, 399–401
    contextual information, 401–402
    literary criticism, 406–410, 410–412
    vs. other disciplines, 419
    passages, 403
    quotations and, 402
    sample, 429–432
    sample using literary criticism, 433–437
    thesis statement, 401
    topics, decoding assigned, 412–416
    topics, devising your own, 417
Literature class goals, 398
Logical argument, 273–276
Logical fallacies, 276–282
    Ad Hominem, 279
    argument to ignorance, 282
    bandwagon, 281–282
    begging the question, 280
    equivocating, 280
    false analogy, 279
    false causes, 279–280
    false dilemma, 281
    guilt by association, 278
    ignoring the question, 280
    jumping to conclusion, 281

S

CPSIA information can be obtained
at www.ICGtesting.com
Printed in the USA
LVHW01s1707260718
584938LV00001B/1/P